Practical Numerical Computing Using Python

Scientific & Engineering Applications

Mahendra Verma

IIT Kanpur

Copyright © 2021 Mahendra Verma

All rights reserved. No part of this book may be reproduced or used in any manner without written permission of the copyright owner.

First paperback edition November 2021

ISBN: 9798767314713 (paperback)

CONTENTS

Preface 1

Part One: Computers and Python Programming 3

Chapter One: Introduction 5
    1.1 Introduction to Computing 6
    1.2 Computer Hardware 8
    1.3 Supercomputers & Computation Complexity 15
    1.4 Computer Software 20
    1.5 Brief Overview of Python 24
    1.6 Anaconda Python, Notebooks, and Prutor 31
    1.7 Applications of Computers 35

Chapter Two: Python Data Types: Integers and Floats 41
    2.1 Integers 42
    2.2 Floating Point and Complex Numbers 50
    2.3 Python Variables and Logical Variables 65

Chapter Three: Python Data Types: Strings, List, and Arrays 73
    3.1 Character & Strings 74
    3.2 List 82
    3.3 Numpy Arrays 91
    3.4 Dictionary 106
    3.5 Mutable and Immutable Objects in Python 109

Chapter Four: Control Structures in Python 119

4.1 Simple Statements 120

4.2 Conditional Flows in Python 121

4.3 Looping in Python 125

Chapter Five: Functions in Python 133

5.1 Functions in Python 134

5.2 Python Namespace and Scope 142

5.3 Recursive Functions 155

Chapter Six: Solving Complex Problems Using Python 165

6.1 Good Progamming Practices 166

6.2 Prime Numbers 168

6.3 Searching and Sorting 173

Chapter Seven: Plotting in Python 183

7.1 Matplotlib & Field Plots 184

7.2 Miscellaneous Plots 199

7.3 Animation Using Python 205

Chapter Eight: Input/Output in Python 209

8.1 Reading & Writing Text Files in Python 210

8.2 Reading & Writing Numerical Data in Python 215

Chapter Nine: Errors & Nondimensionalization 221

9.1 Error Analysis 222

9.2 Nondimensionalization of Equations 237

Part Two: Numerical Methods 245

Connections Among the Numerical Methods 247

Chapter Ten: Interpolation 249

    10.1 Lagrange Interpolation 250

    10.2 Splines 260

Chapter Eleven: Numerical Integration 267

    11.1 Newton-Cotes Formulas 268

    11.2 Gaussian Quadrature 279

    11.3 Python's Quad & Multidimensional Integrals 294

Chapter Twelve: Numerical Differentiation 299

    12.1 Computing Numerical Derivatives 300

Chapter Thirteen: Ordinary Differential Equation: Initial Value Problems 309

    13.1 General Overview 310

    13.2 Euler Forward Method, Accuracy & Stability 314

    13.3 Implicit Schemes 322

    13.4 Higher-order Methods 327

    13.5 Multistep Method 335

    13.6 Solving a System of Equations 340

    13.7 Stiff Equations 347

Chapter Fourteen: Fourier Transform 351

    14.1 Fourier Transform 352

    14.2 One-dimensional Discrete Fourier Transforms 357

    14.3 Multidimensional Fourier Transform 365

Chapter Fifteen: Spectral Method for PDEs 371

15.1 General Procedure & Diffusion Equation 372

15.2 Solving Wave, Burgers, and KdV Equations 378

15.3 Spectral Solution of Naiver-Stokes Equation 387

15.4 Spectral Solution of Schrödinger Equation 391

Chapter Sixteen: Solving PDEs using Finite Difference Method 399

16.1 General Overview & Diffusion Equation Solver 400

16.2 Solving Wave Equation 408

16.3 Burgers and Navier-Stokes Equations 412

16.4 Schrodinger Equation 415

Chapter Seventeen: Solving Nonlinear Algebraic Equations 421

17.1 Root Finders 422

Chapter Eighteen: Boundary Value Problems 435

18.1 Shooting Method 436

18.2 Eigenvalue Calculation 442

Chapter Nineteen: Solvers for Laplace and Poisson Equations 447

19.1 Solving Laplace Equation 448

19.2 Solving Poisson Equation 457

Chapter Twenty: Linear Algebra Solvers 461

20.1 Solution of Algebraic Equations 462

20.2 Eigenvalues and Eigenvectors 471

Chapter Twenty-One: Monte Carlo Methods and Data Science 477

21.1 Random numbers 478

21.2 Integration Using Random Numbers 484

21.3 Regression Analysis ... 487

21.4 Applications in Statmech ... 493

21.5 Machine Learning ... 502

Epilogue ... 505

Appendix A: Errors in Lagrange Interopolation ... 509

Appendix B: Improving Accuracy Using Richardson Method ... 512

References ... 515

Preface

At present, friendly, yet, powerful tools have been developed for computer programming. One such tool, the programming language Python is versatile, but easy to learn. It is being used in wide range of applications: scientific computing, data analysis, machine learning (ML) and artificial intelligence (AI), internet programming, GUI, etc. At present, researchers are employing Python for numerical computing, as well as for AI and ML.

Keeping this in mind, I chose Python as the programming language for teaching numerical computing in my *Computational Physics* course (PHY473A). I also use Python for post processing and for writing large softwares including parallel programs. The present book is a compilation of the course material and the tools developed in our computational laboratory. The contents and the usage of the book is discussed below.

Contents of the book: The book has two parts. The first part covers the Python programming language in a reasonable detail, while the second part contains the numerical algorithms and associated Python codes. The book contains discussions on important numerical tools: interpolation, integration, differentiation, solvers for ordinary and partial differential equations, Fourier transforms, boundary value problems, linear algebra, and Monte Carlo methods. In addition, I also include plotting tools, error analysis, nondimensionalization, and an overview of computer hardware and software.

The computer programs in the book have been tested. These codes are available at the website https://sites.google.com/view/py-comp. The website will also host affiliated material, such as PPTs, video lectures, color figures, etc.

Usage of the book: This book is suitable for advanced undergraduate and graduate students. It does not assume any programming background, but it does require basic understanding of calculus and differential equations. The material could be covered in 40 lectures at a fast pace. However, I recommend that the instructor and students can skip topics that they find complex or somewhat unnecessary.

Programming is learnt by practice. Hence, I strongly urge the students to program enthusiastically. One could start with the examples and then do all the exercises of the book. In my course, we used *Prutor* (https://prutor.ai) for evaluating the exercises submitted by the students. We plan to provide the exercises of the book on *Prutor*.

Acknowledgements: For the significant contents of the book, I am grateful to the PHY473A's TAs (teaching assistants), especially Soumyadeep Chatterjee, Abhishek Kumar, and Manohar Sharma. Special thanks to PHY473A's enthusiastic students, whose interesting questions led to clarity in the presentation in the book. I also thank Mani Chandra for introducing me to Python way back in 2008, and to the members of *Simulation and Modelling Laboratory* (https://turbulencehub.org), where coding is done for fun.

Next, thanks to Python creator, Guido van Rossum, and many developers for creating such a wonderful programming environment, that too for free! Also, thanks to *Anancoda* for the free Python distribution, and to the creators of *Scrivener* that has made writing a joy. I gratefully acknowledge *Wikipedia* and *Wikieducator* for Figures 3, 4, 5, 33, and 138 of the book.

I am also thankful to my friends, Harshawardhan Wanare, Rajesh Ranjan, Prateek Sharma, Anurag Gupta, Rahul Garg, and Prachi Garg for the encouragement, and Manmohan Dewbanshi for help in the manuscript preparation. Finally, I am grateful to pothi.com, especial Jaya Jha and Pratibha, for the assistance in publication of this book, and for publishing it in India. The front cover was prepared using *Canva*, while the full cover was designed by pothi.com.

Feedback request: I request the readers to send their comments and feedback to me at mkv@iitk.ac.in. Even though I have strived to make this book error-free, I am sure some lacuna still remain. I will be grateful if such errors are brought to my attention.

Mahendra Verma
IIT Kanpur

PART ONE

COMPUTERS AND PYTHON PROGRAMMING

CHAPTER ONE
INTRODUCTION

Synopsis

"Computers themselves, and software yet to be developed, will revolutionize the way we learn."
—Steve Jobs

This chapter gives a brief introduction to computer hardware and software. We also describe how to install Python on computers.

1.1 Introduction to Computing

Computer is one device that has impacted all walks of life. It is employed for scientific research, e-commerce, banking, cloud computing, etc. On a personal level, we use computers for surfing internet, emailing, social networking, etc. See Section 1.7 for some of the computer applications.

ENIAC (*Electronic Numerical Integrator and Computer*, made in 1945) was the first general-purpose digital computer. It was used for making Hydrogen bomb and Monte Carlo simulations. A succession of better and faster computers have been built since then. Scientists and engineers have used these machines for research in physics, chemistry, biology, fluids, engineering, geophysics, and astrophysics. In this book, we will focus on generic computation tools used in science and engineering.

Both hardware and software have evolved leaps and bounds over the years. In early days, *Fortran*, short form for *Formula Translation*, was the de facto programming language for scientific applications. Even though Fortran is still a dominant language in scientific programming, many scientists and engineers have moved to modern languages such as C, C++, and Python. Among these languages, Python has become very popular due to its simplicity and availability of large number of Python modules. In this book, we will use Python language for writing programs. An added benefit of Python is that it has excellent post-processing tools, such as plotting, reading/writing data, etc. In addition, Python is widely used in machine learning (ML) and artificial intelligence (AI). Python is also becoming popular for high-performance computing (HPC). However, in this book we will not cover ML, AI, and HPC.

Traditionally, a scientist was either an *experimentalist* or a *theorists*. The former primarily work on experiments, while the latter on theoretical modelling. However, after the prominence of computers, a new category of researchers called *computational scientists* have emerged. These researchers excel in designing computers and writing large softwares. Another important point to note is that computers are often used to simulate physical systems, e.g., Earth's atmosphere, stars, galaxies, large molecules, automobiles, etc. Thus, computers perform virtual experiments. Scientists strive to make accurate models of physical systems using the inputs from experiments and/or computer simulations. Thus, computers provide an interesting and powerful window of opportunity for understanding the world.

Often, experiments and computer simulations complement each other. For example, hydrodynamic experiments can achieve very high Reynolds numbers, but computer simulations can reach only moderate Reynolds numbers (10^5). However, computer simulations can probe velocity field at any point of the flow, which may not be possible in many experiments (e.g., in an opaque liquid). Also, it is impossible to perform experiments on a star, but we can comfortably simulate stars on a computer, at least, approximately.

This book is ideally suited for advanced undergraduate and early graduate students. Part-I of the book includes discussions on Python language. In this part, I also cover error analysis and basics of computer hardware, whose knowledge is required for estimating memory and time complexity of a computational problem. Part-II of the book covers introduction to computational methods—numerical interpolation; integration; differentiation; solvers of ordinary and partial differential-equations; Fourier transforms; linear algebra; Monte Carlo methods; etc. I have attempted to present these topics coherently by highlighting connections among them. For example, the formulas of numerical integration are derived using Lagrange interpolation.

I hope you will enjoy learning these tools.

1.2 Computer Hardware

For an efficient use of a car, it is best to know some of its details: its milage, power of the engine, nature of the brakes, etc. Similarly, an optimal use of a computer requires knowledge about its memory capacity and power of the processors. In this chapter, we provide a basic overview of a computer and its components.

von Neumann Architecture

The present computers are essentially based on *von Neumann architecture* (1945). According to this design, a computer has the following components:

1. *Processor*: A unit that performs arithmetic and logical operations
2. *Memory*: Data and program instructions are stored here.
3. *Input/Output*: Computer takes data from input devices, e.g., keyboard, mouse; and sends results to output devices, such as, printer, terminal, etc.

The *processor, memory, I/O controller* (for connecting input/output devices to the processor), and many other small units reside on a *printed circuit board* (*PCB*) called *Motherboard* or *logic board*. A schematic diagram of these units is shown in Figure 1. Note that *hard disk* (*HD*) or *solid-state drive* (*SSD*), battery, wireless device, and camera are kept inside the computer. The processor of a computer receives inputs from ports, keyboard, and camera through I/O controller; the processor operates on the inputs, and sends the results to the memory or to appropriate output units (for example, screen or printer). The website https://www.nemolaptops.com/post/2018/09/11/antamoy-of-a-laptop provides a good overview of these units.

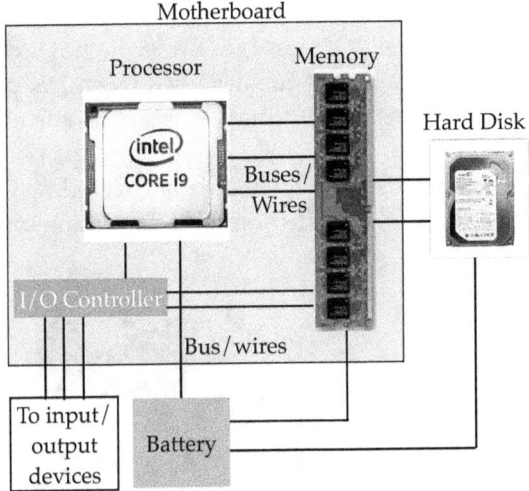

Figure 1: A schematic diagram of the internal parts of a computer: Processor, Memory, Hard Disk, Battery.

Let us get a deeper perspectives on the processor, memory, and hard disk.

Processor: The processor, also called *central processing unit* (CPU), is the most complex and critical component of a computer. This unit can perform billions of arithmetic and logical operations per second. For example, the processor adds two numbers A and B. An important thing to note is that the numbers A, B, and $A+B$ are stored in a small memory, called *registers*, of the CPU.

Now we provide a quick overview of the capabilities of one of the best processors of today. Rome processor (EPY 7002) contains 64 cores residing in 16 blocks of 4 processors each (see Figure 2). The cores of the processor communicate with each other via the memory block in the middle. Note that each core has its own L1 and L2 caches, but 4 cores of a block share 16 MB of L3 cache. Cache, being closer to the core, is faster than RAM. The cores communicate with each other, as well as to the RAM and PCI devices, via buses.

The clock speed of the processor is 2.5 GHz, which can boosted up to 3.4 GHz. A Rome processor can perform 16 floating-point operations per clock cycle. Hence, the peak performance of each core can be estimated to be 16x2.24 ≈ 35 Giga *floating-point operations/second* (*FLOPS* in short). Consequently, a Rome processor can perform maximum of 35 × 64 cores ≈ 2.24 *TeraFLOPS* or *TFLOPS*. Note however that this is the peak performance, which is not achieved in typical programs due to various constraints. Such information is useful for estimating the time for a computing job.

Intel too has fast processors, which are not covered here. Apple's M1 chip has 8 compute cores, 8 GPU (graphical processing unit) cores, and 8 neural engine cores.

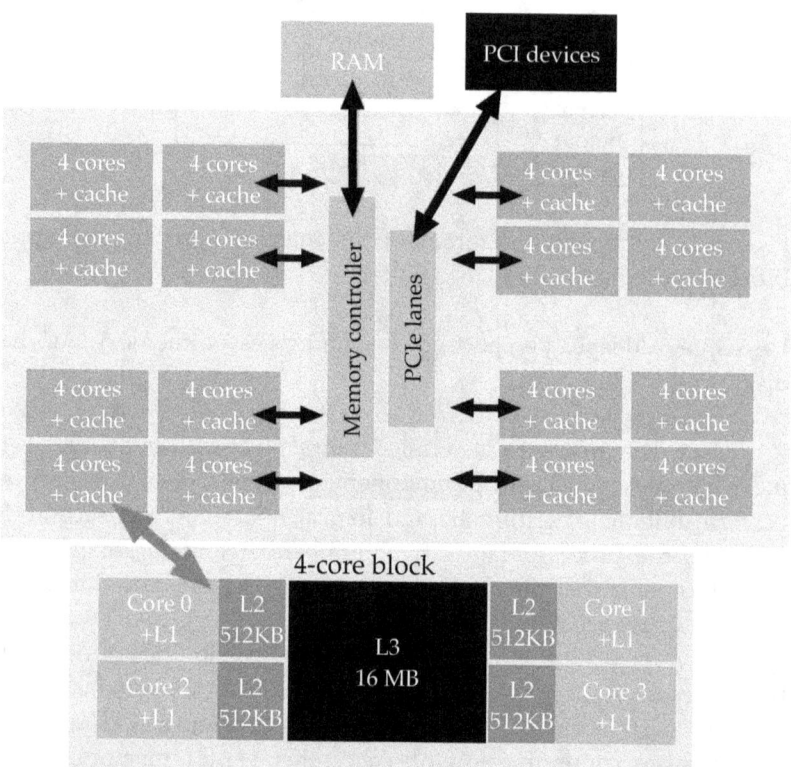

Figure 2: Inside Rome 7742 processor, black bidirectional arrows are the buses that transmit data both ways.

Memory: The data and programs reside in computer's *memory* (the vertical strip inside the motherboard of Figure 1), also called *random access memory* (RAM). The CPU reads the program and data from RAM and write the results back on it. Note that RAM is active only when the computer is powered on, hence it is a temporary memory. We need to write the data to the hard disk for permanent storage.

A laptop or desktop has RAM in the range of 4 Gigabytes to 64 Gigabytes. Note that 1 byte = 8 bits, and

1 Kilobyte = 1 KB = $2^{10} \approx 10^3$
1 Megabyte = 1 MB = $2^{20} \approx 10^6$
1 Gigabyte = 1 GB = $2^{30} \approx 10^9$
1 Terabyte = 1 TB = $2^{40} \approx 10^{12}$
1 Petabyte = 1 PB = $2^{50} \approx 10^{15}$
1 Exabyte = 1 EB = $2^{60} \approx 10^{18}$

The clock speed of RAM ranges from 200 MHz to 400 MHz, which is slower than processor's clock speed. The fastest RAM available at present, DDR4 (double data rate 4), transfers data at the rate of 12.8 to 25.6 Gigabits/second, which is quite slow compared to CPU's data processing capability. Following strategies are adopted to offset this deficiency of RAM:

1. The motherboard has multiple channels or roads for data travel between the CPU and the RAM.
2. The CPU has its own memory called *cache*. The data which is needed immediately is kept in the cache for a faster access.

Hard disk (HD) and Solid-state disk (SSD): HD and SSD are permanent storage of a computer. Programs and data reside here safely after the computer is powered off. When a computer is powered on, the required programs and data are transferred from the HD to the RAM; this process is called *boot up*. Hence, the CPU, RAM, and hard disk continuously interact with each other.

A hard disk is an electro-magnetic device in which magnetic heads read data from the spinning magnetic disks. In these devices, the data transfers rate to RAM is 100-200 Megabytes (MB) per second. Due to the moving parts, HDs are prone to failure, specially in laptops during their movements. In the market, we can buy HDs with capacities ranging from 1 TB to 20 TB.

On the other hand, a SSD is purely an electronic device with no spinning parts. Hence, SSDs are safer than hard disks, but they cost more. The data transfer rate in SSD is around 500 MB per second. The capacity of SSD ranges from 128 GB to 1 TB.

Graphical processing units (GPU): It is efficient to off-load video and image processing to a specialised processor, called *Graphical processing units (GPU)*. GPUs have many processors that perform certain operations, such as matrix rotation and Fourier transforms, very efficiently. In the last 15 years, GPUs are also being used for supercomputing. See Section Supercomputers & Compute Complexity.

Interface of a Computer: Input/Output Units

A keyboard, a trackpad, a mouse, and a camera transmit inputs to the CPU via *bluetooth* or *Universal Serial Bus (USB)* or *USB-C* ports. The CPU processes these inputs and sends outputs to an external monitor, a TV, a projector, or a printer. The data is exchanged among the input/output devices via ports, bluetooth, or *wifi* (see Figure 3).

Computers come in different avatars, but their basic design remains the same. *Desktops*, which are typically more powerful than laptops, sit on desks. *Workstations* or *compute servers* have stronger CPUs and larger memory, hence they are more powerful than desktops. Supercomputers are built using many servers. We will provide brief description supercomputers in Section 1.3.

Mobiles and *tablets* too are computers. They too have processors and memory, and they perform similar operations as a desktop/laptop. However, these mobile devices are weaker than laptops and consume much less power.

The aforementioned *hardware* units by themselves cannot perform any task. A complex program called *Operating System (OS)* gives life to these systems. The OS, applications (such as Microsoft Word), and user programs are called *software*, and they will be briefly described in Section 1.4.

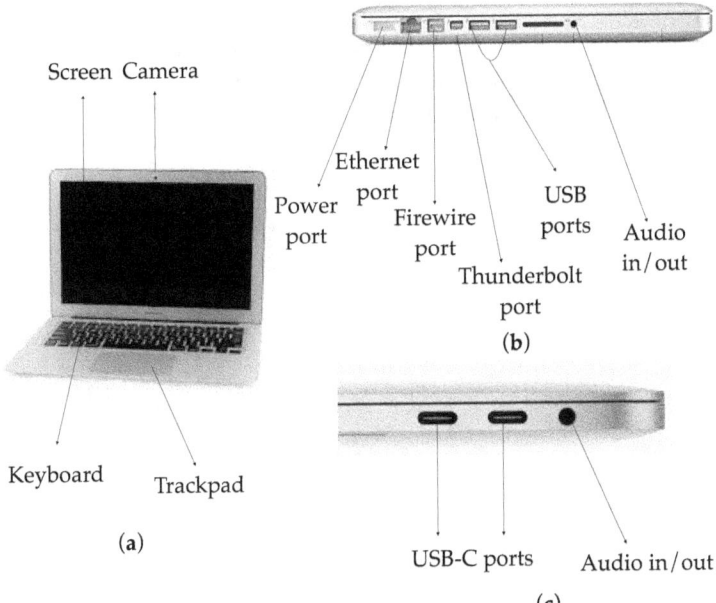

Figure 3: (a) Laptop; (b,c) Ports of a laptop. Adopted from a figure of wikipedia.org

****

Conceptual Questions

1. Why do computers have memory hierarchy—cache, RAM, hard disk?
2. What are the advantages and disadvantages of USB-C port over USB port?
3. What are the similarities and dissimilarities between the functioning of a computer and a human brain?

Exercises

1. List the following for your laptop/desktop and your mobile

phone: RAM size, CPU clock speed, Hard disk, and/or SSD capacity.
2. It is best to see the parts of an opened-up desktop. However, do not open your laptop because it is tricky.
3. Read more about the processors.

1.3 Supercomputers & Computation Complexity

Laptops/Desktops have limited power, hence, they cannot perform complex tasks, such as banking, weather predictions, simulations of aircrafts. For such operations, we employ servers or *supercomputers*, also called *high performance systems*. Supercomputing is also called *High performance computing*.

Modern supercomputers consist of a large number of processors and memory units. *Fugaku*, the fastest supercomputer as on June 2021, consists of large number of racks, each of which contains many nodes with multiple processors. Figure 4 illustrates many racks of Fugaku. The nodes are connected to each other via a fast switch called *interconnect*, through which the processors exchange data. Note that *Fugaku* requires 30 Megawatts of power, which is the power consumed by a typical small town. For reference, we provide the following specifications of *Fugaku*:

1. 158,976 nodes each with 48-core A64FX processor (2 GHz clock speed). Total number of cores: 7,630,848; Power: 29.899 kilowatts
2. Total memory: 4,866,048 GB
3. Peak speed: 442,010 *Tera floating-point operations per second* (*TFLOPS*)
4. Interconnect: Tofu interconnect D

We remark that supercomputers employ high-end processors, e.g., Rome processor, discussed in Section 1.2. Graphical processing units (GPUs) too are being used heavily in supercomputers. Each GPU contains thousands of processors, and it can perform huge number of floating-point operations. GPUs are heavily used in machine learning. Nvidia's top-end GPU A100 has 6912 compute cores, and its peak double-precision performance is 7.8 TFLOPS.

Figure 4: Fugaku, the fastest supercomputer as on June 2021. From wikipedia.org. Work of Hiroko Hama; reprinted under the agreement of CC BY-SA 4.0 license.

Memory and Interconnect

One of the major bottlenecks in the performance of supercomputers is the slow data transfer rate from RAM to CPU. As described in the previous section, the data transfer rate from memory to CPU is several GB's per second. In comparison, CPUs can operate on 1000 GB's of data per second.

Similar bottleneck exists in the interconnects. One of the fastest interconnect, *FDR Infiband*, can transfer data at the rate of 56 Gbps (Giga bits per second). Considering that an interconnect is connected to many nodes, the net transmission speed is much slower than 56 Gbps.

In contrast, the CPUs can process data at much faster pace. CPU is like a giant who can compute very fast, but it remains idle because RAM is not giving it enough data. The performance disparity between the CPU and RAM/interconnect is one of the biggest challenges of supercomputing. These bottlenecks are summarised in the following quote, "FLOPS are free, but data communications are expensive".

Memory and Time Complexity

It is critical to estimate the memory and time requirements for a numerical problem. Significant efforts and resources would be wasted if we do not have a proper estimate of the computation complexity of a given task. For example, the matrix multiplication of two $10^5 \times 10^5$ arrays requires 24 GB of RAM (see Example 1 below), hence we should not try this exercise on a laptop/desktop.

In the following discussion, we present two examples that illustrate how to estimate the memory and time complexities of a problem. To estimate the memory requirement, we need to keep in mind that the storage of an integer and a float normally require 4 and 8 bytes respectively.

Example 1: We need to multiply two arrays A and B of sizes $10^4 \times 10^4$ and store the result in array C. For this problem we need 3 arrays of 10^8 elements each. Storage of 3×10^8 real numbers requires $8 \times 3 \times 10^8 = 24 \times 10^8$ bytes of storage, which is 0.24 GB. For $10^5 \times 10^5$ arrays, the corresponding requirement is 24 GB.

The simplest algorithm for multiplication of two $N \times N$ arrays requires approximately N^3 multiplications and additions. Therefore, for $N = 10^4$, we need 10^{12} floating-point multiplications and additions. We estimate the peak performance of a typical laptop with a 4-core CPU to be 50 GFLOPS. Hence, in the best case scenario, the 2×10^{12} floating-point operations would require $2 \times 10^{12} / (50 \times 10^9) \approx 40$ seconds. Here, the prefactor 2 is for the addition and multiplication.

The retrieval and storage the array elements from/to memory require additional time. In addition, a laptop/desktop also performs other operations such as system management, internet browsing, email checking, etc. The processor works on these tasks in a round-robin and time-sharing manner. Consequently, we expect that multiplication program to take much longer than 40 seconds. However, we do not expect the run to go much beyond several (say 10) minutes.

For $N = 10^5$, the time complexity will be 1000×40 seconds ≈ 666 minutes ≈ 11 hours. Hence, the space and time requirements for $N = 10^5$ are respectively 24 GB and 11 hours that go beyond the capabilities of a typical laptop.

Example 2: For weather prediction, a computer solves the equations for the flow velocity, temperature, humidity, etc. For the same, Earth's surface is divided into a mesh, as shown in Figure 5. High-resolution simulations employ grid resolution of 3 km x 3 km that leads to 12000x12000 horizontal grid points. Suppose, we take 1000 points along the vertical direction, then the total number of grid points for the simulation is 144×10^9. At each grid point, we store the three components of the velocity field, pressure, temperature, humidity, and CO_2 concentration. Hence, to store these seven variables at each grid point, we need $8 \times 7 \times 144 \times 10^9$ = 8.064 TB of memory, which is way beyond the capacity of a laptop/desktop. Clearly, we need a supercomputer for weather prediction. The estimation of time requirement for a weather code is quite complex, and it is beyond the scope of this book.

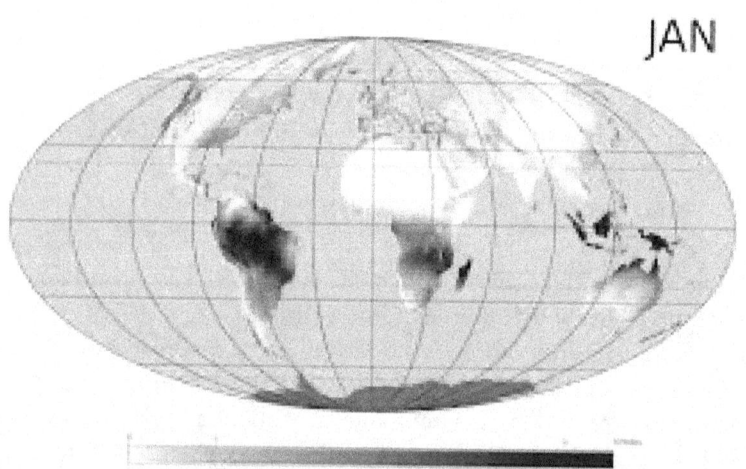

Figure 5: For weather simulation, a sample grid on the surface of the Earth. Courtesy: Wikipedia

With this, we close this section.

****

Conceptual Questions

1. How are the supercomputers helping scientists and engineers in their research?
2. How does one estimate the peak computational performance of a supercomputer? Why don't we achieve performance close to the peak value?
3. Why is memory access a major bottleneck for supercomputers?

Exercises

1. A processor has 20 cores that operate at clock speed of 3 GHz. Each of its cores can perform 20 floating-point operations per clock cycle. Estimate the peak FLOPS of the processor.
2. Visit the website top500.org and study the top 10 supercomputers of the world. Compute the maximum FLOP rating of their processor, and then compute the peak performances of the supercomputers.
3. Estimate the memory requirements for storing the following arrays:
    a. Three-dimensional integer array of size 1000x1000x1000.
    b. Three-dimensional float array of size 1000x1000x1000.
    c. 10^8 spins that can take values up or down.
4. We want to search for a word in text of 300 words. How many comparisons are required in the worst-case scenario?
5. Estimate the number of comparisons required to search for a word in a dictionary with N words.
6. Consider a matrix multiplication operation $A = BxC$, where each of them are NxN matrices. If you were to perform the above multiplication on a server with 4 TB RAM and 4 Rome processors, estimate the largest possible N for this server. How long will it take to perform this operation?

1.4 Computer Software

Computer software is a vast field. This section is not meant to discuss the nuances of various softwares. Rather, we provide provide a bird's-eye view of the operating system and Python programming language. In addition, we relate the programming languages to various programs of a computer.

Operating System and System Software

The *Operating System* (*OS*) makes a computer aware of its hardware—CPU, memory, hard disk—and the connected input/output units—computer screen, keyboard, mouse, printer, etc. For example, a computer responds to the inputs from the keyboard; executes programs; etc.

The OS is loaded from the hard disk to the RAM as soon as a computer is turned on; this process is called *boot up*. The OS performs the following tasks:

1. Memory management
2. Process management
3. Management of input/output devices (keyboard, display, printer, mouse, etc.)
4. Computer security
5. Management of application softwares (to be described below)
6. Interactions with users via input/output devices
7. Compilation and execution of user programs

The leading OS of today's computers are *Unix* and *Windows*. *Linux* and *MacOS* (the OS of Apple Computersis) are another variants of Unix. Unix itself consists of many programs, which are categorised into two classes: *Unix Kernel* and *Unix Shell*. See Figure 6 for an illustration. Note that OS of mobile devices—*iOS*, *Android*, and *Windows*—have limited capabilities.

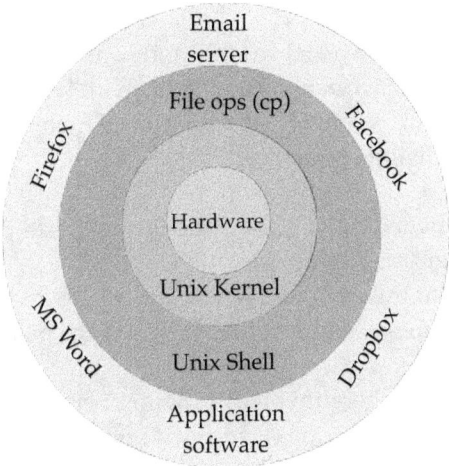

Figure 6: A schematic diagram of various components of Unix OS.

Application Softwares

Everyday we use computers for many jobs: sending/receiving emails, browsing internet, watching movies, playing songs, writing documents, and occasionally programming. Each of these tasks are performed using application softwares. For example, we write documents using Microsoft Word or Pages (on a Mac); browse internet using Firefox, Internet Explorer, Safari, etc.; watch movies using Mplayer, VLC, etc.

In addition to the above, we can employ computers to record videos for surveillance, and to control robots and home devices such as air conditioners, TV, etc. Supercomputers are employed for more complex and data-intensive tasks such as banking, weather forecasting, climate modelling, simulations of airplanes and cars, etc. Note that the application softwares are at the top of Unix shell in system hierarchy. See Figure 6.

System Software and Programming Languages

At the base level, a computer understands only two alphabets—0 and 1. Therefore, all the instructions and data are to be converted to strings of 0's and 1's. For example, an addition of two numbers A and B involves the following operations:

1. Get numbers A and B from the memory and put them into the CPU registers.
2. Add the numbers and put result $A+B$ into another register.
3. Transfer the result from the register to the memory.

The addition of numbers involves bitwise operations, such as 0+0=0, 1+0=1, 1+1=0 with a carry of 1, etc. Such instructions, coded in binary, are called *object code*.

It is cumbersome to write object codes for complex tasks, e.g., weather forecasting code. *Compilers and Interpreters* help overcome this difficulty. A user writes programs in a higher-level language; then *Compilers and Interpreters* translate these programs into object codes. These softwares save the programmer from the drudgery of writing object codes.

The leading programming languages are C, C++, *Fortran, Java, Python, Matlab,* etc. In C, C++, and Fortran, complete computer programs is written first, after which the programs are converted to object codes using compilers. Hence, C, C++, and Fortran are called *compiler languages*. On the other hand, Python and Matlab interpreters execute the codes in pieces, hence Python and Matlab are called *interpreter languages*. The following snippet illustrates how a Python interpreter interacts with a user.

```
In [1]: x=3

In [2]: x
Out[2]: 3

In [3]: y=9

In [4]: print(x+y)
12
```

In the above, the statements after *In* [1], *In* [2], *In* [3], and *In* [4] are typed by the user, while *Out* [2] and the number 12 after *In* [4] are the response of the interpreter. Note that the interpreter replies to the user instantly, unlike compliers who respond to the user after executing the complete code.

In the next section we will provide an overview of Python programming language.

****

Conceptual Questions

1. What are the differences between computer hardware and computer software? Illustrate your answer using examples.
2. What are the differences between a compiler and an interpreter?
3. List all the application softwares and system softwares that are used often in your laptop/desktop.
4. Locate *Ipython* interpreter in your computer.

1.5 Brief Overview of Python

Guido van Rossum created Python programming language, which appeared in 1991 for the first time. Python is an interpreter language, and it is very easy to learn and program, which makes it one of the most attractive and popular languages. Python is used for a large number of applications, for example,

1. Numerical and scientific computing
2. Data analysis
3. Big data and Machine learning
4. Image processing
5. Software development
6. Interface to experimental devices and control
7. GUI (graphical user interface) development
8. Audio and video applications
9. Internet programming

A Cursory View of Python

As on 2021, Python 3 is the standard and supported version of Python. Some of the major differences between Python 3 and its earlier version, Python 2, are given below:

1. In Python 3, the arguments of print statement are within brackets, but it is not so in Python 2.
2. In Python 2, the division operator, "/" performs integer division for two integer operands; for real division, one of the operands of "/" must be float or complex. But, in Python 3, the integer-division and float-division operators are different, and they are "//" and "/" respectively.

The other differences between Python 2 and Python 3 are quite technical to be discussed here. In this book, we follow Python 3.

Using Python Interpreter: We start Python interpreter from a unix terminal by typing *python* at the prompt. After that, we can proceed to write Python statements. For example:

```
(base) ~/python
Python 3.7.4 (default, Aug 13 2019, 15:17:50)
[Clang 4.0.1 (tags/RELEASE_401/final)] :: Anaconda, Inc.
on darwin
Type "help", "copyright", "credits" or "license" for more
information.
>>> 2+3/4
2.75
>>>
```

In this book, we recommend *Ipython* interactive shell with *pylab* option, which imports *Numpy* and *Matplotlib.pyplot* modules. *Ipython* does not consume as much RAM as GUI packages, e.g., *Spyder*. For invoking *ipython*, we type the following at the terminal prompt:

```
(base) ~/ipython --pylab
Python 3.7.4 (default, Aug 13 2019, 15:17:50)
Type 'copyright', 'credits' or 'license' for more
information
IPython 7.8.0 -- An enhanced Interactive Python. Type '?'
for help.
Using matplotlib backend: MacOSX

In [1]: 2+3/4
Out[1]: 2.75
```

Python modules: A major benefit of Python is its large number of libraries—*Numpy, Matplotlib, Scipy, Math, Pandas, Sympy*, etc. Technically, Python libraries are called *modules*. A brief description on some of the important Python libraries are here.

1. *Numpy*: *Numpy* is a short form for *Numerical Python*. This module contains mathematical functions, such as *sin, cos, log, sqrt*, etc. Also, *Numpy* contains optimized functions for array operations.
2. *math*: This module contains various mathematical functions. Many mathematical functions, e.g., trigonometric, logarithm, exist in both *Math* and *Numpy*, but some exist in only one of them. For example, the function *factorial* exists in *Math* module, but not in *Numpy*.
3. *Matplotlib*: This Python module helps create beautiful plots.

4. *Scipy*: This module contains advanced scientific functions for integration and differentiation, interpolators, differential equation solvers, linear algebra operations, special functions, etc.
5. *Pandas*: This module is useful for data analysis and plotting.
6. *Turtle*: Using *turtle* module, we can create geometrical figures.
7. *Sympy*: This module is used for symbolic processing.

In this book we will deal with *Numpy, Math, Matplotlib,* and *Scipy* modules extensively. To use these libraries, we need to import them. An illustration of import operation is given below. Here, math module is imported as *ma*.

```
In [6]: import math as ma

In [7]: ma.factorial(5)
Out[7]: 120
```

Python documentation and Help: Python is one of the best documented programming languages. There are a large number of websites and books on various topics of Python. You can just type what you are looking for in google, and you will find an answer.

Python offers useful online help in the interpreter itself. For example, you can get description of plot, sqrt, etc. by just typing the requisite functions after ?. This is useful if you have forgotten the syntax. Two examples are here:

```
In [1]: ? plot

In [2]: ? sqrt
```

Creating a Python File Using an Editor

Small Python program can be written in *Ipython* window itself. However, it becomes cumbersome to type large codes on a *Ipython* window. Instead, large codes are written in a file using a text editor. You may choose a text editor among many available at present: *Vim, IDLE, Atom, Spyder, Sublime, Xcode, Vi,* etc. However, I recommend *Sublime Text* (https://www.sublimetext.com), which is available for all the three platforms: Windows, Mac, and Linux.

Typing in *Sublime* is very easy. A screenshot of a Python code typed in Sublime is shown below (Figure 7):

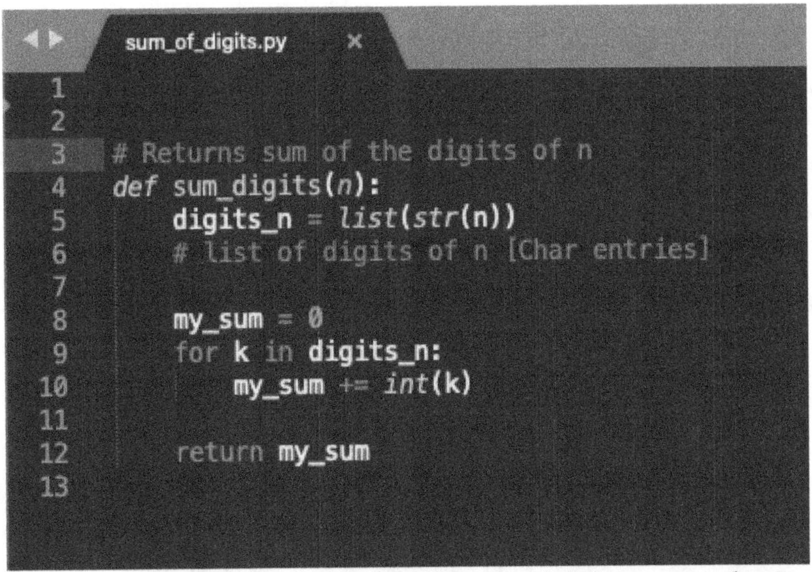

```
sum_of_digits.py
1
2
3    # Returns sum of the digits of n
4    def sum_digits(n):
5        digits_n = list(str(n))
6        # list of digits of n [Char entries]
7
8        my_sum = 0
9        for k in digits_n:
10           my_sum += int(k)
11
12       return my_sum
13
```

Figure 7: A screenshot of a Python file *sum_of_digits.py* created using the *sublime* text editor.

Note that a Python program needs to be properly *indented*. That is, we need to put blocks of code together by placing same number of blank spaces for each line of the block. In the code of Figure 7, lines 5 to 12 belong to the function *sum_digits(n)*, hence they are shifted by equal number of spaces, here 4 spaces. Note however that line 10 is indented further by placing another 4 spaces. This is because the statement *my_sum += int(k)* is within the *for loop*, i.e, it executed for each *k* of the loop. Note that you can choose any number of spaces for indentation; the only condition is that this number must be the same for all the lines of the code block. Keep in mind that if we do not provide these spaces, the code will not run. Indentation is a must for Python codes!

We can save the file in the same folder in which *Ipython* is running. This file can be executed in *Ipython* window using a command ``run filename". For example, a file named *sum_of_digits.py* that contains the function definition of *sum_digits()* is run in *Ipython* as follows:

```
In [115]: run sum_of_digits.py

In [116]: sum_digits(128)
Out[116]: 11
```

The best way to learn programming is to actually program. Programming is like sports and art, which can be mastered by practice. I recommend that students should just starting coding without fear and laziness.

Python vs. C

Python has certain advantages and disadvantages over other programming languages. Here, we contrast Python with another popular language, C. *This section is meant for advanced students, and it can be skipped by students who are not familiar with C.*

We list several important differences between C and Python in Table 1. A C program has to be written completely and then compiled, while Python codes can be developed piece by piece. Due to this reason and because of extensive Python modules, Python codes are easy to develop. A flipside, however, is that Python codes are not optimised, hence, they are slow during the execution. It is often said that a large Python code can be developed 10 times faster than the corresponding C code, but ir is 10 times slower than its C counterpart.

Table 1: Comparison between the features of Python and C.

	Python	C
1	An Interpreter language	A compiler language
2	No variable declaration	Variables need to be declared
3	No need to declare variable type	Defining variable type is mandatory
4	Dynamically typed	Statically typed
5	Python has a large set of libraries. Python is used heavily in Machine Learning and Artificial Intelligence.	A limited set of libraries available.

6	Easy syntax	Relatively harder syntax
7	Easy testing and debugging	Relatively harder to test and debug.
8	Code development is fast	Code development is slow
9	Used heavily for postprocessing	Used for developing systems programming and large codes.
10	Code execution is slow	Code execution is fast
11	Interpreters do not generate as efficient codes as compilers.	Compilers optimise the object codes by taking into considerations the data structures and loop structures.
12	Parallel programming in Python using multithreading and multiprocessing	Parallel programming in C using MPI and OpenMP.
13	Reference Type (see Sec. 3.5)	Value Type

Items 1-8 of Table 1 make programming in Python very easy. Variable declaration is an important programming practice for large codes, but it is relaxed in Python. These features make execution of a Python code slower than C (see item 10). Note however that we can speed up a Python code by making use of fast libraries written in C or C++. For example, Python FFT library *pyfftw* is quite fast because it makes use of the library FFTW, which is written in C.

Due to the above reasons, large parallel programs (e.g., for atmospheric and advanced physics applications) are not written in Python. It is best to write such codes in C, C++, or in Fortran with parallel features. Compilers generate efficient object codes for such applications by taking into considerations the loop and data structures. However, it is customary to write a Python prototype first and test it for a complex and small data set. A comprehensive C/C++ or Fortran code is written after this. This exercise saves time on the whole. Recall that in experiments, researchers work on a prototype aeroplane before venturing into a real-sized aeroplane.

In the next section, we will describe how to run Python on your own computer.

Mahendra Verma

****

Conceptual Questions

1. Why are C codes typically faster than Python codes?
2. List the benefits and drawbacks of Python relative to C.

1.6 Anaconda Python, Notebooks, and Prutor

In this section, we describe some of the popular ways to install and run Python.

Anaconda Python

Anaconda Python is one of the most popular Python distributions. It is available for free for individual use. Anaconda Python can download from Anaconda's website (https://www.anaconda.com) and installed on Windows, Linux, and Mac platforms. Anaconda takes significant disk space because of numerous packages contained in it. Once anaconda Python is installed, you are ready to run *Ipython*, as well as various Python modules.

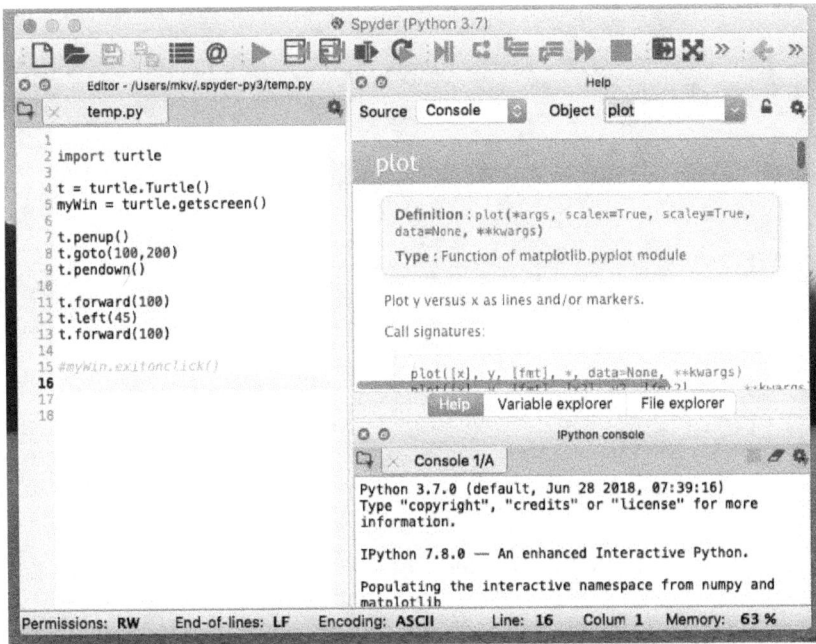

Figure 8: Spyder GUI with Editor, Help, and Ipython consoles.

Anaconda Python also comes with a GUI (graphical user interface) called *spyder*. To start *spyder*, first launch Anaconda-Navigator, after which click the *spyder* package. A typical Spyder GUI has three windows—Editor, Help, and Ipython consoles. We can type Python commands in the Ipython console of Spyder. See Figure 8 for an illustration.

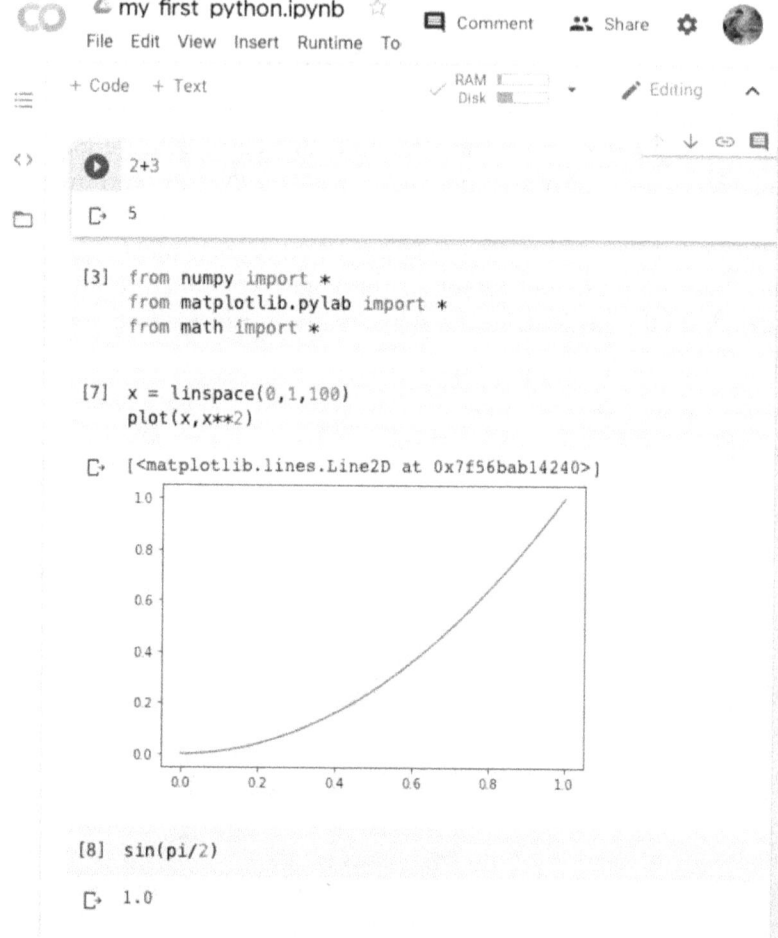

Figure 9: Working with *collab notebook*

Python Notebooks

Several versions of Python notebooks are available at present. A major advantage of Python notebooks is that you do not need to install Python locally on your computer. We list two major Python notebooks below.

Google's Python notebook is called *Google Colab* that can be opened by typing https://colab.research.google.com/notebooks/ on your browser. The browser pops up a window in which you can write Python codes. Figure 9 illustrates how to plot the function $y = x^2$. *Jupyter notebook* too offers a similar interface as Collab.

Prutor

Prutor, a short form for *Program Tutor*, is an intelligent tutoring system for programming. This platform, developed by Prof. Amey Karkare and his team at IIT Kanpur. Prutor is hosted at https://prutor.ai. See Figure 10 for an illustration of a programming session on Prutor.

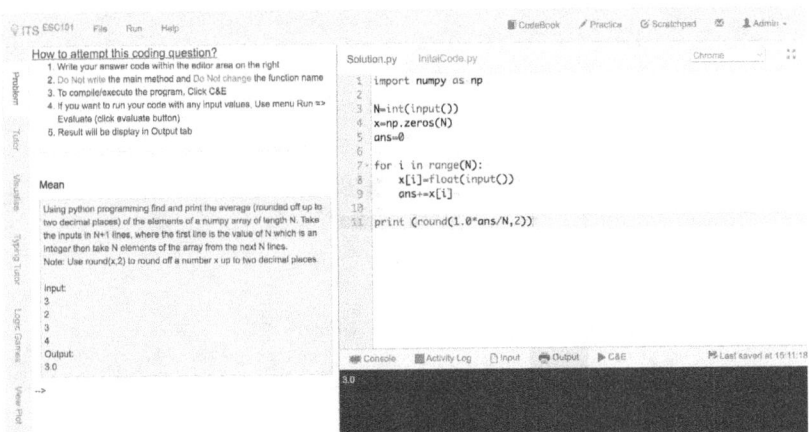

Figure 10: A snapshot of Prutor window.

Prutor hosts a large number of programming exercises on Python. A student can attempt a solution of a programming exercise on the Prutor platform itself. On submission, Prutor evaluates the submitted Python code against given test cases and provides the student with an immediate feedback whether the program's output matches with the expected answer. In case of error, a revised code may be submitted on Prutor.

Thus, Prutor provides an automated tutoring to a student for programming. This is a useful tool for learning how to program.

****

Excercises

1. Install Anaconda Python on your computer.

1.7 Applications of Computers

Most of the present-day science and engineering problems are quite complex. It is impossible to solve many of them analytically. For example, analytical solution for weather forecast is impossible to find. Computers have become ideal tools for addressing such complex problems.

In this section we provide an overview of various computational applications in science and engineering. I have classified them thematically.

Flows

Computers are used heavily for solving flow problems. Some of the leading examples are

- *Weather and climate forecast:* This complex problem of fluid mechanics and nonlinear dynamics requires enormous computing resources. The major challenges in this field are global warming, climate forecast, formation of clouds and rains, etc. Every nation employs their best computers for these applications.

- *Flows around automobiles, aeroplanes, space vehicles, and rockets:* Such flows are quite complex. Scientists and engineers employ advanced numerical techniques and supercomputers to study them. Combustion is another problem with many unsolved issues for which computers are used heavily.

- *Oil exploration:* Major supercomputing efforts are on oil exploration due to economic issues. Here we simulate oil flows between the rocks, buried deep inside the Earth.

- *Physics of turbulence:* There are many unsolved issues in turbulence. For example, we do not fully understand monsoon dynamics, global warming, physics of convection in the atmosphere, and mechanism of generation of magnetic field in stars and planets. Computers have become handy for getting insights into these problems.

- *Flows in and around stars, blackholes, galaxies, and planets:* Some of the challenges in astrophysical fluid dynamics are planet formation, accretion of matter to the central star, stellar winds, corona heating in the Sun, physics of magnetohydrodynamic turbulence. Supercomputers are heavily used for solving such problems.

- *Quantum turbulence:* Turbulence in superfluid and Bose-Einstein condensate yields interesting insights into the quantum world, namely quantum dissipation, multiscale interactions, etc. Computers play an important role in this field of research.

Materials and Quantum Systems

- *Simulations of quantum matter:* Schrödinger's equations for Hydrogen atom and quantum oscillator have been solved analytically. However, no other atom (even Helium) or molecule have an exact solution. This is due to the complex many body interactions in these systems. Hence, computers are used heavily to solve such problems. Simulations of complex molecules have immediate practical applications in drug design and material science (e.g. strong material, noncorrosive steel, etc.).

- *Quantum Monte Carlo:* Simulations of a collection of quantum particles are performed using quantum Monte Carlo. The other popular methods in this field are *density functional theory* (DFT), *particle simulation*, etc.

Nonlinear Physics, Health

Most processes in the world are nonlinear. In fact, large number of problems discussed earlier involve complex nonlinearities. Besides them, nonlinear systems of current interests are

- *Epidemic evolution:* This field has become prominent due to COVID-19 pandemic. Epidemic growth occurs via nonlinear interactions involving people, government, intervention mechanisms, etc. Computer simulations and modelling are heavily used in this field.

- *Drug design:* Computers are employed for drug discovery. These studies involve interactions of drug molecules with human cells.

- *Understanding brain:* We hardly understand human or animal brain. At present, researchers are attempting to simulate brain and understand its behaviour. Some groups simulate billions of neurons and their interactions.

- *Networks:* Interactions in social network, biological and ecological networks, computer networks are quite complex. Computers provide interesting avenue to learn their dynamics.

- *Human body:* Medical scientists are studying heart, brain, blood flow, etc. using computers.

- *Tectonics and earthquakes:* Researchers are trying to understand the physics of earthquakes, and, possibly, predict earthquakes.

Machine learning, Defence, Economics

- *Machine learning:* This field has become very important at present. Here, the emphasis is on understanding the patterns of data, not on the underlying physics. For example, a computer learns to contrast a cow from a horse by observing thousands of images of cows and horses.

- *Defence:* Computers are used heavily for war games, surveillance, cracking passwords, and making weapons.

- *Economics:* Large computers are employed in stock market for data management, predictions of stock market, etc.

Complex Physics

- *Dark matter/energy and evolution of the universe:* Researchers model the matter and energy in the universe, and compare the model predictions with the astronomical observations. Some researchers aim to simulate the whole universal.

- *Fusion and Tokomak simulation:* Nuclear fusion and inertial confinement (imploding matter using high-powered lasers) involve complex physics. In these problems, we have to deal with charged particles, plasmas, electromagnetic fields, as well as large-scale flow dynamics. Computer simulations provide important clues for understanding these complex systems.

- *Lattice quantum chromodynamics:* Even though the equations for nuclear matter (quarks and gluons) are known for sometime, their solution still remains elusive. Hence, researchers simulate the quantum fields of quarks and gluons and try to model properties of nuclei.

- *Accelerator simulations and data analysis:* Particle colliders generate huge amount of data that can be analysed only using computers. Large groups of scientists are involved in such efforts.

There are many more applications, but we will stop here.

****

Conceptual Questions

1. How are computers useful in science and engineering?

Exercises

1. Identify appliances at your house and in your classrooms that rely on computers.
2. Identify computer applications that have not been listed in this section.
3. Discuss some of the engineering applications where computers are being used.

Chapter Two
PYTHON DATA TYPES: INTEGERS AND FLOATS

Synopsis

"Most good programmers do programming not because they expect to get paid or get adulation by the public, but because it is fun to program"
— Linus Torvalds

This chapter describes how numbers are stored in computers.

2.1 Integers

Primary Python data structures are of the following types:

1. Integer
2. Floating point number
3. String
4. List
5. Array
6. Dictionary

In this section, we will discuss the *integer* data type.

Representation of Integers

Recall how the numbers are represented in *decimal system* or *base-10* system. The decimal number 953 is

$$953 = 9 \times 10^2 + 5 \times 10^1 + 3 \times 10^0 = 9 \times 100 + 5 \times 10 + 3.$$

In 953, the digits 9, 5, and 3 have different weights: 9 multiplied by 100, 5 by 10, and 3 by 1.

Classical computers employ *binary system* (*base-2*), whose digits are 0 and 1. These digits called *bits*. Using these bits, a general binary number is represented as follows:

$$(b_{N-1} b_{N-2} \ldots b_2 b_1 b_0)_2 = b_{N-1} \times 2^{N-1} + b_{N-2} \times 2^{N-2} + \ldots$$
$$+ b_2 \times 2^2 + b_1 \times 2^1 + b_0 \times 2^0, \ldots.(1)$$

where b_i is the bit at the ith index. A particular example, illustrated in Figure 11, is

$$(101)_2 = 1 \times 2^2 + 0 \times 2^1 + 1 \times 2^0 = (5)_{10}.$$

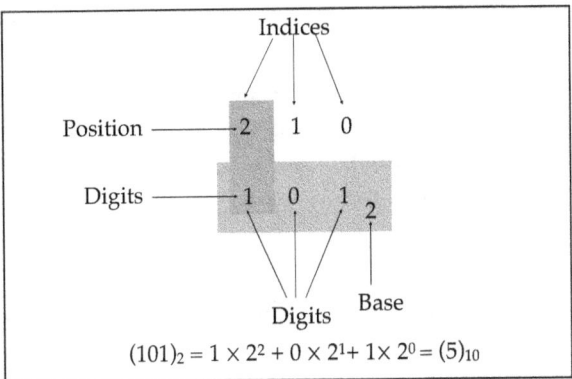

Figure 11: An example of binary number number: $(101)_2$

Some other examples of binary numbers are

$(11)_2 = 1 \times 2^1 + 1 \times 2^0 = (3)_{10}$,
$(1101)_2 = 1 \times 2^3 + 1 \times 2^2 + 0 \times 2^1 + 1 \times 2^0 = (13)_{10}$.

We need both positive and negative integers. The first digit is reserved as a sign bit: 0 for positive integers, and 1 for negative integers. Representation of negative numbers in computers will be discussed at the end of this section.

We require many bits to represent large integers. *Hexadecimal* or *base 16* (*hex*, in short) system becomes handy on such occasion. In hex system, the digits are 0, 1, 2, ..., 9, A, B, C, D, E, F. Here,

$$(h_{N-1} h_{N-2} \ldots h_2 h_1 h_0)_2 = h_{N-1} \times 16^{N-1} + h_{N-2} \times 16^{N-2} + \ldots$$
$$+ h_2 \times 16^2 + h_1 \times 16^1 + h_0 \times 16^0. \quad \ldots (2)$$

The decimal number $(251)_{10}$ in hexadecimal is $(FB)_{16}$:

$(1111\ 1011)_2 = (FB)_{16} = 15 \times 16 + 11 = (251)_{10}$.

Octal number system, which has base 8 and digits 0, 1, 2, 3, 4, 5, 6, and 7, are defined similarly. An example of a number in octal system is

$(11\ 111\ 011)_2 = (373)_8 = 3 \times 8^2 + 7 \times 8 + 3 = (251)_{10}$.

We, thus, show how an integer can be represented in different number systems. Note that a number is the same, but its representations are different.

It is intriguing why humans chose decimal system over others. It is possibly because we have 10 fingers to count. Note that binary representation of large numbers requires too many bits, hence it is not a practical system for daily use.

Conversions Between Different Number Systems

We employ decimal number system in our daily lives, but computers employ binary number system. Hence, we need to convert one representation to another. Conversion from binary to decimal, and from hex to decimal are straightforward. We can employ Eq. (1) and Eq. (2) for these conversions.

The converse, conversion from decimal to binary, is performed as follows. Suppose we want to convert $(19)_{10}$ to binary. Since $16 < 19 < 32$, we write $19 = 16+3$. Now $3 = 2+1$. Therefore, $(19)_{10} = 16+2+1 = (10011)_2$. Following similar process, we convert a decimal number to hex system. For example, $(251)_{10} = 16 \times 15 + 11$. Therefore, $(251)_{10} = (FB)_{16}$.

Python provides functions for binary, octal, and hex equivalents of a decimal number. For example, the following functions provide binary, octal, and hex equivalents to decimal number $(100)_{10}$.

```
In [18]: x=100

In [21]: bin(x)
Out[21]: '0b1100100'

In [22]: oct(x)
Out[22]: '0o144'

In [23]: hex(x)
Out[23]: '0x64'
```

In the above code segment, 0b, 0o, and 0x represent respectively the binary, octal, and hex representations. Using inverse functions, we can obtain decimal representations of numbers in base 2, 10, or hex. For example,

```
In [86]: int('1110',2)   # in base 2
Out[86]: 14

In [89]: int('1110',10)  # in base 10
Out[89]: 1110

In [91]: int('111F',16)  # in base 16
Out[91]: 4383
```

Integers in Computers

Computers typically employ 4 bytes or 32 bits to store an integer. Among the 32 bits, the first bit is reserved for *sign* representation: 0 for positive integers and 1 for negative integers. Hence, the range of integers that can be represented with 4 bytes is -2^{31} to $2^{31}-1$, or -2147483648 to 2147483647. Considering that $2^{10} = 1024 \approx 10^3$, we estimate 2^{31} as $2 \times (10^3)^3$ or 2×10^9. The range of integers that can be represented with 8 bytes is -2^{63} to $2^{63}-1$, which is approximately $8 \times (10^3)^6$ or 8×10^{18}.

However, in python, an integer can of any length. We can demonstrate this statement by the following Python code.

```
In [4]: x=12345678901234567890123456789

In [5]: x
Out[5]: 12345678901234567890123456789

In [7]: x*10
Out[7]: 123456789012345678901234567890
```

In the above example, the integer x contains 29 digits, which is beyond what can be represented with 4 bytes or 8 bytes in C programming language.

The addition, subtraction, multiplication, and integer-division operators in Python are +, −, *, and // respectively. The expression a^b is evaluated in Python as a**b with ** as the power operator. Note that the operator / is used for real division (to be discussed in the next section). For example, 95//45 = 2, but 95/45= 2.111111111111111.

Often we have expressions involving several integers and operators.

Under such situations, we follow the rules given in Table 2.

Table 2: Precedence of arithmetic operators involving integers.

Operator	Function
** (Highest precedence)	Power
*,//,%	Multiplication, Integer division, Modulus
+,- (Lowest precedence)	Add, Subtract

Note that

1. The operators *, //, and % have the same precedence.
2. The operators + and − have the same precedence.
3. Operators with highest precedence are evaluated first.
4. When there are multiple operators with the same precedence, they are evaluated from left to right.
5. Brackets are used to override precedence.

We illustrate some of the above operations using the following examples.

```
In [45]: 2**31-1
Out[45]: 2147483647

In [46]: 5//3
Out[46]: 1

In [47]: 5/3
Out[47]: 1.6666666666666667

In [48]: 3+16//9//3
Out[48]: 3
```

Representation of Negative Integers in Computers

In Python, negative numbers are stored as *two's complement*. Here, a negative number b is stored as $2^N - b$, where is N is the maximum number of bits representing the integer.

We illustrate *two's complement* using examples. For simplicity, we consider a 4-bit computer that can store integers in the range −8 to 7. Note that the first bit is reserved for the sign. The positive integers 0 to 7 are represented as 0000, 0001, 0010, 0011, 0100, 0101, 0110, 0111. To store −3, two's complement of 3 is computed as follows:

1. Bit-flip 3: ~3 = ~0011 = 1100, which is *one's complement* of +3.
2. Add one to the above: ~3+1 = 1101, which is *two's complement* of +3. −3 is stored as 1101.

Using the same method, we deduce that −1, −2 are stored as 1111 and 1110 respectively. See Table 3 for the full list.

Table 3: 1's and 2's compliments of binary numbers from 0000 to 0111 with 4 bits.

number	1's compliment	2's compliment
0000 (0)	1111	No representation (−8)
0001 (1)	1110	1111 (−1)
0010 (2)	1101	1110 (−2)
0011 (3)	1100	1101 (−3)
0100 (4)	1011	1100 (−4)
0101 (5)	1010	1011 (−5)
0110 (6)	1001	1010 (−6)
0111 (7)	1000	1001 (−7)

Using two's compliment we can easily perform the subtraction operation, which is

$$a - b = a + (2^N - b) - 2^N.$$

That is, we add a and two's complement of b, which is $(2^N - b)$. The removal of 2^N is trivially achieved by a bit overflow.

Example 1: Let us see how 4 − 3 is computed in a computer. For the computation, −3 is represented using its 2's complement, which is

1101. After which we add the two numbers as follows:

4 − 3 = 0100 + 1101 = 0001 (with carry of 1 discarded),

which is the correct answer. Note the overflowing bit 1 is discarded.

Example 2: Let us compute 3 − 4 using 2's complement.

3 − 4 = 0011 + 1100 = 1111, which is −1.

The above idea also applies to other number systems. For decimal system, the respective representation is 10's complement. For example, in a three-digit decimal system, −14 would be stored as 1000−14 = 986. Here too, subtraction can be easily performed using 10's complement.

With this, we end our discussion on integers in Python.

****

Conceptual Questions

1. Why is binary system employed for computer memory?
2. Why is the decimal system more suitable than the binary system for daily lives?

Exercises

1. What are the largest and smallest signed and unsigned integers that can be stored in 16-bit, 32-bit, 64-bit, and 128-bit machines?
2. Convert the following binary numbers to decimal numbers. Verify your results using Python functions.
    (a) 11001 (b) 11111111 (c) 1001001
3. Convert the following decimal numbers to binary numbers. Verify your results using Python functions.

(a) 100 (b) 129 (c) 8192

4. Convert the following decimal numbers to hexadecimal numbers. Test your results using Python functions.

   (a) 100 (b) 129 (c) 8192

5. Convert the following hexadecimal numbers to decimal numbers. Test your answers with Python functions.

   (a) 1F (b) DD (c) F54 (d) 555

6. Assume a 1-byte storage for positive and negative integers. Compute 1's and 2's compliments for the following binary numbers. What do these numbers and their 2's complement represent in decimal system?

   (a) 00101010 (b) 01111111 (c) 00001111

7. Perform the following subtraction using 2's compliment and verify your result: 01111111 − 00001111

8. Evaluate the following integer expressions in Python:

   3**3, 9//2, 9/2, 4−6−3, 4−(6−3), 10+90//7, 4//3*7, 4*7//3, 9*2**3

9. Two server have 16GB and 96GB RAM. What are the respective RAM sizes in decimal representation? How many integers can be stored in the RAM of the servers?

2.2 Floating Point and Complex Numbers

To represent real numbers, humans employ decimal number system, while computers use binary number system. Note, however, that there are several ways to describe a real number. For example, half is represented as ½ or 0.5, which are fraction notation and decimal-point notation respectively. In computers, real numbers are represented using binary-point notation (no fraction, except in *sympy*, which is for symbolic processing). An important point to remember is that in computer languages, real numbers are also called *float*, which is a short form for *floating point number*.

A real number can be rational or irrational. Irrational numbers (for example, $\sqrt{2}$, π, and e) require infinite number of digits. Some rational numbers too need infinite number of digits for their representation. For example, in decimal-point notation, ⅓ = 0.3333... with 3 repeating forever.

First, we describe the decimal representation of real numbers.

Fixed Point Notation

We humans represent real numbers as

$$(d_n\, d_{n-1}\, \ldots\, d_0\, .\, d_{-1}\, \ldots\, d_{-m})_{10} = (d_n \times 10^n + d_{n-1} \times 10^{n-1} + \ldots$$
$$+ d_0 + d_{-1} \times 10^{-1} + \ldots + d_{-m} \times 10^{-m}).$$

The number of digits in the above decimal number is $n+m+1$. The number to the left of the decimal point is called *integer*, while to the right of decimal point is called *fraction*. The point separating the integer and fraction is the *decimal point*. Clearly, the weights of the digits decrease as we go rightwards. In addition to the above, we also need a sign symbol: + for positive and − for negative. A specific example of real number is

$$(32.54)_{10} = 3 \times 10 + 2 \times 1 + 5 \times 10^{-1} + 4 \times 10^{-2},$$

which is illustrated in Figure 12(a).

With 4 decimal digits (2 for integer and 2 for fraction), the largest and smallest positive (nonzero) numbers in this notation are 99.99 and 00.01 respectively. Thus, we can represent 10^4 real numbers in this scheme, with the difference between two consecutive real numbers as 0.01, a constant value. The above notation is called *fixed point notation*.

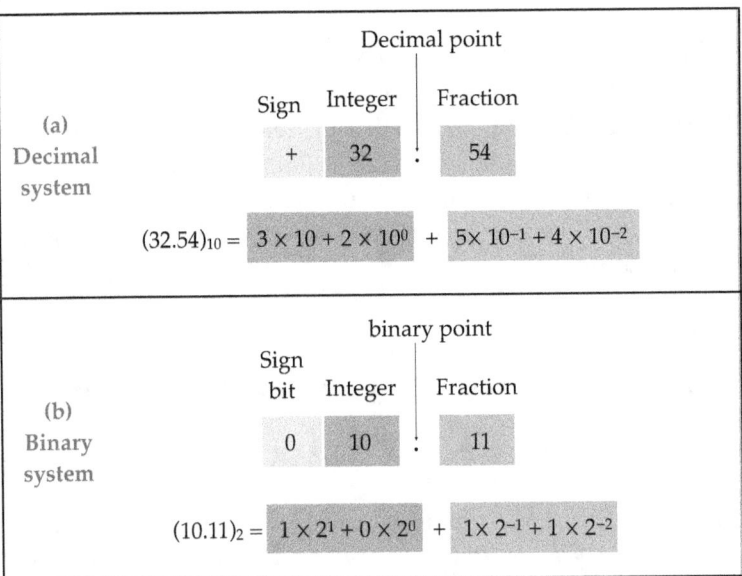

Figure 12: (a) An example of a decimal number, $(32.54)_2$. (b) An example of binary number, $(10.11)_2$

A real number in binary system is

$$(b_n\, b_{n-1}\, \ldots\, b_0\, .\, b_{-1}\, \ldots\, b_{-m})_2 = (b_n \times 2^n + b_{n-1} \times 2^{n-1} + \ldots$$
$$+ b_0 + b_{-1} \times 2^{-1} + \ldots + b_{-m} \times 2^{-m})\, . \quad \ldots(3)$$

Here, similar to the decimal system, the middle point, called *binary point*, separates the integer and fraction. For example, as shown in Figure 12(b),

$$(10.11)_2 = 1 \times 2^1 + 0 \times 2^0 + 1 \times 2^{-1} + 1 \times 2^{-2} = 2 + 0 + 0.5 + 0.25$$
$$= (2.75)_{10}\, .$$

Similarly,

$$(11.1011)_2 = 1 \times 2^1 + 1 \times 2^0 + 1 \times 2^{-1} + 0 \times 2^{-2} + 1 \times 2^{-3} + 1 \times 2^{-4}$$

$$= 2 + 1 + 0.5 + 0.125 + 0.0625 = (3.6875)_{10}.$$

A real number could also be represented in hex and octal systems by replacing the base in Eq. (3) by 16 and 8 respectively.

In the binary system with 1 bit for sign, 5 bits for integer, and 5 bits for fraction, the largest and smallest positive (nonzero) numbers are $(11111.11111)_2$ and $(0.00001)_2$ respectively; they translate to respectively $(31.96875)_{10}$ and $(0.03125)_{10}$ in decimal system.

The above discussion indicates that the range of numbers that can be represented using fixed point scheme is limited, which is a big obstacle for representing a wide range of numbers observed in nature. To achieve this task, we use *floating point scheme*, which will be discussed later in this section.

Conversions Between Binary and Decimal Number Systems

The *integer* part of a real number (e.g., 12 of 12.67) is converted from decimal to binary as described in Section 2.1. Here, we show how to convert the *fraction* part of a real number from decimal to binary. For the same, we keep multiplying the number with 2 and keep taking away the resulting integer, which is either 0 or 1. In the following, we illustrate this conversions process for two fractions, $(0.375)_{10}$ and $(0.80)_{10}$.

In Figure 13(a), we convert $(0.375)_{10}$ to binary representation. For the same, we multiply 0.375 by 2, and collect the integer part (0) as the first binary digit after the binary point. Now, the new fraction, 0.75, is multiplied by 2, and the resulting integer part, 1, is collected as the second binary digit. We continue this process until fraction becomes 0. This process yields $(0.375)_{10} = (0.011)_2$ Thus, representation of 0.375 requires finite number of digits in both decimal and binary representations.

	frac	integer			frac	integer	
0.375 × 2 = 0.75	0.75	0	b_{-1}	0.8 × 2 = 1.6	0.6	1	b_{-1}
0.75 × 2 = 1.5	0.5	1	b_{-2}	0.6 × 2 = 1.2	0.2	1	b_{-2}
0.5 × 2 = 1	0	1	b_{-3}	0.2 × 2 = 0.4	0.4	0	b_{-3}
				0.4 × 2 = 0.8	0.8	0	b_{-4}

$(0.375)_{10} = (0.011)_2$ $(0.8)_{10} = (0.11001100\ldots)_2$

(a)   (b)

Figure 13: Conversion of a decimal number to binary number: (a) 0.375; (b) 0.8.

This conversion process does not converge for some decimal numbers. As shown in Figure 13(b), 0.8→1.6→0.6→1.2→0.2→0.4→0.8. Therefore, $(0.8)_{10} = (0.1100\ 1100\ 1100\ \ldots)_2$ with 1100 recurring. Note that $(0.8)_{10}$ requires finite number of digits in the decimal system, but infinite number of bits in the binary system.

Following similar arguments, we deduce that $(⅓)_{10} = (0.01\ 01\ 01\ \ldots)_2$ with 01 recurring. Note that $(⅓)_{10} = (0.3333\ \ldots)_{10}$. Thus, both decimal and binary representations of $(⅓)_{10}$ require infinite number of digits. However, $(⅓)_{10}$ requires only one digit in tertiary (base-3) system: $(⅓)_{10} = (0.1)_3$.

More examples:

$(1.1)_{10} = (1.0001\ 1001\ 1001\ 1001\ \ldots)_2$ with recurrence of 1001
$(1.5)_{10} = 1 + 1/2 = (1.1)_2$
$(15.0)_{10} = 8 + 4 + 2 + 1 = (1111)_2 = 1.111 \times 2^3$
$(150.0)_{10} = 9 \times 16 + 6 = (1001\ 0110)_2 = 1.001\ 0110 \times 2^7$
$(1.75)_{10} = 1 + 1 \times 2^{-1} + 2^{-2} = (1.11)_2$

In computers, a finite number of bytes is allocated for number representation. Hence, even in principle, some numbers (e.g., ⅓, √2, and 0.8) cannot be represented accurately in a computer. We discuss this issue at the end of the section.

We convert a decimal number to hexadecimal number by following the same procedure as in Figure 13. For example, we can convert $(0.375)_{10}$ and $(0.8)_{10}$ to hexadecimal number by multiplying the fraction with 16. We multiply 0.375 with 16 that yields 6, which is h_{-1}. We stop at this stage because the fraction is zero. Hence, $(0.375)_{10} = (0.6)_x$, where the subscript x represents the hex number system. Note, however, that the iteration does not terminate for some numbers. For example, for 0.8, the next fraction remains as 0.8. You can easily verify that $(0.8)_{10} = (0.CC\ldots)_x$.

	frac	integer			frac	integer
0.375 x 16 = 12	0	C h_{-1}	0.8 x 16 = 12.8	0.8	C	h_{-1}

$(0.375)_{10} = (0.C)_x$ $\qquad$ $(0.8)_{10} = (0.CC\ldots)_x$

(a) $\qquad\qquad\qquad$ (b)

Figure 14: Conversion of a decimal number hexadecimal number: (a) 0.375; (b)0.8.

Following similar lines, we can convert the other numbers discussed earlier.

$(1/3)_{10} = (0.55\ldots)_x$ with recurrence of 5
$(1.1)_{10} = (1.1999\ldots)_x$ with recurrence of 9
$(1.5)_{10} = (1.8)_x$
$(1.75)_{10} = (1.C)_x$

Floating Point Notation

In this notation, a real number is written as

$$\text{real number} = \text{mantissa} \times b^{\text{exponent}}$$

where b is the *base*. Note that we need sign bits for both fraction (called *mantissa*) and exponent. For a unique representation, we need to make certain rules for the mantissa. For example, for the decimal system, we may impose a condition that the integer part is zero, and that the first digit after the decimal must be nonzero. Hence, the number 0.540×10^E is allowed, but 0.054×10^E is not allowed; here E is the exponent. This is because 0.054×10^E is represented as $0.54 \times 10^{E-1}$.

With the above rule, in decimal system, the largest and smallest positive numbers that could be represented using 2 digits each for mantissa and exponent are 0.99×10^{99} and 0.10×10^{-99} respectively. Thus, the range of numbers in floating point representation is much larger than that in the fixed point representation. Another important property of this number system is that for a given exponent E, the gap between two consecutive real numbers is 0.1×10^E. Note that the gap jumps by a factor of 10 when the exponent is incremented by 1.

Interestingly, the above *multiscale* feature is observed in nature. In the animal kingdom, first comes viruses whose sizes are in nanometers, after which comes bacteria, whose sizes are of the order of micrometers. Then comes insects (of size cms) and mammals (of size meters). Thus, the sizes of the animals within a class vary gradually, but there are jumps in the size when we go from one class of animals to another. Physical systems too exhibit similar multiscale structures. We start with nuclei (at femtometer) and then go to atoms and molecules (nanometers), polymers (microns), ..., objects for daily use (meters), oceans and planets (1000 kms), stars (10^6 km), galaxies (light years), and universe (10^9 light years). Thus, the floating point number system is suitable for representing natural systems.

Binary system is used in computers. For floating-point binary numbers, a constraint is imposed that the integer part of the mantissa is always 1. For example, 1.1×2^{-2} is a valid representation. However, 101.1×2^{-2} and 0.0111×2^{-2} are invalid; they can be written as 1.011×2^0 and 1.11×2^{-4} respectively. With 5 bits each for mantissa and exponents (apart from sign bits), the largest and smallest numbers representable in the binary system are 1.11111×2^{31} and 1.00000×2^{-31} respectively; in decimal system, they translate to $(1.96875) \times 2^{31}$ and 1.0×2^{-31} respectively. Similar procedure can be used to represent numbers in hex and octal number systems.

Next, we discuss the details of real number representation in a computer.

Real Numbers in Computers

Computers store real numbers in floating point representation. Typically, 64 bits are employed to store a real number. Among the 64 bits, 52 bits are reserved for the mantissa, 11 bits for the exponent, and 1 bit for the sign (see Figure 15). The integer part of the mantissa is always taken to be 1, and it is not stored. There is no sign bit for the exponent, rather, the exponent is computed as $E-1024$, where E is the value of the 11 bits. Since E lies in the range of 0 to 2047, the exponent varies from -1024 to 1023. Thus, the real number is

$$\text{Number} = (-1)^{\text{sign}} (1.b_{-1}b_{-2}\ldots b_{-52}) \times 2^{E-1023}.$$

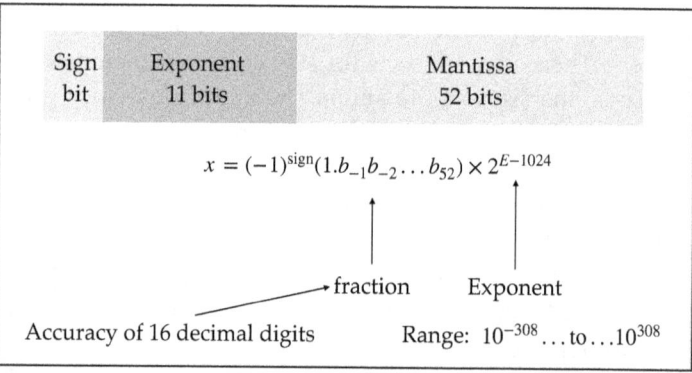

Figure 15: Computer representation of a real number using 64 bits.

Special numbers are represented in the following way:

1. *Actual zero*: $E = 0$, Mantissa $= 0$.
2. *Infinity*: $E = 2047$, Mantissa $= 0$; $+\infty$ when sign $= 1$, but $-\infty$ when sign $= 0$.
3. *Not a number* (NaN): $E = 2047$ and nonzero mantissa.

Python offers function *float.hex* to convert decimal to hex. For example,

```
In [95]: float.hex(1.5)
Out[95]: '0x1.8000000000000p+0'
```

In Out[95], `x' stands for hex. The mantissa for $(1.5)_{10}$ in binary is 100... (with 51 zeros), which corresponds to 13 hex digits, 8000000000000. The exponent is 0, as is evident from p+0. Similarly,

```
In [1]: float.hex(15.0)
Out[1]: '0x1.e000000000000p+3'

In [2]: float.hex(150.0)
Out[2]: '0x1.2c00000000000p+7'

In [3]: float.hex(-150.0)
Out[3]: '-0x1.2c00000000000p+7'

In [5]: float.hex(0.8)
Out[5]: '0x1.999999999999ap-1'

In [6]: float.hex(0.375)
Out[6]: '0x1.8000000000000p-2'

In [7]: float.hex(1/3)
Out[7]: '0x1.5555555555555p-2'

In [8]: (1.1).hex()
Out[8]: '0x1.199999999999ap+0'
```

The above results are consistent with the fact that $(15.0)_{10} = 1.111 \times 2^3$. Thus, mantissa is E in hex and it is written as e in Out[1]), while the exponent is 3. Next, $(150.0)_{10} = 1.0010\ 1100 \times 2^7$ with the mantissa as 2C, and the exponent is 7. Note that +150.0 and −150.0 differ only in the sign bit.

The Python function, float.fromhex() is the inverse function, that is from hex to float. For example,

```
In [4]: float.fromhex('0x1.199999999999ap+0')
Out[4]: 1.1

In [5]: float.fromhex('0x1.e000000000000p+3')
Out[5]: 15.0
```

In Python, infinity and NaN are represented as

```
In [165]: math.inf
Out[165]: inf

In [170]: math.nan
Out[170]: nan

In [153]: myzero = '0x0.0000000000000p-1023'

In [154]: float.fromhex(myzero)
Out[154]: 0.0
```

Since $E = 2047$ is reserved for the infinity, the largest positive floating-point number has $E = 2046$ or exponent = 1023. Therefore,

$$f_{max} = (1.111\ldots1)_2 \times 2^{1023} = (1.\text{FFFFFFFFFFFFF})_{16} \times 2^{1023}$$
$$\approx (1.7976931348623157)_{10} \times 10^{308}$$

```
In [106]: float.fromhex('0x1.FFFFFFFFFFFFFp+1023' )
Out[106]: 1.7976931348623157e+308

In [104]: sys.float_info.max
Out[104]: 1.7976931348623157e+308

In [105]: (sys.float_info.max).hex()
Out[105]: '0x1.fffffffffffffp+1023'
```

Note that $1023 \times \log_{10}(2) \approx 308$. The smallest positive float represented in a computer is computed in a similar manner. Since $E = 0$ is reserved for zero, we take $E = 1$ for the smaller float number. Also, mantissa = 0 for this case. Therefore,

$$f_{min} = (1.000 \ldots 000)_2 \times 2^{-1022} \approx (2.2250738585072014)_{10} \times 10^{-308}$$

The corresponding Python statements are

```
In [19]: float.fromhex('0x1.0p-1022')
Out[19]: 2.2250738585072014e-308

In [106]: sys.float_info.min
Out[106]: 2.2250738585072014e-308

In [107]: sys.float_info.min.hex()
```

```
Out[107]: '0x1.0000000000000p-1022'
```

Also note that the numbers beyond the allowable range are either zero or infinite, depending on whether the number is lower than the minimum number or larger than the maximum number.

In [27]: print(1e308)
1e+308

In [28]: print(1e309)
inf

In [29]: print(3*1e308)
Inf

In [33]: print(1e-500)
0.0

The floating point operators along with their precedence are listed in Table 4. Keep in mind the difference between the integer division (//) and real division (/).

Table 4: Precedence of arithmetic operators involving real numbers

Operator	Function
** (Highest precedence)	Power
*, /	Multiplication, Division
+,- (Lowest precedence)	Add, Subtract

The precedence rules for the float operators are given below. These rules are similar to those for integer operators.

1. The operators * and / have the same precedence.
2. The operators + and − have the same precedence, but they have lower precedence than * and /.
3. Operators with highest precedence are evaluated first.
4. In case of multiple operators with the same precedence, they are evaluated from left to right.
5. Brackets are used to override precedence.

There are many float functions that are part of *Numpy* module. Some of the functions are *sqrt()*, *log()*, *log10()*, *sin()*, *cos()*, *int()* and *round()*. The function *int()* truncates the real number and returns a integer value, while *round()* rounds off the real number.

```
In [113]: int(13.5)
Out[113]: 13

In [115]: round(13.6)
Out[115]: 14

In [21]: round(13.5)
Out[21]: 14

In [21]: round(13.1)
Out[21]: 13
```

Precision, Round-off or Truncation Errors

We estimate the *precision* of a 64-bit computer as follows. The nearest floats differ in bit b_{-52} while keeping E fixed. Consecutively, the difference between two consecutive numbers with the same exponent would be $2^{-52} \times 2^{E-1024}$. Therefore, the precision of a 64-bit real computer is

$$P = 2^{-52} \approx 2.22 \times 10^{-16}$$

that corresponds to 16 decimal digits. Therefore, the maximum significant digits for Python float is 16.

As we discussed earlier in this section. many real numbers can not be represented precisely due to finite number of bits available to save a number. Such an error, called *round-off error* or *truncation error*, could arise due to one or more of the following reasons:

1. Finite number of bits used: For example, consider a number 1.CC...with 20 C's. In a 64-bit machine, we can only save 13 C's, while the rest 7 C's will be ignored.
2. Truncation of digits in the expansion of rational numbers (as in ⅓).
3. Conversion from decimal to binary representation (as in

$(0.8)_{10}$).

On many occasions, an exact arithmetic operation and the corresponding computer output do not match due to truncation errors. For example,

```
In [23]: 0.8*3
Out[23]: 2.4000000000000004

In [24]: 0.8*3-2.4
Out[24]: 4.440892098500626e-16

In [25]: 1.5*3
Out[25]: 4.5

In [26]: 1.5*3-4.5
Out[26]: 0.0
```

Computer-generated 3*0.8 does not match with exact value of 2.4. The difference 0.8*3-2.4 is nonzero, and it is around 10^{-16}, which is the machine precision. The above error is because 0.8 is not representable exactly in binary system (($0.8)_{10}$ = $(0.CC \ldots)_x$). On the contrary, 1.5*3 matches with its exact value 4.5 because 1.5 is represented exactly in a computer.

For more precise calculations, special tricks are employed to achieve better computing precision than 16 digits. For example, π has been computed with precision of billions of digits using advanced mathematical tricks. In Section 9.1 we will discuss errors and precision in more detail.

We relate the precision of a computer to the finite number of states representable by 64 bits. With 64 bits, we can represent 2^{64} distinct numbers, irrespective of schemes (fixed point, float point, or whatever). The rest of the numbers can be stored only approximately. This is the origin of errors in floating-point arithmetics. Note that integers do not have round-off errors because they are represented accurately, as long as they are within the limit, e.g., -2^{63} to $2^{63}-1$ for a 64-bit machine.

32-bit and 64-bit Processors

Some processors employ 32-bit or 16-bit representations for real numbers, and they called 32-bit and 16-bit processors respectively. The ranges of real numbers in these machines are smaller than those of 64-bit processors. Examples of such processors are *GPUs* (*Graphical Processor Units*) and those inside cars, air conditioners, TV sets, etc. Applications in these devices do not require extreme precision.

In a *32-bit* or *single-precision floating-point format*, the exponents and mantissa are represented using 8 and 23 bits respectively. In *16-bit* or *half-precision floating-point format*, the corresponding bits are 5 and 10 respectively. One bit is reserved for the sign.

In a 32-bit machine, the exponent = $\pm 2^7 = \pm 128$, which translates to

$-128*\log_{10}(2) <$ decimal exponent $< 128*\log_{10}(2)$.

That is, the decimal exponent lies in the range of -38 to $+38$. The precision $2^{-23} \approx 1.19 \times 10^{-7}$ that corresponds to 7 significant decimal digits. Similarly we can deduce that the precision of a 16-bit machine is $2^{-10} \approx 9.7 \times 10^{-4}$, while its exponent lies in the range of -4.8 to $+4.8$ ($16*\log_{10}(2)$).

Complex Float

A complex number in Python is a combination of two real numbers, one for the real part and the other for the imaginary part. The syntax for a complex number assignment is as follows:

```
In [12]: z = 1.0+2.0j
```

where 1.0 and 2.0 are the real and imaginary parts of *z, and j* represents $\sqrt{-1}$. The operations on complex numbers are illustrated using the following Python statement. Here, * performs complex multiplication, while the functions *abs*() and *conj*() return respectively the absolute value and complex conjugate of the complex number.

```
In [13]: x*x, x*2, abs(x), conj(x)
```

Practical Numerical Computing Using Python

```
Out[13]: (2j, (2+2j), 1.4142135623730951, (1-1j))
```

With this, we close our discussion on Python's floats and complex numbers.

****

Conceptual Questions

1. For a computer implementation of real numbers, what are the advantages of floating-point representation over the fixed-point representation? Provide examples to support your arguments.
2. Nature has multiscale structure. Which among the two, floating-point representation and fixed-point representation, is more suitable for describing nature?
3. What are the advantages of two's complement representation of negative numbers over signed representation?
4. Derive the precision of a 16-bit processor?

Exercises

1. Convert the following binary numbers to decimal numbers:
    (a) 1.01 (b) 11.1 (c) 0.1001 (d) 1111.11 (e) 11.101
2. Convert the following decimal numbers to binary numbers. Verify your results using Python function.
    (a) 1/8 (b) 1/10 (c) 14.0 (d) 7/10 (e) 256.0
3. Convert the following hexadecimal numbers to decimal numbers:
    (a) 0.F (b) F.F (c) 1.8 (d) 0.C (e) 0.A
4. Convert the following decimal numbers to hexadecimal numbers. Verify your results using Python function.
    (a) 1.6 (b) 1.4 (c) 0.9 (d) 1/3 (e) 0.256
5. What are the largest and smallest positive floats that can be stored in 32-bit and 64-bit computers? What are the corresponding negative floats? How many distinct real

numbers can be represented in these computers?

6. Give examples of real numbers that have inexact representations in both binary and decimal.
7. Give examples of real numbers that have exact representation in decimal, but inexact in binary.
8. Give examples of real numbers that have exact representation in base 3, but inexact in base 10.
9. In a hypothetical computer, double-precision representation requires 1 bit for sign, 7 bits for the exponent, and 13 bits for the mantissa. What are the smallest and largest positive real numbers that can be represented in such a machine? What is the precision of this machine?

2.3 Python Variables and Logical Variables

Like any programming language, Python too has variables. A python variable is associated with an object, which could be integer, float, or other data type. For example, in the following Python statement

In [1]: x=8,

x is associated with the object 8 ($x \longleftrightarrow 8$). Here, $x = 8$ does not mean equality, rather, = is an assignment operator.

We can obtain the value of x by just typing x:

In [2]: x
Out[2]: 8

We can perform operations on x, which is equivalent to operating on its associated object 8. For example,

In [3]: x**3
Out[3]: 512

We can print x or any expression involving x using the *print* function:

In [4]: print(x, x**3)
8   512

We can reassign x to another number, say 5.5, as shown below:

In [5]: x = 5.5

In [6]: x
Out[6]: 5.5

After the statement *In* [5], x is associated with the new number 5.5, which is a real number. Note that data-type of a Python variable is not fixed; after assigning a Python variable to an integer, it can be reassigned to a real number, or a string, or an array (strings and arrays will be discussed in the next chapter).

In Python, the integers, as well as other data types, are objects. The location and size of the objects can be determined using the *Python methods* (or *functions*), *id*() and *sys.getsizeof*() respectively. For example,

```
In [67]: x = 100

In [68]: sys.getsizeof(x)
Out[68]: 28

In [76]: id(x)
Out[76]: 4563550448

In [77]: y=x

In [78]: id(y)
Out[78]: 4563550448
```

The *address* of the object 100 is 4563550448. That is, 100 is stored at this memory location. Note that after *In* [77], both the variables x and y are labels to the same object 100, hence, they have the same address. In Section 3.5 we cover this topic in more detail.

Note that the size of the *data object* 100 is 28 bytes. Since $x \leq 2^{30}-1$, 4 bytes are used to store x, while the remaining 24 bytes are used for storing other attributes of the object. Note that the integers which are greater than 2^{30} but less than 2^{60} take 8 bytes to store. Larger integers require even larger number of bytes.

We can clear all the Python objects of a python session using the *reset* function:

```
In [10]: reset
Once deleted, variables cannot be recovered. Proceed (y/
[n])? y
```

We remark that several Python statements can be written in a single line with semicolons separating them. For example,

```
In [47]: x=5; y = 6; z = x*y; print("x = ", x, "y =", y,
"z = ",  z)
x =   5 y = 6 z =   30
```

In the print statement, "x =", "y = ", and "z =" are strings that are printed as they are.

Variable Names and Keywords

The names of Python variables can be of any length. However, variable names obey the following rules:

1. A variable name must start with a letter or an underscore (_).
2. A variable name cannot start with a number.
3. A variable name can contain alpha-numeric characters (A-Z, a-z, 0-9) and underscore (_). It cannot contain any other character including special characters, such as $,%, etc.
4. Variable names are case-sensitive. For example, *a* and *A* are different variables, so are India and india.

It is a good programming practice to choose appropriate names for the variables. For example, for the city temperature, *temperature* is a good variable name, while *temp* is a terrible choice because *temp* is also used as a short form for *temporary*.

Python *keywords* are used for specific purposes, and they should not be used as variable names or function names. Here is the list Python keywords:

and, as, assert, break, class, continue, def, del, elif, else, except, False, finally, for, from, global, if, import, in, Is, lambda, none, nonlocal, not, or, pass, raise, return, True, try, while, with, yield.

Logical Variables in Python

Logical variables and *logical expressions* play an important role in Python programming. We encounter them everywhere, specially in conditional statements and in loops (see Chapter Four). In honour of George Boole, who pioneered the study of modern logic, logical variables are also also called *Boolean variables*.

Logical data types and logical expressions take two values, *True* or *False*. For example,

```
In [28]: 5 < 6
Out[28]: True

In [29]: 5>6
```

```
Out[29]: False

In [33]: 5 == 6
Out[33]: False

In [34]: 5 == 5
Out[34]: True
```

In the above expressions, <, >, == are comparison operators that compares two operands and return True or False. See Table 5 for a list of comparative operator.

Table 5: A list of comparative operators

Operator	Name	Example
==	Equal	x == y
!=	Not equal	x != y
>	Greater than	x>y
<	Less than	x<y
>=	Greater than or equal to	x>= y
<=	Less than or equal to	x<=y

We can combine logical expressions using boolean operators *and, or, xor* (exclusive or), and *not*, whose functions are as follows:

1. *A and B* yield True only if both the operands are True. Otherwise, the result is False. For example, *True and True = True*.
2. *A or B* yield True if any one of the operands is True. *A or B* is False if both *A* and *B* are False. For example, *True or False = True*.
3. *A xor B* is True if and only one argument is True and the other argument is False. For example, *True xor True = False*, and *True xor False = True*.
4. *not A* is opposite of *A*. For example, *not True = False*.

Note that the logical operations are analogous to its English usage. Also note that *xor* operator is not available in Python. Refer to Table 6 for the results of these operators.

Table 6: Truth table ($T = True$ and $F = False$)

A	B	A and B	A or B	A xor B	not A
T	T	T	T	F	F
T	F	F	T	T	F
F	T	F	T	T	T
F	F	F	F	F	T

In case of multiple boolean variables and operators, the sequence of operations is decided by the precedence of the operators, which is listed in Table 7.

Table 7: Precedence of logical operator (from highest to lowest)

Operator	Function
`<, <=, > , >=, !=, ==` (highest)	Comparison
`not`	Boolean not
`and`	Boolean AND
`or` (lowest)	Boolean OR

We illustrate logical operators using the following examples. First, we start with the *or* operator.

```
In [38]: is_summer = (month == 5) or (month == 6) or
(month == 7)

In [40]: month = 5

In [41]: is_summer
Out[41]: True
```

is_summer is a logical variable that takes value *True* when the *month* is May (5th month), June (6th month), or July (7th month); it is *False* otherwise. After this, we illustrate the *and* operator.

```
In [7]: angles_equal = True

In [8]: sides_equal = True

In [9]: is_square = (angles_equal == True) and
(sides_equal == True)

In [10]: is_square
```

```
Out[10]: True

In [11]: sides_equal = False

In [13]: is_square = (angles_equal == True) and
(sides_equal == True)

In [14]: is_square
Out[14]: False
```

A quadrangle is a square if and only if all the sides, as well as angles, of the quadrangle are equal. The boolean variable *is_square* is True when both the conditions are True. The variable *is_square* is false when either of the two conditions is false. The above example illustrates operator *and*.

After this, we illustrate the *not* operator. A person is well if he/she is not sick. Hence *is_well* = *not*(*is_sick*).

```
In [16]: is_sick = True

In [17]: is_well = not(is_sick)

In [18]: is_well
Out[18]: False
```

Some more examples of boolean operations are here.

```
In [96]: P = True

In [97]: Q = False

In [98]: P and Q
Out[98]: False

In [99]: P or Q and P
Out[99]: True

In [100]: not P and Q
Out[100]: False
```

Another interesting feature of Python is that boolean values of any nonzero Integer, nonzero float, and string are *True*, while those of 0 and 0.0 are *False*. See the illustration below.

```
In [108]: bool(5), bool(-5.0)
Out[108]: (True, True)

In [112]: bool(0), bool(0.0)
Out[112]: (False, False)
```

Bitwise Operations

At the end of this section we discuss bitwise operations on binary bits. Since 1 and 0 are treated as *True* and *False* respectively, we can extend the logical operations listed in Table 6 to binary numbers. For example, 1 & 1 = 1, where & stands for the bitwise AND operator. The symbols used for other binary operators are listed in Table 8.

Table 8: A list of bitwise operators

Operator	Name	Example
&	Bitwise AND	5 & 6 = 4
|	Bitwise OR	5 | 6 = 7
^	Bitwise XOR	5^6 = 3
~	Bitwise NOT	~5 = −6
<< m	Bitwise left shift by m bits	5 << 1 = 10
>> m	Bitwise right shift by m bits	5 >> 1 = 2

We illustrate the above operations as follows:

1. 5 & 6 = (101)&(110) = 100 = 4
2. 5 | 6 = (101)|(110) = 111 = 7
3. 5 ^ 6 = (101)^(110) = 011 = 3
4. ~5=~(101) = 010, whose negative equivalence is −6 (for 3 bit numbers, −(8−2)). This convention differs from that of Table 3.
5. ~11=~(1011)=0100, whose negative equivalence is −12 (for 4 bit numbers, −(16−4) = −12).
6. In fact, ~n = −(n+1). Prove it!
7. 5 << 1 = (0101) << 1 = 1010 = 10
8. 5 >> 1 = (0101) >> 1 = 0010 = 2

Note that shift left by m bits yields multiplication by 2^m, while shift right by m bits yields integer division by 2^m. Thus, we can perform fast multiplication or division using bit-shift operators. Such tricks are used in computers.

****

Conceptual Questions

1. What are the differences between = and == operators of Python?
2. List efficient ways to divide an integer by 8?

Exercises

1. In Ipython, type the statement: $y = 89$. Obtain the memory location where 89 is stored.
2. Suppose x = 5 and y = 10. What are the outputs of the following logical expressions?
    - $x < y$, $x <= y$, $x == y$, $x\ != y$, $x < y$ or $x > y$, $x < y$ and $x > y$
3. Given three logical variables, A = True, B=True, and C=False, evaluate the following logical expressions:
    - A and C, A or C, not C, A and B and C, A and B or C, not A or B or C, bool(10.0), bool(0)
4. State the results of the following bitwise operations:
    - 7 & 9, 7 | 8, 7 ^ 9, ~7, ~9, 6 << 2, 6 >> 2

Chapter Three
Python Data Types: Strings, List, and Arrays

Synopsis

"Python is the most powerful language you can still read." — Paul Dubois

"Words and Ideas can change the world" — Dead Poet Society (movie)

In this chapter, we describe strings, list, and Numpy arrays.

3.1 Character & Strings

Text manipulation is required in many computing applications, for example, text editing, shell scripting, web applications, etc. In this section, we will discuss characters and strings, which are Python's primary data structures for text manipulation.

Characters in Python

We encounter different characters in English (e.g., a, b, c), Hindi (e.g., अ, आ, ब, म), in various languages, and in mathematics (e.g., =, +, /). In addition, we have special characters (@, &), as well as characters for currencies ($, €, ₹). These characters are symbols or images. It is too expensive to store such images in a computer. Instead, the characters are *encoded* as numbers in a computer (a level of abstraction). We will discuss this aspect later in this section.

In Python, characters are enclosed within single quotes ('.') or double quotes ("."); both these quotes are used interchangeably. For example, in the following Python statement,

```
In [1]: x='2'

In [2]: ord(x) # returns ascii representation of x
Out[2]: 50
```

Here, x represents character '2', which is represented using decimal number 50 in ASCII (*American Standard Code for Information Interchange*) format. The Python function *ord*() provides the corresponding ASCII value. Note that '2' differs from number 2, which is represented as 10 in binary format.

For a given decimal number y, Python function *chr(y)* provides the corresponding character in ASCII representation. For example,

```
In [36]: chr(50)
Out[36]: '2'
```

Encoding/Decoding in Python

ASCII (*American Standard Code for Information Interchange*) encoding was proposed in 1960 in order to represent English characters (0..9, A..Z, a..z) and special characters (e.g., $) using numbers 0 to 255. For example, '2' and 'A' are encoded using decimal numbers 50 and 65 respectively. Clearly, ASCII characters can be represented using a single byte.

Later, the characters of different languages, which are in thousands, were included in computers using *Unicode* (*Universal Coded Character Set*) scheme. At present, Unicode includes all international languages, as well as more special characters. For example, Hindi characters 'अ' and 'ह' are represented using hex numbers 905 and 939 respectively.

Another complex issue is the storage of Unicode characters in computers. The hex numbers corresponding to the unicode characters are further encoded. Python employs UTF-8 (*Unicode Transformation Format*) encoding scheme, where the ASCII characters are stored using a single byte as they are. However, 2 to 4 byes are employed for other characters.

Example 1: In UTF-8 encoding scheme, the character 'ह' is U+0939 (hex 0939).

    0000 1001 0011 1001

This number is represented using 3 bytes as follows:

    1110**0000** 10**100100** 10**111001**

where the condensed-bold bits represent the data bits (the number 0939), while the other bits 1110, 10, and 10 represent the control bits.

Several other character encoding schemes are employed for encoding emails, HTML files, JavaScript, etc. The leading encoding schemes are UTF-16, UTF-32, EBCDIC, Latin A. We refer the reader to web resources for more details on encoding schemes.

Strings in Python

A Python *string*, which is an ordered sequence of characters, is an important data types of Python. A character is treated as a string with a single element. Python strings too are enclosed within single quotes (' ') or double quotes (".").

```
In [7]: x = "This is a string."

In [8]: x
Out[8]: 'This is a string.'
```

Two strings can be added together using *concatenation operator*, +. Multiplication of a string by an integer, a *replication operation*, yields a larger string with its multiple copies strung together. Note that a string cannot be added to an integer. For example, 3+'9' is an invalid Python expression. We illustrate the above operations using the following examples:

```
In [70]: 'SS'+'T'
Out[70]: 'SST'

In [71]: 5*'S'
Out[71]: 'SSSSS'

In [72]: x = "This is a string."

In [74]: x + "  Hi, string"
Out[74]: 'This is a string.  Hi, string'
```

We also present several important Python escape sequences: \n for Linefeed (or next line), \u for unicode character, and \x for hex-encoded byte. The backslash '\' is called the *escape* character.

```
In [121]: y= "abs \ncde"

In [123]: print(y)
abs
cde

In [126]: print('\u0905')
अ
In [132]: print('\x55')
```

U

Note that 0905 (*hex*) is a unicode representation for Hindi letter अ, and 55 (hex) is a representation of roman letter U.

Two more important issues related to the string data type are in order. To continue a string to the next line, one can use \ to indicate a line break to the interpreter. For example,

```
In [173]: 'I am going to the center of the \
    ...: Earth'
Out[173]: 'I am going to the center of the Earth'
```

Also, we define a *raw string* by prefixing the string using a letter r.

```
In [177]: r'$\alpha$'
Out[177]: '$\\alpha$'

In [178]: print(r'$\alpha$')
$\alpha$
```

This feature is useful while printing symbols using latex (see Section 7.1). Without *r*, the character *a* of *alpha* is not printed because \a represents an empty character (a special character).

```
In [175]: print('$\alpha')
$lpha
```

The character \b represents backspace. Hence,

```
In [35]: print('$\beta$'); print(r'$\beta$'); print('$
\gamma$')
eta$
$\beta$
$\gamma$
```

Function *str*() converts an integer or a float to the corresponding strings. For example,

```
In [150]: str(345), str(20.9), str(14.9e10)
Out[150]: ('345', '20.9', '149000000000.0')
```

We can read a string from the keyboard using the function *input*().

```
In [134]: x = input("Enter the value of x =")
Enter the value of x =10

In [135]: x
Out[135]: '10'
```

Note that *input()* returns a string. Hence, in the above statement, *x* is not an integer. For the same, we need convert the input to an integer using *int()* function as follows:

```
In [138]: x= int(input("Enter the value of x ="))
Enter the value of x =10

In [139]: x
Out[139]: 10
```

The *int()* function takes an string as an input and converts it to an integer. In the above, '10' to converted to integer 10. Similarly we can employ *float()* and *complex()* functions to convert input string to float and complex number respectively. These functions help us read real and complex numbers as shown below.

```
In [145]: complex( input("Enter the value of x =") )
Enter the value of x =4+5j
Out[145]: (4+5j)
```

Note that the *input()* function need not have an argument, as shown below. However, it is better to use a prompt, such "Enter the value of x =", because we want the interpreter to talk to us all the time.

```
In [25]: x = input()
10
```

The function *print()* outputs *string, integer, float,* or a combination of them to the screen. For example,

```
In [154]: x=5; y=10.0; z='hello'

In [156]: print('x = ', x,'; ', 'y = ', y, '; ', 'z = ', z)
x =  5 ;  y =  10.0 ;  z =  hello
```

In the above example, the final output is a string containing all the objects and separators.

String Formatting in Python

Formatting of data plays a crucial role in input/output. Here we provide a brief introduction to formatting in Python using several examples.

```
In [21]: print('My name is {}, and I am {} years
old.'.format('Vijay Verma', 18))
My name is Vijay Verma, and I am 18 years old.

In [24]: print('My first name is {1}, and the last name is
{0}.'.format('Verma', 'Vijay'))
My first name is Vijay, and the last name is Verma.
```

In the above examples, {} are black boxes, whose values are filled using the arguments of the format(). We can also specify which arguments of format() fills which {}. For *In*[24], the indices 0 and 1 correspond to 'Verma' and 'Vijay' respectively.

In the above examples, the arguments are either strings or integer. We can also have formatted floats with specified number of digits before and after the decimal point. For example, {:2.2f} prints 2 digits before and after the decimal point.

```
In [26]: print('Pi is {:2.2f}'.format(12.3456))
Pi is 12.35
```

In exponential notation, we specify the number of significant digits after the decimal point as follows.

```
In [28]: print('Pi is {:.2e}'.format(12.3456))
Pi is 1.23e+01
```

In Table 9, we specify formatting for hexadecimal and octal integers, as well as for ASCII characters.

Table 9: Formatting of different data types in Python

	Data type	Example
{}	string	`In [166]: '{}'.format('Vijay')` `Out[166]: 'Vijay'`
{:d}	decimal integer	`In [169]: '{:d}'.format(22)` `Out[169]: '22'`
{:x}	hexadecimal integer	`In [170]: '{:x}'.format(22)` `Out[170]: '16'`
{:o}	octal integer	`In [171]: '{:o}'.format(22)` `Out[171]: '26'`
{:.2f}	float	`In [172]:'{:.2f}'.format(22.435)` `Out[172]: '22.43"`
{:.2e}	float exponent	`In [173]:'{:.2e}'.format(22.435)` `Out[173]: '2.24e+01'`
{:c}	ASCII char	`In [176]: '{:c}'.format(98)` `Out[176]: 'b'`

With this, we close our discussions on strings.

****

Conceptual Questions

1. What are the advantages of special characters such as '\n'?

Exercises

1. A book contains 5 million characters. Estimate the memory requirement for storing this book in a computer.
2. Using python formatting, print floating point numbers to 5 significant digits after decimal. Write them in both float and exponential formats.
3. What are the outputs of the print() function with the following Python expressions?
   - 2*'Hi', 'Hi' + 2020, 'Hi'+'2020', 2*3*"Hi", 'Hi' + ' friend', 'x'+'y'+'=5', '$\alpha', '$\beta', r'α', r'\beta', 'xyz\babc', 'abc\axyz'
4. What is the output of the following Python statement?

Practical Numerical Computing Using Python

- In [75]: x=5; y=10; print('x+y');
- In [76]: print(r'$\alpha\beta$')
- In [77]: print('$\alpha\beta$')
- In [78]: print('{:.3e}'.format(20.00159))
- In [79]: print('{:2.3f}'.format(20.00159))
- In [80]: print('{:1.3f}'.format(20.00159))

5. What are the differences between the following two Python statements?
    - x = input("Enter the value of x =")
    - x = float(input("Enter the value of x ="))

3.2 List

A Python *list* is an *ordered* set of objects. The ordered set implies that the elements of the list have their assigned places and they cannot be interchanged. Also note that the elements of a list could of different data types.

For a list with N elements, the items of the list can be accessed using indices 0, 1, .., N–1; or using indices –N, –N+1, ...,–1. Note that the index in Python starts from 0, and that the last element of the list can be accessed using index N–1 or –1. See the following example and Table 10 for an illustration.

```
In [187]: y = [1,2,'hi']

In [188]: print (y[0], y[1], y[2], y[-1], y[-2])
1 2 hi hi 2
```

Table 10: Indices of array elements of $y = [1,2,\text{'hi'}]$

Index	0	1	2
Index	–3	–2	–1
y	1	2	'hi'

Interestingly, a string is also a list. For example,

```
In [189]: z = 'Python'

In [191]: z[0], z[1], z[2], z[3], z[4], z[5], z[-1], z[-2]
Out[191]: ('P', 'y', 't', 'h', 'o', 'n', 'n', 'o')
```

The functions associated with a list are given in the following table.

Table 11: Functions associated with a list.

Function	Description
append(element)	Appends *element* at the end of the list.
pop()	Removes the last *element* from the list and returns this element.

pop(i)	Removes the ith element of the list, and returns it.
remove(element)	Removes the first occurrence of element from the list.
reverse()	Reverses the list.
sort()	Sorts the list.
copy()	Returns a copy of the list.
index(x)	Returns the lowest index of the list where the element x is stored.
count(x)	Returns the number of occurrence of the element x in the list.
insert(ind,x)	Insert the element x into the list at index ind.

Usage of list functions:

```
In [192]: a = [1, 3, 5, 9, 15]

In [193]: a.append(21)

In [194]: a
Out[194]: [1, 3, 5, 9, 15, 21]

In [196]: a.insert(2,4)

In [197]: a
Out[197]: [1, 3, 4, 5, 9, 15, 21]

In [199]: a.reverse()

In [200]: a
Out[200]: [21, 15, 9, 5, 4, 3, 1]
```

In addition, we can change an element of the list. For example,

```
In [212]: a[0]=100

In [213]: a
Out[213]: [100, 15, 9, 5, 4, 3, 1]
```

We can add two lists using + operator.

```
In [223]: a+[0,1]
```

```
Out[223]: [21, 15, 9, 5, 4, 3, 1, 0, 1]
```

Two useful list functions of Python are *size(a)* and *len(a)*. For one-dimensional list, these functions yield the size of its argument, *a*.

```
In [89]: a = [100, 15, 9, 5, 4, 3, 1]

In [90]: len(a)
Out[90]: 7

In [91]: size(a)
Out[91]: 7
```

Note that we can alter a list, i.e., change some of its elements. Hence, a list is a *mutable* (or changeable) object. Consequently, the *id* of a list remains the same after its elements have been altered. For example,

```
In [1]: a = [100, 15, 9, 5, 4, 3, 1]

In [2]: id(a)
Out[2]: 140602671466208

In [3]: a[0]=500

In [4]: id(a)
Out[4]: 140602671466208
```

Contrast these observations with those for integers and floats. When a variable associated with an integer or a float was assigned to another integer/float, its id changed as well. Also note that a string is an immutable object, and hence its contents cannot be changed, as shown in the following example. However, you may convert a string to a list using the list function, and then change the contents of the list.

```
In [9]: x='abcd'

In [10]: print(x[0], x[1], x[2], x[-1])
a b c d

In [11]: x[0]='s'

TypeError: 'str' object does not support item assignment
```

```
In [12]: x=list('abcd')

In [13]: x
Out[13]: ['a', 'b', 'c', 'd']

In [14]: x[0]='S'

In [15]: x
Out[15]: ['S', 'b', 'c', 'd']
```

Slicing

A *sublist* (a part of a list) can be accessed using *slice()* function:

```
slice([start,] end [, step])
```

where the arguments in the square brackets are optional, and.

1. *start*: Start position of slice. This argument is optional, and its default value is 0.
2. *end*: End position of slice. This argument is mandatory.
3. *step*: Step of slice. This argument is optional, and its default value is 1.

For example,

```
In [227]: x = [100, 15, 9, 5, 4, 3, 1]

In [236]: s = slice(1,4)

In [237]: x[s]
Out[237]: [15, 9, 5]

In [238]: s = slice(1,4,2)

In [239]: x[s]
Out[239]: [15, 5]
```

Note that index of a slice goes up to *end*−1. For example, *In* [237] lists $x[1]$... $x[3]$, not till $x[4]$.

Python offers a shortcut to *slice* function. We can skip defining the intermediate variable s, and directly apply x[start:end:step]. For example, $x[1:4:2]$ yields the same result as In [239]. That is,

```
In [169]: x[1:4:2]
Out[169]: [15, 5]
```

For a list x, $x[i:j:k]$ produces a sublist containing elements between indices i (inclusive) and j (exclusive) with steps of k. Note that

1. In case an argument is skipped, its default value is taken ($i \to 0; j \to$ end; $k \to 1$).
2. Consequently, $x[:j]$ contains elements $x[0]$, ... , $x[j-1]$; while $x[j:]$ contains elements $x[j]$, ... , $x[-1]$ (including the last element).
3. When $j = -1$, then take $j =$ end-1.

We illustrate these features in the following examples.

```
In [227]: x = [100, 15, 9, 5, 4, 3, 1]

In [228]: x[1:4]
Out[228]: [15, 9, 5]

In [229]: x[1:-1]
# j = -1 or  end-1, hence last item is skipped.
Out[229]: [15, 9, 5, 4, 3]

In [230]: x[::]   # full array
Out[230]: [100, 15, 9, 5, 4, 3, 1]

In [231]: x[::-1]    # revsed array
Out[231]: [1, 3, 4, 5, 9, 15, 100]

In [232]: x[:3]
Out[232]: [100, 15, 9]

In [233]: x[4:]
Out[233]: [4, 3, 1]

In [234]: x[4:-1]
Out[234]: [4, 3]

In [235]: x[4::-1]
Out[235]: [4, 5, 9, 15, 100]
```

```
In [236]: x[:-1]
Out[236]: [100, 15, 9, 5, 4, 3]
```

Function *range()*

Python function *range([start,] end [, step])* generates a sequence of integers from *start* to *end*−1 in steps of *step*. Here, *start* and *step* are optional, with their default values being 0 and 1 respectively. The rules for the *range()* are same as those for slice. Some illustrative examples of *range()* function are as follows:

1. *range*(1,10,2) will generate a sequence [1, 3, 5, 7, 9].
2. *range*(5) will generate a sequence [0,1,2,3,4]
3. *range*(1,5) will generate a sequence [1,2,3,4]
4. *range*(5,1,−2) will generate a sequence [5,3]

Note that *range()* does not return a *list*. It produces the integers on demand. This is to ensue that range() can take a very large integer as an argument. Note however that we can access the elements of range object by casting it into a *list*.

Examples:

```
In [239]: x=range(1,10,2)

In [240]: x[2]
Out[240]: 5

In [241]: list(x)
Out[241]: [1, 3, 5, 7, 9]
```

Array vs. List vs. String vs. Tuple

Python has a module called *array*, which is similar to *list* with a difference. All the elements of array are of same data type, and they are stored at contiguous memory locations. The allowed data types for *array* are *signed char, unsigned char, Py_UNICODE, signed short, unsigned short, signed int, unsigned int, signed long, unsigned long, signed long long, unsigned long long, float, double*. We need to specify the data type code for them in the function. See Table 12 for a list of data types along with their codes (https://www.geeksforgeeks.org/python-arrays/).

Table 12: Various data types of *array*() along with their codes

code	C Type	Python Type	Size in bytes
'b'	signed char	int	1
'B'	unsigned char	int	1
'u'	Py_UNICODE	unicode char	2
'h'	signed short	int	2
'H'	unsigned short	int	2
'i'	signed int	int	2
'I'	unsigned int	int	2
'L'	signed long	int	4
'q'	signed long long	int	8
'Q'	unsigned long long	int	8
'f'	float	float	4
'd'	double	float	4

Usage:

```
In [248]: import array as arr

In [249]: a = arr.array('i', [1, 2, 3])   # 'i' for integers

In [250]: a[0]
Out[250]: 1

In [251]: type(a)
Out[251]: array.array
```

Though *string* is a list of characters, it differs from a *list* in a significant way. No character of a *string* be replaced. Also, neither a character can be appended to a string, nor popped from a string. This is because a *string* is an *immutable* object, but a *list* is a *mutable* (changeable) object.

We will discuss these features in more detail in Section 3.5.

Similarly, a *tuple* is *immutable* list. That is, a *tuple* can be indexed and sliced as in a list. However, no element of a tuple can be destroyed or altered. A *tuple* is created using a slightly different syntax. For example, a *tuple y* is created as follows:

```
In [244]: y = (1,2,3)

In [245]: y[1]
Out[245]: 2

In [246]: y.pop()

AttributeError: 'tuple' object has no attribute 'pop'
```

Clearly, *pop()* function is not allowed for a *tuple*.

In the next section, we describe a new data type called *Numpy array*, which are much more efficient than *list* for numerical computing. Note that *Numpy arrays* differ from *array* data structure discussed above.

****

Conceptual Questions

1. What are the differences between a list and a tuple?

Exercises

1. Given a list y = [10, 20, 40, 60], what are the Python outputs for the following list operations? For each operation, start with the original y.
    - y.pop(), y.append(10), y.reverse(), y.insert(2,3)
2. Given a list y = [10, 11, 12, 13, 14, 15, 16], what are the Python outputs for the following slicing operations?
    - $y[0:2]$, $y[1:3]$, $y[2:-1]$, $y[:-1]$, $y[::-1]$, $y[:2]$, $y[-1:3]$, $y[-1:3:-1]$

3. What are the outputs of the following Python statements?
   - range(10), range(5,10), range(1,10,3), range(5,1,–1)
4. For a string s = "The Sun", what are the outputs of s[0], s[2], s[3], s[−1], s[-2]?

3.3 Numpy Arrays

Numpy, an important Python package for scientific computing, provides an efficient implementation of multidimensional arrays. A *Numpy* array contains data of same type, and its array size is *fixed*. The numpy arrays and associated functions are written in C language because of which arrays and associated functions are quite fast.

We need to *import numpy* to use Numpy arrays. We could use the following statements (see Section 5.2 for more details):

```
import numpy as np
from numpy import *
```

Or, more simply, import *pylab* by invoking the following command at the terminal prompt (see Section 1.5).

```
ipython --pylab
```

Python statements in this section and in some later parts of the book correspond to either the later option or import using *from numpy import* *. We meant to keep our discussion and syntax as simple as possible by avoiding constructs such as *np.array()*, *np.len()*.

Among the numpy functions, *array()* creates an array. The method to access array elements is same as that for a *list*.

```
In [265]: y=array([5,9])

In [266]: y[1]
Out[266]: 9

In [267]: y.dtype   # yields data type of y
Out[267]: dtype('int64')

In [268]: y*2   # multiply each element by 2
Out[268]: array([10, 18])

In [269]: size(y)   # yields count of elements in the array
Out[269]: 2

In [270]: len(y)
Out[270]: 2
```

Here, y*2 yields a new array with each element of y multiplied by 2.

Note that unlike *list*, we cannot insert an element in an array or delete an element of the array. For example, y.append(10) and remove(5) are not allowed.

In a mixed array containing *int* and *float*, *numpy* converts types of all the elements to *float*.

```
In [275]: y=array([1.0,2])

In [276]: y.dtype
Out[276]: dtype('float64')
```

We can employ real functions, e.g., *sqrt, log, log10, sin, cos*, on the array elements. For example, for y of *In* [265].

```
In [448]: sqrt(y)
Out[448]: array([2.23606798, 3. ])
```

The +, *, / operations on two arrays yield respective element-by-element addition, multiplication, and division of the two arrays.

```
In [449]: z = array([1.0,4.0])

In [450]: y+z
Out[450]: array([ 6., 13.])

In [451]: y*z
Out[451]: array([ 5., 36.])

In [452]: y/z
Out[452]: array([5.   , 2.25])

In [271]: z = y+3

In [272]: z
Out[272]: array([ 8, 12])
```

For a numpy array *a*, the functions *sum(a)* provides the sum of all the elements of the array, while *prod(a)* provides the product of all the elements. These functions work for integer as well as float arrays.

```
In [7]: a=[2,3,6]
```

```
In [8]: sum(a)
Out[8]: 11

In [9]: prod(a)
Out[9]: 36
```

Also note that the integer and float lists can be converted Numpy arrays as follows:

```
In [312]: y=[3,4]

In [313]: array(y)
Out[313]: array([3, 4])
```

Similarly, we can convert a Numpy array to a *list* using the *list()* function:

```
In [21]: z=array([10.0,20.0])

In [22]: list(z)
Out[22]: [10.0, 20.0]

In [23]: z
Out[23]: array([10.0, 20.0])
```

Functions *linspace()* and *arange()*

The following numpy functions create useful arrays:

1. *linspace(start, stop, n)*: Returns uniformly-distributed n real numbers from *start* to *stop*.
2. *arange([start,] stop[, step,])*: Returns real numbers from *start* to *stop* (excluding) in steps of *step*. The arguments *start* and *step* are optional, with their default values as 0 and 1 respectively.

Examples:
```
In [310]: arange(1,10,1.5)
Out[310]: array([1. , 2.5, 4. , 5.5, 7. , 8.5])

In [311]: linspace(1,10,6)
Out[311]: array([ 1. ,  2.8,  4.6,  6.4,  8.2, 10. ])
```

```
In [317]: arange(5.0)
Out[317]: array([0., 1., 2., 3., 4.])
```

Note that

1. The number *stop* is excluded in the function *arange()*.
2. *arange()* returns an array, while *range()* does not return a list.
3. In the functions *arange()* and *linspace()*, *dtype* is an optional argument. If dtype is skipped, arange() deduces the type of the array elements from the types of start, stop, and step. For the above examples, *dtype* is *float*.

In Numpy, *int64* (8-byte integers) and *float64* (8-byte floats) are default integers and floats. In addition, Numpy offers arrays of the types listed in Table 13. If our data consists of positive integers in the range 0 to 255, then it is best to use *uint8* that takes much less computer memory. Also, the operations on *uint8* are much faster than those on *int64*. To create an *int8* array x, we insert an argument dtype='u1' in the array function. See the example below.

```
In [189]: x=array([1,3,5],dtype='u1')

In [190]: x.dtype
Out[190]: dtype('uint8')
```

To create numpy arrays with other data types, use the appropriate option listed in the first column of Table 13.

Table 13: Numpy data types

Data type	Description	Size (bytes)	Range
int_ ('i8')	default type int64	8	-2^{63} to $2^{63}-1$
int8 ('i1')	1-byte integer	1	−128 to 128
int16 ('i2')	2-byte integer	2	32768 to 32767
int32 ('i4')	4-byte integer	4	−2147483648 to 2147483647
int64 ('i8')	8-byte integer	8	-2^{63} to $2^{63}-1$
uint8 ('u1')	unsigned 1-byte integer	1	0 to 255

uint16 ('u2')	unsigned 2-byte integer	2	0 to 65535
uint32 ('u4')	unsigned 4-byte integer	4	0 to 4294967295
uint64 ('u8')	unsigned 8-byte integer	6	0 to to $2^{64}-1$
float_	default type float64	8	~10^{-308} to 10^{308}
float32 ('f4')	4-byte float	4	~10^{-38} to 10^{38}
float64	8-byte float	8	~10^{-308} to 10^{308}
complex_	default complex128	16	See float64
complex64	(float32,float32)	8	See float32
complex128	(float64,float64)	16	See float64
bool_	Default boolean	1	0, 1

Multi-dimensional Arrays

The following examples illustrate creation of two-dimensional (2D) arrays and several numpy functions associated with them. We create a two-dimensional array x as follows:

```
In [25]: x=array([[4,5,6], [7,8,9]])

In [26]: x
Out[26]:
array([[4, 5, 6],
       [7, 8, 9]])
```

Numpy array x has 6 elements arranged in 2 rows and 3 columns as shown below. Note that x is an ordered array, that is, the elements have their assigned places, and they cannot be interchanged.

4	5	6
7	8	9

We can access the elements of a 2D array using two indices $[i,j]$ or $[i]$ $[j]$. A diagram representing the variations of the two indices of the array x is shown below. Both the indices (for rows and columns) start from 0.

| [0,0] | [0,1] | [0,2] |
| [1,0] | [1,1] | [1,2] |

The first index represents the row, while the second index represents the column. In Python, the data is stored in such a way that the column index moves faster than the row index. For example, the elements of array x is stored in sequence as [0,0], [0,1], [0,2], [1,0], [1,1], and [1,2]. Note that the array elements can be also accessed as [0][0], [0][1], [0][2], [1][0], [1][1], and [1][2]. This arrangement, called *row-major order*, is also followed in C and C++. However, the array storage in Fortran follows *column-major order*, that is, its elements are stored as [1,1], [2,1], [1,2], [2,2], [1,3], [2,3]. Note that the Fortran index starts from 1.

We illustrate the Python indexing using the following statement:

```
In [320]: print(x[0,1], x[0][1])
5, 5
```

Numpy contains linear algebra module that helps us compute *eigenvalues* and *eigenvectors* of an array. For example,

```
In [300]: x=array([[0,1],[1,0]])

In [301]: x
Out[301]:
array([[0, 1],
       [1, 0]])

In [316]: det(x)   # determinant of x
Out[316]: -1.0

In [323]: y=eig(x)

In [324]: y
Out[324]:
(array([ 1., -1.]), array([[ 0.70710678, -0.70710678],
       [ 0.70710678,  0.70710678]]))
```

In *Out* [324], $y[0] = [1., -1]$ are the eigenvalues of x, while $y[1]$ contains two lists that are the associated eigenvectors of eigenvalues 1 and -1. Note that y is a three-dimensional array, whose elements are accessed as follows:

```
In [328]: print(y[0][0], y[1][1], y[1][1][1])
1.0 [0.70710678 0.70710678] 0.7071067811865475
```

Note that $y[1,1,1]$ gives an error because y is a nonuniform array. We employ $y[i][j][k]$ to access the elements of a 3D nonuniform array.

The following array is an example of a uniform 3D array (of size 2x2x2).

```
In [100]: y = array([[[1, 2], [3, 4]], [[5, 6], [7, 8]]])

In [101]: y
Out[101]:
array([[[1, 2],
        [3, 4]],

       [[5, 6],
        [7, 8]]])

In [102]: y[1,1,1]
Out[102]: 8
```

We can treat y as 2 layers of 2D arrays. Since y is a uniform array, we can access an element using $y[i,j,k]$.

Operations on Numpy Arrays

The following Numpy functions are used to extract size and shape of an array, as well as create new arrays.

size(a, axis = None): Returns the number of elements of array a along the argument *"axis"*. However, *size(a)* yields the total number of elements of array a.

shape(a): Returns array's shape, which is a tuple whose entries are the numbers of elements along the axes of the array.

zeros(shape, dtype=float): Returns a new array of a given *shape* and type filled with zeros.

ones(shape, dtype=float): Returns a new array of given *shape* and type filled with ones.

vstack(tuple): Stacks numpy arrays along the first dimension (row-wise).

column_stack(tuple): Stacks numpy arrays along the second dimension (column-wise).

empty(shape, dtype=float): Returns a new empty array of given shape and type.

random.rand(shape): Returns a float array of given *shape* with random numbers sampled from a uniform distribution in [0,1].

random.randn(shape): Returns a float array of given *shape* with random numbers sampled from a Gaussian (normal) distribution with zero mean and unit standard deviation.

random.randint(low, high=None, size=None, dtype=int): Returns an integer array of given size with random numbers sampled from a uniform distribution in [*low, high*). If high is None, the random numbers are sampled from [0, *low*).

concatenate(a1, a2, ...): Concatenates arrays given as arguments. Its short form is c_.

Examples:

```
In [357]: a = ones((3,3))

In [358]: a
Out[358]:
array([[1., 1., 1.],
       [1., 1., 1.],
       [1., 1., 1.]])

In [359]: size(a)
Out[359]: 9
```

```
In [360]: shape(a)
Out[360]: (3, 3)
```

We can use the function *resize()* to convert an array from one shape to another.

```
In [361]: a = ones((4,4))

In [362]: a
Out[362]:
array([[1., 1., 1., 1.],
       [1., 1., 1., 1.],
       [1., 1., 1., 1.],
       [1., 1., 1., 1.]])

In [363]: a.resize(2,8)

In [364]: print(a)
[[1. 1. 1. 1. 1. 1. 1. 1.]
 [1. 1. 1. 1. 1. 1. 1. 1.]]

In [204]: random.rand(3,2)
Out[204]:
array([[0.03303746, 0.2236998 ],
       [0.20059688, 0.1309394 ],
       [0.68722795, 0.54985967]])

In [207]: random.randint(2,5, size=10)
Out[207]: array([3, 4, 3, 2, 2, 4, 3, 4, 2, 4])

In [209]: random.randint(2,5, size=(2,4))
Out[209]:
array([[4, 3, 4, 3],
       [2, 3, 3, 3]])

In [1]: x = array([1,2,3])

In [2]: y = 2*x

In [3]: vstack((x,y))
Out[3]:
array([[1, 2, 3],
       [2, 4, 6]])

In [29]: column_stack((x,y))
```

```
Out[29]:
array([[1, 2],
       [2, 4],
       [3, 6]])

In [107]: x=array([3,4,5]); y = array([45, 50])
In [109]: concatenate((x,y))
Out[109]: array([ 3,  4,  5, 45, 50])

In [7]: a = ones((4,4))*4

In [8]: c = array([1,1,1,1])

In [9]: combined =  c_[a,c]    # c_ is a short form of concatenate

In [10]: combined
Out[10]:
array([[ 4., 4., 4., 4., 1.],
       [ 4., 4., 4., 4., 1.],
       [ 4., 4., 4., 4., 1.],
       [ 4., 4., 4., 4., 1.]])
```

Numpy function *transpose()* performs transpose operation on an array. For example,

```
In [1]: a = ones((2,8))

In [2]: a
Out[2]:
array([[1., 1., 1., 1., 1., 1., 1., 1.],
       [1., 1., 1., 1., 1., 1., 1., 1.]])

In [3]: a.transpose()
Out[3]:
array([[1., 1.],
       [1., 1.],
       [1., 1.],
       [1., 1.],
       [1., 1.],
       [1., 1.],
       [1., 1.],
       [1., 1.]])
```

An array is indexed by a *tuple* of integers, as illustrated earlier. *Slicing* an array along any direction follows a similar rule as that for a *list* (discussed in Section 3.2).

Examples:

```
In [375]: y
Out[375]:
array([[  1.        ,   2.26666667,   3.53333333,
         4.8       ],
       [  6.06666667,   7.33333333,   8.6       ,
         9.86666667],
       [ 11.13333333,  12.4       ,  13.66666667,
        14.93333333],
       [ 16.2       ,  17.46666667,  18.73333333,
        20.        ]])

In [381]: y[0,:]
Out[381]: array([1.        ,  2.26666667,  3.53333333,
         4.8       ])

In [382]: y[0,0:2]
Out[382]: array([1.        ,  2.26666667])

In [383]: y[0,0:3:2]
Out[383]: array([1.        ,  3.53333333])

In [405]: y[0:2,1:3]
Out[405]:
array([[2.26666667,  3.53333333],
       [7.33333333,  8.6       ]])
```

We can also create a subarray by choosing a set of indices.

Examples:

```
In [416]: ia = array( ((1,0), (2,1)) )

In [417]: ja = array( ((0,1), (1,2)) )

In [418]: y[ia,ja]
Out[418]:
array([[  6.06666667,   2.26666667],
```

```
              [12.4         ,  8.6         ]])
```

Here, *ia* and *ja* provide two columns of the subarray.

Another useful function is *meshgrid()*, which is used to create X and Y coordinates at the grid points. For example,

```
In [1]: row_x = linspace(0,0.3,4)

In [2]: col_y = linspace(0,0.2,5)

In [3]: X,Y=meshgrid(row_x, col_y)

In [4]: X
Out[4]:
array([[0. , 0.1, 0.2, 0.3],
       [0. , 0.1, 0.2, 0.3],
       [0. , 0.1, 0.2, 0.3],
       [0. , 0.1, 0.2, 0.3],
       [0. , 0.1, 0.2, 0.3]])

In [5]: Y
Out[5]:
array([[0.  , 0.  , 0.  , 0.  ],
       [0.05, 0.05, 0.05, 0.05],
       [0.1 , 0.1 , 0.1 , 0.1 ],
       [0.15, 0.15, 0.15, 0.15],
       [0.2 , 0.2 , 0.2 , 0.2 ]])

In [6]: X[0,:]
Out[6]: array([0. , 0.1, 0.2, 0.3])

In [7]: Y[:,0]
Out[7]: array([0.  , 0.05, 0.1 , 0.15, 0.2 ])
```

The above example is an illustration of *meshgrid*. It follows the default indexing option, *indexing* = 'xy', in which X[*i*,:] gives row_x, while Y[:,*j*] gives col_y. This choice follows from the way plots are made—x coordinates vary as in *Out*[4] and y coordinates vary as in *Out*[5]. If we need *meshgrid* as in Python array notation, then we need to give option as *indexing* = 'ij'.

```
In [12]: X1,Y1=meshgrid(row_x, col_y, indexing = 'ij')
```

```
In [13]: X1
Out[13]:
array([[0. , 0. , 0. , 0. , 0. ],
       [0.1, 0.1, 0.1, 0.1, 0.1],
       [0.2, 0.2, 0.2, 0.2, 0.2],
       [0.3, 0.3, 0.3, 0.3, 0.3]])

In [14]: Y1
Out[14]:
array([[0. , 0.05, 0.1 , 0.15, 0.2 ],
       [0. , 0.05, 0.1 , 0.15, 0.2 ],
       [0. , 0.05, 0.1 , 0.15, 0.2 ],
       [0. , 0.05, 0.1 , 0.15, 0.2 ]])

In [16]: X1[:,0]
Out[16]: array([0. , 0.1, 0.2, 0.3])

In [17]: Y1[0,:]
Out[17]: array([0. , 0.05, 0.1 , 0.15, 0.2 ])
```

The x and y meshgrid would be more complex for a nonuniform mesh. The function *meshgrid()* is useful for making *surface plots* and *contour plots*. See Section 7.1 for more details.

Vectorization

A processors can perform many operations in a single clock cycle if the data is arranged consecutively in the memory. The speedup by this process is significant for multicore processors and supercomputers. We illustrate this idea using a simple example where we multiply two Numpy arrays of the same size.

```
a = np.random.rand(10**8)
b = np.random.rand(10**8)
c=(a*b)
```

In the above example, the computer operations are streamlined as in an assembly line of a car manufacturer. As a result, element-by-element multiplication could be performed for a large chunk of data in a single clock cycle. This process, called *vectorization*, is supported for Numpy arrays. Here, optimised array operations like $c = a^*b$ is much faster than that performed using a loop.

We illustrate the speedup by timing the code segments. We employ the Python function *datetime.datetime.now()* to capture the current time of the computer.

```
from datetime import datetime
import numpy as np

a =  np.random.rand(10**8)
b =  np.random.rand(10**8)
c =  np.empty(10**8)

t1 = datetime.now()
c=(a*b)
t2 = datetime.now()
print ("for vectorised ops, time = ", t2-t1)

t1 = datetime.now()
for i in range(10**8):
    c[i] = a[i]*b[i]
t2 = datetime.now()
print ("for loop, time = ", t2-t1)
```

In my MacBook Pro 2014 model, vectorised array multiplication took 2.10 seconds, while the multiplication by an explicit loop took 20.06 seconds. Thus, vectorised array multiplication is approximately 10 times faster than the loop-based array multiplication. We remark that we could also capture time using *timeit* module:

```
import timeit
t1 = timeit.default_timer()
```

With this, we end our discussion on Numpy arrays.

****

Conceptual Questions

1. What are the differences between the features of a Python list and a Numpy array?
2. Contrast the array access methods of Python, C, and Fortran.

Exercises

1. An image consists of 2048x1536 pixel, with each pixel represented by 8 bits. Estimate the image size in kilobytes. Construct a Numpy array to host this image.
2. Create a numpy *bool* array to work with 10^8 spins that take values 0 and 1. Store 1 in all of them. This arrangement will be useful for many applications related to Ising spins. One problem is that the Ising spins take values ±1. How will you adopt the *bool* array for Ising spins?
3. Consider an array $x = array([1,2,3,4,5])$. What are the outputs of $x[1]$, $x[3]$, $x[-1]$?
4. Consider a list of integers $x = [4,5,6]$. Find square root of all the elements using Python. You code should work for a general integer list.
5. For the array $x = array([1,2,3,4,5])$, what are the outputs of $sqrt(x)$ and $x^{**}2$?
6. What is the output of $linspace(0,10,11)$?
7. What are the outputs of the following?
   - $arange(1,5,0.5)$, $arange(1,5)$, $arange(5)$, $arange(5,1,-0.5)$
8. Construct a 3x3 array $A[i,j] = (i+1)^*(j+1)$. Find its eigenvalues and eigenvectors. Work with a float32 array.
9. Construct a 3D array of 1000x1000x100 size with random entries. Sum the numbers using *sum()* function and using a loop. Compare the timings for the two operations. Verify that the mean values of the number match with the expected results.

3.4 Dictionary

We access an element of a list using its index. However, often, we need more advanced features for data access. For example, in a class, we may need to find the roll number of a student given his/her name. In systems programming, we need memory address corresponding to a variable. Python's *dictionary* provides such features as *key-value* pair. For a class, a student's name (*key*) and roll number (*value*) form a pair. Similarly, for Python's symbol table, variable's name (*key*) and address (*value*) form a pair. The (*key, value*) pair is represented as *key:value*, and the pairs are separated by commas.

We illustrate the above dictionaries using concrete examples. Consider a dictionary, named *myclass*, that contains three students along with their roll numbers, which are 101, 102, and 103. The roll number (*value*) of a student x (*key*) can be accessed using *myclass*[x].

```
In [1]: myclass = {'Rahul': 101, 'Arjun':102, 'Krishna': 103}

In [3]: myclass['Rahul']
Out[3]: 101
```

Consider another dictionary *vars* containing Python variables x and y, and their addresses.

```
In [8]: var = {'x': 4533028272, 'y' : 4533028304}

In [9]: var['x']
Out[9]: 4533028272
```

The dictionaries have the following properties:

1. The *keys* of a dictionary are unique, but the *values* are not. Note that *values* may repeat in a dictionary.
2. Dictionaries are unordered, and hence the items of a dictionary cannot be accessed using indices. Rather, the value of an item is accessed using its key.
3. Dictionaries are changeable. That is, we can delete an entry of the dictionary; modify an element corresponding to a key; etc.

Note that the keys cannot be changed, but they can be deleted.

We illustrate the addition and deletion of items in a dictionary as follows. To the dictionary *myclass,* we add a student named Radha whose roll number is 104. In addition, we delete *Rahul* from the dictionary.

```
In [12]: myclass['Radha'] = 104

In [13]: myclass
Out[13]: {'Rahul': 101, 'Arjun': 102, 'Krishna': 103,
'Radha': 104}

In [15]: del myclass['Rahul']

In [16]: myclass
Out[16]: {'Arjun': 102, 'Krishna': 103, 'Radha': 104}
```

We can implement a French-to-English dictionary in Python with pairs of French words and their English synonyms. For example,

```
In [20]: french_eng = {'bon':'good', 'merci':'thanks you'}

In [21]: french_eng['bon']
Out[21]: 'good'

In [22]: french_eng['Oui'] = 'yes'   # add an entry

In [23]: french_eng
Out[23]: {'bon': 'very good', 'merci': 'thanks you',
'Oui': 'yes'}
```

We can also create a dictionary using Python loop:

```
In [9]: sqr = {x: x**2 for x in (2, 4, 6, 8)}

In [10]: sqr
Out[10]: {2: 4, 4: 16, 6: 36, 8: 64}
```

Python's *Pandas* module contains more powerful features than Python dictionary. However, we will skip discussion on Pandas in this book.

Conceptual Questions

1. What are the key differences between Numpy arrays and Python Dictionary?

Exercises

1. Create a dictionary of five countries whose key:value pairs are country's name and its population.
2. To the dictionary of Exercise 1, add another country. Print the dictionary.

3.5 Mutable and Immutable Objects in Python

This section is a somewhat advanced, and it can be skipped by an uninitiated programmer.

The Python data types—*integer, float, complex, string, list, array, tuples*—are objects. Python employs *reference type* to represent these objects. Here, a variable "points to" or "refers to" an object. In particular, a variable contains the address where the object is being stored. We illustrate it using the following code segment.

```
In [32]: x = 10

In [33]: id(x)
Out[33]: 4477371824
```

As shown in Figure 16, x stores the address (4477371824) of object "10".

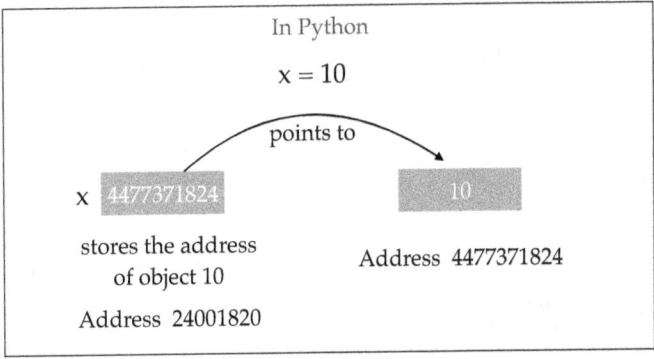

Figure 16: An illustration of a Python variable and its contents

In contrast, in C and C++ programming languages, variables are of *value type*. A C or C++ variable refers to the value of the variable. We illustrate this feature in Figure 17. Here, the variable x refers to the integer 10.

However, C's pointer is similar to a Python variable. A pointer contains the address of the variable. As shown in Figure 17, p is the pointer to x, and it contains the address of x, which is 4477371856. Note that the address of p differs from that of x.

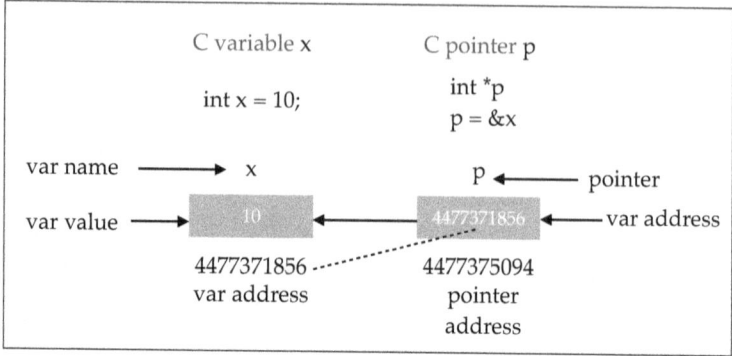

Figure 17: An illustration of a C variable and a C pointer. The variable x refers to integer 10, while the pointer p contains the address of the location where the integer 10 is stored.

The above property of Python variables has consequence on handling of Python data and functions. We discuss this below.

Referencing Python Objects

Let us illustrate the immutability of a Python integer using an example.

```
In [32]: x = 10

In [33]: id(10)
Out[33]: 4477371824

In [34]: id(x)
Out[34]: 4477371824

In [35]: id(11)
Out[35]: 4477371856

In [36]: sys.getsizeof(10)
Out[36]: 28
```

Python statement *In* [32] creates an integer 10, which is an object. The location of the object is 4477371824, which can be obtained using *id*(10). Since x *refers to* the object 10, *id*(x) too yields the address of 10, which is

Practical Numerical Computing Using Python

4477371824. Next, as in *In* [35], an object 11 was created whose id is 4477371856. Also, note that the objects 10 and 11 take 28 bytes each for storage.

Let us explore some more intricacies of Python objects.

```
In [37]: y=x

In [38]: id(y)
Out[38]: 4477371824

In [39]: x = 100

In [40]: id(x)
Out[40]: 4477374704

In [52]: id(100)
Out[52]: 4477374704

In [53]: id(y)
Out[53]: 4477371824
```

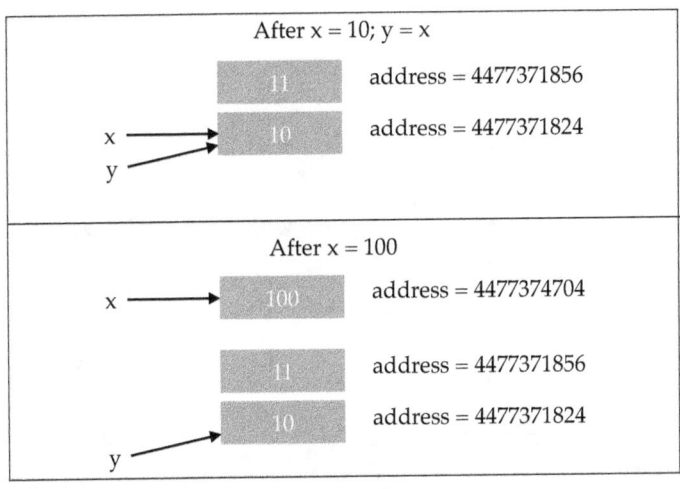

Figure 18: An illustration of Python's *immutable* objects related to Python statements from *In* [32] to *In* [53].

In Python statement *In* [37], we create another variable, y, that points to the object 10. Thus, both the variables, x and y, refer to the same object. Refer to Figure 18 for an illustration. Note that $id(y) = id(10)$.

111

In statement *In* [39], we create another object 100, to which *x* refers to now. The variable *x* no more points to the object 10. Consequently, $id(x) = id(100) = 4477374704$. Note, however, that the variable *y* still points to the object 10. See Figure 18.

In contrast, the corresponding C constructs have very different behaviour. As shown in Figure 19, after execution of $y = x$, a new variable *y* is created at a different memory location. After the statement $x = 100$, the contents of *x* is changed to 100 at the same location. The corresponding C code is given below.

```
#include <iostream>
using namespace std;

int main() {
  int x =10;
  int y;
  int *px, *py;
  px = &x;
  y = x;
  py = &y;
   x = 100;
}
```

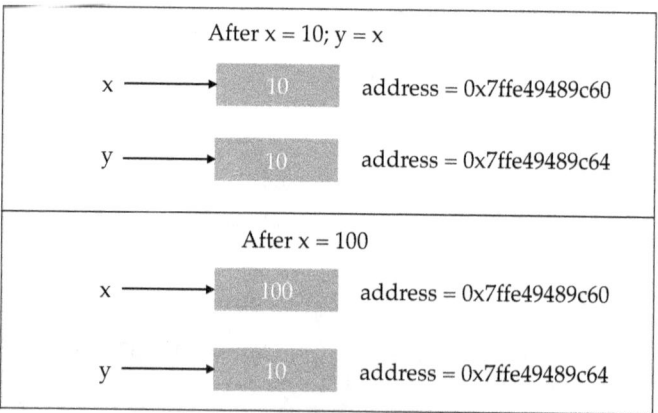

Figure 19: Illustration of C variables and their storage.

After this brief introduction to Python variables, we discuss immutable and mutable Python objects.

Immutable Python objects

In the examples discussed earlier, the objects 10, 11, and 100 cannot be altered. Such objects are called *immutable objects*. In fact, among the Python data types, *integer*, *float*, *complex*, *string*, and *tuples* are immutable. The value of an immutable object is unchangeable once it has been created. However, *lists* and *arrays* are mutable objects because their contents can be altered (discussed later in this section). In the following discussion we will discuss the subtleties of immutable and mutable Python objects.

Example 1: In the following example, $x = 5$, and the operation x**2 creates a new object, which is 25. Hence, after the execution of statement *In* [149]: $x = x^{**}2$, x points to the new object (25).

In [147]: x=5

In [148]: print(id(x))
4540589328

In [149]: x = x**2

In [150]: print(x, id(x))
25 4540589968

Example 2: We swap two variables a and b using the following code:

In [152]: a, b = 5,6

In [153]: print(id(a), id(b))
4540589328 4540589360

In [154]: tmp = a; a = b; b = tmp

In [156]: print(a, b, tmp)
6 5 5

In [157]: print(id(tmp), id(b), id(a))
4540589328 4540589328 4540589360

Note that after the execution of *In* [156], the variables *tmp* points to the object 5 (previous value of a), *a* points to 6 (previous value of b), and then *b* points to 5 (value of tmp). Thus, the the variables *a* and *b* have been swapped.

Example 3: The following Python code swaps variables *a* and *b*. This version is simpler than the code of Example 2. In this scheme, after an execution of $b, a = a, b$, the variable *a* points to object *b*, and vice versa.

```
In [303]: a, b = 5,6

In [304]: print(id(a), id(b))
4540589328 4540589360

In [305]: b,a = a,b

In [306]: print(id(a), id(b))
4540589360 4540589328

In [307]: a,b
Out[307]: (6, 5)
```

After this, we briefly discuss the properties of mutable objects.

Mutable Python objects

Lists and *arrays* are mutable objects, that is, these objects can be altered after their creation. We illustrate their mutability using the following examples.

```
In [1]: a = [1,2,3]

In [2]: b=a

In [3]: print(id(a), id(b))
4630230512 4630230512

In [4]: a.pop(1)
Out[4]: 2
```

```
In [6]: print(a, b)
[1, 3] [1, 3]

In [7]: print(id(a), id(b))
4630230512 4630230512
```

In the above statements, the variables *a* and *b* point to the *list* [1,2,3], and they have the same address (4630230512). In statement *In* [4], we pop the element 2 from the list. Consequently, both *a* and *b* refer to the new list [1,3]. Note that the addresses of *a* and *b* remain the same after *pop* (see *In*[7]). See Figure 20 for an illustration. Contrast the above feature with the earlier example where the address of *x* got changed on reassignment.

We create a copy of *a* using the statement:

```
In [8]: c = a[:]

In [9]: print(c, id(a), id(c))
[1, 3] 4630230512 4627991840
```

Note that *c* is a new array, and hence its address differs from that of *a*. Thus, c = a and c = a[:] have different effects. Similarly, a = 5*a creates a new list, whose *id* differs from that of original *a*.

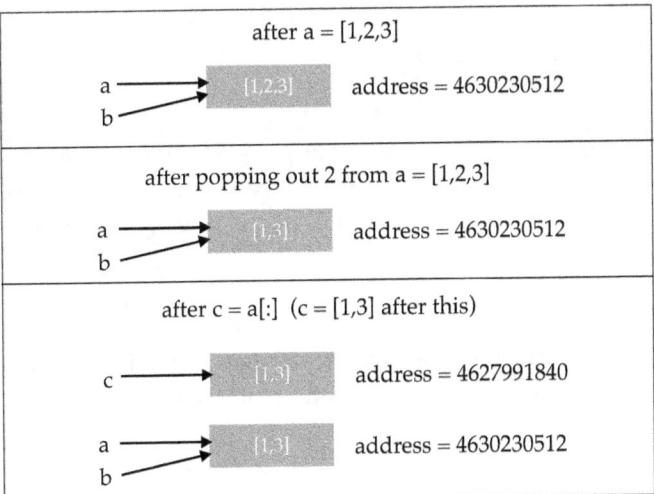

Figure 20: Illustrations of Python's *mutable* objects related to Python statements from *In*[1] to *In*[9].

If *a* points to another list, then the *id* of *a* is changed, but *b* continues to point to the original object [1,2,3].

```
In [88]: a = [5,6]

In [89]: print(id(a), ' ' , id(b))
4846573760    4630230512
```

Why do we choose lists and arrays as *mutable* objects? In computing, *arrays* and *lists* can be large objects with many elements. Often, we need to modify the contents of these objects. It is not advisable to create a completely new array after a minor modification of an array, especially when the array is long.

Example 4: The following code segment squares the elements of the numpy array.

```
In [166]: x = array([1,2,3])

In [167]: print(id(x))
140562475313552

In [168]: x = x**2

In [169]: print(x, id(x))
[1 4 9] 140562590651216
```

The operation $x^{**}2$ creates the array [1, 4, 9], which is a new object. Therefore, $id(x)$ changes to a new address after the execution of *In* [168]. Similar behaviour is observed for other array functions, such as $sin(x)$, $cos(x)$.

Example 5: The following code exchanges two lists *a* and *b*. The exchange process is exactly same as that for Example 2.

```
In [158]: a, b = [1,2], [10, 20]

In [160]: print(id(a), id(b))
140562475473008 140562569714096
```

```
In [163]: tmp = a; a = b; b = tmp

In [164]: print(a, b, tmp)
[10, 20] [1, 2] [1, 2]

In [165]: print(id(tmp), id(b), id(a))
140562475473008 140562475473008 140562569714096
```

With this, we end our discussion on immutable and mutable Python objects of Python.

****

Conceptual questions

1. What are the differences between Python variables and C variables in terms of storage?
2. List three main differences between the mutable and immutable Python variables.

Exercises

1. Execute the following Python statements: $x = 60.9; y = x; x = 99$. What are the id's of x and y at each stage of the code segment?
2. Execute the following Python statements: $x = $ array([3,4]); $y = x; x = 99$. What are the id's of x and y at each stage of the code segment?
3. Consider the following Python statements: $a=[1,2,3]; b=[4,5,6]; a[:]=b$. What do the lists a and b contain after the statement, $a[:]=b$? What are their id's? Test your code.
4. We change the statements of Exercise (3) to $a=[1,2,3]; b=[4,5,6]; a=b$. Contrast your results with those of Exercise (3).

Chapter Four
CONTROL STRUCTURES IN PYTHON

Synopsis

"The good news about computers is that they do what you tell them to do. The bad news is that they do what you tell them to do." — Ted Nelson

This chapter describes basic program structures: statements, conditionals, and loops.

4.1 Simple Statements

Computer programs, including Python codes, consists of the following basic structures:

1. Simple sequential statements
2. Conditional or Branching statements
3. Repetitive structures

In the present section and next two sections, we will cover these structures along with simple example. We start with sequential statements.

In the following sequential code segment, a set of Python statements are written one after the other. These statements are separated by semicolons (;). Python interpreter executes these statements one after the other.

```
In [482]: x=50; \
     ...: y=100; \
     ...: print(x,' ' ,y)
50    100
```

Sequential statements are quite simple. We end this discussion here.

****

Exercises

1. Write a program to compute the roots of an equation $a x^2 + b x + c = 0$. Read the values of the parameters a, b, c (assume real) from the keyboard.
2. A projectile is fired with velocity v and at angle θ from the horizontal. Write a Python code that prints the trajectory of this projectile, i.e., x and y coordinates of the projectile.

4.2 Conditional Flows in Python

In a computer program, we perform operations based on certain conditions. The code segments related to conditionals are called *conditional* or *branching* program structures.

The following Python code segment illustrates a conditional flow of an *if* statement.

```
In [491]: x = 3

In [492]: if (x%2 == 1):
    ...:     print('x is odd')
    ...:
x is odd
```

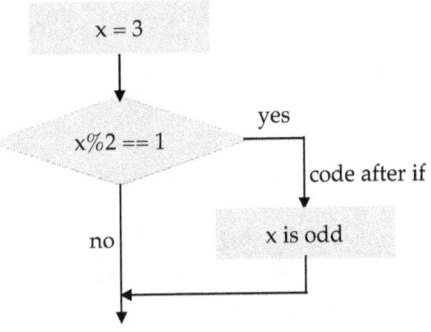

Figure 21: An illustration of an *if* conditional flow in Python. The rhombus contains the condition for the *if* statement.

Often, flow control of a program is illustrated using a diagram, which is called *control-flow diagram*. Figure 21 is the control-flow diagrams for the above code segment involving an *if* statement.

In the code segment of *In* [492], *if* ($x\%2 == 1$) is a conditional statement. The subsequent statement *print('x is odd')* is executed only if the logical expression ($x\%2 == 1$) is True. The indentation of the code block tells the Python interpreter what to execute after the *if* statement. An improper indentation will give an error. Also, there may be many lines of code in the *if* branch.

Now we illustrate the conditional flow of *if-else* statement using a code segment and Figure 22.

```
In [493]: x=2

In [500]: if (x%2 == 1):
     ...:     print('x is odd')
     ...: else:
     ...:     print('x is even')
     ...:
x is even
```

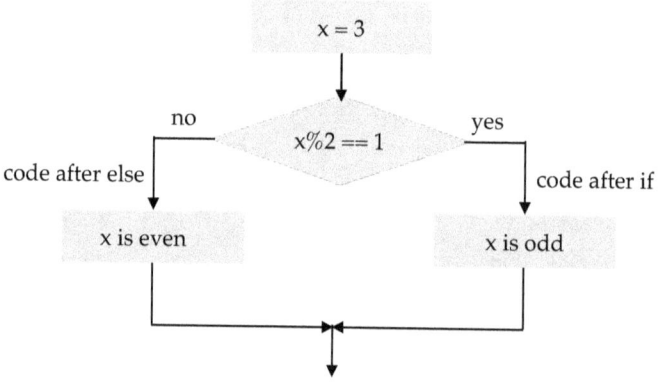

Figure 22: An illustration of an *if-else* conditional flow.

In the code segment, if $(x\%2 == 1)$ is True, then the first print statement, *print ('x is odd')* is executed. Otherwise, the print statement after *else*, *print ('x is even')*, is executed.

The conditional segments themselves may contain further conditional branches. See the example below, which is illustrated in Figure 23. In this example, among the odd numbers, we further test if the number x is divisible by 3 or not.

In [501]: x=27

In [502]: if (x%2 == 0):
    ...:   print('x is even')
    ...: elif(x%3 == 0):
    ...:   print('x is divisible by 3')
    ...: else:
    ...:   print('x is not divisible by 2 or 3')
    ...:

x is divisible by 3

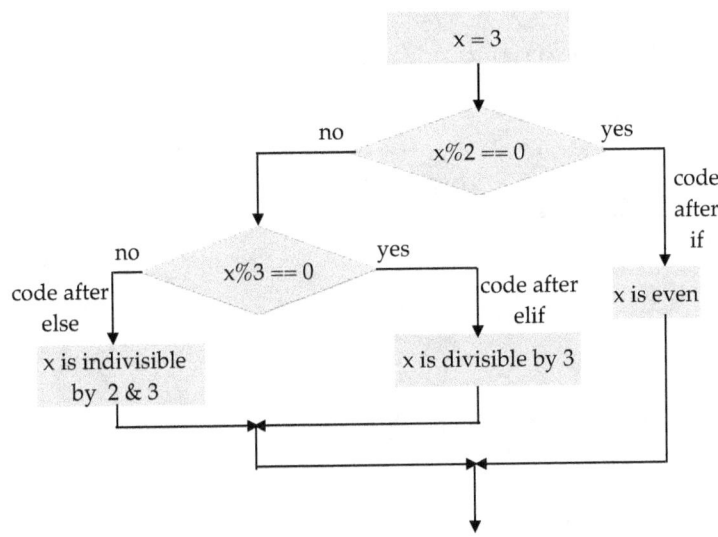

Figure 23: An illustration of an *if-elif-else* conditional flow.

Identification of a leap year involves more complex conditional statements. Consider year = yr.

```
If yr is divisible by 400
    then yr is  a leap year
else if yr is divisible by 100
    then yr is not a leap year
else if yr is divisible by 4
    then yr is  a leap year
else yr is  not a leap year
```

Python code for the above computation is as follows.

```
In [37]: yr = 1984

In [61]: if (yr%400 == 0):
   ...:     print ('A leap year')
   ...: elif (yr%100 == 0):
   ...:     print ('Not a leap year')
   ...: elif (yr%4 == 0):
```

```
...:        print ('A leap year')
...: else:
...:        print ('Not a leap year')
```

A shorter but a more cryptic code is as follows:

```
In [37]: yr = 1984
In [39]: if (yr%400 == 0):
...:        print('A leap year')
...: elif (yr%4 ==0) & ~(yr%100==0):
...:        print('A leap year')
...: else:
...:        print('Not a leap year')
...:
A leap year
```

With this, we end this section.

****

Exercises

1. Perfect square is a number whose square root is an integer. Examples of perfect squares are 25 and 36. Write a Python code to test if a number is perfect square or not.

2. Armstrong number is a number that is equal to the sum of cubes of its digits. One such number is 153 because 1+125+27=153. Write a Python program to test if a number is an Armstrong number or not. Hint: Use the functions *str()* and *int()*.

3. A palindrome string is one that reads the same forward and backward. Examples of palindrome strings are 'lal', 'KAK', and '010'. Write a Python code that tests whether a string is a palindrome or not.

4. Write a program to compute the roots of an equation $a x^3 + b x^2 + cx + d = 0$. Read the values of the parameters a, b, c, d (assume real) from the keyboard. Test your result for $a = 1, b = 6, c = 11$, and $d = 6$.

4.3 Looping in Python

Computer programs typically involve repetitive structures. For example, to compute the sum of the elements of a numpy array, we need to repeatedly add the array elements. Python offers two repetitive structures—*for loop* and *while loop*—that are described below.

For Loop

The structure of a *for loop* is as follows:

for elements *in* list:
    body of the loop

The body of the loop is executed for all the elements of the list. We illustrate the loop structures using several examples.

Example 1: The following Python code prints the names of all students in the *student_list*.

```
In [508]: student_list = ['Rahul', 'Mohan', 'Shyam', 'Shanti']

In [509]: for student in student_list:
     ...:     print(student, '\n')
     ...:
Rahul

Mohan

Shyam

Shanti
```

Figure 24 illustrates the control flow of the *for* loop. The loop is carried out for all students in *student_list*. We start with index = 0, and continue till the *student_list* is exhausted. Note that the initialisation of index and increment of indices are not required in the code segment;

they are performed by the Python interpreter internally.

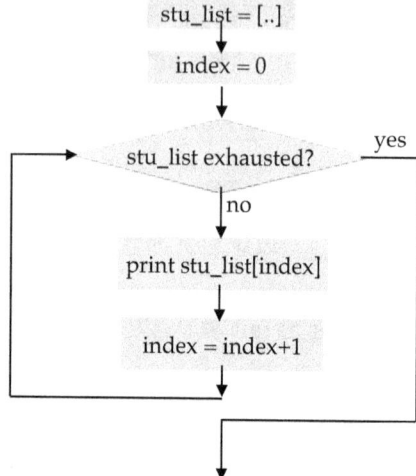

Figure 24: Illustration of the *for* loop of Example 1.

Example 2: The following code computes factorial(n) using for loop.

```
In [510]: n = 5
     ...: fact=1
     ...: for i in range(2,n+1):
     ...:     fact = fact*i
     ...:

In [511]: print("Factorial of ", n, '= ', fact)
Factorial of  5 =  120
```

Here, *range*(2,n+1) creates a list containing integers 2 to n (excluding n+1). Hence, *for loop* is carried out for *i* ranging from 2 to n.

Example 3: Find the maximum number in a list.

```
In [42]: A =  [6, 0, 4, 9, 3]
In [43]: max = -inf

In [44]: for x in A:
```

```
   ...:     if (x > max):
   ...:         max = x
```

```
In [45]: max
Out[45]: 9
```

In this example, we initialise *max* to −inf (−∞). After that we loop over all the elements of A. If the element > *max*, then we replace *max* with the new element. In the end, *max* contains the maximum number of the list.

Another way to compute the maximum is as follows:

```
In [43]: max = A[0]
```

```
In [44]: for x in A[1:]:
   ...:     if (x>max):
   ...:         max = x
   ...:
```

An index-based loop implementation is given below. Here, we start with *max* = A[0], and loop using the index *i*.

```
In [45]: for i in range(1, len(A)):
   ...:     if (A[i] > max):
   ...:         max = A[i]
   ...:
```

```
In [46]: max
Out[46]: 9
```

Example 4: In an integer array, send the maximum element to the end of the array.

```
n [46]: A = [6, 0, 4, 9, 3]
```

```
In [47]: for i in range(len(A)-1):
   ...:     if (A[i] > A[i+1]):
   ...:         A[i], A[i+1] = A[i+1], A[i]
   ...:
```

```
In [48]: A
Out[48]: [0, 4, 6, 3, 9]
```

In this example, among $A[i]$ and $A[i+1]$, the larger number is pushed to the right. The loop is carried out from $i=0$ to $n-2$, where n is the length of the array A. The above process is similar to the bubbling operation in which the lightest element rises to the top.

While Loop

The structure of a *while* loop is as follows:

    while (expression):
        body of while loop

The body of while loop is executed until condition of *while*(expression) statement remains *True*. The loop is terminated as soon as the condition becomes false. See examples below for illustrations.

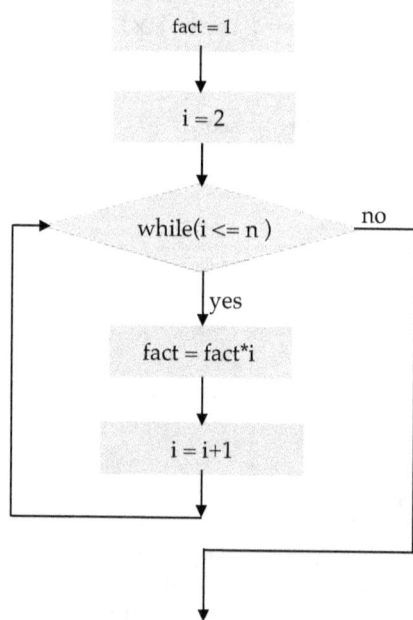

Figure 25: An illustration of the *while* loop of Example 5.

Example 5: The following code computes *factorial*(n) using a while loop. The control-flow diagram is shown in Figure 25.

```
In [514]: n = 5
     ...: fact = 1
     ...: i = 2
     ...: while (i <= n):
     ...:     fact = fact*i
     ...:     i = i+1
     ...:
```

The while loop is executed until the running index $i <= n$. The loop terminates as soon as $i = n+1$.

Example 6: Compute the greatest common divisor (gcd) of two integers a and b using Euclid's algorithm.

```
In [525]: a, b = 2277, 1633
```

```
In [526]: while b:
     ...:     a, b = b, a%b
     ...:
In [527]: print(a)
23
```

In the above algorithm, $b < a$. The loop is continued till $b = 0$. Within the loop, a ⟵ b and b ⟵ a%b. Refer to wikipedia for details on Euclid's algorithm.

Infinite Loop and *Break* Statement

It is mandatory that all loops in a program terminate. If not, the loop will continue forever. Such a loop, called *infinite loop*, must be avoided at all cost. An example of infinite loop is given below.

```
In [54]: i=1
```

```
In [55]: while (i>0):
    ...:     i = i+2
    ...:
```

You can easily check that the above loop does not terminate. You will have to kill the program using Cntrl-C (control-C). We may wish for a system software that can detect an infinite loop in any program; this is called *halting problem*. Unfortunately, using a mathematical proof, Turing showed that it is impossible to write such a program. This celebrated theorem is important an construct in theoretical computer science.

A loop can be broken using a *break* statement. For example, we can break the above infinite loop using the following *break* structure.

```
In [263]: i=1

In [266]: while (i>0):
    ...:     i = i+2
    ...:     if (i>100):
    ...:         break
```

The above loop terminates as soon as *i* exceeds 100.

For ... Else and Repeat ... Until

Python allows usage of *else* after *for* or *while* loop. The *else* block is executed when the loop finishes normally. We illustrate this structure using a code that tests if number *n* is a prime or not. In this program we use a property that one of the factors of a prime number must be less than or equal to $\sqrt{n}$.

```
n=15

# i ranges from 2 to sqrt(n) in steps of 1.
for i in range(2, int(sqrt(n))+1):
    if (n%i == 0):
        print ("n is divisible by ", i, ")
        Print("Hence, n is not  a prime")
        break
else:
    print ("n is a prime")
```

In this example, the *else* structure is executed if the condition ($n\%i ==$ 0) is not satisfied for any *i*. Here, this construct provides a simple way to contrast the nonprime numbers with prime numbers. Without *else* construct, the code gets more complex.

Python does not provide *repeat ... until* structure. However, it can be easily implemented using the following construct:

```
while (True):
    body of the loop
    if <logical condition>
        break
```

In the next chapter, we will discuss Python functions.

****

Exercises

1. Write a Python code to find the minimum number in a list of numbers.
2. Write your own Python function to sum the numbers of a Numpy array.
3. Write your own Python code to convert a binary number to decimal number. Assume the number to be a positive integer.
4. Write a Python code to construct a 5x5 two-dimensional array $A[i,j] = (i+1)*(j+1)$.
5. Pingala-Virahanka-Fibonacci numbers are defined as follows: $F_{n+2} = F_{n+1} + F_n$ with $F_0 = 0$ and $F_1 = 1$. Write a Python program to compute the first 15 Pingala-Virahanka-Fibonacci numbers. Compute the ratio F_{n+1} / F_n. Verify that the ratio converges to the goden mean, $(\sqrt{5}+1)/2$.
6. Iterate the function $x_{n+1} = f(x_n)$ where $f(x) = 4x(1-x)$. Start with $x_0 = 0.3$.
7. Write a computer program to find out the time taken to perform 10^9 addition, subtraction, multiplication, division for both integers and floating point numbers. Generate random numbers for the operation. Do the same for $x^{**}n$ with $n = 2,4,8,16$, and $exp(x)$ for $x = 1.939389$.

Chapter Five
FUNCTIONS IN PYTHON

Synopsis

"Doing mathematics should always mean finding patterns and crafting beautiful and meaningful explanations." — Albert Einstein

In this chapter, we describe how to write Python functions.

5.1 Functions in Python

A code segment that is used often can be abstracted as a function. For example, the function *sqrt(x)* computes the square root of x. We do not need to or want to write codes again and again for this often-used function. It is better to use an optimised *sqrt()* function written by experts.

Functions in a programming language provide the following benefits:

1. We can avoid repetition of codes.
2. The user codes become smaller and readable with functions.
3. Functions help modularise complex problems into smaller tasks. It is much better to write separate functions (each with 100 lines or less) for different tasks of a code and then combine them. It leads to bug-free and readable codes. Imagine debugging a single file with 5000 lines of code!
4. Different functions can be kept in different files; this arrangement makes programming manageable.
5. Modification of a program becomes easier with functions. For example, we may just replace a function by its optimised version. This will not alter the main program and other functions at all.

Similar to mathematical functions, a typical Python function takes arguments and returns results after computation. The *return* statement provides the result of the function. See the following lines and Figure 26 for illustrations.

> def function_name (parameters):
> Body of the function
> Typically includes a return statement

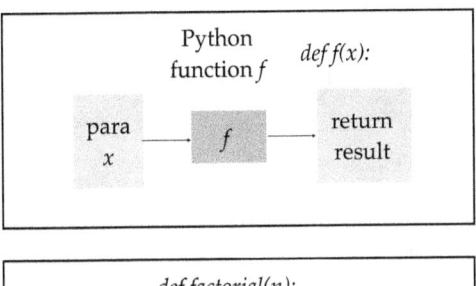

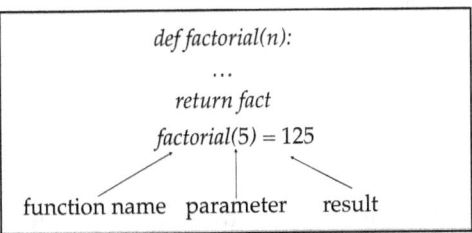

Figure 26: An illustration of a Python function.

We illustrate several python functions below.

Example 1: Function factorial(n) to compute $n!$

```
def factorial(n):
    fact = 1
    for i in range(2,n+1):
        fact = fact*i
    return fact
```

```
Usage:
In [16]: factorial(8)
Out[16]: 40320

In [17]: factorial(9)
Out[17]: 362880
```

Example 2: A function that returns the sum the digits of an integer. Here, $str(n)$ converts integer n to a string of digits, while $int(k)$ converts digit-characters (e.g., '1') to the corresponding integers.

```
import numpy as np

# Returns sum of the digits of n
```

```
def sum_digit(n):
    digits_n = list(str(n))
    # list of digits of n [Char entries]

    my_sum = 0
    for k in digits_n:
        my_sum += int(k)

    return my_sum
```

Usage:
```
In [94]: sum_digit(456)
Out[94]: 15
```

Example 3: A function that returns the maximum value of an array A.

```
# Returns maximum number of an array A.
def max_array(A):

    my_max =  -inf

    for x in A:
        if (x > max):
            my_max = x

    return my_max
```

Usage:
```
In [92]: a=[5, 0, 9, 4]

In [93]: max_array(a)
Out[93]: 9
```

Example 4: A function that tests if number n is a Harshad number or not. Harshad number is one that is divisible by sum of its digits. For example, 21 is Harshad number. In the code we make use of the function *sum_digits(n)*.

```
import numpy as np

# Harshad number is one that is divisible
# by sum of its digits
# is_harshad(n) returns 1 if n is a Harshad number,
```

0 otherwise.

```
def is_harshad(n):
    return not(n % sum_digit(n))
```

Usage:
```
In [95]: is_harshad(21)
Out[95]: True
```

Example 5: A function that tests if number *n* is a Armstrong number or not. Armstrong number is one that is equal to the sum of cubes of its digits. For example, 153 is an Armstrong number.

```
# An Armstrong number is one that is
# equal to sum of cubes of its digits.

# is_armstrong(n) 1 if n is an Armstrong number,
# 0 otherwise.

def is_armstrong(n):
    digits_n = list(str(n))
    # list of digits of n [Char entries]

    sum_cube = 0

    for k in digits_n:
        sum_cube += int(k)**3

    return (sum_cube == n)
```

Usage:
```
In [96]: is_armstrong(153)
Out[96]: True

In [97]: is_armstrong(154)
Out[97]: False
```

Example 6: A function that tests if a string is a Palindrome or not. A Palindrome string is one that is same as its inverse.

```
# A Palindrome string is one that is same as its inverse.
```

```
# Here, x[::-1] returns a new string which is
# reverse of x.
# In x[::-1] means from end to 0 in steps of -1

# is_palindrome(x) 1 if x is Palindrome, 0 otherwise

def is_palindrome(x):
    return(x == x[::-1])
```

Usage:
In [100]: is_palindrome('ABCD')
Out[100]: False

In [101]: is_palindrome('ABCCBA')
Out[101]: True

In the next chapter, we will construct more complex functions.

Python Function as an Object

A Python function is an object, and its identity is obtained by the function *id()*. This feature makes function and data indistinguishable in many respects. As illustrated in the following example, we can pass a function as an argument to a function.

```
In [138]: def mysqr(x):
     ...:     return x*x
     ...:

In [139]: def mycube(x):
     ...:     return x**3
     ...:

In [140]: def func(x, f):    # f is a function
     ...:     return f(x)
     ...:

In [141]: func(2,mysqr)
Out[141]: 4

In [142]: func(2,mycube)
Out[142]: 8
```

Lambda Function

A *lambda function* in Python in an anonymous function. Such functions are defined as follows:

    lambda arguments: expression

A lambda function can have any number of arguments but only one expression, which is evaluated and returned on a function call. A lambda function can be substituted for an object.

Example 7: The following function computes the derivative of a function $f(x)$ at x using two points: $x+dx$ and $x-dx$.

```
def my_deriv(f,x,dx):
    return((f(x+dx)-f(x-dx))/(2*dx))
```

We can define $f(x)$ and then employ *my_deriv()* on that function. For example, for *my_sqr()* function defined in the previous subsection, the derivative is at $x = 1$

```
In [59]: my_deriv(my_sqr, 1, 0.1)
Out[59]: 2.0000000000000004
```

A simpler version using lambda function is as follows. In this version, we can skip the definition of my_sqr().

```
In [61]: my_deriv(lambda x: x**2, 1, 0.1)
Out[61]: 2.0000000000000004
```

Clearly, lambda function makes the code simpler and concise.

Example 8: The following Python statement computes $\int_0^1 x\,dx$ using Python's builtin function *quad(f, lower_lim, upper_lim)*. We will describe this function in Section 11.3.

```
from scipy.integrate import quad
```

```
print (quad(lambda x: x, 0,1))    # 1D
```

Here, the quad() function integrates the lambda function *lambda x: x* in the interval 0 and 1.

Examples 7 and 8 illustrate the power of lambda function. In the next section, we will discuss namespace and scope of variables.

****

Conceptual Questions

1. What are the advantages of functions in a programming language?

Exercises

1. Write a Python function that returns second minima of an integer array.
2. Write a function to generate nth Pingala-Virahanka-Fibonacci numbers.
3. For $x_{n+1} = a\, x_n(1 - x_n)$, write a function that returns $\{x_n\}$ for a given n. Here, a and the initial condition, x_0, are the parameters of the function.
4. Write a function that takes two $n \times n$ matrices A and B and returns their matrix product. Solve for 3x3 and 4x4 matrices. You could try $A[i,j] = i*j/100$ and $B[i,j] = (i+1)*(j+1)/100$.
5. Write a Python function that returns the number of digits of an integer.
6. Write a Python function that returns the number of digits of the mantissa of a real number.
7. Write your own Python function that converts a positive real number in decimal format to binary format. Assume fixed point format.
8. Write a computer program to discover positions of 4 queens on a 4x4 chess board so that the queens do not kill each other. List

all possible solutions.
9. Solve problem 8 for n queens on a $n \times n$ chess board for $n = 5, 6, 7, 8$.
10. Knight's tour: Consider a 4x4 chess board. Write a computer program to construct move sequence of a knight tour such that the knight visits every square of the board exactly once. List all possible solutions.
11. Solve problem 10 for a $n \times n$ chess board.
12. We have 4 coins with one among them heavier than the rest. Write a computer program to identify the defective coin using least possible weighings. Make a tree diagram for the solution. Hint: For 4 coins, weigh coins 1 and 2 in one side, and coins 2 and 3 in the other side.
13. Extend Exercise 12 to 8 and 12 coins.
14. We have 4 coins among which one of them is defective (could be lighter or heavier). How will you identify the defective coin?
15. Do Exercise 14 for 8 coins and 12 coins.

5.2 Python Namespace and Scope

In this section, we will discuss scope and namespace in Python, as well as how arguments are passed in Python. We start with a description of *namespace* in Python.

Namespace in Python

In programming languages, namespace is employed to identify objects. Namespaces in computing are organised hierarchically that helps in identifying variables. To make an analogy, *Rahul* is a common name in India. However, *Rahul Dravid* brackets Rahul within a family named *Dravid*. Note however that there may be more than one Rahul Dravid, but Rahul Dravid, famous cricketer, is unique. Here, we employ three levels of identification—name (Rahul), family name (Dravid), and profession (cricketer). Similar organisation is used in programming languages.

Python variables are organised hierarchically into four namespaces: *Built-in*, *Global*, *Enclosing*, and *Local* (see Figure 27). It helps in clear identification of a variable. For example, we may have a global variable x, and a local variable with the same name. These two variables are identified by their scopes (global and local).

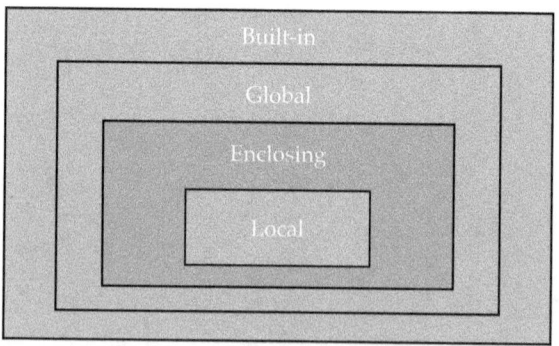

Figure 27: A hierarchy of namespaces in Python

A brief description of these namespaces are as follows:

1. *Built-in namespace*: It is a collection of names of Python's built-in objects, such as *True, False, bool, bin,* etc. The Python interpreter creates the built-in namespace at the start itself. This namespace exist till the termination of the interpreter.
2. *Global namespace*: Global namespace contains names at the level of main program. This namespace is created when the main program starts, and it terminates with the main program.
3. *Local namespace*: When a function is executed, a new namespace specific to the function is created. This namespace is destroyed when the function terminates.
4. *Enclosing namespace*: Python functions are often organised hierarchically. A variable defined inside a function is local to that function, but it is inaccessible to functions defined at a higher level. For example, in the following code segment, the function *inner()* is enclosed within the function *outer()*. The variable *xlocal* is local to inner(), and, hence, it is inaccessible to *outer()*. However, the variables *xencl* and *xglobal* are accessible inside the function *inner()*. In this example, *xencl* is an example of enclosing namespace.

```
In [64]: xglobal = 100
    ...:
    ...: def outer():
    ...:     xencl = 10
    ...:
    ...:     def inner():
    ...:         xlocal = 1
    ...:         print(xlocal)
    ...:         print(xencl, xglobal)
    ...:
    ...:     inner()

In [65]: outer()
1
10 100
```

We illustrate an application of namespace using module import.

Module Import

To use Python modules, we need to import them, which can be done in three ways:

import module: This way we make the module available in the current program as a separate *namespace*. Here, we need to refer to a function of the module using *module.function*. For example,

In [1]: import math

In [2]: math.factorial(5)
Out[2]: 120

from module import item: Here, the item of the module is referred to in the namespace of the current program. For example,

In [3]: from math import factorial

In [4]: factorial(10)
Out[4]: 3628800

import module as alias: The new namespace is referred to using an alias. This feature provides convenience when the module name is large. For example,

In [6]: import math as ma

In [7]: ma.factorial(5)
Out[7]: 120

Scope of Python Variables

Scope of a variable refers to its visibility in a program. Thus, it is connected to the namespace described above. A variable created inside a function is within the local scope of that function, while a variable created in the main body of a code belongs to the global scope. Note that a variable can be used within its scope only.

In a computer code, a variable name may be used at different levels.

In the following example, variable name x appears thrice in *global*, *enclosing*, and *local* scopes.

```
In [64]: x = 100 #global
   ...:
   ...: def outer():
   ...:     x = 10 #enclosing
   ...:
   ...:     def inner():
   ...:
   ...:         x = 1 #local
   ...:         print(x)
   ...:
   ...:     inner()

In [65]: outer()
1
```

Note that different namespaces or scopes (global, enclosing, local) segregate the variables so as to clearly differentiate them. The Python interpreter first searches for the variable inside a function. If it isn't available, then the interpreter searches for the variable in the enclosing function's scope. After that, the interpreter looks for the variable in the global scope. At last, the interpreter searches for the name in built-in scope. If the variable isn't available even after that, an error message is flashed.

After this, we discuss how arguments are passed to Python functions.

Passing of Arguments to Python Functions

A Python function communicates to outside world via *arguments* or *parameters*. Immutable variables (integer, float, string) and mutable variables (list and arrays) behave differently when they are passed as parameters. When an immutable global variable (say x) is passed as an argument to the function, any change in x inside the function does not affect x outside the function. We illustrate this feature using an example. See Figure 28 for an illustration.

```
In [90]: def test_fn(x):
   ...:     print('inside function, step 1: ', x, ' ',
```

```
        id(x))
        ...:    x = 999.0
        ...:    print('inside function, after x = 999.0: ',
x, ' ' , id(x))
        ...:

In [91]: a = 100.0

In [92]: id(a)
Out[92]: 4846932752

In [93]: test_fn(a)
inside function, step 1:   100.0    4846932752
inside function, after x = 999.0:   999.0    4846935088

In [94]: print(a, id(a))
Out[94]: 100.0.  4846932752
```

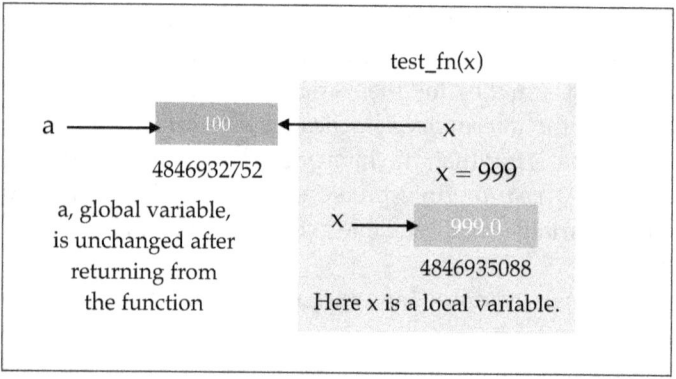

Figure 28: Behaviour of a immutable object in a Python function

In the above example, during the function call test_fn(a), the object a is passed to the function as x. Inside the function, after the execution of x=999.0, x points to the object 999.0. Note however that the global variable a is unaffected during these operations.

However, when a list or an array, which are mutable variables, is passed as an argument to a function, any alteration in the list or array inside the function reflects on the global variable. See the example below, which is illustrated in Figure 29.

```
In [216]: b=[1,2,3]

In [217]: def change_array(x):
```

Practical Numerical Computing Using Python

```
   ...:         print('Starting of fn: x,
                 id(x) ', x, id(x))
   ...:         x[0] = 100
   ...:         print('End of fn: x, id(x)',
                 x, id(x))
   ...:         return
   ...: 

In [218]: id(b)
Out[218]: 140562590748992

In [219]: change_array(b)
Starting of fn: x, id(x)   [1, 2, 3] 140562590748992
End of fn: x, id(x)   [100, 2, 3] 140562590748992
```

During the function call *change_array(b)*, list *b* is passed to *change_array(x)* for *x*. Inside the function, *x*[0] takes value 100. This change is reflected in *b* (see *Out* [219]) because *x* and *b* point to the same object. This is unlike immutable variables that are unaffected by similar operations inside the function.

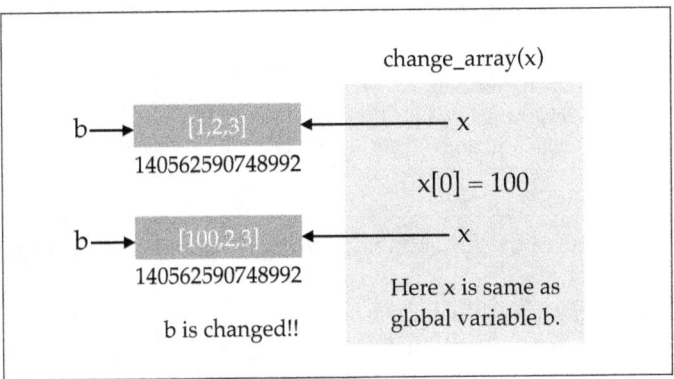

Figure 29: Behaviour of a mutable object in a Python function

Example 1: In the following code, global variable *a* is passed to function my_sqr(*x*).

```
In [6]: a = 5

In [209]: id(a)
```

```
Out[209]: 4540589328

In [214]: def my_sqr(x):
     ...:     print('Starting of fn: x, id(x) ', x, id(x))
     ...:     x = x**2
     ...:     print('End of fn: x, id(x) ',x, id(x))
     ...:     return

In [234]: my_sqr(a)
Starting of fn: x, id(x)  5 4540589328
End of fn: x, id(x)    25 4540589968
```

As illustrated in Figure 30, first, x of the function $my\_sqr(x)$ points to a. Next, x points to a new object 25, and it becomes a local variable. Note that a is unchanged after the execution of the function $my\_sqr(a)$.

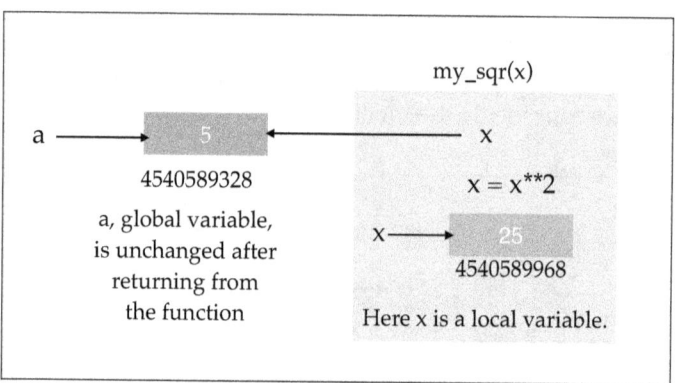

Figure 30: Effects of the function $my\_sqr(a)$ on variables of the function.

The above examples illustrate how arguments are passed to Python functions, and how variables behave inside and outside the functions.

Global Variables

A Python variable that is declared in the main program (outside functions) is called a *global variable* (see Figure 27). Such variables have *global scope*. In Python, the global variables have the following properties.

1. Global variables are accessible inside a function, but they cannot be modified inside the function, unless it is declared with *global* keyword (e.g., *global count*).
2. Once a variable has been declared inside a function using *global* keyword, the function can modify the global variable. These modifications are permanent and they visible outside the function. See Example 5.

We illustrate these features using the following examples.

Example 2: A global variable *count* is defined outside function $f()$. It is available inside the function $f()$.

```
In [262]: count = 0

In [265]: def f():
     ...:     print("count = ", count)

In [266]: f()
count =  0
```

Example 3: We cannot alter *count* inside a function, as shown in the following code:

```
In [267]: def f():
     ...:     count = count+1

In [268]: f()
UnboundLocalError: local variable 'count' referenced before assignment
```

Example 4: In the following code, count is passed as a parameter to $f()$.

```
In [273]: def f(count):
     ...:     print("Start of fn: count = ", count, id(count))
     ...:     count = count+1
     ...:     print("End of fn: count = ", count,id(count))
```

```
   ...:

In [274]: count=0

In [275]: f(count)
Start of fn: count =  0 4540589168
End of fn: count =   1 4540589200

In [277]: print(count, id(count))
0 4540589168
```

At the start of the function, *count* is a global variable. However, after the execution of the statement, *count* = *count*+1, the variable *count* points to a new object, which is 1. The variable *count* (1) now becomes a local variable, and the above increment has no effect on the global variable *count*. Look at the *id(count)* at various stages.

Example 5: Inside *f()*, we declare *count* to be a global variable. Under this arrangement, the increment of the global variable *count* is visible outside the function.

In [294]: def f():
  ...:   global count
  ...:   print("Start of fn: count = ", count, id(count))
  ...:   count = count+1
  ...:   print("End of fn: count = ", count,id(count))
  ...:

In [295]: count=0

In [296]: f()
Start of fn: count = 0 4540589168
End of fn: count = 1 4540589200

In [297]: print(count, id(count))
1 4540589200

Example 6: The following *swap* function for integers does not work.

```
#  This function does not swap the vars a,b
```

```
# of the main program
# (Reference Type, or call by value in some sense)
def swap_not_working(a,b):
    temp = a
    a = b
    b = temp
    print (a, b, temp, id(a), id(b), id(temp))
    return a, b

In [323]: a
Out[323]: 5

In [324]: b
Out[324]: 50

In [325]: id(a), id(b)
Out[325]: (4453578000, 4453579440)

In [329]: swap_not_working(a,b)
50 5 5 4453579440 4453578000 4453578000

In [330]: print(a, b, id(a), id(b))
5 50 4453578000 4453579440
```

In the python statement *In* [325], we pass the global variables *a* and *b* as arguments to the function. Inside the function, the variables *a* and *b* have been swapped (see *In* [329]), but the changes are lost when the function exits. This is because *a* and *b* inside *swap_not_working(a,b)* are local variables of the function. The global variables remain unaffected by the operations performed inside the function (see *In* [330]).

The variables *a* and *b* inside the function and outside are different even though their id's are the same. This is because their scopes are different. It is important to note that the two different variables can have same names if their scopes are different. Also, a variable can point to different objects at different times, hence its *id* can vary with time.

A side remark: Contrast the above behaviour with C functions. If *a* and *b* were passed as pointers to integers, then swap would work. However, the C function will not swap the arguments when they are passed by value.

Example 7: The *swap* function of Example 5 can be made to work by modifying the function and the function call as follows.

```
return → return (a,b)

swap_not_working(a,b)  →  (a,b) = swap_not_working(a,b)
```

The latter statement passes function's *a* and *b* (that are swapped) to global variables *a* and *b*.

Another version (simpler one) of swap function that works is given below.

```
# Swap a and b
def swap(a,b):
    return b,a

Usage: a , b = swap(a,b)
```

Even a simpler way to swap is the following:

```
In [308]: a, b = b,a
```

Example 8: The swap function of Example 6 can take lists/arrays as inputs, but two lists are not swapped due the arguments given earlier. Instead, the following function, swap_list(a,b), enables swapping of lists *a* and *b*, which are global variables.

```
# Swaps two lists a and b
def swap_list(a,b):
    temp = a[:]
    # copies elements of a into tmp (new array).
    # differs from temp = a

    a[:] = b
    # copies elements of b into a

    b[:] = temp
    # copies elements of tmp to b

    print (a, b, temp, id(a), id(b), id(temp))
    Return

In [365]: a = [1,2]
```

Practical Numerical Computing Using Python

```
In [366]: b = [10,20]

In [367]: id(a), id(b)
Out[367]: (140716150723760, 140716130405904)

In [369]: swap_list(a,b)
[10, 20] [1, 2] [1, 2] 140716150723760 140716130405904
140716132670352

In [371]: a, b, id(a), id(b)
Out[371]: ([10, 20], [1, 2], 140716150723760,
140716130405904)
```

In the function *swap_list(a, b)*, the lists *temp* and *a* behave differently than the previous swap example because *list* is mutable.

Example 9: Squaring a numpy array

```
In [47]: b = array([1,2,3])

In [48]: id(b)
Out[48]: 140708012226560

In [49]: def my_sqr(x):
    ...:     x = x**2
    ...:     print (x, id(x))
    ...:     return(x)
    ...:

In [50]: print(my_sqr(b))
[1 4 9] 140708036299952
[1 4 9]

In [51]: print(b, id(b))
[1 2 3] 140708012226560
```

In the above example, array b is passed to the function $my\_sqr(x)$. Hence, Inside the function, $x = b$. However, the operation $x = x^2$ creates a new array to which x points to. The new array is the output of the function $my\_sqr(x)$, as is evident from *In* [50].

Note however that original b remains unaffected by the squaring operation (see *In* [51]). Similar behaviour would be observed for other array functions such as *sqrt()*, *sin()*, *exp()*, etc.

The above examples show that the argument passing in Python is tricky. Sometimes codes do not produce expected outputs due to the subtle reasons mentioned above. We need to be careful on such occasions.

****

Conceptual Questions

1. What are the differences between Python's local and global variables?
2. Arguments to a Python function could be immutable and mutable objects. What are their behavioural differences?

Exercises

1. Execute all the codes given in this section and verify the results.
2. What are the outputs of the print() in the following code segment?

    ```
    def mult(a,b)
        a *= b
        return(a)

    X = 3
    mult(x,4)
    print(x)

    a=np.array([4,8])
    print (mult(a,4))
    print(a)
    ```

5.3 Recursive Functions

In mathematics, a recursive function is one that is defined using its own definition. For example, *factorial(n)* or n! can be defined as

$n! = n\,(n-1)!$ for $n > 1$, and
$1! = 1$

Such a definition is called a *recursive* definition.

The above function works as follows. For $n = 3$, $3! = 3 \times 2!$, $2! = 2 \times 1!$, and $1! = 1$. The last condition, $1! = 1$, helps terminate the recursive process. After the last step, reverse substitution yields $2! = 2$ and $3! = 3 \times 2 = 6$, which is the answer.

We can define recursive functions in Python and in many modern languages, e.g., C, C++. In the following discussion, we provide some examples of recursive Python functions.

Example 1: Recursive implementation of factorial(n)

```
def factorial(n):
    if (n==1):
        return 1
    else:
        return n*factorial(n-1)
```

It works as follows:

```
factorial(3) = 3*factorial(2),
factorial(2) = 2*factorial(1),
factorial(1) = 1.
```

After this, the reverse substitution yields

```
factorial(2) = 2*1 = 2,
factorial(3) = 3*2 = 6.  (Answer)
```

The above recursive implementation of *factorial(n)* yields the same result as in Example 1 of Section 5.1. However, the recursive function is quite expensive because it makes forward calls to itself, and then performs reverse substitutions. Each function call requires significant bookkeeping (e.g., saving local variables at each stage).

Recursion does not provide any real benefit in the implementation of factorial. However, some problems are much easier to solve using recursion than using iteration. One such problem is *Tower of Hanoi*.

Example 2: *Tower of Hanoi*: Consider 3 pegs, A, B, C, as shown in the initial configuration of Figure 31. Peg A has n discs, but pegs B and C have none. We need to transfer n disks from peg A to peg C under the following rules:

1. Only one disk can be moved at a time.
2. Only the top disk of a peg can be moved.
3. A larger disk cannot be placed on top of a smaller disk.

A recursive solution for the above problem is as follows. For $n > 1$,

1. Transfer $n-1$ disks from A to B.
2. Transfer one remaining disk from A to C.
3. Transfer $n-1$ disks from B to C.

However, for $n = 1$, the disk can be transferred in a single step, as long as rule 3 is obeyed. We illustrate the above steps in Figure 31. A Python implementation is given below.

```
def tower_of_hanoi(n,source,dest,intermediate):
    if (n==1):
        print("transfer disk ", source , " dest ", dest)
    else:
        tower_of_hanoi(n-1, source, intermediate, dest)
        print("transfer disk ", source , " dest ", dest)
        tower_of_hanoi(n-1, intermediate, dest, source)


In [2]: run tower_of_hanoi.py

In [3]: tower_of_hanoi(3,"A","B","C")
transfer disk   A   to   B
transfer disk   A   to   C
transfer disk   B   to   C
transfer disk   A   to   B
transfer disk   C   to   A
```

```
transfer disk  C  to  B
transfer disk  A  to  B
```

In the above function definition, we employ *source*, *dest*, and *intermediate* as the peg labels. This is because source and destination pegs vary at different stages of function calls.

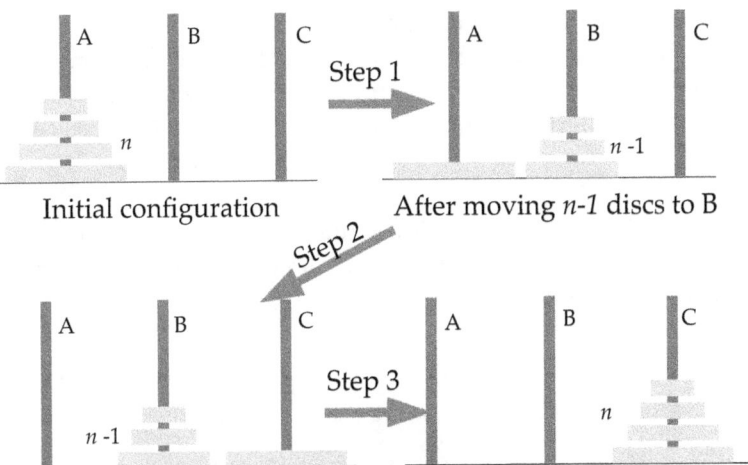

Initial configuration   After moving *n-1* discs to B

After moving the first discs to C   After moving *n-1* discs to C

Figure 31: Illustrations of the three steps for solving the tower of Hanoi problem.

Based on the steps of the algorithm, we can estimate the number of moves required to transfer n disks. If $N(n)$ is the total number of moves to transfer n disks, then the recursive definition yields the following relation between $N(n)$ and $N(n-1)$:

$$N(n) = 2\,N(n-1) + 1 \quad \ldots(4)$$
and $N(1) = 1$

We attempt solution of the form $N(n) = a^n + b$. The condition $N(1) = 1$ yields $a+b = 1$. Substitution of $N(n) = a^n + b$ in Eq. (4) and usage of $a+b = 1$ yields

$$a^n = 2\,a^{n-1} + 2 - a.$$

For $n = 2$, the above equation becomes $a^2 = a + 2$, whose solutions are $a = -1$ and 2. The former solution is invalid because $N(n)$ is an increasing function of n. Therefore,

$$N(n) = 2^n - 1, \quad \ldots(5)$$

which is a valid solution of Eq. (4). Thus, $N(n) = 2^n - 1$ is the time complexity of the above algorithm.

We remark that Tower of Hanoi has an iterative solution as well. However, it is much more complex to implement. The recursive solution is very intuitive and straight forward.

Example 3: *Sierpinski triangle*: We write a computer program to draw *Sierpinski triangle* shown in Figure 32. Refer to the website https://sites.google.com/view/py-comp for the color figure.

Figure 32: Sierpinski triangle of degree 3. Refer to the website https://sites.google.com/view/py-comp for the color figure.

In Figure 32, we illustrate a Sirpiński triangle of fractal degree 3. Note that each triangle has three sub-triangles, whose dimension is half of its predecessor (for example, blue triangle within a red triangle). Further, the sub-triangles have even smaller triangles (subsub-triangles) within them. For fractal degree 3, the recursive iteration stops at the innermost green triangles. Here, the white, red, blue, and green triangles have *fractal degrees* of 3, 2, 1, 0 respectively. Such objects are *self-similar*. That is, smaller triangles have similar structure as the large ones.

An algorithm to construct Sirpiński triangle is as follows.

```
def draw_sirpinski(vortex_coords, fractal_degree):

    Draw a triangle of fractal_degree.

    if (fractal_degree > 0):
        Find the coordinates of the triangle
            at the left corner
        draw_sirpinski(left_triange_vortex_coords,
            fractal_degree-1)

        Find the coordinates of the triangle at
            the right corner
        draw_sirpinski(right_triagle_vortex_coords,
            fractal_degree-1)

        Find the coordinates of the triangle at
            the top corner
        draw_sirpinski(top_triangle_vortex_coords,
            fractal_degree-1)
```

The code that produces the Sierpinski triangle with fractal degree of fractal_degree is given below. It employs *turtle module* of Python. The *turtle* could move forward by a distance d (*forward*(d)), turn left by any angle θ (*left*(θ)), turn right by an angle ζ (right(ζ)), go to a point (x,y) (*goto*(x,y)), and perform several other tasks. Refer to the turtle manual for more details.

```
import turtle

colormap = ['red','green','blue',
'white','yellow','violet','orange']

# Draws a triangle of color 'color' and whose vortices are
in the list vortex_coords.
def drawTriangle(vortex_coords,color,fractalTurtle):
    fractalTurtle.fillcolor(color)
    fractalTurtle.up()
    fractalTurtle.goto(vortex_coords[0][0],
        vortex_coords[0][1])
    fractalTurtle.down()
    fractalTurtle.begin_fill()
    fractalTurtle.goto(vortex_coords[1][0],
        vortex_coords[1][1])
    fractalTurtle.goto(vortex_coords[2][0],
        vortex_coords[2][1])
```

```
        fractalTurtle.goto(vortex_coords[0][0],
            vortex_coords[0][1])
        fractalTurtle.end_fill()

# Returns the mid point of points p1 and p2
def mid_point(p1,p2):
    return ( (p1[0]+p2[0]) / 2, (p1[1] + p2[1]) / 2)

# Draws sierpinski triangle of fractal_degree with its
def
sierpinski(vortex_coords,fractal_degree,fractalTurtle):

    drawTriangle(vortex_coords,colormap[fractal_degree],fracta
    lTurtle)
    if fractal_degree > 0:
        sierpinski([vortex_coords[0],
            mid_point(vortex_coords[0], vortex_coords[1]),
            mid_point(vortex_coords[0], vortex_coords[2])],
            fractal_degree-1, fractalTurtle)

        sierpinski([vortex_coords[1],
            mid_point(vortex_coords[0], vortex_coords[1]),
            mid_point(vortex_coords[1], vortex_coords[2])],
            fractal_degree-1, fractalTurtle)

        sierpinski([vortex_coords[2],
            mid_point(vortex_coords[2],vortex_coords[1]),
            mid_point(vortex_coords[0],vortex_coords[2])],
            fractal_degree-1, fractalTurtle)
def main():
    fractalTurtle = turtle.Turtle()
    Win = turtle.getscreen()
    vortex_coords = [[-200,-100],[0,200],[200,-100]]
    sierpinski(vortex_coords,3,fractalTurtle)
    Win.exitonclick()

main()
```

The above code appears quite complex, but it is not so. Some of the key features of the code are as follows.

1. The centre of the largest triangle is at the origin, while its three vortices are at (−200,−100), (0,200), (200,−100). The vortices are stored in the array *vortex_coords*. The vortices of the inner triangles are computed iteratively.

2. In main(), we create *fractalTurtle* using the function *turtle.Turtle()*; this *fractalTurtle* is passed as an argument to the functions *sierpinski()* and *drawTriangle()* because the same turtle moves in these functions.
3. Using the array *colormap*, we set the colours of the triangles of levels 3, 2, 1, 0 as white, red, blue, and green respectively. Note that level n triangles are at the top of level $n-1$ triangles, hence only the remnants of the earlier triangles are visible in the figure.
4. The color-filling of the triangles is achieved by the functions *fillcolor()*, *begin_fill()*, and *end_fill()*. The colors are filled after the triangles have been drawn.

Since the turtle moves on turtle console, the above code cannot run on *Ipython*. It is best to run this code on *Spyder* that supports turtle console.

Example 4: *Pingala-Virahanka-Fibonacci* (PVF) sequence is defined recursively as follows:

$$f(n) = f(n-1) + f(n-2)$$

with $f(0) = 1$ and $f(1) = 1$. Using this definition, we compute $f(2)$ onwards as 2, 3, 5, 8, and so on. Asymptotically (for large n), $f(n) = C a^n$ with a satisfying

$$a^2 = a + 1,$$

whose solution is a = $(\sqrt{5}+1)/2$, which is called *golden ratio*.

The Pingala-Virahanka-Fibonacci sequence is used to describe growth models. For example, as shown in Figure 33, the numbers of petals in flowers are PVF numbers. Also, the growth of the flowers and shells follow the PVF spiral, which is shown in the first subfigure of Figure 33. See https://en.wikipedia.org/wiki/Fibonacci_number for more details.

Figure 33: Illustrations of Pingala-Virahanka-Fibonacci sequence and spirals in nature. From https://wikieducator.org/images/f/f1/Fibonacci.png. Credits: wikieducator.

The following recursive code generates the Pingala-Virahanka-Fibonacci sequence:

```
def pingala(n):
    if (n==0):
        return 1
    elif (n==1):
        return 1
    else:
        return (pingala(n-1)+pingala(n-2))
```

Usage:

```
In [5]: pingala(3)
Out[5]: 3

In [6]: pingala(4)
Out[6]: 5
```

Recursion is a powerful tool for many computational problems, e.g. binary search, Fast Fourier Transform, etc. However, majority of scientific algorithms employ iterative solutions because they are faster than their recursive counterparts.

With this, we end our discussion on recursive functions.

Conceptual Questions

1. State five examples of mathematical recursive functions.
2. List five recursive structures found in nature.
3. Why are recursive functions more expensive than their iterative counterparts?

Exercises

1. Write an iterative Python function to compute x_n of function $x_{n+1} = f(x_n)$ where $f(x) = ax(1-x)$. Here, a and initial x_0 are the parameters of the function.
2. Modify the code for Sierpinski triangle so as to produce white-grey triangles of different darkness intensities.
3. Using turtle module write Python functions to create the following fractal objects: Sierpinski carpet, Koch curve, Lévy fractal. See wikipedia for their description.

CHAPTER SIX
SOLVING COMPLEX PROBLEMS USING PYTHON

Synopsis

"First, solve the problem. Then, write the code."
-- John Johnson

"Any fool can write code that a computer can understand. Good programmers write code that humans can understand." -- Martin Fowler

This chapter describes good programming practices, and simple algorithms on prime numbers, searching, and sorting.

6.1 Good Progamming Practices

Computational problems can be very complex. Here, we list a small sample of often-encountered complex computational problems.

1. Compression of a music file.
2. Weather prediction
3. Making a document writer (e.g., Microsoft Word)
4. Making a web browser

Writing computer programs for such applications requires major planning and team work. These problems, of course, are beyond the scope of this introductory book where we solve much simpler problems. Yet, it is best to learn the best practices of programming during early stages itself. In this chapter, we will illustrate how to solve computational problems as a good computer scientist.

In the following we list some important tips that are helpful for writing good programs:

1. A computer has a fast processor, but it does not have an intuituion or intelligence. It has to be told exactly what is to be done. A step-by-step process to arrive at the final solution is called an *algorithm*. It is important to write down an algorithm before we start to code. This way, we arrive at a correct and error-free code.
2. Think about the problem at hand before you start to program. In fact, *first solve the problem, and then write an algorithm, after which start to code.*
3. Think simple! Simple solutions are easy to code and easy to explain to colleagues. Simple codes often yield efficient results, and they are easy to modify. KISS—*Keep it simple, stupid!*—is an important proverb in computer programming. Follow this guideline! When you get back to your code after a year, you should be able to understand it without strain.
4. Think carefully about extreme cases. For example, your search program should work even when the item is not in the list.
5. Choose variable names wisely. For example, use *mass* as a variable name to denote the mass of a particle. Do not use x for mass! Your code should be readable.

6. Follow consistent choice of variables. For example, use i, j, k for loop variables consistently.
7. Comment your code, but avoid excessive commenting.
8. Computer programming is an art. Write beautiful codes! Of course, mastering this art takes a lot of effort, practice, and patience.

For further guidance on the art of programming, refer to the following books:

1. B. W. Kernighan and R. Pike: The practice of Programming
2. G. Polya and J. H. Conway: How to Solve It: A New Aspect of Mathematical Method
3. R. G. Dormy: How to Solve It by Computer

6.2 Prime Numbers

In this section, we focus on three problems related to prime numbers. In addition, we will illustrate how to write algorithms and then write the corresponding codes.

Test if an Integer is Prime or Not

Many clever algorithms are available to test whether a given number is prime or not (also called *primality test*). In this section we will present a simple algorithm for this test.

Idea: If n is not a prime, then one of its factors will be in the range 2 to $\sqrt{n}$. For example, 15 is divisible by 3, which is less than $\sqrt{15}$. Therefore, we test whether n is divisible by integers 2, 3, ..., $\sqrt{n}$. As soon as we find a factor in this band of numbers, we declare n to be a non-prime. Otherwise n is a prime number.

Algorithm:

```
function is_prime(n):
    for i: 0 to √n
        if (n%i == 0):
            n is non-prime; return
    else  # after the loop
        n is indivisible by a factor.
        Declare n to be prime; return
```

Code:

```
import numpy as np

# Returns 1 if n is prime, 0 otherwise  #s
def is_prime(n):

    # First test if n is divisible by 2.
    if (n%2 == 0):
        return 0
```

```
# Test if i divides n.
# i ranges from 3 to sqrt(n) in steps of 2.
for i in range(3, int(np.sqrt(n))+1, 2):
    if (n%i == 0):
        return 0
else:
    return 1
```

In the code, we save computation effort by eliminating $i = 2,4,6..$ (even numbers) in the first loop. The present code is more efficient than that in Section 4.3.

Generating Prime Numbers up to n

Here, we present the algorithm—*Sieve of Eratosthenes*—to generate prime numbers up to n.

Idea: The algorithm consists of following steps.
1. Construct a sieve of integers from 2 to n.
2. From the sieve, eliminate numbers that are multiples of prime numbers 2, 3, 5, 7, ..., $\sqrt{n}$ one after the other.
3. At the end of the process, the remaining numbers in the sieve are the desired prime numbers.

Algorithm: Here we remove the non-prime numbers using *pop()* function.

```
function prime_sieve(n):

    Create sieve (2:n)
    prime = prime_no[0]

    loop (prime***2 < n):

        for the given prime:
            Eliminate all the multiples of of prime
                up to the last number n.
            Retain other numbers.

        Pick the next prime and loop.
```

Code:

```
import numpy as np

# The function prime(n) returns a list of primes up to n.
# Adopts the Sieve of Eratosthenes algorithm
# Pops the non-prime numbers from the sieve ones
# a prime is able to divide it.

def prime(n):

    nos = list(range(2,n+1))
    # Sieve containing integers from 2 to n

    prime_index = 0
    prime_now = nos[prime_index]
    # prime_now = 2 is the first prime

    while(prime_now**2 < n):

        # remove all multiples of prime_now from nos
        index = prime_index + 1

        while (index <= (np.size(nos)-1)):
            # Loop till the last number in the Sieve
            # if prime_now divides the number,
            # then delete it from the sieve.
            # Otherwise let it be,
            # move on to the next number
            if ((nos[index] % prime_now) != 0):
                index += 1
            else:
                nos.pop(index)

        # Goto the next prime number
        prime_index += 1
        prime_now =  nos[prime_index]
    return nos
```

Compute the Prime Factors of a Number

Computing *prime factors* of a number is an important problem of number theory, and it has wide applications in cryptography, statistical physics, combinatorics, etc. In the following discussion, we present one of the simplest algorithms to obtain a list of prime factors of a number.

Idea: To compute the prime factors of number n:

1. Start with 2. If n is divisible by 2, then add 2 as a factor, and set $n \rightarrow n/2$. Repeat this process until 2 is unable to divide n.
2. Repeat the same process for subsequent prime numbers: 3, 5, 7, ...
3. This process is continued till n becomes 1.

Algorithm:

```
prime_no = [2,3,5, ...]

function prime_factor(n):
    factor = [] # empty arrays
    i=0
    while (n > 1):
        loop:
            For prime(i),
            if (prime[i] divides n):
                n ← n/prime[i]; Append prime[i] to factor.
        increment i
    return factor
```

Code:

```
import numpy as np

# Prime numbers up to 100
prime_nos = [2, 3, 5, 7, 11, 13, 17, 19, 23, 29, 31, \
37, 41, 43, 47, 53, 59, 61, 67, 71, 73, 79, 83, 89, 97]


# Returns prime factors of integer n
def prime_factor(n):
    factor_array = []
    i = 0
    while (n > 1):
        # loop for prime[i]
        # Inner loop for multiple factors of prime[i]
        while(n%prime_nos[i] ==0):
```

```
        n /= prime_nos[i]
        factor_array.append(prime_nos[i])

    # Go to the next prime factor
    i += 1

return factor_array
```

With this, we end our preliminary discussions on prime numbers using Python.

****

Exercises

1. Compute the first 50 prime numbers.
2. Consider two integers a and b. Compute their prime factors. Using these prime factors, compute the greatest common divisor (GCD) and least common multiple (LCM) of a and b.
3. Twin prime numbers are those who differ by 2. For example, (5,7), (11,13). List all the twin prime numbers up to 500.
4. Consider the primality code discussed in this section. Rewrite the code without the for-else structure.
5. Find the first 10^7 prime numbers from the internet. Label them as P_n and plot P_n vs. n. Also plot $P_{n+1} - P_n$ vs. n. Fit the second plot with $log(n)$.

6.3 Searching and Sorting

Search is an important problem and it is employed everywhere. Some examples involving search operations are

1. Searching for a person, research topic, as in google search
2. Recognition of a person in our head via search through the stored images in our brain.
3. Search for a word in a dictionary

Many search algorithms are quite complex. Google has become world famous and very rich due to their sophisticated search algorithms. Such complex schemes are beyond the scope of this book; here, we present two elementary search algorithms.

As we show below, search in sorted and unsorted arrays have different time complexities. Note that a sorted array is one in which the elements (numbers) are arranged either in ascending or descending order. We describe the respective algorithms below.

Searching in an Unsorted Array

An unsorted array has no pattern. Hence, we need to look for the element to be searched in the whole array one by one. Algorithmically, it is prudent to start searching from the beginning of the array and continue to search till the element is found. This algorithm is called a *linear search*. The following code performs a linear search of element x in array A. The function returns the array index of x. The linear search process is illustrated in Figure 34.

Algorithm:

```
function linsearch(A, x):
    Loop:
        Starting from the first element \
        to the last element of A.
            Test if the A[i] == x:
                if success, report the index.
```

```
    else: report that x is absent in A.
```

Code: The function returns the array index of x. It returns -1 if x does not belong to A.

```
# Searches x in an unsorted array A.
# Return index i, A[i]=x
# If x does not belong to A, then return -1
# Linear search

def linsearch(A, x):

    for i in range(len(A)):
        if (A[i] == x):
            return i

    else:   # x does not exist in A
        return -1
```

Usage:
```
In [382]: A = ['Rohit', 'Sita', 'Ahilya', 'Laxmi']

In [383]: linsearch(A, 'Sita')
Out[383]: 1

In [384]: linsearch(A, 'Ahilya')
Out[384]: 2

In [385]: linsearch(A, 'Jaya')
Out[385]: -1
```

How many comparisons are required in the above search operation? The best and worst scenarios require 1 and n comparisons respectively. It is easy to verify that the average number of comparison is $n/2$. Hence, the time complexity of linear search algorithm is $O(n)$, where O stands for "order of".

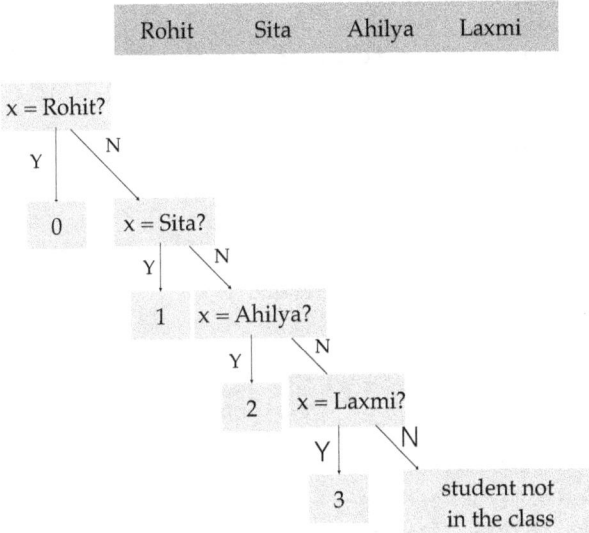

Figure 34: Linear search of an element x in list A = [Rohit, Sita, Ahilya, Laxmi]. Here, Y and N represent *yes* and *no*.

Searching in an Sorted Array: Binary Search

It is faster to search for an element in a sorted array. The algorithm makes use of the sorted nature of the array. Let us we assume that the integer array A is sorted in an ascending order.

Idea: First we locate the mid index of the array and denote it by *mid*. If $x = A[mid]$, then search is complete. If $x < A[mid]$, then we search in the left half of the array, else we search in the right half of the array. The above procedure is recursively applied to the subarrays (left half or right half). We continue till we succeed. In case of failure, return −1 indicating that the element is not in the list. This procedure is called *binary search*.

Code: The function returns the array index of x. It returns −1 if x does not belong to A.

```
# Search x in an sorted array A.
# Return index i, A[i]=x
# If x does not belong to A, then return -1
# Binary search
def binsearch(A, x):
    n = len(A)
    lower = 0
    upper = n-1
    mid = (lower+upper)//2

    # if x is outside array, return -1
    if ((x < A[0]) | (x>A[-1])):
        return -1

    # If x == A[mid], exit the loop.
    # else, search left or right half depending
    # on x < A[mid] or x>A[mid].
    while (A[mid] != x):
        if (lower == upper):
            # search exhausted. x not found.
            break
        if (x<A[mid]):
            upper = mid-1
        else:
            lower = mid+1
        mid = (lower+upper)//2

    # Check with the returned mid if A[mid]==x.
    if (A[mid] == x):
        return mid
    else:
        return -1
```

Usage:
In [72]: A = [1,3,7,8,11,15,20,25,30]

In [73]: binsearch(A,11)
Out[73]: 4

In [74]: binsearch(A,35)
Out[74]: -1

In [75]: binsearch(A,9)
Out[75]: -1

We illustrate the binary search described above using a diagram shown in Figure 35. The search process starts from the top of the tree ($x == 11$), and goes down to lower branches. In the diagram, the elements are shown inside the nodes (circle), and the index range for the tree at the node, (*lower, mid, upper*), is shown by its side. If *lower* = *upper*, then we list the *middle* index at the node.

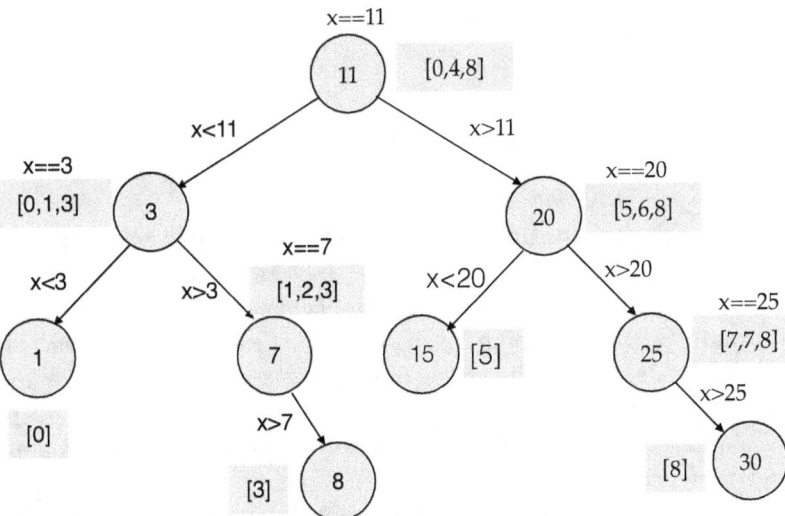

Figure 35: An illustration of a binary search tree for the array A = [1,3,7,8,11,15,20,25,30]. The nodes contain the array elements, while the list in the side contains the index range of the tree at the node.

Recursive code: A recursive code provides a more transparent implementation of binary search. However, this code is more expensive than the iterative code described above.

```
# Search x in an sorted array A between A[lower:upper].
# Return index i, A[i]=x
# If x does not belong to A, then return -1
# Recursive binary search
def binsearch_recursive(A,lower,upper,x):

    mid = (lower+upper)/2
    if ((x < A[lower]) | (x>A[upper])):
        return -1
    elif ((lower==upper) & (A[mid] != x)):
```

```
        return -1
else:
    if (A[mid] == x):
        ans = mid
    elif (x < A[mid]):
        ans = binsearch_recursive(A,lower,mid-1,x)
    else:
        ans = binsearch_recursive(A,mid+1,upper,x)
    return ans
```

Usage:
In [76]: binsearch_recursive(A,0,8,11)
Out[76]: 4

We can compute the time complexity of binary search as follows. As illustrated in Figure 35, at each stage, the data is divided into two parts. Array A of the above example has 9 elements. For this array, the maximum number of comparisons (==, <, >) required is 5, which is maximum depth of the tree plus one. We need these many comparisons when $x = 30$ or 8.

For an array of size n, the corresponding number is approximately $log_2(n)$. Hence, the time complexity for binary search is $O(log_2(n))$, which is much smaller than that for a linear search ($O(n)$). The difference becomes significant for large n. Hence, binary search is more efficient than linear search.

The above binary search algorithm is for an integer list. However, the algorithm is equally applicable to any ordered list, for example, a language dictionary. In a dictionary, we can search for a word much more quickly because the words are sorted. It would be nightmare to search for a word in a set of unsorted words.

Sorting an Array: Bubble Sort

As described above, a sorted array facilitates efficient search. Hence, sorting an array is an important problem. Computer scientists have devised many efficient sorting algorithms. Here, we present *bubble sort*, which is one of the simplest sorting algorithms.

Idea: We first push the largest element of the array to the end of the array. For the same, we start from the first element of the array and move forward comparing the neighbours. On comparison, if $A[j] > A[j+1]$, we swap the integers. As a result, the last element of A becomes the largest number.

After this, we need to push the largest number among $A[0:N-2]$ to the end of $A[0:N-2]$. We follow exactly the same procedure as above. We continue this process till we are left with a single number, which is the smallest number of the array, which stays at $A[0]$.

We implement the above idea in the following program.

Python code:

```python
# Compare two neighbours: if A[i] < A[i-1], swap.
# In the first round, A[N-1] is the largest integer.
# In the next round, A[N-2] is the second largest number.
# We carry out this process till the end.

# Sort A in increasing order.
def bubble_sort(A):
    n = len(A)

    for i in range(n):

        # A[n-i-1:n-1] is sorted.
        # So go only up to n-i-2.
        for j in range(0, n-i-1):

            # Swap if the prev number is greater
            # than the last number.
            if A[j] > A[j+1]:
                A[j], A[j+1] = A[j+1], A[j]
```

Usage:
In [76]: run bubble_sort.py

In [77]: A = [8,7,3,10,6]

In [78]: bubble_sort(A)

In [79]: A
Out[79]: [3, 6, 7, 8, 10]

Figure 36 illustrates the sorting procedure for array $A = [8,7,3,10,6]$. In the first iteration, the program bubbles the largest integer, which is 10.

In the next iteration, the second largest integer 8 is bubbled up. This process is continued till the whole array is sorted.

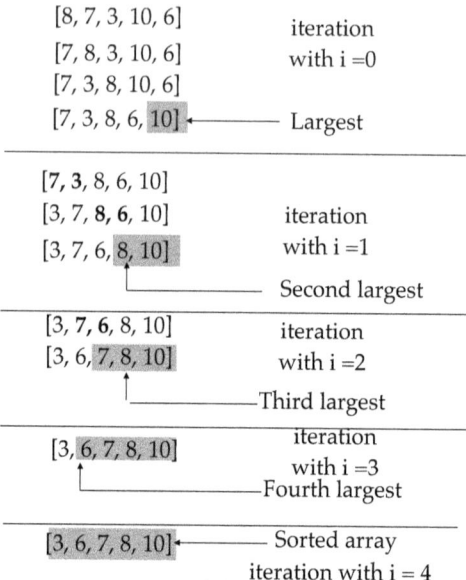

Figure 36: Sorting of array $A = [8,7,3,10,6]$ using bubble sort. The shaded list indicates the numbers that have been sorted.

With this, we end our discussion on search and sort algorithms.

****

Exercises

1. Compare the time complexities (number of comparisons) of linear and binary searches for $n = 16, 256, 4096, 2^{30}$.
2. How many comparisons are required to bubble sort an array of size n?
3. Given an integer array, write a Python function that prints the

fourth largest integer of the array.
4. Write a Python function that sorts an integer array in descending order.
5. Consider a list of strings, for example, A = ["Python", "C", "Java", "Pascal"]. Write a computer program to sort A.

Chapter Seven
PLOTTING IN PYTHON

Synopsis

"A picture is worth a thousand words."
— Napoleon Bonaparte

Python offers many tools to make plots and animations, a topic of the present chapter.

7.1 Matplotlib & Field Plots

Experiments, observations, and computer simulations generate data. Most often, just staring at the numbers do not provide valuable insights, but plots do. For example, a plot of Earth's surface temperature reveals much more information than the raw data. Similarly, business and demographic data too are presented using plots. This is the reason why most scientific and business presentations and publications contain plots of various kinds.

Python provides extensive plotting and visualisation tools. These functions are part of *Matplotlib module* of Python. In this chapter, we will cover only basic plotting features of *Matplotlib*. In this section, we will show how to make plots for scalar and vector fields.

We start with the usage of *Pyplot* module of Matplotlib.

Using Pyplot

Pyplot within *Matplotlib* is an important module for plotting. This module can be imported within *Ipython* by typing the following in the terminal.

```
$ipython --pylab
```

We employ the following Python statements to plot $sin(x)$ for $x = [0, 2\pi]$.

```
In [114]: x=linspace(0,2*pi,100)

In [115]: y=sin(x)

In [116]: plot(x,y); xlabel('x',size=20);
ylabel('y(x)',size=20)
Out[116]: Text(0, 0.5, 'y(x)')

In [117]: xlim([0,2*pi]); grid();
# X axis is fixed as [0,2π].

In [118]: savefig("test.pdf")
```

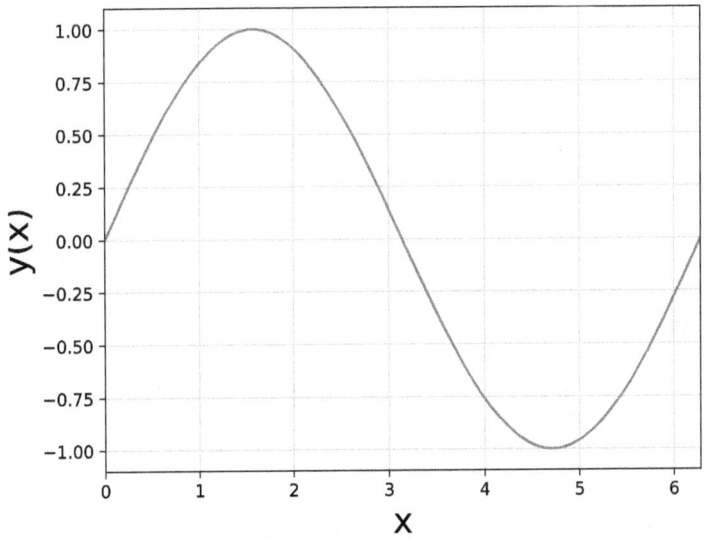

Figure 37: Plot of $y = \sin(x)$.

We save the plot in the file *test.pdf* using the function *savefig()*. We display the plot in Figure 37. Note that Python allows the plot to be saved in *png, jpg,* and *svg* formats as well.

It is much more convenient to put the axis labels, legends, etc. in a file and then run the file in *Ipython*. It is easier to tinker some Python statements in the file, rather than modify the features interactively in *Ipython*. In the following, we present contents of a file that plots $y = x^2$ and $y = x^3$.

```
import numpy as np
import matplotlib.pyplot as plt
from pylab import rcParams
rcParams['figure.figsize'] = 5, 3
# figure of the size 5in x 3in

x = np.linspace(-1,1,40)
y = x**2
y1 = x**3

plt.plot(x,y, 'r.', label = r'$y=x^2$')
```

```
plt.plot(x,y1, lw = 3, color = 'g', label = r'$y=x^3$')
# The labels appear in the legend.
# Helpful for identifying the curves

plt.axhline(0, color='k')
plt.axvline(0, color='k')
# Axis properties

plt.xlim(-1,1)
plt.ylim(-1,1)
# Limits of x and y axes

plt.xlabel(r'$x$', fontsize=20)
plt.ylabel(r'$y$', fontsize=20)
# Axis labels

plt.xticks(np.linspace(-1, 1, 5, endpoint=True))
# Ticks on the xaxis.
# 5 points in the interval (-1,1).

plt.legend(loc=4)
# Legends appear at the fourth quadrant,
# which is the bottom right

plt.tight_layout()
# Helps in fitting plots within
# the figure cleanly

plt.savefig('plot2d.pdf')
# Save the plot in a file plot2d.pdf
plt.show()
# Show the plot on the console.
```

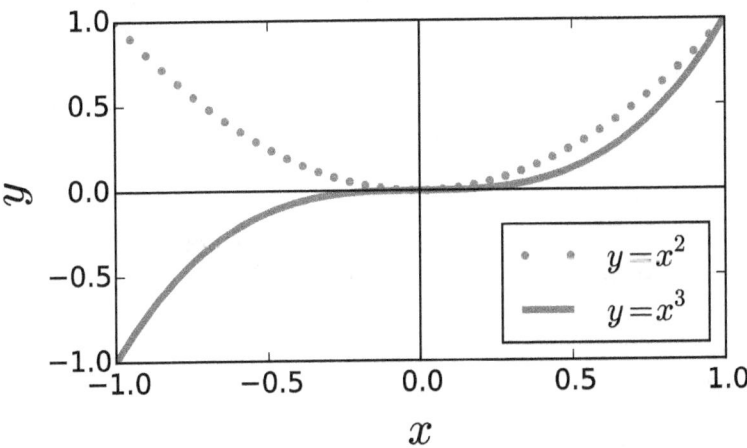

Figure 38: Plot of $y = x^2$ and $y = x^3$ vs. x.

The generated pdf file is shown in Figure 38. In the code, the comments provide a brief description of the *Matplotlib* functions, such as *legend, xlim, xlim*. In the following we make several important remarks about the plot script.

1. Key arguments of the plot() function are
    - color: Color of the curve, which could be blue (b), green (g), red (r), cyan (c), magenta (m), yellow (y), black (k), or white (w).
    - linewidth (lw): Line width of the curve in units of points. Note that 72 points = 1 inch.
    - marker: Markers could one of the following: hline ('-'), point ('.'), Circle ('o'), triangle_down ('v'), triangle up ('^'), triangle_left ('<'), triangle_right ('>'), octagon ('8'), square ('s'), pentagon ('p'), star ('*'), hexagon ('h' or 'H'), diamond ('d' or 'D'), plus ('+'), x ('x'), and more. See https://matplotlib.org/api/markers_api.html for more details.
    - markersize: Size of the above markers.
    - linestyle: solid ('-'), dashed ('- -'), chained ('-.'), dotted (':')
    - label: Labels are used for the legends.

2. plt.xticks, plt.yticks: We can place the axis ticks at the desired locations.
3. plt.show(): Display all the open figures.
4. plt.legend(loc = x): Place legend at location given by x. See Table 14 for the location code.

Table 14: Location code for placing *legends* in a plot

Location string	Location code
'best'	0
'upper right'	1
'upper left'	2
'lower left'	3
'lower right'	4
'right'	5
'center left'	6
'center right'	7
'lower center'	8
'upper centre'	9
'center'	10

Objects of Matplotlib

Numerous functions and features of Matplotlib can be quite confusing. It is best to understand these functions in relation to two key objects of *Matplotlib.pyplot*:

1. *Figure object*
2. *Axes object*

Figure is the top level object containing all the elements of a figure. A *Figure object* contains one or more *Axes objects* with each *axes object* representing a plot inside the figure. *Figure class declaration* is as follows:

```
class matplotlib.figure.Figure(figsize=None, dpi=None,
facecolor=None, edgecolor=None, linewidth=0.0,
frameon=None, subplotpars=None, tight_layout=None,
```

```
constrained_layout=None)
```

We create a *figure object* of size 5 inch x 5 inch using the following Python statement:

```
fig = plt.figure(figsize = (5,5))
```

A single plot or several plots are embedded inside the figure. This is done by a function *add_subplot()*. It adds an *Axes* to the figure. The function *add_subplot* can be called in several ways:

```
add_subplot(nrows, ncols, index, **kwargs)
add_subplot(pos, **kwargs)
add_subplot(ax)
add_subplot()
```

Example 1: In the following code, we create 4 *Axes objects* within object *fig*. Here,

```
Nrows = ncols = 2
```

and the *axes objects ax1, ax2, ax3, ax4* are created using

```
ax1 = fig.add_subplot(2,2,1)
ax2 = fig.add_subplot(2,2,2)
ax3 = fig.add_subplot(2,2,3)
ax4 = fig.add_subplot(2,2,4)
```

In the figure, *ax1, ax2, ax3,* and *ax4* appear at the *top left, top right, bottom left,* and *bottom right* parts of the figure, respectively.

```
import numpy as np
import matplotlib.pyplot as plt

fig = plt.figure(figsize = (5,5))

x = np.linspace(0,1,100)

# Generate a grid of 2x2 subplots.

# Axes plot at 1st location
ax1 = fig.add_subplot(2,2,1)
ax1.plot(x,x,label=r'$y=x$')
```

```
ax1.set_xlim(0,1)
ax1.set_ylim(0,1)
ax1.legend(loc = 'upper left')
ax1.set_ylabel(r'$y$', fontsize=20)
#ax1.xaxis.set_major_locator(plt.NullLocator())
ax1.xaxis.set_major_formatter(plt.NullFormatter())
ax1.xaxis.set_major_locator(plt.MaxNLocator(3))


# Axes plot at 3nd location
ax2 = fig.add_subplot(2,2,2)
ax2.plot(x,x**2,label=r'$y=x^2$')
ax2.set_xlim(0,1)
ax2.set_ylim(0,1)
ax2.legend(loc = 'upper left')
ax2.xaxis.set_major_formatter(plt.NullFormatter())
ax2.xaxis.set_major_locator(plt.MaxNLocator(3))
ax2.yaxis.set_major_formatter(plt.NullFormatter())
ax2.yaxis.set_major_locator(plt.MaxNLocator(6))


# Axes plot at 3rd location
ax3 = fig.add_subplot(2,2,3)
ax3.plot(x,x**3,label=r'$y=x^3$')
ax3.set_xlabel(r'$y=x^3$')
ax3.set_xlim(0,1)
ax3.set_ylim(0,1)
ax3.legend(loc = 'upper left')
ax3.set_xlabel(r'$x$', fontsize=20)
ax3.set_ylabel(r'$y$', fontsize=20)
ax3.xaxis.set_major_locator(plt.MaxNLocator(3))


# Axes plot at 4th location
ax4 = fig.add_subplot(2,2,4)
ax4.plot(x,x**4,label=r'$y=x^4$')
ax4.set_xlabel(r'$y=x^4$')
ax4.set_xlim(0,1)
ax4.set_ylim(0,1)
ax4.set_xlabel(r'$x$', fontsize=20)
ax4.legend(loc = 'upper left')
ax4.xaxis.set_major_locator(plt.MaxNLocator(3))
ax4.yaxis.set_major_formatter(plt.NullFormatter())
ax4.yaxis.set_major_locator(plt.MaxNLocator(6))

plt.savefig('plot_axes.pdf')
plt.show()
```

The above code produces

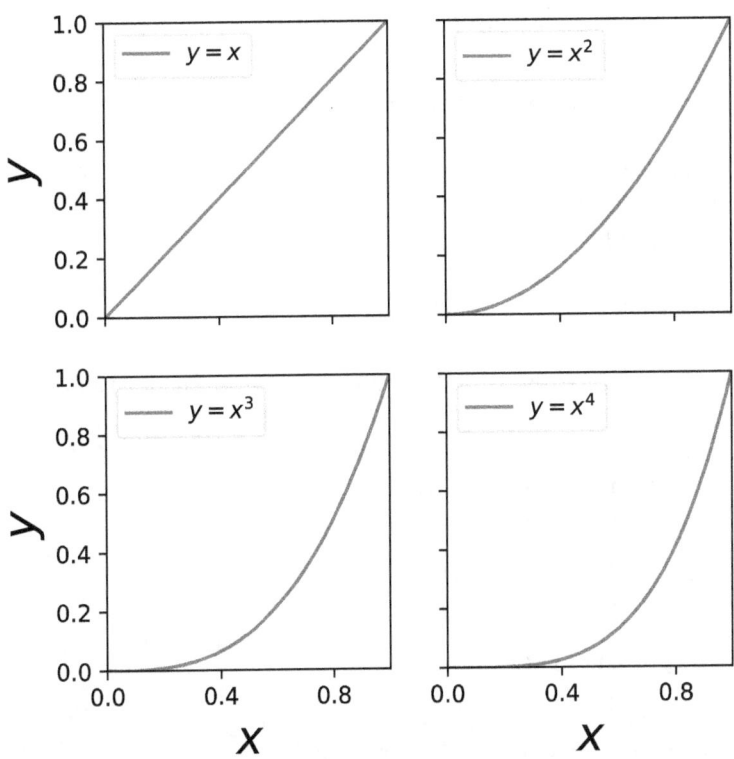

Figure 39: Plot produced by Example 1. It illustrates the usage of Axes and subplots.

An important point to note in the figure is control of the *xticks* and *yticks* in the figure.

```
ax1.xaxis.set_major_locator(plt.MaxNLocator(3))
ax2.yaxis.set_major_locator(plt.MaxNLocator(6))
```

The above statements produce 3 *xticks* and 6 *yticks* respectively. The other interesting options for the above functions are *NullLocator, LogLocator, AutoLocator, FixedLocator*. The other ticks function is Tick formatter. For example, *NullFormatter()* puts no labels on ticks. Refer to

Matplotlib documentation for more details.

Python offers features for producing variety of plots. In the following discussion, we will show how to make plots to present scalar and vector fields.

Visualising $z = f(x,y)$

We can visualise a function $z=f(x,y)$ in the following ways:

1. Contour plot
2. Density plot
3. Surface plot

We describe each one of them below:

Contour plot: The following code segment creates a *contour plot* of the function $z = x^2 + y^2$.

```
fig = plt.figure(figsize = (3,3))
ax = fig.add_subplot(1,1,1)

x = np.linspace(-10,10,100)
y = np.linspace(-10,10,100)

xv, yv = np.meshgrid(x,y)
z = (xv**2 + yv**2)/2

# contour plot, contours (6 contours)
curves = ax.contour(xv,yv,z, 6)
ax.clabel(curves, inline=1, fmt='%.1f', fontsize=10)
```

The function *ax.contour(xv, yv, z, 6)* produces six *contour lines*. *ax.clabel()* controls the formatting of *contour labels*. Alternatively, the function

```
curves = ax.contourf(xv,yv,z, 5, cmap = cm.Reds)
```

produces contours with *color map*. The resulting plot is show in Figure 40.

Practical Numerical Computing Using Python

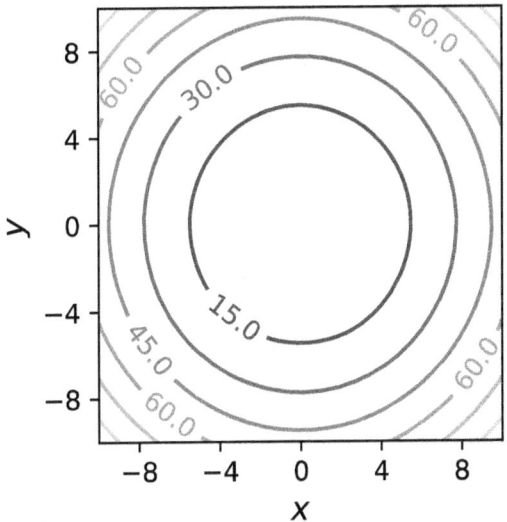

Figure 40: Contour plot of function $z = x^2 + y^2$. The contours are labelled.

Density plot: We can also make *density plot* of the function $z = x^2 + y^2$ using the functions *imshow()*, *pcolor()*, and *pcolormesh()*. The function *pcolormesh()* is faster than *pcolor()*. The code segment is given below, and the plots are shown in Figure 41.

```
import numpy as np
import matplotlib.pyplot as plt
from mpl_toolkits.axes_grid1 import make_axes_locatable

x = np.linspace(-1,1,100)
y = np.linspace(-1,1,100)
xv, yv = np.meshgrid(x,y)
z = (xv**2 + yv**2)/2

fig = plt.figure(figsize = (6,3), tight_layout= True)
ax1 = fig.add_subplot(121, aspect='equal')

# Using imshow (image show)
c1 = ax1.imshow(z, vmin=abs(z).min(), vmax=abs(z).max(),
     extent=[-1,1,-1,1])
ax1.set_title('using imshow')
ax1.set_xlabel('$x$',size=12)
ax1.set_ylabel('$y$',size=12)
```

```
divider = make_axes_locatable(ax1)
cax2 = divider.append_axes("right", size="5%", pad=0.05)
fig.colorbar(c1, cax=cax2)

# Using pcolor

ax2 = fig.add_subplot(1,2,2)
ax2.set_title('using pcolormesh')
c2 = ax2.pcolormesh(xv,yv, z)
ax2.set_xlabel('$x$',size=12)
ax2.set_aspect(aspect=1)
#Another way to set aspect ratio
```

Two important points to note:

1. The arrays *xv* and *yv* provide the *x* and *y* coordinates at the grid points. They are 2D arrays. We compute *z* at each grid point using *xv* and *yv* arrays.
2. The colormap is resized to dimension of the plot using make_axes_locatable(). There are variety of colormaps. Choice of colormap is subjective. For some advice on colormaps, refer to https://matplotlib.org/tutorials/colors/colormaps.html and https://www.kennethmoreland.com/color-advice/

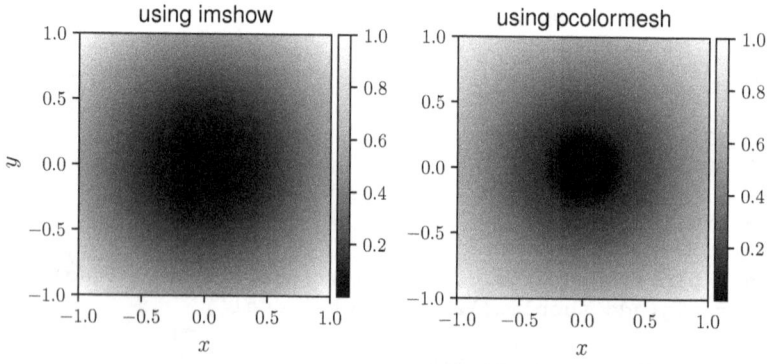

Figure 41: Density plot of function $z = x^2 + y^2$ using functions *imshow*() and *pcolormesh*(), which are in the left and right sides respectively.

Surface plot: In *surface plots*, which are three-dimensional in nature, the z coordinate specifies the value of the function. In the following code segment we present how to make *surface plot* and *wireframe plot* of the function $z = exp(-x^2 - y^2)$. The functions used are *plot_surface()* and *plot_wireframe()*.

```
import numpy as np
import matplotlib.pyplot as plt
from mpl_toolkits.mplot3d import Axes3D
# import matplotlib.cm as cm
from pylab import rcParams
rcParams['figure.figsize'] = 7, 3.5

x = np.linspace(-2,2,100)
y = x.copy()
xv, yv = np.meshgrid(x,y)
z = np.exp(-(xv**2 + yv**2))

fig = plt.figure()
ax1 = fig.add_subplot(121, projection = '3d')
ax1.plot_surface(xv, yv, z, rstride=5, cstride=5, color = 'm')

ax2 = fig.add_subplot(122, projection = '3d')
ax2.plot_wireframe(xv,yv,z, rstride=5, cstride=5)
ax2.set_title('Wireframe')
```

In the above code, we make use of *mpl_toolkits.mplot3d.Axes3D module* to set the axis as three dimensional. This is achieved using

```
ax1 = fig.add_subplot(121, projection = '3d')
```

The surface plots are shown in Figure 42.

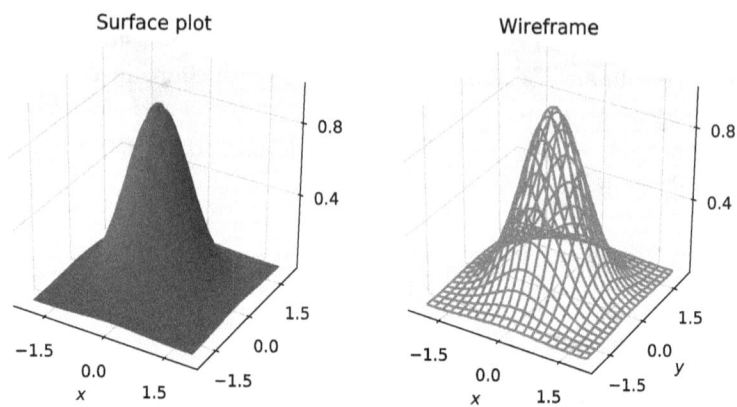

Figure 42: Surface plots of function $z = x^2 + y^2$ using functions *plot_surface()* and *wireframe()*, which are in the left and right sides respectively.

Vector Plots

The following code segment produces 2D and 3D *vector plots* for the fields **v** = (–x, –y) and **v** = (–x, –y, –z) respectively. Here, we employ the function *quiver()*.

```
import numpy as np
import matplotlib.pyplot as plt
from mpl_toolkits.mplot3d import Axes3D
import matplotlib.cm as cm
from pylab import rcParams
rcParams['figure.figsize'] = 7, 3.5

# Vector plot for the field v = (-x, -y)
L = 10
x = np.linspace(-L,L,10)
y = x
xv, yv = np.meshgrid(x,y)

fig = plt.figure()
ax1 = fig.add_subplot(121, aspect ='equal')
ax1.quiver(xv, yv, -xv, -yv)

#3D vector plot for the field v = (-x, -y)
ax2 = fig.add_subplot(122, projection = '3d')
```

```
x = np.linspace(-L,L,5)
y = x
z = x
xv, yv, zv = np.meshgrid(x,y,z)
ax2.quiver(xv, yv, zv, -xv, -yv, -zv)
```

The 2D and 3D *vector plots* are shown in the left and right sides of Figure 43, respectively.

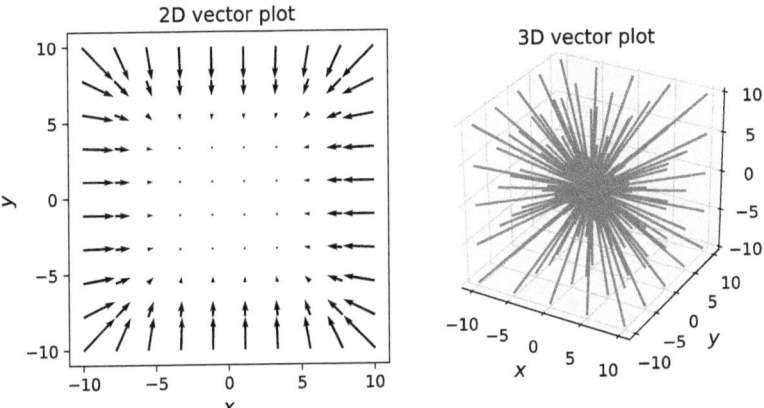

Figure 43: (Left figure) 2D vector plot of the vector field $\mathbf{v} = (-x, -y)$. (Right figure) 3D vector plot of the vector field $\mathbf{v} = (-x, -y, -z)$.

With this, we end this section on scalar and vector plots.

****

Exercises

1. Plot $\log(x^2)$ vs. x and $\cos^2 x$ vs. x.
2. Make contour, density, and surface plots for the electric potential of a line charge with charge density of λ. Make appropriate scaling for the plot.
3. Plot the electric field for the above line charge.
4. Plot the electric potential and electric field of an electric dipole. You will need to moderate the singularity near the origin.
5. Plot the wavefunction of the ground state and first-excited

state of a quantum oscillator. Use nondimensionalized wave functions.

6. The wavefunction of Hydrogen atom for $n = 2$, $l = 1$, $m = 0$ is $r \exp(-r/2) \cos\theta$. Make a contour, density, and surface plots of the wave function for a cross section of xz plane. Make similar plots for other wave functions of Hydrogen atom.

7.2 Miscellaneous Plots

In this section, we will show how to plot particle trajectories, histograms, and Pie diagrams.

Plotting Particle Trajectory

Using Python we can easily plot 3D trajectory of a particle. The following code segment yields the helical trajectory of a particle whose coordinates are described by

$$\mathbf{r} = (x, y, z) = (b\sin(t), b\cos(t), b\,t),$$

where b is a constant, and t is time that varies from 0 to 8π.

```
import numpy as np
import matplotlib.pyplot as plt
from mpl_toolkits.mplot3d import Axes3D
from pylab import rcParams
rcParams['figure.figsize'] = 3,3.5

fig = plt.figure()
axes = fig.add_subplot(111, projection = '3d')
t = np.linspace(0, 8 * np.pi, 1000)
b = 1
r = b

x = r * np.sin(t)
y = r * np.cos(t)
z = b*t

axes.plot(x, y, z, lw=2, color='r')
```

The generated plot is shown in Figure 44(a). The code employs *mpl_toolkits.mplot3d.Axes3D module* for the 3D plot.

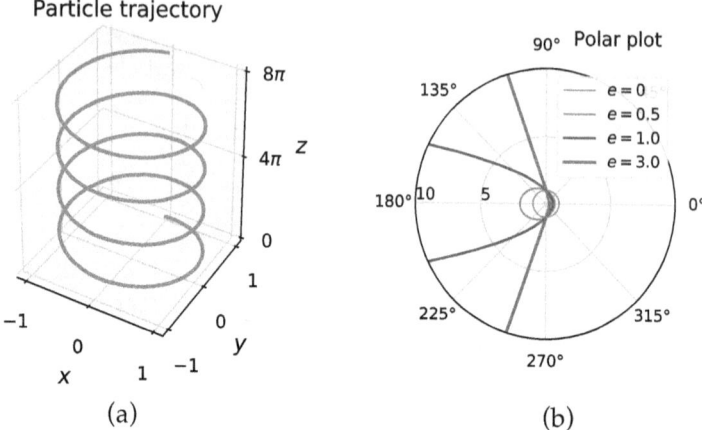

Figure 44: (a) A 3D plot of a helical trajectory of a particle. (b) Radial polar plot of various conic section curves, whose eccentrics are listed in the legend.

Radial-polar Plot

Using Python we can make plots in radio-polar (r-θ) coordinate system. The following code segment plots conic-section curves, which are described by

$$r = 1/(1 + e \cos(\theta)),$$

where e is the eccentricity of the curve. In Figure 44(b) we plot the conic-section curves for $e = 0, 0.5, 1$ and 3.

```
import numpy as np
import matplotlib.pyplot as plt
from pylab import rcParams
rcParams['figure.figsize'] = 4,3

phi = np.linspace(0,2*np.pi,100)
```

```
r1 = 1.0/(1 + 0*np.cos(phi)) #Circle
r2 = 1.0/(1 + 0.5*np.cos(phi)) #Ellipse
r3 = 1.0/(1 + 1*np.cos(phi)) #Parabola
r4 = 1.0/(1 + 3*np.cos(phi)) #Hyperbola


fig = plt.figure()
axes = fig.add_subplot(111, projection = 'polar')

axes.set_title('Polar plot')
axes.plot(phi, r1, lw=1, color='r', label=r'$e = 0$')
axes.plot(phi, r2, lw=1.25, color='g', label=r'$e = 0.5$')
axes.plot(phi, r3, lw=1.5, color='b', label=r'$e = 1.0$')
axes.plot(phi, r4, lw=2, color='m', label=r'$e = 3.0$')
plt.ylim(0, 10)
axes.set_rgrids([5,10], angle=180)
plt.legend()
```

Here, the statement,

```
axes = fig.add_subplot(111, projection = 'polar')
```

plays a key role. The *projection = 'polar'* instructs the interpreter to make a radial-polar plot. The resulting plot is shown in Figure 44(b).

Histogram

Python helps us plot a histogram of a given data set. The following code creates a histogram of random numbers which are Gaussian distributed with mean of ½ and standard deviation of 1.

```
import matplotlib.pyplot as plt
import numpy as np

avg = 0.5 # mean of distribution
sig = 1.0 # standard deviation of distribution
x = avg + sig * np.random.randn(100000)
# generates 100000 random numbers with normal distribution

fig = plt.figure(figsize = (3.5,2.5))
num_bins = 50
n, bins = plt.hist(x, num_bins)
```

```
# Creates histogram of x using num_bins bins.
```

The above code generates 10^5 random numbers with Gaussian distribution with average of ½ and standard deviation of 1.0. After this, the numbers are divided into 50 (*num_bins*) bins and a histogram is created, which is displayed in Figure 45. The function *plt.hist()* provides the following information about the histogram:

1. *n*: Array of size *num_bin*, with $n[i]$ as the number of data points in the *i*th bin.
2. *bins*: Array of size *num_bin+1*; it contains the edges of the bins.

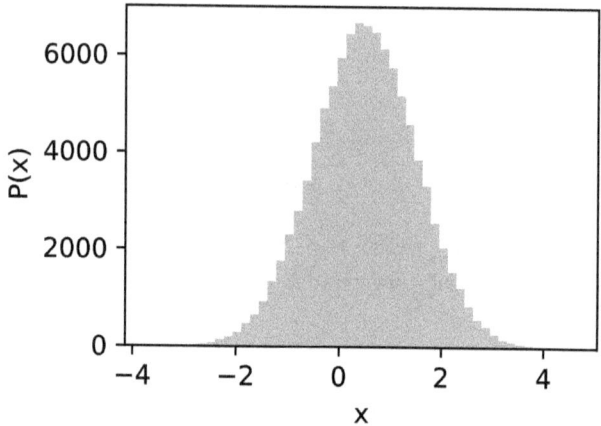

Figure 45: Histogram of random numbers which are Gaussian distributed with mean of ½ and standard deviation of 1.

Pie diagram

We create a *Pie diagram* using the following code. Imagine that a student obtains 90, 80, 60, 90 marks (out of 100 each) in Physics, Chemistry, Mathematics, and in Hindi. Using Pie diagram we can illustrate the distribution of student's marks (from the total marks) in various subjects. The function

```
pie(y,labels=mylabels)
```

creates a pie diagram of elements of array *y*, and labels the elements using the entries from the list *mylabels*. The plot is show in Figure 46.

In [5]: y = array([90,80,60,90])

In [6]: mylabels = ["Phy", "Chem", "Math", "Hindi"]

In [7]: pie(y, labels=mylabels)

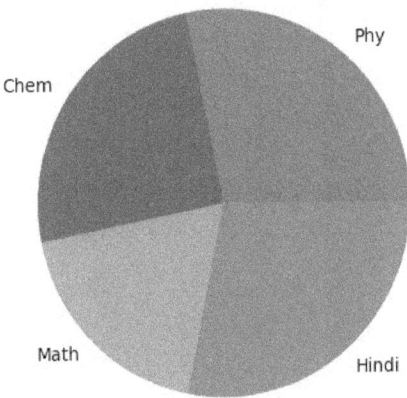

Figure 46: A Pie diagram illustrating marks distribution in various subjects.

Pie diagram is often used in business. For example, the income of Apple company from various device segments (MacBook, iPhone, iwatch, ..) could be presented using a Pie diagram.

Python has additional libraries for plotting. Two popular libraries are *Seaborn* and *Plotly*. They are often used along with *Pandas* for data visualisation. In this book, we skip these topics to save time and space.

****

Exercises

1. Generate a million random number with uniform distribution in the interval (0,4). Make a histogram of the data.
2. Collect area and population of various states of India. Make Pie diagrams for them.
3. Collect daily temperature data of your city over the full year. Make a histogram for the temperature.

7.3 Animation Using Python

In this section, we will will show how to create animations in Python. The following code animates the function

$$f(x,t) = \exp(-(x-bt)^2/\sigma^2),$$

where t is time, and b and σ are constants. The code is a modified version of the original code written by Jake Vanderplas (http://jakevdp.github.com).

```
"""
Matplotlib Animation Example

author: Jake Vanderplas
email: vanderplas@astro.washington.edu
website: http://jakevdp.github.com
license: BSD
Please feel free to use and modify this, but keep the
above information. Thanks!
"""
import numpy as np
from matplotlib import pyplot as plt
from matplotlib import animation

# First set up the figure, the axis, and the plot element
we want to animate
fig = plt.figure()
ax = plt.axes(xlim=(0, 2), ylim=(-0.5, 1.5))
line, = ax.plot([], [], lw=2)

# initialization function: plot the background of each
frame
def init():
    line.set_data([], [])
    return line,

# animation function. This is called sequentially
def animate(i):
    x = np.linspace(-2, 2, 1000)
    y = np.exp(-((x-0.01*i)**2)/0.01)
    line.set_data(x, y)
    return line,
```

```
# call the animator.  blit=True means only re-draw
#the parts that have changed.
# interval in milisec. There are 200 frames.
anim = animation.FuncAnimation(fig, animate,
init_func=init,frames=200, interval=10, blit=True)


# save the animation as an gif using
# the writer='PillowWriter')

anim.save('gaussian.gif',writer='matplotlib.animation.Pill
owWriter')
```

A brief explanation of the above code is as follows. The function

```
anim = animation.FuncAnimation(fig, animate,
init_func=init, frames=200, interval=20, blit=True)
```

animates the time-dependent curves generated by function *animate()*. The background frame is generated by *init()*. These two functions generate *line* object, which is a curve, for *Matplotlib*. The output of the animation is saved in gaussian.gif file using *PillowWriter* of *matplotlib*. Other animation writers that could also be used are *ffmpeg, avconv,* etc. In Figure 47 we illustrate frame numbers 30 and 100 for illustration.

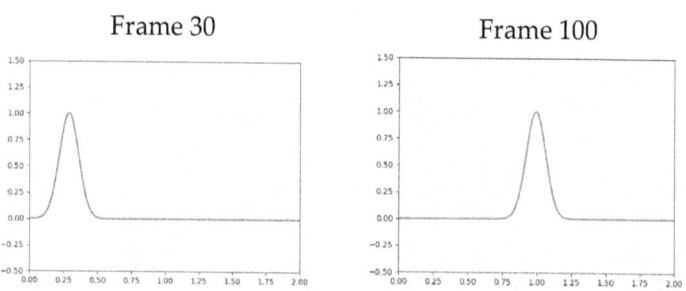

Figure 47: Plots of $f(x)$ for frames 30 and 100.

With this, we end this section on plotting and creating animations.

****

Exercises

1. Animate a moving sin wave, $f(x,t) = sin(k\,x - \omega t)$, for a given k and ω.
2. Consider a free quantum particle modelled as a gaussian wave packet. Animate its motion.

Chapter Eight
INPUT/OUTPUT IN PYTHON

Synopsis

"Your memory is a monster; you forget - it doesn't. It simply files things away. It keeps things for you, or hides things from you - and summons them to your recall with a will of its own. You think you have a memory; but it has you!" — John Irving

In this chapter, we discuss how to save data to a file and how to read data from a file.

8.1 Reading & Writing Text Files in Python

The data (numbers, strings, data structures) is stored permanently in a hard disk. Note that the data in RAM is temporary, hence we need to transfer useful data from RAM to permanent storage. In reverse, we read the data from hard disk (stored earlier) or from internet and transfer it to RAM. We can analyze this data or make plots.

In Section 3.1, we read data from the keyboard using *input*() function and wrote output to the screen using *print*() function. These functions are specific to the standard input (keyboard) and the standard output (screen). In this section, we will describe how to read text or binary data from a file, and how to write data to a file.

Files in Python

Python facilitates reading from a file, as well as writing to a file. In Python, a *file* is an object, while its associated functions allows read/write operations on the file. For example, the following Python statement creates an object, *f*, for writing data on to a physical file whose name is *data.txt*.

In [98]: f = open('data.txt', "w")

Python supports many access modes to a file. Some of them are listed in Table 15. We will discuss these modes in some detail in the following discussion.

Table 15: Access modes for files

argument	format	Access mode
r	text	read-only
w	text	write
a	text	append
r+	text	read and write
rb	binary	read-only
wb	binary	write
ab	binary	append
rb+	binary	read and write

Writing Text to a File

Python treats a *text* as a set of *strings*. We write strings to a file using the following set of statements.

```
In [100]: f = open('data.txt', "w")

In [101]: f.write("Hi! \n")
Out[101]: 5

In [102]: str_list = ["This is month of June. \n", "It is
very hot here. \n", "Expect rains next month. \n"]

In [103]: f.writelines(str_list)   # write lines of text

In [104]: f.close()

In [105]: !cat data.txt
Hi!
This is month of June.
It is very hot here.
Expect rains next month.
```

The first statement creates file object *f*, which is associated with the physical file *data.txt*. We write a single *string* using function *f.write()* and multiple lines using *f.writelines()*.

Note that *f.write*(20) will give an error because 20 is not a string. Instead, you need to use *f.write*('20'). The file *data.txt* has four lines that are separated by the *nextline* character '\n'. We can view the data.txt using *cat* or *vi* commands, e.g., *vi data.txt*.

Another way to write data to a file is as follows. We can use the *print* function with an additional argument, *file = file_name*, to send the data to the file whose name is *file_name*. For example, the following statement prints variables *x* and *y* to file *f*.

```
In [90]: f2 = open('data2.txt', "w")

In [97]: x=5; y=6

In [110]: print(x, y, file = f2)
```

In [111]: f2.close()

In the above example, the variables x and y are stored as a string. After the above operations, file's contents are "5 6 \n".

Reading Text from a File

Now, we read the contents of the file *data.txt* using *readline*() and *read*() functions.

In [127]: f = open('data.txt', "r+")

In [128]: print(f.readline())
    ...: print(f.readline())
Hi!

This is month of June.

In [129]: print(f.read())
It is very hot here.
Expect rains next month.

In [130]: f.seek(0)
Out[130]: 0

In [131]: str_read = f.read()

In [132]: str_read
Out[132]: 'Hi! \nThis is month of June. \nIt is very hot here. \nExpect rains next month. \n'

In [133]: f.seek(0)
Out[133]: 0

In [134]: for line in f:
    ...:   print(line, end='')
    ...:
Hi!
This is month of June.
It is very hot here.
Expect rains next month.

Important points for reading text from a file are as follows:

1. Python starts to read the data from a file from the beginning of the file.
2. The function *f.readline*() reads the current line from a file *f*.
3. The function *f.read*() reads the remaining part of the file, that is, from the current location to the end of file (EOF).
4. The function *f.seek*(*n*) takes the file pointer to the *n*th byte from the beginning. *f.seek*(0) would take the file pointer to the beginning of the file.
5. A convenient way to read lines from a file *f* is using the statement *for line in f:*. The text is extracted from the file line by line.

Next, we will discuss how to work with binary files.

Working with Binary Format

Python also facilitates reading/writing strings in the binary format. As shown in Table 15, we need to use options 'wb' to write to a binary file, and 'rb' to read from a binary file. The following code segment illustrates the procedure for writing a string "ABCɛ" to a file *data.bin* and then reading the same string from the file.

```
f = open('data.bin', 'wb')
bin_str = bytearray("ABCɛ", 'utf-8')
f.write(bin_str)
f.close()

f = open('data.bin', 'rb')
bin_str_read = f.read()
f.close()
```

The above code segment has several tricky issues:

1. The function *bytearray*() returns an object *bin_str* for the string "*ABCɛ*". This procedure however requires an encoding

scheme. In the above example, we employ utf-8 scheme (see Section 3.1). The other prominent encoding schemes are *ascii*, *latin-1*, *utf16*, and *utf32*.
2. bin_str is an array of bytes: 41 42 43 e0 a4 b9, with the first three bytes corresponding to characters 'A', 'B', 'C' respectively, and the last three bytes for the unicode character 'ह' (see Section 3.1). We obtain these values from the terminal using *hexdump* command. The numbers in the left of the lines (e.g., 0000000) are the byte addresses.
   - `$hexdump data.bin`
   - `0000000 41 42 43 e0 a4 b9`
   - `0000006`
3. bin_str Note that we cannot write a string to a binary file. For example, f.write('Hi') is not allowed for 'data.bin' file. We can write only binary strings to a binary file.
4. Ipython prints the following where b of b'ABC' represents binary.
   - `In [206]: bin_str`
   - `Out[206]: bytearray(b'ABC\xe0\xa4\xb9')`
   - `In [207]: bin_str_read`
   - `Out[207]: b'ABC\xe0\xa4\xb9'`

We remark that it is convenient to use text format, rather than binary format, for working with text or strings.

****

Exercises

1. Write a poem in a text file, and save it in a file named "poem.txt". Read back the poem and store it as a list of strings. Make sure that the read text is same as the original text.

8.2 Reading & Writing Numerical Data in Python

In scientific computing, we often encounter large datasets. Some examples of large datasets are as follows:

1. Weather data: temperature, humidity, and wind velocity of Earth's atmosphere
2. Wind velocity in a simulation of a moving car
3. Quantum wave function of a complex molecule
4. Population data of a country
5. Matter density inside a star or galaxy

Such datasets are saved or stored on a hard disk. Subsequently, they are *read* by a computer program for further processing.

Numerical data can be stored on a hard disk in various formats. Some of the popular formats are ASCII, binary, HDF, HDF5, CSV, NASACDF, etc. A brief description of some of the above formats are given below.

1. *ASCII*: Here, the numbers are stored as a set of characters. For example, "13.5" consists of 4 characters including the decimal point, all of whom need to be stored. In ASCII representation, we truncate the binary number to a limited precision. Hence, there is a loss of accuracy during the storage. A similar loss of accuracy occurs while reading data from a hard disk.
2. *Binary*: Recall the discussion of Chapter Two where we showed how numbers are represented in binary format, e.g., $(2.75)_{10}$ = $(10.11)_2$. Clearly, binary format is accurate because the numbers are saved as they are. Note that we need 4 bytes for integers, 4 bytes for single-precision floats, and 8 bytes for double-precision floats.
3. *HDF5* or *Hierarchical Data Formats*: This is a complex data format for storage. HDF5 supports binary format. Refer to https://www.hdfgroup.org/solutions/hdf5/ for more details.
4. *CSV* or *Comma Separated Values*: It is a plain text format. It is popular because Microsoft Excel uses CSV format for data import/export.

Python can read/write numerical data in all the above formats. In addition, Python can also work with movie formats (e.g., mp4, png) and image formats (e.g., png, pdf). In this section we will briefly discuss how to work with files with some of the above formats.

For the following examples, we will consider two Numpy arrays x and y containing 629 numbers each:

```
import numpy as np
x = np.arange(0,2*np.pi,0.01)
y = np.sin(x)
```

In the following discussion, we show how to store these arrays in ASCII format, which is the simplest of all formats.

Input/Output of Numpy Arrays in ASCII Format

Python's *Numpy module* provides functions *save()* and *savetxt()* to save an array to a file, and *load()* and *loadtxt()* to load an array in the memory from a txt file. We illustrate these functions using the following code segment.

```
np.save('data_x.npy', x)
np.save('data_y.npy', y)
x_read_txt = np.load('data_x.npy')
y_read_txt = np.load('data_y.npy')

np.savetxt('data_x.txt', x)
np.savetxt('data_y.txt', y)
x_read_txt = np.loadtxt('data_x.txt')
y_read_txt = np.loadtxt('data_y.txt')
```

The functions *save()* and *load()* work with *.npy* files, while *savetxt()* and *loadtxt()* work with *.txt* files. Note that, by default, ASCII real data is saved in exponential format. However, we can save the data in float format with finite precision using fmt option. In the following, we save x to the file *data.txt*. Using format, we save only 3 digits after the decimal.

```
np.savetxt("data.txt", x, fmt="%0.3f", delimiter=",")
```

After this, we discuss how to save and read numbers in binary format.

Input/Output for Numpy Arrays in Binary Format

Writing to and reading from binary files (with *.bin* extension) are described below. For reading a binary file, we need to provide the number of bytes to be read as an argument to the file. In the following example, the number of bytes is 629*8 because each double-precision float takes 8 bytes of storage.

```
f=open('sin.bin', 'wb')
f.write(x); f.write(y); f.close()

f=open('sin.bin', 'rb')
xraw=f.read(629*8)   # no of data elements = 629
yraw=f.read(629*8)   # each float takes 8 bytes

import struct
x_read_bin=np.array(struct.unpack('d'*629, xraw))
y_read_bin=np.array(struct.unpack('d'*629, yraw))
```

The operations *f.read*(629*8) creates two strings, *xraw* and *yraw*, but not floating-point arrays. We employ the *struct* module to convert the above strings to float arrays. The function *struct.unpack*() returns a tuple containing the data. The character 'd' in the argument of *struct.unpack*() stands for the double precision, while 629 is the number of data elements to be read.

In the above example, we read arrays containing real numbers in double precision. However, Python can read/write integers, single-precision real numbers, and boolean arrays as well. We need to employ 'f' for float, 'i' for integer, and '?' for _Bool as arguments of *struct.unpack*() function.

Input/Output for HDF5 Data

In the following code segment we write two arrays x and y to a HDF5 file 'data.h5'. Here we use *h5py module* of Python. The file object *hf* is created to write the arrays to the hard disk. The file object *hf* contains information about the file size, file type (integer, float, character), and the data.

```
import numpy as np
import h5py

# Create file object, hf, for writing
hf = h5py.File('data.h5', 'w')

#Creates dataset  array_x and array_y
hf.create_dataset('array_x', data=x)
hf.create_dataset('array_y', data=y)

# close the file
hf.close()
```

The function *hf.create_dataset()* creates datasets *array_x* and *array_y* for x and y arrays respectively. These datasets are saved on the hard disk. We close the file at the end. For reading the file *data.h5*, we reverse the operation.

```
# Create file object hf2 for reading data.h5 file
hf2 = h5py.File('data.h5', 'r')

# keys() tells us datasets stored in the file
hf2.keys()

# Returns dataset objects array_x_read  & array_y_read
# They are not numpy arrays
array_x_read = hf2.get('array_x')
array_y_read = hf2.get('array_y')

# Converts dataset objects to numpy arrays
x_read = np.array(array_x_read)
y_read = np.array(array_y_read)

#Close the file
hf2.close()
```

In the above code, *hf2* is created to read the datasets *array_x* and *array_y* from the hard disk. Remember that the arrays x and y are stored as *array_x* and *array_y* in *data.h5*. The function *hf2.keys()* tells us about the datasets stored in the file, while the function *hf2.get()* reads the datasets and transfers the arrays to *array_x_read* and *array_y_read*. These objects are converted to numpy arrays *x_read* and *y_read* using *array*() function. We close the file at the end.

Reading an Image in Python

Often we need to import images and rework them. Here we show how to read an image in python using *mpimg* function.

```
In [65]: import matplotlib.image as mpimg

In [69]: imag = mpimg.imread('amaltas.jpg')

In [70]: plt.imshow(imag)
```

The function *mpimg.imread*(file) generates an array *imag*($n,m,3$) that contains the pixel map of the picture. The array imag is of the size $n \times m$ with three layers (argument 3) that provide the values of red, green, and blue components of the image. We print the image using plt.imshow(imag) that regenerates the original picture (see Figure 48). In the figure, the x and y axes represent the pixel indices.

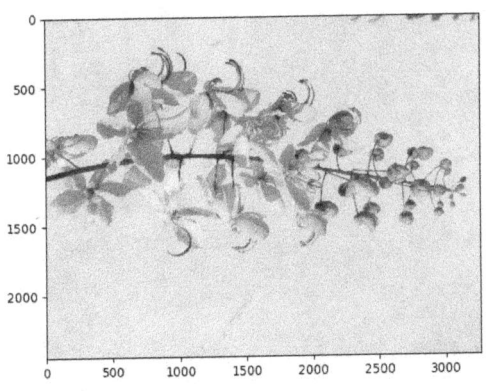

Figure 48: Output of plt.imshow(imag). Refer to the website https://sites.google.com/view/py-comp for the color figure.

With this, we close our discussion on input/output from/to files.

Exercises

1. Download the yearly population data of India from worldometer.org. Read the data using loadtxt(), and plot the yearly population.
2. Download the COVID-19 data for India and several other countries from worldometer.org and plot the daily infection count.
3. Create a *Numpy* array of 100 random numbers. Save this array in a file in (a) ASCII format, (b) binary format, (c) HDF5 format. Read the array back from the files. Verify that you recover the original array.
4. Take picture of yourself. Read its pixel values using matplotlib.image library.

Chapter Nine
ERRORS & NONDIMENSIONALIZATION

Synopsis

"Fast is fine, but accuracy is everything."
— Wyatt Earp

This chapter describes error analysis and nondimensionalization of systems.

9.1 Error Analysis

Most numerical or computer solutions have errors due to various reason—imprecision of computers, inaccurate measurements of data, approximations involved in algorithms, etc. In this section, we will briefly describe the origins of errors in computations, as well as steps taken to minimize these errors.

Precision and accuracy are important and generic issues in error analysis; these topics will be addressed first.

Precision vs. Accuracy

Precision and accuracy are often considered to be the same thing. However, they are not the same! Contrasting these two terms yields interesting insights into the error analysis, as we show below.

A marksman aims to hit the bullseye all the time. See Figure 49 an illustration. The distance of a shot from the bullseye is a measure of inaccuracy, while the scatter of shots is a measure of imprecision. Accurate shots are close to the centre, while precise ones are clustered together. In Figure 49, case (a) corresponds to accurate and precise shooting, (b) to precise but inaccurate shooting, (c) to accurate but imprecise shooting, and (d) to inaccurate and imprecise shooting. Needless to say that a marksman desires accurate and precise shots at the target.

Even though both accuracy and precision of shots depends on the quality of the gun and the skills of the marksman. Note, however, that a good marksman can shoot accurately, but the precision of the shot depends on the quality of the gun. For example, sniper shots are precise. Note that precision is related to random errors, while accuracy to systematic errors. More on these errors in later part of the section.

In later part of this section, we will show similar features in numerical computation. Now, we discuss some important issues— precision of an instrument, significant digits, and quantification of errors.

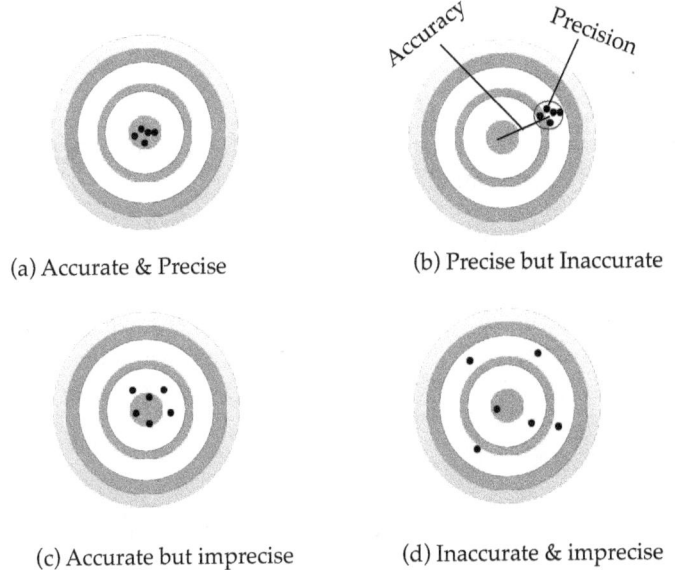

(a) Accurate & Precise (b) Precise but Inaccurate

(c) Accurate but imprecise (d) Inaccurate & imprecise

Figure 49: Illustration of accuracy and precision in target practice. (a) accurate and precise shots; (b) precise but inaccurate shots; (c) accurate but imprecise shots; (d) inaccurate and imprecise shots.

Precision of an instrument: Instruments record measurements only up to a certain precision. For example, the real temperature of 25.789° will be recorded as 25.7° by a thermometer whose precision is 0.1°.

Similarly, a ruler with milimeter marks provides accurate measurements only up to a milimeter. For this ruler, we can trust only one digit beyond the decimal place (in cm). A correct measurement would be 10.3 cm, 1.9 cm, but not 10.34 cm. In computers, real numbers are represented with a precision of 16 digits. Hence, computers too have a limited precision.

Significant digits: The number of non-zero digits and zeros between the extreme non-zero digits is called *significant digits*. We illustrate significant digits using several examples.

1. The numbers 10.3, 10.300, 010.30 are the same, and they have only 3 significant digits. Here, the zeros of the integer part prior to the first nonzero digit is ignored. In addition, we also ignore the zeros in the fraction beyond the last nonzero digit.

2. Following the above rule, 0.0019 has only two significant digits.

Error is defined as the difference between the actual value (V_{actual}) and the measured or computed value (V_{comp}), that is

$$\text{Error} = V_{actual} - V_{comp}.$$

Absolute error is defined as the absolute value of the difference between the actual value (V_{actual}) and the numerical value (V_{num}), that is

$$\text{Absolute error} = |V_{actual} - V_{comp}|.$$

Relative error is defined as the ratio of absolute error and the actual value:

$$\text{Relative error} = |V_{actual} - V_{comp}| / |V_{actual}|$$

Relative error is a better measure of errors. For example, an error of 0.1 kg for the weight of a baby is significant, but it is not so for an elephant.

After this discussion, we categorise the errors encountered in numerical computations.

Errors in Numerical Solutions

Numerical errors can be categorised into the following two broad categories:

Round-off error: Most real numbers cannot be represented accurately in a computer. For example, as discussed in Section 2.2, 0.8 cannot be represented accurately in computer memory. Consequently, 0.8*3-2.4 ≠ 0. The errors due to an approximate representation of real numbers is called *round-off error* or *truncation error*. Note that such a truncation of floats occurs at almost all stages of a numerical computation. These inaccuracies compound the numerical errors of simulations. The round-off errors are related to the limitation of a computer. We also remark that imprecision of physical instruments lead to round-off errors.

The round-off errors are typically random, and they are not reproducible. Complex computations on different computers may differ within error limits (here, we are ignoring the chaos theory in which errors have amplifying effects). Thus, simulation results of an ensemble of an application are expected to be scattered around a mean value, similar to what was shown in Figure 49. Round-off errors affect the precision of a computer simulation. Larger round-off errors lead to larger scatter in the computation results. The round-off errors are often presented in terms of absolute error due to their random distribution.

A consequence of radom errors is that the weather forecast beyond 5 days exhibits large scatter from the actual value (measured afterwards). This error is due to the imprecision in the numerical computation, and due to the random errors in the initial condition of the simulation. Note that instruments supply the weather data, hence, instrument errors too are responsible for the errors in weather prediction.

Systematic error: Measuring instruments may have systematic error. For example, if the zero of a weighing machine is not set properly, all the measurements would be shifted from the real weights in a certain direction. Such errors are called systematic errors.

Systematic errors are present in numerical computations as well. For example, we approximate a quadratic function $f(x)$ using a linear function $\tilde{f}(x)$ (see Figure 50). Under such approximation, we observe a systematic error for $f(x) - \tilde{f}(x)$. This is because $f(x) - \tilde{f}(x) < 0$ for intermediate values of x, but $f(x) - \tilde{f}(x) > 0$ for x's near the ends.

Weather forecast may show systematic deviation from the real value, possibly due to some approximations in the algorithm or due to some new event that may have arisen. For example, forecasts may be several degrees lower than the actual value due to an incumbent tornado. This systematic error is analogous to the inaccuracy in the target practice discussed earlier.

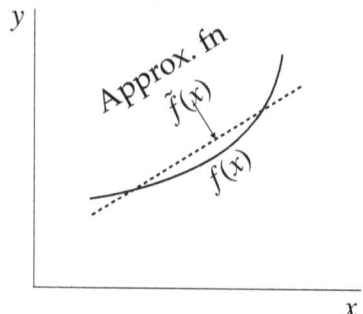

Figure 50: A quadratic function $f(x)$ is approximated using a linear function $\tilde{f}(x)$. The error, $f(x) - \tilde{f}(x)$ is negative for intermediate x, but positive for x near the ends. Here, the error is systematic.

Even though we broadly classify the computational errors in the above two categories, these errors are more complex. The numerical solution of a differential equations depends quite critically on the discretization scheme employed, for example, the time-difference Δt for an ordinary differential equation. Since differential equations assume that $\Delta t \to 0$, any discretization leads to errors that could be random and/or systematic. Space discretization in PDE (partial differential equation) solvers too leads to similar errors. Error propagation is another complex issue that will be sketched at the end of this section.

Next we discuss syntax and logical errors that are encountered during a program development.

Errors Encountered During Program Development

Random and systematic errors occur when a computer program is executed. However, we encounter errors during program development itself. Such errors are given below:

Syntax errors: Python interpreter understand only valid Python statements. For example, the statement "x =^4" is syntactically (or grammatically) incorrect and it leaves the computer clueless. A computer can not apply intuition to correct such statements. When a computer encounters a syntactically incorrect Python statement, it raises a flag to the programmer that the code has syntax error. The programmer has to correct such statements to proceed further.

Logical error: A syntactically correct program may not yield correct results due to incorrect algorithm. An obvious example is an infinite loop. Also, we may have some errors in the algorithm. Such errors, called logical errors, need to be fixed by the programmer.

Numerical error: A syntactically and logically correct program may still yield incorrect answer due to numerical errors. In the following discussion, we will elaborate numerical errors encountered in arithmetic operations and in series solutions.

Errors in Arithmetic Operations

As described in Section 2.2, real numbers are prone to round-off errors. Consequently, most arithmetic operations (such as sum, multiplication, division) have numerical errors. In the following we discuss the errors in subtraction and multiplication operations.

First, we estimate the error in a subtraction operation. Imagine two floats x and y that are represented in computers as x_c and y_c. We denote the relative errors in x and y using ε_x and ε_y respectively. Therefore,

$$x_c = x\,(1+\varepsilon_x); \quad y_c = y\,(1+\varepsilon_y).$$

Further, we assume that ε_x and ε_y are small numbers.

The real difference between x and y is $r = x - y$. However, a computer will report the difference to be

$$r_c = x_c - y_c = x(1+\varepsilon_x) - y(1+\varepsilon_y).$$

Therefore, the relative error is

$$\frac{r_c}{r} = 1 + \epsilon_r = 1 + \epsilon_x \frac{x}{r} - \epsilon_y \frac{y}{r}. \quad \ldots..(6)$$

Clearly, the error ϵ_r explodes when $r \to 0$. This limit occurs when we subtract two nearly equal numbers. We estimate the relative error ϵ_r as

$$\langle \epsilon_r \rangle = \frac{x}{r} \sqrt{<\epsilon_x^2> + <\epsilon_y^2>}, \quad \ldots..(7)$$

where $\langle \rangle$ stands for averaging. The above analysis shows that we need to be cautious while taking a difference between nearly equal numbers.

Following similar procedure we can estimate the relative error in a multiplication operation. For the operation $r = x\, y$, we deduce that

$$\frac{r_c}{r} = \frac{x_c y_c}{x y} = 1 + \epsilon_r \approx 1 + \epsilon_x + \epsilon_y.$$

Hence, the relative error ϵ_r is

$$\epsilon_r \approx \epsilon_x + \epsilon_y. \quad \ldots..(8)$$

Clearly, the error in multiplication of two numbers is bounded, and it is not as dangerous as in the difference between nearly equal numbers.

Example 1: We estimate the error in 1.5*3 and in 1.1*16. As shown below,

```
In [2]: 1.5*3-4.5
Out[2]: 0.0

In [3]: 1.1*1.5-1.65
Out[3]: 2.220446049250313e-16
```

1.5*3 is accurate with zero error, but 1.1*1.5 has error of the order of 10^{-16}. This is because 1.5 and 3 are accurately represented by computers, but 1.1 is not. As we show in Section 2.2, $(1.1)_{10}$ = $(1.1999\ldots)_x$ with 12 ocurrences of 9. Hence, the truncation error in the representation of $(1.1)_{10}$ is of the order of $9 \times 16^{-14} \approx 1.25 \times 10^{-16}$. The net error 1.1*1.5 is of the order of this truncation error (see Eq. (8)). Further discussion on this topic will take us beyond the scope of this book.

Example 2: We estimate the errors in the computations of 1.1−0.8 and 1.1000001−1.1 in single precision. They are

```
In [82]: float32(1.1)-float32(0.8)
Out[82]: 0.3

In [83]: float32(1.1000001)-float32(1.1)
Out[83]: 1.1920929e-07
```

The relative errors for the two cases are

```
In [85]: (float32(1.1)-float32(0.8))/float32(0.3)-1
Out[85]: 0.0

In [86]: (float32(1.1000001)-float32(1.1))/float32(1e-7)-1
Out[86]: 0.1920928955078125
```

Clearly, the error for 1.1000001−1.1 is quite significant. This is because 1.1000001 and 1.1 close to each other.

Example 3: Now we estimate the errors in 1.1−0.8 and 1.1000001−1.1 for double precision, which are

```
In [13]: 1.1-0.8
Out[13]: 0.30000000000000004

In [14]: 1.1000001-1.1
Out[14]: 9.999999983634211e-08
```

The relative errors for the two cases are

```
In [16]: (1.1-0.8)/0.3-1
Out[16]: 2.220446049250313e-16

In [17]: (1.1000001-1.1)/1e-7-1
Out[17]: -1.6365788724215236e-09
```

The situation is much better for double precision. For 1.1000001−1.1, the relative error is approximately 10^{-9}, which is close to zero. For double precision, the relative error is significant for 1.100000000000001−1.1.

```
In [89]: 1.100000000000001-1.1
Out[89]: 8.881784197001252e-16

In [90]: (1.100000000000001-1.1)/1e-12 -1
Out[90]: -0.9991118215802999
```

That is, the relative error is significant when the difference between the two numbers is close to the machine precision.

A question is why worry about such small numbers. It turns out that we encounter such small numbers in physics. For example, the atomic and nuclear sizes are in nano (10^{-9}) and femto meters (10^{-15}) respectively. Therefore, we need to be cautious in quantum calculations that involve small numbers. In the next section, we will present strategies for overcoming the above issues using nondimensionalization.

Example 4: The roots of a quadratic equation

$$a x^2 + b x + c = 0$$

are

$$x_1 = \frac{-b - \sqrt{b^2 - 4ac}}{2a}, \quad (9)$$

$$x_2 = \frac{-b + \sqrt{b^2 - 4ac}}{2a}. \quad (10)$$

For small c, $\sqrt{b^2 - 4ac}$ is close to $|b|$. Hence, one of the solutions is close to zero, which is vulnerable to round-off errors. For $a = b = 1$, and $c = 10^{-15}$, single precision yields

```
In [1]: c=1e-15

In [2]: x1=float32((-1-float32(sqrt(1-float32(4*c))))/2)

In [3]: x2=float32((-1+float32(sqrt(1-float32(4*c))))/2)
```

```
In [4]: print(x1, x2)
-1.0 0.0
```

This is incorrect because $x_2 = c/(a\, x_1) \approx 10^{-15}$. In fact, for this problem, we should compute x_1 using the formula of Eq. (9), and x_2 using $c/(a\, x_1)$.

The situation however is much better with double precision:

```
In [42]: c=1e-15

In [43]: x1=(-1-sqrt(1-4*c))/2

In [44]: x2=(-1+sqrt(1-4*c))/2

In [7]: print(x1, x2)
-0.999999999999999 -9.992007221626409e-16
```

For double precision, we will face problems when c is smaller than 10^{-30}.

Example 5: For large x, $\sqrt{x+1} - \sqrt{x} \to 0$. Hence, it is best to evaluate the above using

$$\sqrt{x+1} - \sqrt{x} = \frac{1}{\sqrt{x+1} + \sqrt{x}}.$$

For $x = 10^{18}$, $\sqrt{x+1} - \sqrt{x} = 0$, but the correct answer is

$$\frac{1}{\sqrt{x+1} + \sqrt{x}} = 5 \times 10^{-10}.$$

Errors in Series Expansion

In computational science, many quantities are computed using series expansion. For example, we compute $\cos(x)$ and $\exp(x)$ using the following series:

$$\cos(x) = \sum_{n=0}^{\infty} (-1)^n \frac{x^n}{(2n)!} = 1 - \frac{x^2}{2!} + \frac{x^4}{4!} - \frac{x^6}{6!} \cdots$$

$$\exp(x) = \sum_{n=0}^{\infty} \frac{x^n}{n!} = 1 + x + \frac{x^2}{2!} + \frac{x^3}{3!} + \frac{x^4}{4!} + \cdots$$

In the following code, we compute $\cos(x)$ and $\exp(x)$ for $x = 1$ using series solution with n terms. We vary n from 1 to 19.

```
import numpy as np
import matplotlib.pyplot as plt
import math

plt.tick_params(axis='both', which='minor', labelsize=10)

plt.figure(figsize = (3,2))

N = 20
x = 1

# for exp(x)
print ("Exp(x) expansion for x=1")

##
error_expx = []

sum = 0
for n in range(0,N):
    sum += x**(n)/math.factorial(n)
    error_expx.append(np.exp(x)-sum)
    print (n, sum, np.exp(x)-sum, x**(n+1)/
math.factorial(n+1))

x_axis = np.arange(1,N+1,1)
error_expx = np.array(error_expx)

plt.semilogy(x_axis, abs(error_expx),'g.-', label='error in $\exp(x)$')


# for cos(x)
print ("cos(x) expansion for x=1")

error_cosx = []

sum = 0
```

```
for n in range(0,N):
    sum += (-1)**n * x**(2*n)/math.factorial(2*n)
    error_cosx.append(np.cos(x)-sum)
    print (n, sum, np.cos(x)-sum, x**(2*n+2)/
math.factorial(2*n+2))

x_axis = np.arange(1,N+1,1)
error_cosx = np.array(error_cosx)


plt.semilogy(x_axis, abs(error_cosx),'b.-', lw = 2,
label='error in $\cos(x)$')


plt.xticks([1,4,8,12,16,20])

plt.xlabel(r'$n$',fontsize=10)
plt.ylabel('Errors',fontsize=10)
plt.tight_layout()
plt.show()
```

We compute the numerical errors for each n and plot them. As shown in Figure 51, cos(x) converges quickly to the actual answer. For $n = 8$, the error is approximately 1.11×10^{-16}. However, the convergence is slow for exp(x); the accuracy of 10^{-16} is achieved for $n = 17$.

The above series expansions describe simple approximate solutions. Ramanujam came up with an amazing series solution for π that yields correct answer up to 7 significant digits with three terms only (reference: wikipedia.org):

$$\frac{1}{\pi} = \frac{2\sqrt{2}}{9801} \sum_{k=0}^{\infty} \frac{(4k)!(1103 + 26390k)}{(k!)^4 396^{4k}}.$$

In later parts of the book, we will discuss various approximate solutions for computing derivatives, integrals, roots of equations etc.

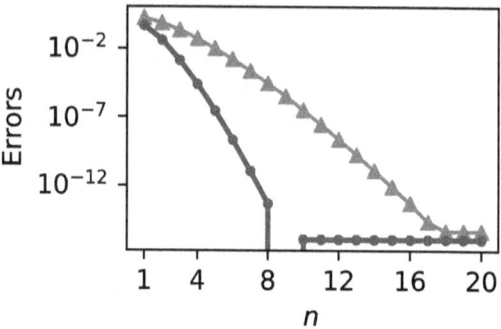

Figure 51: Errors in the series solution for $\cos(x)$ (circles) and $\exp(x)$ (triangles) for various n's of the series.

In Figure 52 we illustrate how one approaches the correct answer using better and better approximations. A marksman improves his/her accuracy with better techniques, while better algorithms improve the accuracy of a numerical solution. In the examples of $\sin(x)$, we obtain better solution by increasing the number of terms of the series solution.

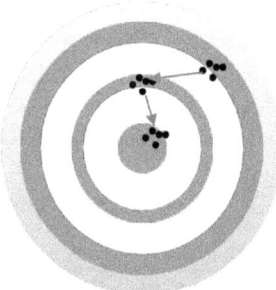

Figure 52: A schematic diagram illustrating how to obtain accurate solution successively using better and better algorithms.

Propagation of Numerical Errors

Error propagation is an important area of research in computation science. We illustrate propagation of numerical errors using weather prediction. We run weather codes for forecasting up to five to seven days. Propagation of uncertainty in such simulations is a complex issue. Yet, we know from experience that the forecasts get worse for longer periods. This is because errors tend to accumulate with time in the following two ways:

1. *In a random manner:* In some applications, the errors in every step is random and uncorrelated (say ε), hence the total error after N steps will be approximately $\varepsilon\sqrt{N}$.
2. *In a systematic manner:* Systematic errors add up algebraically. Here, the total error after N steps is approximated as εN, where ε is the error in each step.

Another important issue in numerical schemes is stability of numerical solutions, which will be discussed in Section 13.2.

According to chaos theory, errors in chaotic systems grow exponentially with time. Consequently, we may expect most numerical solutions to be useless due to the propagation of initial errors. However, large weather simulations yield meaningful results for several days. This contradiction is unresolved and it is a topic of present-day research. Klaus Hasselmann won the Nobel prize for physics in 2021 for a work related to this topic.

Among many factors, multiscale interactions may be suppressing the numerical errors to some degree. It is known that in multiscale systems, the energy cascade from large scales to small scales leads to effective dissipation. Such dissipation may be responsible for the suppression of expanding errors arising due to chaotic nature.

Before closing this chapter we remark that

1. Integer operations do not have round-off or truncation errors. For example, we obtain a definite result for nth prime number.
2. Experiments have random and systematic errors. An experimentalist has to cautiously avoid systematic errors. For example, there should not be any zero error in thermometer or in any measurement device. However, beyond a certain limit, it is impossible to avoid random errors that arise due to temperature, precision in measuring devices, etc.

With this, we close our discussion on error analysis.

Conceptual Questions

1. Contrast round-off errors and systematic errors using examples.
2. Series solutions have numerical errors. Are they round-off errors or systematic errors?

Exercises

1. Compute the round off errors for the following operations: 1.1*8, 1/3*7, 1.5*2, 0.2*9.
2. Count the significant digits for the following real numbers.
   - 0.0019, 0.00190, 01.980
3. Using Python code, find roots of quadratic equation a x^2 + b x + c = 0 for a = 1, b = 2000.00001, and c=0.002. Employ 32-bit float variables. Compare your numerical result with exact results.
4. Compute cos(x) at x = 1.0 using a series solution by taking various number of terms (n). Plot the errors as a function of n. Compare the results with those for sin(x) discussed in this section.
5. Compute exp(−x) at x = 1.0 using a series solution and compute the errors. Compare the results with those for exp(x) discussed in this section.

9.2 Nondimensionalization of Equations

As we discussed in the previous section, operations with small and large numbers are prone to severe numerical errors (see Examples 2, 3, 4 of Section 9.1). Also, it is inconvenient to work with very large and small numbers. To circumvent such problems, atomic physicists, nuclear physicists, and astrophysicists employ respectively Angstrom (Å) (10^{-10} meter), fermi (10^{-15} meter), and lightyear as units of length.

Similarly, convenient units are chosen for time, velocity, energy etc. For details on the choice of appropriate scales, I refer the reader to Appendix B of Verma [2016].

In this section, we go a step further. We nondimensionalize equations using appropriate scales. For numerical simulations, it is best to work with nondimensionalized equations due to the following reasons:

1. Many parameters of the original equations are eliminated in the nondimensionalized equations. For example, Planck's constant (6.63 x 10^{-34} Joule second), which is a tiny number, does not appear in the nondimensionalized Schrödinger's equation of Hydrogen atom (to be discussed later in this section). The parameters of the nondimensionalized equations are of the order of unity.

2. A nondimensionalized equation has a fewer parameters than its dimensional counterpart. Hence we need fewer simulations (also experiments) of the system. Using these techniques, aeronautical engineers perform experiments on smaller prototypes of aircrafts and deduce the flow behaviour of the real aircraft. Typically, we perform numerical simulations of a nondimensional system and predict the behaviour of the original system by scaling.

3. The variables of the nondimensionalized equations are $O(1)$. Thus, we avoid small or large numbers and minimise round-off errors.

4. We understand the system better in terms of nondimensionalized equations. Also, it is easier to present the relevant numbers in nondimensional units. For example, we may state the size of the atoms and molecules in the units of

size of the Hydrogen atom (0.53 Å).

We illustrate the nondimensionalization procedure using the following examples.

Nondimensionalization of a Projectile With Drag

We solve for the motion of a projectile of mass m moving under gravity (acceleration due to gravity = g) and viscous damping of γv, where v is the velocity of the projective (see Verma [2016], Section 9.1.2). For initial velocity $(v_x(0), v_y(0))$, the solution $(x(t), y(t))$ is

$$x(t) = \frac{m v_x(0)}{\gamma} \left[1 - \exp\left(-\frac{\gamma}{m}t\right)\right], \quad (11)$$

$$y(t) = -\frac{mgt}{\gamma} + \frac{m}{\gamma}\left[\frac{mg}{\gamma} + v_y(0)\right]\left[1 - \exp\left(-\frac{\gamma}{m}t\right)\right]. \quad (12)$$

The above solution appears quite complex with so many parameters $(m, g, \gamma, v_x(0), v_y(0))$. Therefore, we nondimensionalize this solution using the following transformations. We take the velocity scales along the x and y directions as $v_x(0)$ and $v_y(0)$ respectively; the time scale as $v_y(0)/g$, and the length scales along the x and y directions as $v_x(0)v_y(0)/g$ and $[v_y(0)]^2/g$ respectively. In terms of these units, the nondimensionalized time and space coordinates are

$t' = t/[v_y(0)/g]$,

$x' = x/[v_x(0)v_y(0)/g]$,

$y' = y/[(v_y(0))^2/g]$.

Substitution of the above in Eq. (11) and Eq. (12) yields the following solution:

$$x' = \frac{1}{\alpha}\left[1 - \exp(-\alpha t')\right],$$

$$y' = -\frac{t'}{\alpha} + \frac{1}{\alpha}\left[\frac{1}{\alpha}+1\right]\left[1-\exp(-\alpha t')\right],$$

where $\alpha = \gamma v_y(0)/(mg)$ is the only parameter of the nondimesionalized system. The initial velocity is $(v_x(0), v_y(0)) = (1,1)$ in the nondimensional units.

We can analyse (x', y') for various α's. The resulting trajectories are exhibited in Figure 53. Note that we can easily convert (x',y',t') to (x,y,t) using the above transformations and compute the real trajectories.

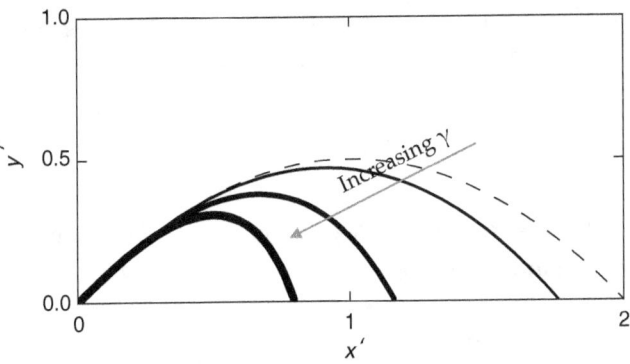

Figure 53: Trajectories of the projectile for various values of $\alpha = \gamma v_y(0)/(mg)$: $\alpha = 0$ (dashed line) for the frictionless case, while $\alpha = 0.1, 0.5,$ and 1 (curves with increasing thickness) for the dissipative cases.

The nondimensionalized solution has many advantages, namely,

1. The original equation has five parameters: m, g, γ, $v_x(0)$, and $v_y(0)$, but the nondimensionalized version has only one (α). Thus, nondimensionalization has reduced the complexity of the system tremendously without sacrificing anything.
2. The nondimensionalized solution is much cleaner, and it can be plotted very easily. It is less prone to errors.
3. We avoid small or large numbers in the nondimensionalized version. For example, the range of the actual projectile could be in tens of kilometres, but x' and y' range from 0 to 2.

Nondimensionalization of Classical Oscillator

The equation of a forced oscillator with mass m and a spring of spring constant k is

$$m\frac{d^2x}{dt^2} + kx = F_0 \cos(\omega_f t), \quad \ldots (13)$$

where F_0 and ω_f are respectively the amplitude and frequency of the external force. Note that the above equation has four parameters: m, k, F_0, and ω_f. The spring constant k is related to the natural frequency ω_0 as $k = m\omega_0^2$. Hence, the oscillator equation can be rewritten as

$$\frac{d^2x}{dt^2} + \omega_0^2 x = \frac{F_0}{m} \cos(\omega_f t).$$

The oscillator has two time scales: ω_0^{-1} and ω_f^{-1}. We nondimensionalize the above equation using ω_0^{-1}:

$$t = t'/\omega_0, \quad \ldots(14)$$

where t' is the nondimensional time. We rewrite the oscillator equation in terms of x and t' that yields

$$\frac{d^2x}{dt'^2} + x = \frac{F_0}{m\omega_0^2} \cos\left(\frac{\omega_f}{\omega_0} t'\right). \quad \ldots (15)$$

The above equation provides us a length scale, $F_0/(m\omega_0^2)$, using which we nondimensional x:

$$x = x'\left(\frac{F_0}{m\omega_0^2}\right). \ldots (16)$$

Substitution of above x in Eq. (14) yields

$$\frac{d^2x'}{dt'^2} + x' = \cos\left(\frac{\omega_f}{\omega_0} t'\right). \ldots (17)$$

The above equation, a nondimensionalized version of the original oscillator equation, has only one parameter, ω_f/ω_0. Thus, there is a significant complexity reduction.

In computer, we solve Eq. (17) for various values of ω_f/ω_0 (including extreme values), e.g., 0.001, 0.1, 1, 10, 1000, and study its properties. We do not need to solve the original equation by varying the four parameters. Note that we can always get $x(t)$ using Eqs. (14, 16).

Nondimensionalization of Hydrogen Atom

Schrödinger's equation for Hydrogen atom in CGS system is

$$-\frac{\hbar^2}{2m_e}\nabla^2\psi - \frac{e^2}{r}\psi = E\psi,$$

where ψ is the wavefunction, $\hbar$ is Planck's constant, m_e is the reduced mass of the electron, e is the charge of the electron, E is the energy of the system, and r is the distance of the electron from the proton. Using dimensional analysis we can deduce the following length scale, r_a, and energy scale, E_a, for the system:

$$r_a = \frac{\hbar^2}{m_e e^2}; \quad E_a = \frac{e^2}{r_a}.$$

Note that r_a is the Bohr radius. We nondimensionalize Schrödinger equation using the above scales, that is,

$$r = r' r_a; \quad E = E' E_a.$$

Substitution of the above in Schrödinger's equation yields

$$-\frac{\hbar^2}{2m_e r_a^2}\nabla^2\psi - \frac{e^2}{r_a r'}\psi = E'\frac{e^2}{r_a}\psi,$$

or

$$-\frac{1}{2}\nabla^2\psi - \frac{1}{r'}\psi = E'\psi,$$

which is the nondimensionalized Schrödinger equation, a simpler version of the original equation. Some of the nondimensionalized wave functions of the Hydrogen atom are

$$\psi_{1,0,0} = \frac{1}{\sqrt{\pi}} \exp(-r'),$$

$$\psi_{2,0,0} = \frac{1}{\sqrt{32\pi}} (2 - r') \exp(-r'/2),$$

$$\psi_{2,1,0} = \frac{1}{\sqrt{32\pi}} r' \exp(-r'/2) \cos\theta,$$

$$\psi_{2,1,\pm 1} = \frac{1}{\sqrt{64\pi}} r' \exp(-r'/2) \sin\theta \exp(\pm i\phi).$$

Note that the normalisation condition in terms of nondimensionalized variables is $\int d\mathbf{r}' |\psi|^2 = 1$.

Nondimensionalization of Quantum Oscillator

Schödinger's equation for a linear oscillator of mass m and frequency ω is

$$-\frac{\hbar^2}{2m} \nabla^2 \psi + \frac{1}{2} m \omega^2 x^2 \psi = E\psi.$$

Using $\sqrt{\hbar/(m\omega)}$ and $\hbar\omega$ as length and energy scales respectively, we derive the nondimensional Schödinger equation as the following:

$$-\frac{1}{2} \nabla^2 \psi - \frac{1}{2} x^2 \psi = E'\psi.$$

The nondimensional stationary wave functions for the oscillator are

$$\psi_0 = \frac{1}{\sqrt{\pi}} \exp(-x'^2/2),$$

$$\psi_1 = \frac{1}{\sqrt{\pi}} \sqrt{2} y \exp(-x'^2/2),$$

$$\psi_2 = \frac{1}{\sqrt{\pi}} \frac{1}{\sqrt{2}} (2x^2 - 1)\exp(-x'^2/2),$$

$$\psi_3 = \frac{1}{\pi^{1/4}} \frac{1}{\sqrt{3}} (2x'^3 - 3x)\exp(-x'^2/2).$$

Thus, we show that nondimensionalization has the following benefits: (a) It simplifies the governing equations and corresponding solution. (b) There is a reduction in number of parameters. (c) Variables are $O(1)$.

With this, we end this section.

****

Conceptual Questions

1. What are the benefits of nondimensionalization of equations? How does it help computer simulations?

Exercises

1. What is the length scale of a quantum oscillator with mass m and frequency ω? Compute $\langle x \rangle$, $\langle x^2 \rangle$, and $\langle E \rangle$ for the ground and first-excited states of the oscillator using nondimensionalized wave functions.
2. Using the nondimensionalized wave functions of Hydrogen atom, compute $\langle r \rangle$, $\langle r^2 \rangle$, and $\langle E \rangle$ for ψ_{100}, ψ_{200}, ψ_{210}, and ψ_{211} states of the H atom.

3. Navier-Stokes equation is given below, where **u** and p are the velocity and pressure fields respectively, and ν is the kinematic viscosity. Nondimensionlize this equation.

$$\partial_t \mathbf{u} + \mathbf{u} \cdot \nabla \mathbf{u} = -\nabla p + \nu \nabla^2 \mathbf{u}$$

4. The equation of a damped oscillator is given below. Here, γ is the damping coefficient, while the other variables are same as that for Eq. (13). What are the time scales of this equation? Nondimensionalize the above equation using one of the time scales.

$$m\frac{d^2 x}{dt^2} + 2\gamma \frac{dx}{dt} + kx = F_0 \cos(\omega_f t)$$

Part Two
Numerical Methods

Connections Among the Numerical Methods

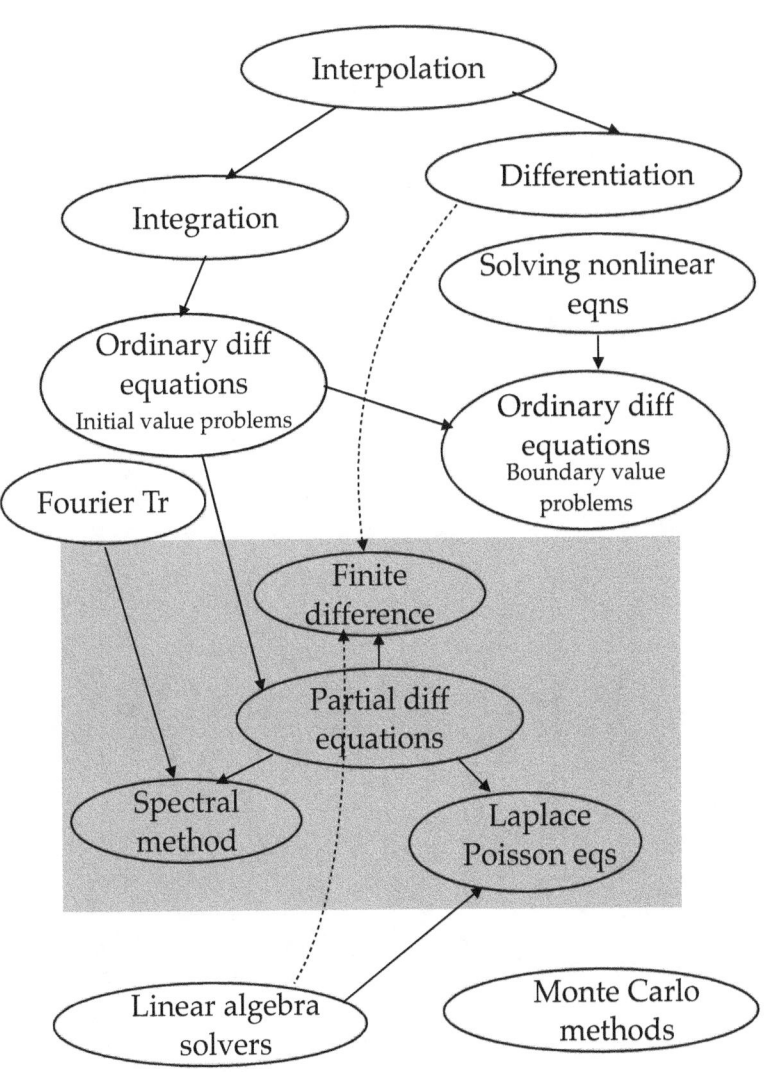

Chapter Ten
INTERPOLATION

Synopsis

"Interpolation is the cornerstone on which other methods are based." — Joel Ferziger

"Numerical computations with clever algorithms can yield exact result."

In this chapter, we show how to interpolate among the data points.

10.1 Lagrange Interpolation

In experiments and simulations, we record values of a function at finite number of points. For further processing we construct a smooth function that passes through these points. A process of construction of such a function is called *interpolation*, which is illustrated below using several example.

1. For weather predictions, weather data (e.g., temperature, wind velocity) is recorded at discrete locations on the Earth. We employ interpolation to decipher the weather data at intermediate points on the Earth.
2. In television or computer games, GPUs (graphical processor units) interpolate the variables at various pixels of an image to reconstruct the full image.

In addition, interpolation forms a basis for many numerical algorithms: integration, differentiation, differential equation solver, etc. This observation will become evident when we discuss these methods in future.

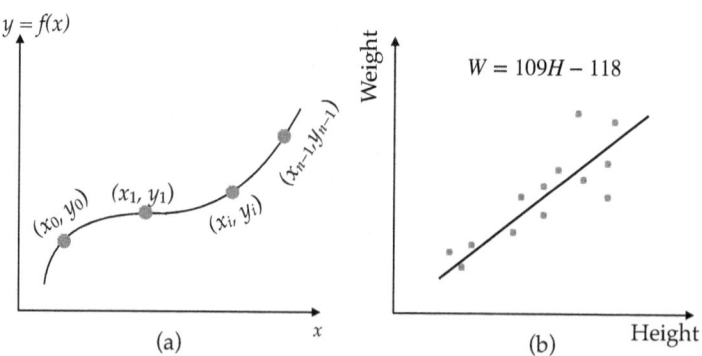

Figure 54: (a) An interpolation function $f(x)$ (black curve) passes through the data points, which are represented as blue dots. (b) The best-fit curve (black curve) passes through a set of data points (blue dots).

In Figure 54(a), we exhibit an extrapolated curve that passes through the data points (x_i, y_i), which are called *knots*. For a smooth interpolation, the uncertainties in the values of the data points need to minimal. However, when the data points have significant spread due to random errors, we employ *regression analysis* (to be discussed in Section 21.3) to find a *best-fit curve* through the data points. See Figure 54(b) for an illustration.

There are many interpolation schemes—Lagrange interpolation, Hermite interpolation, divided difference, splines, etc. We start with one-dimensional (1D) Lagrange interpolation.

Lagrange Interpolation in 1D

Figure 54(a) Illustrates 1D interpolation through a set of data points. Lagrange constructed a $(n-1)$th order *polynomial* that passes through n data points. In the following discussion, we will discuss Lagrange's interpolation procedure.

It is easy to construct a linear interpolation function through two points, (x_0,y_0) and (x_1,y_1), of the function $f(x)$. Note that $f(x_0) = y_0$ and $f(x_1) = y_1$. In Figure 55(a), the dashed line is the linear interpolating curve.

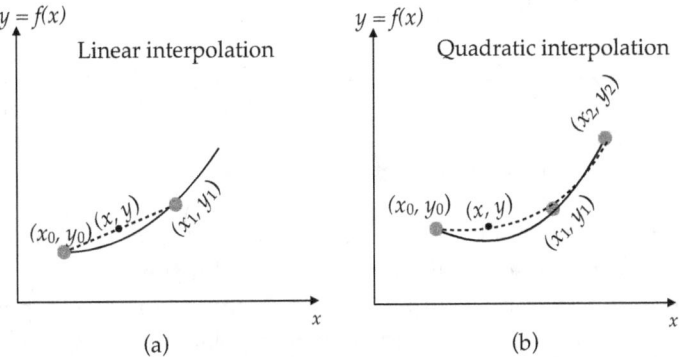

Figure 55: (a) Linear interpolation through (x_0,y_0) and (x_1,y_1). (b) Quadratic interpolation through (x_0,y_0), (x_1,y_1), and (x_2,y_2). The dashed lines are the interpolating curves, while the solid curve are actual $f(x)$.

It is straightforward to derive the following linear interpolating function $P_2(x)$ passing through the two points:

$$P_2(x) = \frac{x-x_1}{x_0-x_1}y_0 + \frac{x-x_0}{x_1-x_0}y_1 = L_0(x)y_0 + L_1(x)y_1,$$

where $L_0(x)$ and $L_1(x)$ are linear functions of x, and they have the following properties: $L_0(x_0) = 1$, $L_0(x_1) = 0$, $L_1(x_0) = 0$, and $L_1(x_1) = 1$. Note that in general, $P_2(x) \neq f(x)$. However, $P_2(x) = f(x)$ when $f(x)$ is a linear function of x.

Now we generalise the above discussion to n data points: (x_0, y_0), (x_1, y_1), ..., (x_{n-1}, y_{n-1}). Lagrange constructed the following interpolation function passing through these points:

$$P_n(x) = \sum_{j=0}^{n-1} L_j(x) y_j,$$

where

$$L_j(x) = \prod_{i, i \neq j} \frac{(x - x_i)}{(x_j - x_i)}.$$

Note that $L_j(x_k) = \delta_{jk}$, and that the interpolation function $P_n(x)$ is a $(n-1)$th degree polynomial. For $n = 2$, $P_2(x)$ is the formula for the linear interpolation described above, while for $n = 3$, $P_3(x)$ is quadratic interpolating function of $f(x)$:

$$P_3(x) = \frac{x-x_1}{x_0-x_1}\frac{x-x_2}{x_0-x_2}y_0 + \frac{x-x_0}{x_1-x_0}\frac{x-x_2}{x_1-x_2}y_1 + \frac{x-x_0}{x_2-x_0}\frac{x-x_1}{x_2-x_1}y_2$$

$$= L_0(x)y_0 + L_1(x)y_1 + L_2(x)y_2.$$

Note that $P_3(x) = f(x)$ if $f(x)$ is a polynomial of degree 2 or lower, and $P_3(x) \neq f(x)$ otherwise. See Figure 55(b) for an illustration.

Like any numerical computation, it is important to compute the error, $f(x) - P(x)$, for the Lagrange interpolation. Using reasonably complex arguments, it has been shown that the error for $P_n(x)$ is

$$E_n(x) = f(x) - P_n(x) = \frac{f^{(n)}(\zeta)}{n!} \prod (x - x_i), \quad \ldots(18)$$

where ζ is an intermediate point, and $f^{(n)}(\zeta)$ is the nth oder derivative of $f(x)$ at $x = \zeta$. The proof of the above statement is somewhat complex, hence it is detailed in Appendix A: Error in Lagrange Interopolation. If $f(x)$ is a polynomial of degree $(n-1)$, then $f^{(n)}(\zeta) = 0$, and hence $f(x) = P_n(x)$. Thus, the Lagrange interpolation function $P_n(x)$ is same $f(x)$ for this case.

The derivation of $E_n(x)$ tells about the existence ζ, but its determination is quite complex. Hence, an accurate error estimation is quite difficult. In practical, we estimate bounds on $E_n(x)$ depending on the bounds of ζ.

The following Python function *Lagrange_interpolate*() evaluates $P_n(x)$ at a given x given dataset $\{(x_i, y_i)\}$. The arrays *xarray* and *yarray* contain $\{x_i\}$ and $\{y_i\}$ respectively.

```
# P(x) = Pi_i (x-x_i)/(x_j-x_i) y_i
# returns value at x
def Lagrange_interpolate(xarray,yarray,x):
    n = len(xarray)
    ans = 0
    for j in range(n):
        numr = 1; denr = 1;
        for i in range(n):
            if (j != i):
                numr *= (x-xarray[i])
                denr *= (xarray[j]-xarray[i])
        ans += (numr/denr)*yarray[j]
    return ans
```

Usage:

```
xarray = np.array([3,4])
yarray = np.array([1/3.0,1/4.0])
P2 = Lagrange_interpolate(xarray,yarray,x)
```

Example 1: Given $f(x) = 1/x$, we construct Lagrange interpolating polynomials using 2, 3, and 4 points between $x = 2$ to 5. Using the function *Lagrange_interpolate*() and the two points $(2,1/2)$ and $(5,1/5)$ we construct a linear $P_2(x)$ illustrated in Figure 56(a). After this, we employ two sets of points, $\{(2,1/2), (4,1/4), (5,1/5)\}$ and $\{(2,1/2), (3,1/3), (5,1/5)\}$, to construct quadratic interpolating functions, which are illustrated in Figure 56(b,c) respectively. In Figure 56(b,c), the errors are significant between $(2,4)$ and $(3,5)$ respectively, which is due to the location of the intermediate points. At the end, we use 4 points $\{(2,1/2), (3,1/3), (4,1/4), (5,1/5)\}$ to derive $P_4(x)$ illustrated in Figure 56(d).

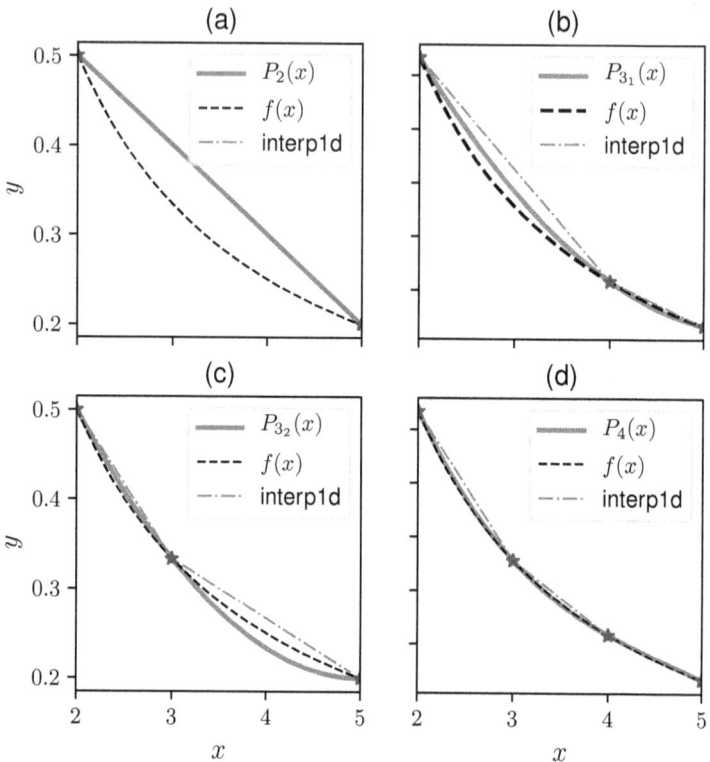

Figure 56: (a) Linear interpolation $P_2(x)$ using 2 points. (b,c) Quadratic interpolation $P_3(x)$ using three points. (d) Interpolation using 4 points ($P_4(x)$). The stars represent the data points. The actual function $f(x)$ is shown using the dashed lines, the Lagrange interpolation polynomials using the solid line, and interpolation function using Python's *interp1d* using the dashed-chained line.

Example 2: Error analysis of the data of Example 1: In Figure 57, we plot the errors $E_n(x) = f(x) - P_n(x)$ for $n = 2, 3, 4,$ and 5. Note that $E(x) = 0$ at the knots. As expected, error decreases with the increase of n.

We estimate the upper bound on $E_2(x) = f(x) - P_2(x)$ as follows. Since

$$E_2(x) = \frac{f^{(2)}(\zeta)}{2}(x-2)(x-5),$$

$E_2(x)$ is maximum somewhere in the middle of the interval. The product $(x-2)(x-5)$ takes maximum value of 2.25 at $x = 3.5$. In addition, $\max(|f^{(2)}(\zeta)|) = 2/\zeta^3 = 1/4$ at $\zeta = 2$. Therefore,

$$|E_2(x)| < \frac{1}{8} \times 2.25 = 0.28125.$$

Thus, the error $|E_2(x)|$ is bounded within 0.2815. This estimate is consistent with the numerical values of $E_2(x)$, which is shown in Figure 57 using the thickest curve. We can perform similar error estimation for other polynomials as well.

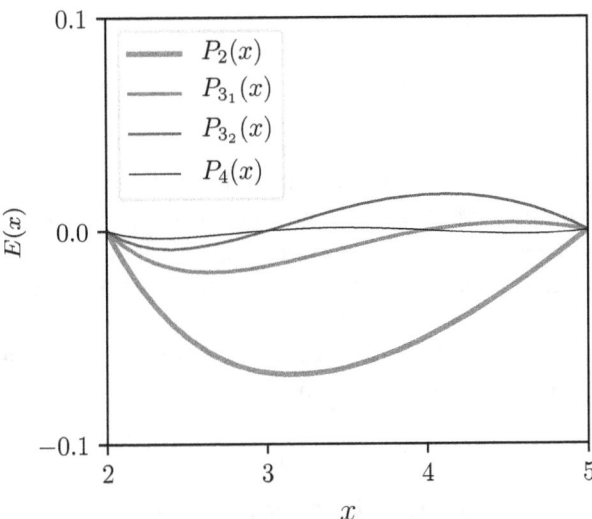

Figure 57: The plots of errors $E_n(x) = f(x) - P_n(x)$ for various Lagrange interpolation polynomials of Example 1.

In addition, we also compute error at a specific point, say at $x = 3.5$, which is the middle point in [2,5]. For the polynomials $P_2(x)$ to $P_4(x)$, the errors $E_n(3.5) = 1/3.5 - P_n(3.5)$ are -0.06429, -0.00804, 0.01071, and 0.00134 respectively. Here too, the error decreases with increase of n.

Lagrange Interpolation Using *Scipy*'s *Interp1d*

Python's *Scipy* module has an interpolating function named *interp1d*. This function makes a linear interpolation between consecutive points of the data. The following Python code illustrates how to use *interp1d* function for the same data as Example 1.

```
from scipy import interpolate

xarray = np.array([2,5])
yarray = np.array([1/2.0,1/5.0])
f = interpolate.interp1d(xarray,yarray)
# f contains the interpolation function.

xinter = np.arange(2.1,5,.1)
P2_scipy = f(xinter)
# P2_scipy is an array containing interpolated values for
xinter array.
```

In the above code sengment, f contains the interpolation function. We use f to generate interpolated values at x coordinates of *xinter* array. The interpolated values are stored in *P2_scipy* array. A point to note that the range of *xinter* must be within extreme abscissa values of the data.

In Figure 56, we exhibit the results of *interp1d*. Note that *interp1d* produces piece-wise linear functions.

Lagrange Interpolation in 2D

One-dimensional Lagrange interpolation descried earlier can be easily generalised to two dimensions (2D). Two-dimensional interpolation is very useful for image processing and other applications.

Assume a Cartesian 2D mesh with points as (x_i, y_i). Consider an arbitrary point (x,y) where we wish to interpolate the function $f(x,y)$. We denote the interpolating function as $P(x,y)$. See Figure 58 for an illustration:

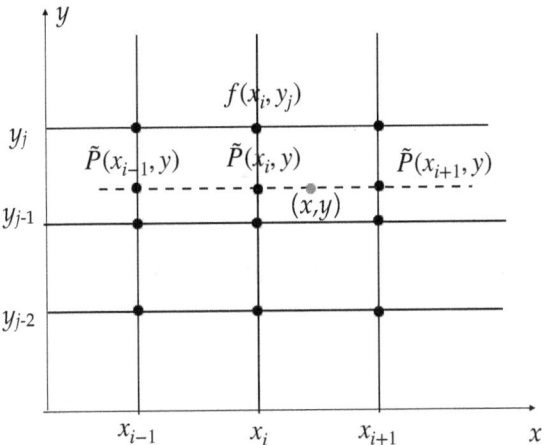

Figure 58: Interpolation of f(x,y) in a 2D mesh.

We derive the 2D interpolating function in the following three steps:

First step: We estimate $f(x,y)$ using interpolation along the x axis. That is,

$$P(x,y) = \sum_i \prod_{i',i'\neq i} \frac{(x-x_{i'})}{(x_i-x_{i'})} \tilde{P}(x_i,y).$$

Second step: We construct $\tilde{P}(x_i, y)$ using interpolation along y:

$$\tilde{P}(x_i,y) = \sum_j \prod_{j',j'\neq j} \frac{(y-y_{j'})}{(y_j-y_{j'})} f(x_i,y_j).$$

Third step: We substitute $\tilde{P}(x_i, y)$ in $P(x,y)$ that yields the desired interpolation function:

$$P(x,y) = \sum_i \prod_{i',i'\neq i} \frac{(x-x_{i'})}{(x_i-x_{i'})} \tilde{P}(x_i,y)$$
$$= \sum_i \sum_j \prod_{i',i'\neq i} \frac{(x-x_{i'})}{(x_i-x_{i'})} \prod_{j',j'\neq j} \frac{(y-y_{j'})}{(y_j-y_{j'})} f(x_i,y_j).$$

Hence,

$$P(x,y) = \sum_i \sum_j L_{i,j}(x,y) y_{i,j},$$

where $y_{i,j}$ is shorthand for $f(x_i, y_j)$, and

$$L_{i,j} = \prod_{i', i' \neq i} \prod_{j', j' \neq j} \frac{(x - x_{i'})}{(x_i - x_{i'})} \frac{(y - y_{j'})}{(y_j - y_{j'})}.$$

Similarly, interpolation polynomials for 3D functions is

$$P(x,y,z) = \sum_i \sum_j L_{i,j,k}(x,y,z) y_{i,j,k},$$

where

$$L_{i,j,k} = \prod_{i', i' \neq i} \prod_{j', j' \neq j} \prod_{k', k' \neq k} \frac{(x - x_{i'})}{(x_i - x_{i'})} \frac{(y - y_{j'})}{(y_j - y_{j'})} \frac{(y - y_{k'})}{(y_k - y_{k'})}.$$

The accuracy of Lagrange interpolation increases with more points. However, large number of data points need high-order interpolating polynomials that have spurious oscillations. Also, the computational cost for the construction of high-order polynomials may be exorbitant. Thus, we need to use optimum number of points for Lagrange interpolation. For a large number of data points, piece-wise interpolation may be employed.

There are several other polynomial-based interpolation schemes, such as *Hermite interpolation* and *Netwon's divided difference*. We will not discuss them here due to lack of space and time. Rather, we move to a different class of interpolation scheme called *splines*, which is topic of the next section.

****

Conceptual Questions

1. List scientific applications where interpolation is used.

Exercises

1. For $f(x) = \sin(x)$ in the domain $x = [0, \pi/2]$, construct Lagrange interpolating polynomials using 2, 3, and 4 points. Plot the interpolating functions, as well as the errors for them. Repeat the exercise when the domain is $x = [0, \pi]$.
2. For $f(x) = \exp(x)$ in the domain $x = [0,2]$, construct Lagrange interpolating polynomials using 2, 3, and 4 points. Analyse the errors associated with them.
3. Consider a 2D function $f(x,y) = \exp(x+y)$ in the domain $x = [0,1]$ and $y = [0,1]$. Construct Lagrange interpolating polynomials using 2, 3, and 4 points along each directions. Make contour plots for the interpolating polynomials along with the original function.

10.2 Splines

As we discussed in the previous section, Lagrange interpolation is not suitable for large number of data points. A way out is to employ piece-wise interpolation. However, such interpolating functions are not smooth at the nodes (x_i's). That is, the first derivatives at the nodes do not match from both sides. For example, the piece-wise linear function generated by *interp1d* has kinks at the nodes (see Figure 56). Splines, to be discussed in this section, help us smoothen the piece-wise interpolating functions.

In this section, we will describe *cubic splines* that are derived using the beam equation. The equation for the beam equation is

$$EI \frac{d^4}{dx^4} f(x) = F(x),$$

where E is the Young's modulus of the material, I is the second moment of beam's cross-section, and $F(x)$ is the applied force. In the spline framework, the force is assumed to be active at the nodes, denoted by (x_i, y_i) with $i = 0:(n-1)$. In Figure 59, the curve represents a beam.

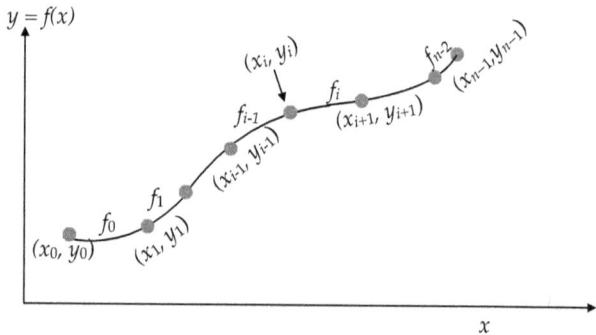

Figure 59: Illustration of a spline with nodes as (x_i, y_i) and the piece-wise functions as $f_i(x)$.

The equation for the beam on which the forces active at x_i is

$$EI \frac{d^4}{dx^4} f(x) = F_i \delta(x - x_i). \quad \ldots (19)$$

Note that F_i acts at x_i. An integration of the above equation yields $f'''(x)$ (triple derivative of $f(x)$) with discontinuities around the nodes. The second derivative exhibits a kink, but $f'(x)$ and $f(x)$ are smooth functions.

In Figure 60, we exhibit $f(x)$ and its derivatives when the RHS of Eq. (19) is $\delta(x-1)$ (forcing of unit amplitude applied at $x = 1$). For such a force, $f'''(x)$ exhibits a jump, $f''(x)$ is piece-wise linear with a kink, but $f'(x)$ and $f(x)$ are smooth functions.

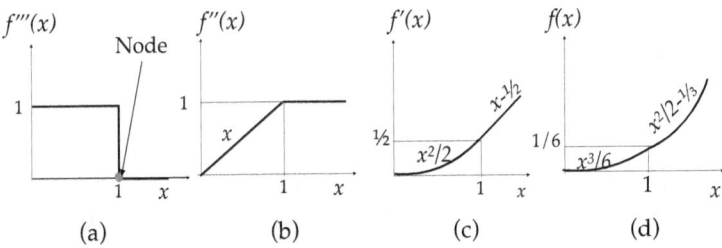

Figure 60: Function $f(x)$ and its derivatives for a spline with forcing function $\delta(x-1)$.

The construction of a spline requires finding a smooth $f(x)$ passing through the nodes (x_i, y_i). As shown in Figure 60, $f(x)$ and its derivatives satisfy the following properties:

1. The second derivative, $f''(x)$, is piecewise linear in each interval (x_i, x_{i+1}).
2. The function $f(x)$ and its first derivative are continuous and smooth everywhere, including at the nodes.
3. The function $f(x)$ passes through (x_i, y_i).

Following property (1), the linear interpolation of $f''(x)$ in the interval (x_i, x_{i+1}) yields

$$f''_i(x) = f''(x_i)\frac{x_{i+1}-x}{x_{i+1}-x_i} + f''(x_{i+1})\frac{x-x_i}{x_{i+1}-x_i}.$$

Double integration of the above equation yields $f(x)$ in the interval (x_i, x_{i+1}) as

$$f_i(x) = f''(x_i)\frac{(x_{i+1}-x)^3}{6h_i} + f''(x_{i+1})\frac{(x-x_i)^3}{6h_i}$$
$$+ \left[\frac{y_i}{h_i} - \frac{h_i}{6}f''(x_i)\right](x_{i+1}-x) + \left[\frac{y_{i+1}}{h_i} - \frac{h_i}{6}f''(x_{i+1})\right](x-x_i),$$

where $h_i = x_{i+1} - x_i$. The two constants of integration have been determined using the conditions: $f_i(x_i) = y_i$ and $f_{i+1}(x_{i+1}) = y_{i+1}$. Similarly, for the interval (x_{i-1}, x_i), the function is

$$f_{i-1}(x) = f''(x_{i-1})\frac{(x_i-x)^3}{6h_{i-1}} + f''(x_i)\frac{(x-x_{i-1})^3}{6h_{i-1}}$$
$$+ \left[\frac{y_{i-1}}{h_{i-1}} - \frac{h_{i-1}}{6}f''(x_{i-1})\right](x_i-x) + \left[\frac{y_i}{h_{i+1}} - \frac{h_{i-1}}{6}f''(x_i)\right](x-x_{i-1}).$$

Now we impose an additional condition that the first derivative at the nodes is continuous at both sides. Applying this condition at $x = x_i$, i.e., $f'_i(x_i) = f'_{i-1}(x_i)$, we obtain

$$-f''(x_i)\frac{h_i}{2} - \left[\frac{y_i}{h_i} - \frac{h_i}{6}f''(x_i)\right] + \left[\frac{y_{i+1}}{h_i} - \frac{h_i}{6}f''(x_{i+1})\right]$$
$$= -f''(x_i)\frac{h_{i-1}}{2} - \left[\frac{y_{i-1}}{h_{i-1}} - \frac{h_{i-1}}{6}f''(x_{i-1})\right] + \left[\frac{y_i}{h_{i-1}} - \frac{h_{i-1}}{6}f''(x_i)\right],$$

which yields

$$\frac{h_{i-1}}{6}f''(x_{i-1}) + \frac{1}{3}(h_i + h_{i-1})f''(x_i) + \frac{h_i}{6}f''(x_{i+1})$$
$$= \frac{y_{i+1}}{h_i} - y_i\left(\frac{1}{h_i} + \frac{1}{h_{i-1}}\right) + \frac{y_{i-1}}{h_{i-1}}.$$

We obtain $(n-2)$ linear equations for nodes at $i = 1...(n-2)$. However we have n unknowns $[f''(x_i)$ for $i = 0...(n-1)]$. To solve this problem, we use one of the following boundary conditions:

1. *Parabolic run-out*: We assume that $f''(x)$ are constant on both end intervals, i.e., $f''(x_0) = f''(x_1)$ and $f''(x_{n-1}) = f''(x_{n-2})$. Hence $f(x)$ is quadratic in these intervals. With these two additional constraints, we have n equations to determine the $n\,f''(x_i)$'s.
2. *Free end*: We assume that $f'' = 0$ at both the ends, or $f''(x_0) = f''(x_{n-1}) = 0$.
3. *Cantilever end*: A intermediate condition between the cases 1 and 2, i.e., $f''(x_0) = \lambda f''(x_0)$ and $f''(x_{n-1}) = \lambda f''(x_{n-2})$ with $0 \le \lambda \le 1$.
4. *Periodic spline*: We assume that the data is periodic with y_0 identified with y_{n-1}, i.e., $y_0 = y_{n-1}$. With this, we have $(n-1)$ matching conditions at $(n-1)$ points to determine all $f''(x_i)$ $((n-1)$ of them).

With the above four boundary conditions, we have equal number of unknowns and linear equations. These equations can be solved using matrix methods that will be discussed in Section 20.1. In the following example, we take a simple case with four points that can be solved analytically.

Example 1: We work out the splines for the data of Example 1 discussed in Section 10.1. We consider the same four points {(2,1/2), (3,1/3), (4,1/4) (5,1/5)} as before. Let us use the free-end boundary condition ($f_0'' = f_3'' = 0$) for this example. Note that $h_i = 1$. The equations for the splines at the intermediate nodes are

$$\frac{2}{3}f_1'' + \frac{1}{6}f_2'' = y_2 - 2y_1 + y_0 = \frac{1}{4} - \frac{2}{3} + \frac{1}{2} = \frac{1}{12}$$
$$\frac{1}{6}f_1'' + \frac{2}{3}f_2'' = y_3 - 2y_2 + y_1 = \frac{1}{5} - \frac{2}{4} + \frac{1}{3} = \frac{1}{30}$$

The solution of the above equations are $f_1'' = 3/25$ and $f_2'' = 1/50$. Using these values and $f''_0 = f''_3 = 0$, we construct the piece-wise functions and plot them together. The plot is shown in Figure 61 as a black dashed curve.

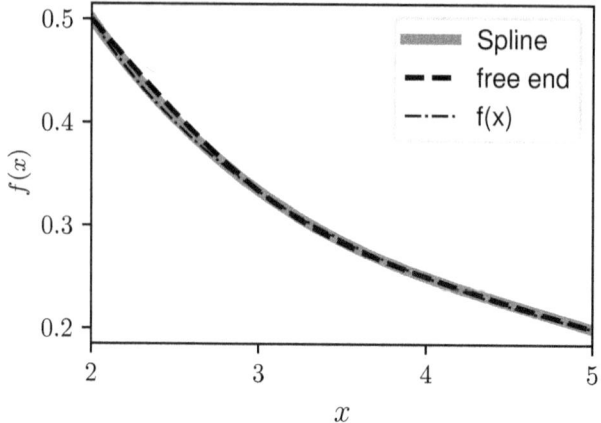

Figure 61: For the data {(2,1/2) (3,1/3), (4,1/4) (5,1/5)}, the plots of splines computed using free-end boundary condition (dashed curve) and Scipy's *CubicSpline* (solid curve). These curves are close to each other, and to the actual function $1/x$. See Figure 62 for errors.

The following Python code computes the splines using free-end boundary condition (as described above) and using Scipy's *interpolate.CubicSpline* function. The function generated using *interpolate.CubicSpline* function is shown as the solid curve in Figure 61. The code for the computation of $f(x)$ is given below.

```
### x-y data
xd = np.array([2,3,4,5])
yd = np.array([1/2.0,1/3.0,1/4.0,1/5.0])
### double derivatives
fdd = np.array([0,3/25,1/50,0])

def f(i,x):
    first_term = (fdd[i]*(xd[i+1]-x)**3 + fdd[i+1]*(x-xd[i])**3)/6
    second_term = (yd[i]-fdd[i]/6)*(xd[i+1]-x) + (yd[i+1]-fdd[i+1]/6)*(x-xd[i])
    return first_term + second_term

# range of x
x0r = np.arange(2,3.1,0.1)
x1r = np.arange(3,4.1,0.1)
x2r = np.arange(4,5.1,0.1)
y0r = f(0,x0r);
```

```
y1r = f(1,x1r);
y2r = f(2,x2r);

xtot = np.concatenate((x0r, x1r, x2r))
ytot = np.concatenate((y0r, y1r, y2r))

# Using splines
cs=interpolate.CubicSpline(xd,yd)
x=np.arange(2,5.1,0.1)
y = cs(x)
```

Even though the splines generated by free-end boundary condition and Scipy functions are quite close to the actual function, $1/x$, there are small errors ($E(x) = f(x) - P(x)$), which are plotted in Figure 62. The dashed and solid curves represent the errors for the two cases. The accuracy of Lagrange polynomial and splines computed using *interpolate.CubicSpline* are comparable. However, the errors of splines computed using free-end boundary condition is quite significant. This is because $f''(x_0) = 1/4$, not zero, as is assumed in free-end boundary condition. The error at the other end, $x = 5$, is less damaging because $f''(x_3) = 2/25 \approx 0$.

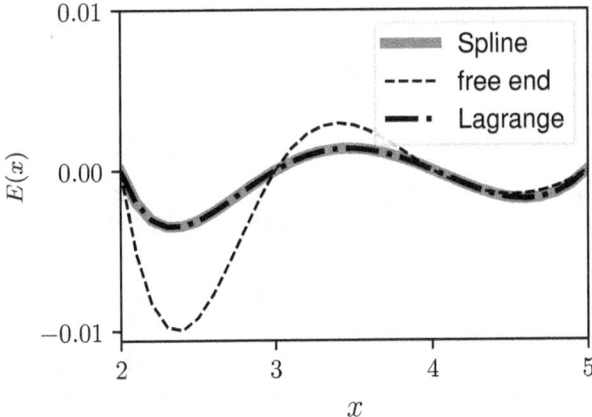

Figure 62: The plots of error $E(x) = f(x)-P(x)$ for the splines calculated using free-end boundary condition (dashed curve), using *CubicSpline* (solid curve), and using Lagrange polynomial with 4 points (black chained curve).

B-Splines is another prominent spline, but it is not covered in this book. For B-splines, you can use Scipy's function *interpolate.splrep()* to compute the spline parameters (*tck*), and then compute the curve by supplying x array to *interpolate.splev(x, tck)*.

In summary, splines provide *smooth* interpolating functions for a large number of points. However, these computations require solution of a matrix equation. Fortunately, the matrix is tridiagonal that can be easily solved using methods that will be described in Section 20.1.

In this chapter, we have assumed that the sampling points (x_i, y_i) have zero noise. In the presence of random noise, regression analysis are used to determine the underlying function $f(x)$. We will discuss regression in Section 21.3.

****

Conceptual Questions

1. In what ways spline interpolation is better than Lagrange interpolation?

Exercises

1. Rework Example 1 with parabolic run-out boundary condition.
2. Consider $f(x) = \sin(x)$ for the domain $x = [0, 2\pi]$. Construct periodic splines using appropriate number of points. After this, rework the splines with parabolic run-out boundary condition.
3. For $f(x) = \exp(x)$ in the domain $x = [0, 2]$, construct splines with free-end boundary condition. Take appropriate number of knots.

Chapter Eleven
NUMERICAL INTEGRATION

Synopsis

"God does not care about our mathematical difficulties. He integrates empirically.."
— Albert Einstein

Numerical integration algorithms are covered in this chapter.

11.1 Newton-Cotes Formulas

Integration, which is summing up of a function in an interval, is encountered in all streams of science and engineering. For example, the velocity of a particle is computed by integrating acceleration, which is force divided by mass. In turn, an integration of the velocity yields the position of the particle. *Numerical integration* is one of the most important topics of computational science.

Numerical integration, also called *quadrature*, of a function $f(x)$ from $x = a$ to $x = b$ is written as

$$I = \int_a^b f(x)dx = \sum_{i=0}^{n-1} w_i f(x_i), \ldots (20)$$

where w_i's are the *weights* and x_i's are *abscissas*. The integration schemes can be classified into two broad categories:

1. *Simple methods*: Here, we choose x_i as evenly spaced n points and then compute w_i. If the error is beyond an admissible limit, the number of points is increased.
2. *Complex methods*: Here, x_i and w_i are chosen in such a way that the integral has a minimum error.

Newton-Cotes Formulas

Newton-Cotes (NC) scheme is one of the *simple methods*. Here, we divide the interval (a,b) into m equal divisions with $\Delta x = (a-b)/m = h$. The abscissas are located at $x_j = a + jh$, where $j = 0{:}m$. Note that the number of points $n = m+1$. Here, m is the *degree of Newton-Cotes scheme*.

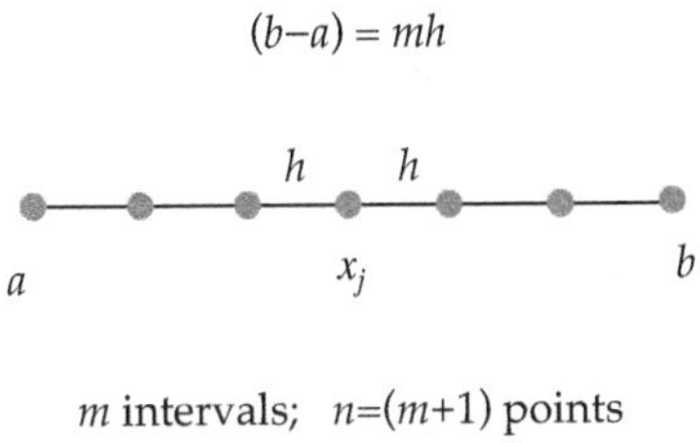

$$(b-a) = mh$$

```
        h    h
a ●—●—●—●—●—●—● b
          x_j
```

m intervals; $n=(m+1)$ points

Figure 63: Division of the domain $(b-a)$ into m interval. $(b-a) = mh$.

We approximate the function $f(x)$ using the Lagrange interpolation:

$$P_n(x) = \sum_{j=0}^{n-1} L_j(x) f(x_j),$$

which is substituted in Eq. (20) that yields

$$I = \int_b^a f(x)dx \approx \int_b^a P_n(x)dx = \sum_{j=0}^{n-1} f(x_j) \int_a^b L_j(x)dx = h \sum_{j=0}^{m} C_j^{(m)} f(x_j), \ldots (21)$$

where

$$C_j^{(m)} = \frac{1}{h} \int_b^a L_j(x)dx \ldots (22)$$

are the coefficients for mth degree NC scheme. Since $L_j(x)$'s are independent of the data $f(x_j)$, we conclude that $C_j^{(m)}$'s are independent of $f(x_j)$. For $f(x) = 1$, Eq. (21) yields $I=(b-a)$. Hence, we conclude that $\sum_j C_j^{(m)} = m$. Note that weights $w_j = h\, C_j^{(m)}$.

Now, let us compute $C_j^{(m)}$ for some of the Legendre polynomials (see Section 10.1). For $n = 2$ (two points), the polynomial is

$$P_2(x) = \frac{x-b}{a-b}f(a) + \frac{x-a}{b-a}f(b).$$

An integration of the above yields

$$I = \int_b^a P_2(x)dx = \frac{h}{2}(f(a)+f(b)).$$

Using the above formula we deduce that $C_0^{(1)} = C_1^{(1)} = ½$. This method, called *trapezoid rule*, is accurate up to machine precision for linear functions. The shaded region of Figure 64(a) is the numerical integral, and the white area **A** below $f(x)$ is the error in the integral.

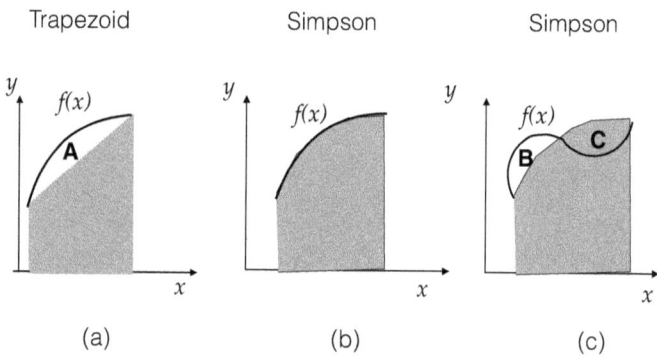

(a) (b) (c)

Figure 64: (a) Trapezoid rule. (b,c) Simpson's rule. The numerical integrals are represented by the shaded regions.

For $m = 2$, we employ the quadratic Lagrange polynomial, $P_3(x)$, with abscissas at x=a, (a+b)/2, b. Note that $h = (b-a)/2$. Hence,

$$I = \int_b^a P_3(x)dx = \frac{h}{3}(f(a) + 4f((a+b)/2) + f(b)).$$

Therefore, $C_0^{(2)} = C_2^{(2)} = ⅓$ and $C_1^{(2)} = 4/3$. This method, called *Simpson's ⅓ rule*, is accurate when $f(x)$ is a polynomials of third-degree or lower (see Figure 64(b,c)). In figure(c), for a cubic $f(x)$, the filled region **C** and unfilled region **B** cancel each other. The coefficients $C_j^{(m)}$ for larger m are derived similarly using higher-order Lagrange polynomials. These coefficients are listed in Table 16.

Table 16: Coefficients for the Newton-Cotes integration schemes.

m	$C_j^{(m)}$	$C_j^{(m)}$	$C_j^{(m)}$	$C_j^{(m)}$	$C_j^{(m)}$	$C_j^{(m)}$
1	½	½				
2	⅓	4/3	⅓			
3	3/8	9/8	9/8	3/8		
4	14/45	64/45	8/15	64/45	14/45	
5	95/288	125/96	125/144	125/144	125/96	95/288

The methods for $m=2$ and 3 are called *Simpson's ⅓* and *Simpson's 3/8 rules* respectively. We can obtain the coefficients for all m's using Python's *scipy.integrate.newton_cotes(m, 1)*, where m is the degree of the scheme. The argument 1 of newton_cotes(m,1) indicates that the abscissas are equally spaced. The function returns a tuple whose first element is a list of coefficient, while the second element is the prefactor for the error, which will be discussed later in this section.

Example 1: A code segment below illustrates how to compute $\int_0^1 dx\, x^4$ using NC method. The integral is exact (0.2) for $m = 4$. However, for $m = 2$ and 3, the integrals are 0.20833333333333331 and 0.20370370370370366 respectively.

```
from scipy.integrate import newton_cotes

def integ_Newton_Cotes(m, f, a, b):
    x = np.linspace(a,b,m+1)
    coeff, error = newton_cotes(m,1)
    h = (b-a)/m
    return  (h * np.sum(coeff * f(x)))

In [74]: print(integ_Newton_Cotes(4, lambda x: x**4, 0,
1))
0.2
```

Error Analysis for Newton-Cote's Method

In Section 10.1, we derived that the error in Lagrange interpolation with n points is

$$E_n(x) = f(x) - P_n(x) = \frac{f^{(n)}(\zeta)}{n!} \prod (x - x_i).$$

Hence, the error in the integration by the Newton-Cotes scheme with n points is

$$E_n = \int_a^b E_n(x)dx = \frac{f^{(n)}(\zeta)}{n!} \int_a^b dx \prod (x - x_i). \quad \dots (23)$$

When $f(x)$ is a $(n-1)$th order polynomial, $f^{(n-1)}(x)$ vanishes, and hence $E_n = 0$, Thus, NC method with n points yields exact integral for a $(n-1)$th order polynomial. However, as we show below, NC method is more accurate than the above for odd n.

By power counting of x or dimensional analysis, we obtain $\int_a^b dx \prod (x - x_i) \approx O(h^{n+1})$. Hence, the integral of Eq. (23) is $O(h^{n+1})$ for even n, but it vanishes for odd n. Note however that $E_n \neq 0$ for odd n unless $f(x)$ is a polynomial of degree n or lower. Hence, to estimate the error for odd n, we approximate $f(x)$ with the $(n+1)$th order Lagrange polynomial that passes through the points $(a, a+h, a+2h, \dots, b, b+h)$, but integrate $E_n(x)$ in the interval $[a,b]$. Hence, a more accurate estimate of the error for odd n is

$$E_n = \int_a^b E_n(x)dx = \frac{f^{(n+1)}(\zeta)}{(n+1)!} \int_a^b dx \left[(x - b - h) \prod (x - x_i) \right]. \quad (24)$$

We illustrate the above estimation for $n = 3$ with $a = 0$, $b=1$, and $h=\frac{1}{2}$. For these parameters, Eq. (23) yields

$$E_3 = \frac{f^{(3)}(\zeta)}{3!} \int_0^1 dx\, x(x - 1/2)(x - 1) = 0$$

because the integrand is an odd function around $x = \frac{1}{2}$. However, an application of Eq. (24) with knots at $x = 0, 1/2, 1$, and $3/2$ yields the following error estimate:

$$E_3 = \frac{f^{(4)}(\zeta)}{4!} \int_0^1 dx\, x(x-1/2)(x-1)(x-3/2) = \frac{1}{2880} f^{(4)}(\zeta),$$

which is same as $(h^5/90)\, f^{(4)}(\zeta)$ with $h = 1/2$. We generalise this result to any odd n. Using dimensional analysis of Eq. (24), we deduce that for odd n, the error in the NC integral is $O(h^{n+2})$.

The errors for various Lagrange polynomials are listed in Table 17. We can obtain the prefactors for the errors using Python's scipy.integrate.newton_cotes(m, 1), where m is the degree of the scheme. We will illustrate the integral and error computations using several examples.

Table 17: Errors for the Newton-Cotes integration. Here, $f^{(6)}$ and $f^{(8)}$ stand for the sixth and eighth derivative of f.

m	Error
1	$(h^3/12)\, f''(\zeta)$
2	$(h^5/90)\, f''''(\zeta)$
3	$(3h^5/80)\, f'''(\zeta)$
4	$(8h^7/945)\, f^{(6)}(\zeta)$
5	$(275h^7/12096)\, f^{(6)}(\zeta)$
6	$(9h^9/1400)\, f^{(8)}(\zeta)$

In the above table, $f^{(4)}(\zeta) = f''''(\zeta) = 0$ for a third-order polynomial. Hence, Simpson's 1/3 rule yields accurate integrals for polynomials up to cubic order. In general, Newton-Cotes scheme with even n points provides accurate integrals for polynomials of degree $(n-1)$ or lower. However, for odd n points, the integral is accurate for polynomials of degree n or lower; this is due to further cancelations of the areas around middle knot. See Figure Figure 64(c) for an illustration. The above statements on exact integrals using numerical methods may sound like an oxymoron, but it is true. *Careful computations with powerful algorithms can yield exact results (with no errors).*

Example 2: We compute $\int_0^1 x\, dx$ using NC method. We employ the Trapezoid rule for which the knots are at 0 and 1, and $h = 1$.

$$\int_0^1 x\, dx = \tfrac{1}{2}[f(0) + f(1)] = \tfrac{1}{2}$$

which is the correct answer. This is because Trapezoid rule gives exact integral for linear functions. Needless to say that higher-order NC methods too yield exact results for $\int_0^1 x\, dx$.

Example 3: We compute $I = \int_0^1 x^2\, dx$ using NC method. The Trapezoid rule yields $I = \tfrac{1}{2}$, which is incorrect. However, Simpson's ⅓ rule with $h = \tfrac{1}{2}$ yields

$$I = \int_0^1 x^2\, dx = \{\, \tfrac{1}{3}[f(0) + f(1)] + 4/3\, f(\tfrac{1}{2}) \,\}\, h = \tfrac{1}{3},$$

which is the correct answer.

Example 4: We compute $I = \int_0^1 x^3\, dx$ using NC method. The Trapezoid rule yields $I = \tfrac{1}{2}$, which is incorrect. However, Simpson's ⅓ rule yields

$$I = \int_0^1 x^3\, dx = \{\, \tfrac{1}{3}[f(0) + f(1)] + 4/3\, f(\tfrac{1}{2}) \,\}\, h = 1/4,$$

which is the correct answer. We obtain an exact result because $x^3 - P_2(x)$ is an odd function around $x = \tfrac{1}{2}$, hence its integral vanishes.

Example 5: We compute $I = \int_0^1 dx\, x^4$ using NC method. The Trapezoid rule yields $I = \frac{1}{2}$, which is incorrect. Simpson's ⅓ and 3/8 rules yield I = 5/24 and 11/54 respectively, which differ slightly from the exact results of 1/5. We compute the errors for these two methods using the formulas of Table 17, and find them to be 1/120 and 1/270 respectively, which are the exact errors of these methods. Note that $f^{(n)}$ (ζ) is easily computable for this case. As illustrated in Example 1, we obtain $I = 1/5$ for $m = 4$.

The results of Examples 2 to 5 are consistent with the discussion of this section. Now we consider a more complex example.

Example 6: We compute $\int_0^{\pi/2} dx \sin x$ numerically by dividing the interval $(0, \pi/2)$ into various intervals and employing Newton-Cotes scheme. Note that the exact answer is 1. We employ n = 2,3,4,5,6 abscissa points, for which the results are 0.7853981633974483, 1.0022798774922104, 1.001004923314279, 0.9999915654729927, 0.9999952613861667 respectively.

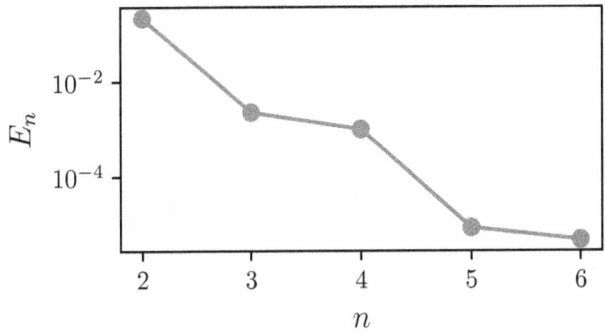

Figure 65: Example 6: Errors in integral $\int_0^{\pi/2} dx \sin x$ computed using Newton-Cotes method with n = 2,3,4,5,6 points.

In Figure 65, we plot the errors in the integral computation. The figure shows that error drops when we go from 2 to 3, but not so much from 3 to 4. Similarly, error does not drop significantly when n increases from 5 to 6. This is because the integrals using odd n's are accurate up to $O(h^{n+2})$, which is also the accuracy with $n+1$ even points.

See Table 17 for details.

Multi-interval Newton-Cotes Method

For a large interval (b-a), it is practical to divide it into many smaller segments, and then employ NC method to each of the segments. For example, we divide an interval (a,b) into n−1 segments, and employ trapezoid rule to all of them. This operation yields the following formula for the integral:

$$I = \int_a^b f(x)dx = \frac{h}{2}\left[f_0 + 2\sum_{i=1}^{n-2} f_i + f_{n-1}\right].$$

We compute $\int_0^{\pi/2} dx \sin x$ using the above formula by dividing the interval $(0,\pi/2)$ into 2 to 9 intervals and employing Trapezoid rule on each segment. In Figure 66 we plot error E_h vs. h for $h = (\pi/2)/2$ to $(\pi/2)/9$. As shown in the figure, E_h is proportional to h^3, which is consistent with the error estimate of trapezoid rule, $E_h = (h^3/12) f'^{(2)}(\zeta)$.

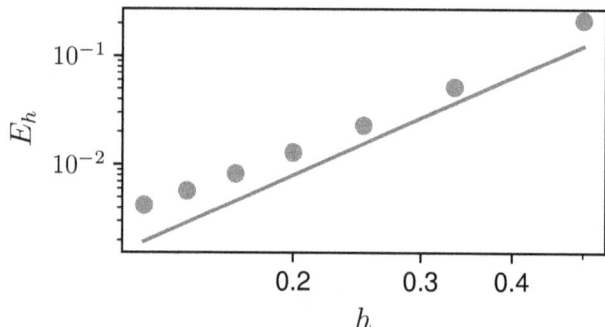

Figure 66: Plot of error E_h vs. h for the integral $\int_0^{\pi/2} dx \sin x$ when h varies from $(\pi/2)/2$ to $(\pi/2)/9$. The straight line represents h^3.

We already know the values of the integrals in the above illustrative examples. Hence, we could study the errors for various m and h. The computation, however, becomes tricky in practice when the integral is unknown. Here, we need to choose h and degree of NC method with care. In such a scenario, for a given NC method, we compare $I(h)$ with $I(h/2)$. If the error, $I(h) - I(h/2)$, is less than the required tolerance, then we can take $I(h/2)$ as the final numerical value of the integral. Also, it is better to use NC method with odd n's because they yield better accuracy compare to even n's.

With this, we close our discussion on the Newton-Cotes method. In the next section we will describe Gaussian quadrature, which is more accurate than the Newton-Cotes method.

****

Conceptual Questions

1. Comment on usefulness of Lagrange interpolation to the derivation of Newton-Cotes formulas.
2. It is better to use odd number of points for integration using Newton-Cotes method. Why?

Exercises

1. Integrate $\int_0^1 x^\alpha dx$ for $\alpha = 5,6$ using 2,3,4,5 points and compare the results with the exact ones. Are your results consistent with the formulas for the error estimates?

2. Integrate $\int_0^5 (x^6 - 5x^5 + 3)dx$ using Newton-Cotes method with 2,3,4,5 points and compare the results with the exact one. Also divide the interval into many segments and sum the integrals for each segment. Employ Trapezoid and Simpson rules for the latter integrals.

3. Integrate $\int_0^1 \exp(-x)\cos(x)dx$ using Newton-Cotes method

with 2,3,4,5 points.

4. Integrate $\int_0^\infty \exp(-x^2)dx$ using Newton-Cotes method. What strategy would you adopt to get accurate integral up to 5%.

5. Compute the time period of an oscillator whose mass is 2 units and whose potential energy is $10\, x^2$.

6. Compute the time period of a pendulum of length is 1 meter and that oscillates between −30 degrees to 30 degrees.

11.2 Gaussian Quadrature

Gaussian quadrature is one of the *complex methods* for integration, and it is more accurate than Newton-Cotes method. This is because in Gaussian quadrature, both the abscissa and weights are chosen so as to improve the accuracy of the integral. Note that Newton-Cotes scheme with odd N (even N) points provides accurate integrals for polynomials of N ($N-1$) degrees. In this section, we show that the Gaussian quadrature with N points yields accurate integrals for polynomials of degree ($2N-1$).

In Gaussian quadrature, our objective is to determine abscissa (x_j) and weights (w_j) to compute the integral to the best possible accuracy. Note that

$$I = \int_a^b f(x)dx \approx \sum_{j=0}^{N-1} w_j f(x_j) \quad ....(25)$$

Example 1: Suppose we demand exact quadrature for $f(x) = 1, x, x^2, ..., x^{2N-1}$ in the interval $[-1,1]$. Substitution of this condition in Eq. (25) yields $2N$ equations, using which we can obtain the $2N$ unknowns (abscissas and weights). Let us compute x_j and w_j for $N = 2$ in the domain $[-1,1]$. We require accurate integrals for $f(x) = 1, x, x^2, x^3$, which yields the following four equations:

$2 = w_0 + w_1$
$0 = w_0 x_0 + w_1 x_1$
$2/3 = w_0 x_0^2 + w_1 x_1^2$
$0 = w_0 x_0^3 + w_1 x_1^3$

whose solutions are $w_0 = w_1 = 1$ and $x_0 = -x_1 = 1/\sqrt{3}$.

The above procedure is quite cumbersome for large N. In the following discussion, we provide a general formulation for determining x_j and w_j using orthogonal polynomials. Note that our formulation should yield an exact quadrature for any polynomial of degree $2N-1$ or less with N data points.

Derivation of Gauss Quadrature

In Gauss quadrature, we take N+1 orthogonal polynomials $\phi_i(x)$ ($i = 0:N$) that satisfy the orthogonality relation:

$$\int_a^b h(x)\phi_i(x)\phi_j(x) = \delta_{ij}\gamma_i \ldots (26)$$

where a and b are the limits of the integral, $h(x)$ is the weight function for the integral (different from the weights w_i for the integral), and γ_i's are constants. In this scheme, the N abscissas are the roots of $\phi_N(x)$, while the weights are

$$w_j = -\frac{a_N \gamma_N}{\phi'_N(x_j)\phi_{N+1}(x_j)}, \quad \ldots (27)$$

where A_N is the coefficient of x^N in $\phi_N(x)$. In terms of these abscissas and weights, the integral is

$$I = \int_a^b h(x)f(x)dx = \sum_{j=0}^{N-1} w_j f(x_j)$$

Note that the weight function $h(x)$ enters in the integral.

The derivation involves interesting applications of functional analysis and orthogonal polynomials. The following derivation can be skipped by those who are not interested in the mathematical details. The derivation is as follows.

Step 1: First, we assume that $f(x)$ is a polynomial of degree 2N−1 or lower. A division of such $f(x)$ with $\phi_N(x)$ yields

$$f(x) = q_{N-1}(x)\phi_N(x) + r_{N-1}(x), \ldots (28)$$

where the quotient $q_{N-1}(x)$ and remainder $r_{N-1}(x)$ are polynomials of degree N−1 or lower. Therefore, the functions $q_{N-1}(x)$ and $r_{N-1}(x)$ can be expanded using polynomials $\{\phi_0(x), \phi_1(x), \ldots, \phi_{N-1}(x)\}$, hence, they are orthogonal to $\phi_N(x)$, or

$$\int_a^b h(x)q_{N-1}(x)\phi_N(x)dx = 0. \quad \ldots(29)$$

Therefore,

$$\int_a^b h(x)f(x)dx = \int_a^b h(x)r_{N-1}(x)dx.$$

When $f(x)$ is a polynomial of degree higher than $2N-1$, the integral with the quotient (Eq. (29)) is not zero.

Step 2: We simplify the integral further. $\phi_N(x)$ is a polynomial of degree N, hence it has N roots (assume real), which are taken to be abscissas $\{x_j\}$ with $j = 0{:}N-1$. Note that

$$f(x_j) = q_{N-1}(x_j)\phi_N(x_j) + r_{N-1}(x_j) = r_{N-1}(x_j).$$

Since $r_{N-1}(x)$ is a polynomial of degree $N-1$ or lower, we expand it using Lagrange polynomials whose knots are located at x_j's. That is,

$$r_{N-1}(x) = \sum_j r_{N-1}(x_j)L_j(x) = \sum_j f(x_j)L_j(x).$$

Therefore,

$$\int_a^b h(x)f(x)dx = \sum_j f(x_j) \int_a^b h(x)L_j(x)dx = \sum_j w_j f(x_j),$$

where $w_j = \int_a^b h(x)L_j(x)dx.$

Step 3: Further, we derive w_j in terms of orthogonal polynomials. Since x_j's are roots of $\phi_N(x)$, $\phi_N(x) = A_N \prod_i (x - x_i)$, while $\phi_N'(x_j) = A_N \prod_{i, i \neq j}(x_j - x_i)$. Note that A_N is the coefficient of x^N in $\phi_N(x)$.

Therefore,

$$L_j(x) = \frac{\phi_N(x)}{(x-x_j)\phi'_N(x)}.$$

Using these properties, we deduce that

$$w_j = \int_a^b dx\, h(x) L_j(x) = \frac{1}{\phi'_N(x_j)} \int_a^b \frac{h(x)\phi_N(x)}{x-x_j} dx. \quad \ldots(30)$$

For further simplification, we employ Christoffel-Darboux identity:

$$\sum_{i=0}^{N} \frac{\phi_i(x)\phi_i(y)}{\gamma_i} = \frac{\phi_{N+1}(x)\phi_N(y) - \phi_N(x)\phi_{N+1}(y)}{a_N \gamma_N (x-y)},$$

where $a_m = A_{m+1}/A_m$, and γ_N is a constant of orthogonality relation (see Eq. (26)). In Christoffel-Darboux identity, substitution of $y = x_j$, a zero of $\phi_N(x)$, yields

$$\sum_{i=0}^{N} \frac{\phi_i(x)\phi_i(x_j)}{\gamma_i} = -\frac{\phi_N(x)\phi_{N+1}(x_j)}{a_N \gamma_N (x-x_j)}.$$

We multiply the above equation with $h(x)\phi_0(x)$ and integrate in the interval $[a,b]$. In addition, we employ the orthogonality property and the fact that $\phi_0(x)$ is a constant. Consequently the above equation simplifies to

$$\frac{\phi_0(x_j)\gamma_0}{\gamma_0} = -\frac{\phi_{N+1}(x_j)}{a_N \gamma_N}\phi_0(x) \int_a^b dx\, \frac{h(x)\phi_N(x)}{(x-x_j)}.$$

Hence,

$$\int_a^b dx\, \frac{h(x)\phi_N(x)}{(x-x_j)} = -\frac{a_N \gamma_N}{\phi_{N+1}(x_j)},$$

substitution of which in Eq. (30) yields the weights as

$$w_j = -\frac{a_N \gamma_N}{\phi'_N(x_j)\phi_{N+1}(x_j)},$$

which is same as Eq. (27). This completes the derivation of Gauss quadrature formulas. Gaussian quadrature with N abscissas and roots is exact when $f(x)$ is a polynomial of order $2N-1$ or lower.

Errors in Gaussian Quadrature

When $f(x)$ is a polynomial of degree higher than $2N-1$, the integral with the quotient (Eq. (29)) is not zero. This integral is the error. A division of a general $f(x)$ with $\phi_N(x)$ yields

$$f(x) = q(x)\phi_N(x) + r_{N-1}(x),$$

where $q(x) = \sum_j b_j \phi_j(x)$. Therefore, the integral of Eq. (29) gets contributions from $q(x) = b_N \phi_N(x)$ and becomes

$$\int_a^b h(x)q(x)\phi_N(x)dx = b_N \gamma_N.$$

This is the error in the integral. The other terms of $q(x)$ ($j \neq N$) vanish due to the orthogonality properties of the polynomials. After algebraic manipulation we derive the error as

$$E_{int} = \frac{\gamma_N}{A_N^2 (2N)!} f^{(2N)}(\zeta), \quad \dots (31)$$

where ζ is an intermediate point in [a.b].

In the following discussion, we discuss specific implementations of Gaussian quadrature.

Legendre-Gauss Quadrature

For Gauss quadrature with finite a and b, it is best to employ Legendre polynomials ($G_n(x)$) whose orthogonality properties are

$$\int_{-1}^{1} G_i(x)G_j(x)dx = \frac{2}{2j+1}\delta_{ij}.$$

Thus, when $a = -1$, $b = 1$, we observe that $h(x) = 1$, $\gamma_j = 2/(2j+1)$. In Table 18, we list the Legendre polynomials $G_0(x)$, ..., $G_5(x)$; these polynomials are also depicted in Figure 67. This method is called Gauss-Legendre quadrature.

Table 18: Legendre polynomials

$G_0(x) = 1$	$G_3(x) = \frac{1}{2}(5x^3 - 3x)$
$G_1(x) = x$	$G_4(x) = \frac{1}{8}(65x^5 - 70x^3 + 15x)$
$G_2(x) = \frac{1}{2}(3x^2 - 1)$	$G_5(x) = \frac{1}{8}(231x^6 - 315x^4 + 105x^2 + 5)$

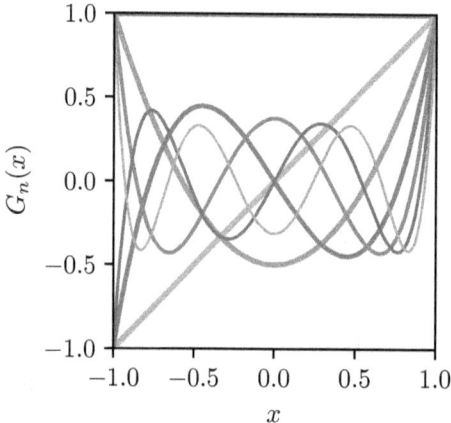

Figure 67: Plots of Legendre polynomials $G_0(x)$ .. $G_6(x)$ by curves with decreasing line thickness.

It can be shown that

$$A_j = \frac{(2j)!}{2^j(j!)^2}, \quad a_N = \frac{2}{N+1}.$$

Using the above properties and an identity

$$(1 - x^2)G'_j(x) = (j+1)x G_j(x) - (j+1)G_{j+1}(x),$$

we can show that

$$w_j = \frac{2}{(1 - x_j^2)[G'_N(x_j)]^2}.$$

The roots x_j and the weights w_j can be computed using the polynomials. In Table 19, we list them for $N = 1$ to 5. Python's module scipy.special.roots_legendre() provides these quantities (see the Python code below). Note that the weights and abscissas of Example 1 match with that shown in Table 19.

Table 19: The roots of Legendre polynomials, and the weights for the Gaussian quadrature

N	x_j	w_j
2	$\pm 1/\sqrt{3}$	1
3	0	8/9
	$\pm 1/\sqrt{(3/5)}$	5/9
4	± 0.339981	0.347855
	± 0.861136	0.568889
5	0	128/225
	± 0.538467	0.478629
	± 0.90618	0.236927

To employ Gauss Quadrature $\int_a^b f(x')dx'$ for an arbitrary interval $[a,b]$, we employ a liner transformation $x' = \alpha x + \beta$ and impose the condition that $x' = a \rightarrow x = -1$ and $x' = b \rightarrow x = 1$. Consequently, $\alpha = (b-a)/2$ and $\beta = (b+a)/2$. Therefore,

$$I = \int_a^b f(x')dx' = \frac{b-a}{2}\int_{-1}^1 f(\alpha x + \beta)dx \quad \dots(32)$$

Now the above integral can be computed using Legendre polynomials in the interval $[-1,1]$.

Example 2: We compute $\int_{-1}^{1} x^8 dx$ using Gauss quadrature. The actual answer is 2/9. For the Gauss quadrature described above, for N=2,3,4,5, the errors are −0.19753086419753085, −0.07822222222222211, −0.01160997732426308, and 0 respectively. This is consistent with the fact that Gaussian quadrature for $N = 5$ is exact for any polynomial of degree 9 or lower. For the above computation, we use the following code:

```
from scipy.special import roots_legendre
def f(x):
    return x**8

for n in range(2,6):
    xi = roots_legendre(n)[0]
    wi = roots_legendre(n)[1]
    yi = f(xi)

    In = sum(yi*wi)
    print(n, In, In-2/9)
```

Note that *scipy.special.roots_legendre*(n) returns a tuple whose elements are the roots and weights of $P_n(x)$.

Example 3: We compute $\int_0^1 \exp(x) dx$ numerically. The actual answer is $e-1$. However, for N=2,3,4,5, the Gauss quadrature of Eq. (32) yields approximate integral with errors of −0.0003854504515410362, −8.240865234654393e−07, −9.329670369595533e−10, −6.534772722943671e−13. Note that the Gaussian quadrature is quite accurate with just 5 points.

Laguerre-Gauss Quadrature

We often encounter integral of the form

$$\int_0^\infty e^{-x} f(x) dx. \quad \ldots(33)$$

The above computation using Newton-Cote's scheme will be very expensive because we have to take many intervals to reach x = ∞ (effectively a large number). Laguerre-Gauss quadrature offers an attractive option.

Table 20: Laguerre polynomials

$L_0(x) = 1$	$L_2(x) = \frac{1}{2}(x^2 - 4x + 2)$
$L_1(x) = -x + 1$	$L_3(x) = \frac{1}{6}(-x^3 + 9x^2 - 18x + 6)$

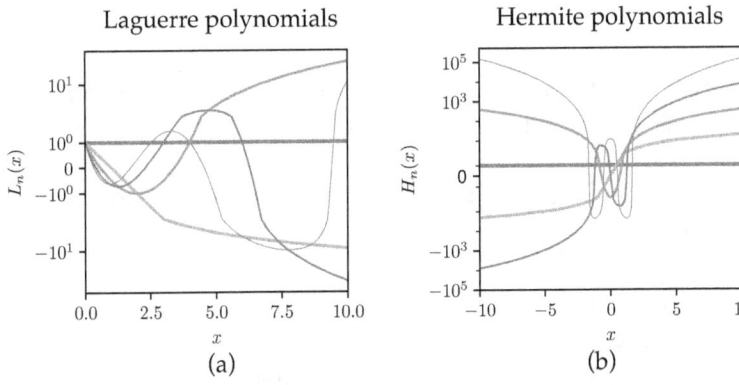

Figure 68: Plots of (a) Laguerre polynomials and (b) Hermite polynomials in semiology format. The thickness of the curves decreases with the increase of the order of the polynomials.

For the above integral, we employ Laguerre polynomials ($L_m(x)$) whose orthogonality relation is

$$\int_0^\infty e^{-x} L_i(x) L_j(x) dx = \delta_{i,j}.$$

Therefore, $a = 0$, $b = \infty$, $h(x) = e^{-x}$, and $\gamma_j = 1$. Some of the low-order Laguerre polynomials are listed Table 20 and exhibited in Figure 68(a). Since the values of the functions are quite large, we employ *plt.yscale('symlog')* for plotting both positive and negative numbers in logscale.

These polynomials satisfy the properties: $A_j = (-1)^j/j!$ and $a_N = -1/(N+1)$. The weights for the Laguerre-Gauss quadrature are

$$w_j = \frac{1}{(N+1)L'_N(x_j)L_{N+1}(x_j)} = -\frac{1}{NL_{N-1}(x_j)L'_N(x_j)}.$$

Using the above ingredients and the identity

$$x_j L'_N(x_j) = -NL_{N-1}(x_j) = (N+1)L_{N+1}(x_j),$$

we deduce that

$$w_j = \frac{1}{x_j[L'_N(x_j)]^2} = \frac{x_j}{(N+1)^2[L_{N+1}(x_j)]^2}.$$

The roots x_j and the weights w_j of leading-order Laguerre-Gauss polynomials are listed in Table 21.

Table 21: Roots of Laguerre polynomials, and the weights for Gaussian quadrature.

N	x_j	w_j
2	0.585786	0.853553
	3.41421	0.146447
3	0.415775	0.711093
	2.29428	0.278518
	6.28995	0.0103893
4	0.322548	0.603154
	1.74576	0.357419
	4.53662	0.0388879
	9.39507	0.000539295
5	0.26356	0.521756
	1.4134	0.398667
	3.59643	0.0759424
	7.08581	0.00361176
	12.6408	0.00002337

Now, using the x_j's and w_j's we compute the integral

$$\int_0^\infty e^{-x} f(x) dx = \sum_{j=0}^{N-1} w_j f(x_j).$$

Example 4: Let us compute $\int_0^\infty \exp(-x) x^n dx$ using Lagurre-Gauss quadrature. The exact value of the integral is $n!$. For $n = 4$, the integral with two points $N=2$ is 20.000000000000007, which is incorrect. However, the quadrature yields 24, correct result, for $N=3$ and beyond. Similarly, for x^9, the quadrature yields correct value for $N = 5$ and beyond.

Example 5: For a stationary state of Hydrogen atom, the average value (or expectation value) of function $f(r)$, $\langle f(r) \rangle$, is defined as

$$\langle f(r) \rangle = \int d\mathbf{r} f(r) |\psi(\mathbf{r})|^2,$$

where $\psi(\mathbf{r})$ is the wave function. The ground state of the H-atom is $\psi_{1,0,0} = \dfrac{1}{\sqrt{\pi}} \exp(-r')$, where $r' = r/r_a$ is nondimensional radius with r_a is the Bohr radius. For this state,

$$\langle r' \rangle = \frac{1}{\pi} \int_0^\infty e^{-2r'} 4\pi (r')^3 dr' = \frac{4}{16} \int_0^\infty e^{-2r'} (2r')^3 d(2r'),$$

which has the same form as Eq. (33). We compute the above integral using Laguerre-Gauss quadrature that yields $\langle r' \rangle = 3/2$ or $\langle r \rangle = (3/2) r_a$. Similarly, we can derive that

$$\langle \frac{1}{r'} \rangle = \frac{1}{\pi} \int_0^\infty e^{-2r'} 4\pi r' dr' = \frac{4}{4} \int_0^\infty e^{-2r'} (2r') d(2r') = 1.$$

Therefore, the average potential energy is $\langle U \rangle = (-e^2/r_a)\langle 1/r' \rangle = -(e^2/r_a)$. Virial theorem tells us that the average kinetic energy $\langle KE \rangle = -\frac{1}{2} \langle U \rangle$. Therefore, the average energy of Hydrogen atom, $\langle E_0 \rangle = \langle U \rangle + \langle KE \rangle$

$= -(e^2/2r_a)$. The other quantities can be computed in a similar manner. Note that $\langle 1/r \rangle \neq 1/\langle r \rangle$.

Example 6: We compute the average radius, $\langle r \rangle$, for Hydrogen atom's $\psi_{2,0,0}$ state, whose normalised wave function (Section 9.2) is

$$\psi_{2,0,0} = \frac{1}{\sqrt{32\pi}}(2 - r')\exp(-r'/2).$$

For this state, we find that

$$\langle r' \rangle = \frac{1}{32\pi} \int_0^\infty e^{-r'}(2-r')^2 4\pi (r')^3 dr' = 6$$

Hence, $\langle r \rangle = 6\, r_a$. Similarly, we find that $\langle 1/r' \rangle = 1/4$. Hence $\langle U \rangle = (-e^2/r_a)\langle 1/r' \rangle = (-e^2/4r_a)$ and $\langle E \rangle = (-e^2/8r_a) = \langle E_0 \rangle /4$.

Hermite-Gauss Quadrature

For integrals of the form $\int_{-\infty}^{\infty} e^{-x^2} f(x) dx$, we employ Hermite's polynomials that satisfy the following orthogonal relation:

$$\int_{-\infty}^{\infty} e^{-x^2} H_i(x) H_j(x) dx = j!\sqrt{2\pi}\delta_{ij}.$$

Hence, $a = -\infty$, $b = \infty$, $h(x) = \exp(-x^2)$, $\gamma_j = j!\sqrt{(2\pi)}$. Some of the low-order Legendre polynomials are listed in Table 22, and depicted in Figure 68(b).

For the Hermite-Gauss quadrature, the weights w_j are

$$w_j = \frac{2^{N-1} N! \sqrt{\pi}}{N^2 [H_{N-1}(x_j)]^2},$$

which are listed in Table 23 along with the abscissas.

Table 22: Hermite polynomials

$H_0(x) = 1$

$H_1(x) = 2x$

$H_2(x) = 4x^2 - 2$

$H_3(x) = 8x^3 - 12x$

$H_4(x) = 16x^4 - 48x^2 + 12$

$H_5(x) = 32x^5 - 160x^3 + 120x$

Table 23: The roots and weights of Hermite polynomials

N	x_j	w_j
2	$\pm(\sqrt{2})/2$	$(\sqrt{\pi})/2$
3	0	$2(\sqrt{\pi})/3$
	$\pm(\sqrt{6})/2$	$(\sqrt{\pi})/6$
4	± 0.524648	0.804914
	± 1.65068	0.0813128
5	0	0.945309
	± 0.958572	0.393619
	± 2.02018	0.0199532

Example 7: Let us compute $\int_{-\infty}^{\infty} \exp(-x^2) x^4 dx$ using Hermite-Gauss quadrature. The exact value of the integral is $(3/4)\sqrt{\pi}$. Numerical computation yields the correct result for $N = 3$ and beyond. For $N = 2$, the numerical integral yields 0.4431134627263788. For $\int_{-\infty}^{\infty} \exp(-x^2) x^n dx$, the quadrature will yield a correct value when $N = (n/2)+1$ and beyond.

Example 8: Hermite-Gauss quadrature is useful for solving quantum oscillator. We take the wave functions of the oscillator given in Section 9.2 and compute $\langle f(x) \rangle$ for ψ_n using

$$\langle f_n(x) \rangle = \int dx f(x) |\psi_n(x)|^2$$

We observe that $\langle 1 \rangle = 1$, indicating normalization of the wave functions. In addition, we observe that for ψ_n, $\langle x^2 \rangle = n+½$. Therefore, average potential potential energy $\langle U \rangle = \langle x^2 \rangle/2 = (n+½)/2$. Using Virial theorem, we infer that $\langle T \rangle = \langle U \rangle = (n+½)/2$. Hence, the total energy = $\langle T \rangle + \langle U \rangle = (n+½)$. In dimensional form, the total energy for ψ_n is $(n+½)\hbar\omega$.

In summary, Gaussian quadratures are much more accurate than the Newton-Cotes methods. In the next section, we will cover multidimensional integration.

****

Conceptual Questions

1. Why is Gaussian quadrature more accurate than Newton-Cotes method?
2. With N data points, list the polynomials that can be integrated accurately using Gaussian quadrature.
3. Derive the expression for the error in Gaussian quadrature (Eq. (31)).
4. Study about Chebyshev-Gauss quadrature.

Exercises

1. Integrate $\int_0^5 (x^6 - 5x^5 + 3)dx$ using Gauss quadrature with $N = 2,3,4,5$ knots and compare the results with the exact ones. Compare the accuracy of the results with those from Newton-Cotes schemes.
2. Compute the following integrals using Gauss quadrature: $\int_0^\infty \exp(-x)(x^6 - 5x^5 + 3)dx$ and $\int_0^\infty \exp(-x^2)(x^6 - 5x^5 + 3)dx$. How many knots do you need for the accurate integration of the above?
3. Integrate $\int_0^\infty \frac{x^3}{\exp(x) - 1} dx$ using Gaussian quadrature. This

integral appears in black-body spectrum.

4. Integrate $\int_0^1 \frac{x^4 \exp(x)}{(\exp(x)-1)^2} dx$ using Gaussian quadrature.

5. Integrate $\int_0^1 \frac{\sin(x)}{x} dx$, $\int_0^1 \exp(-x)\cos(x) dx$, $\int_0^\infty \exp(-x)\cos(x) dx$ using Gaussian quadrature.

6. Consider the wave functions $\psi_{2,1,0}$ and $\psi_{2,1,\pm 1}$ of Hydrogen atom. Show that these wave functions are normalised. Compute the average radii and energies for these quantum states. It is best to work with nondimensionalized wave functions.

7. Consider the ground state and the first, second, and third excited states of quantum oscillator. Compute $\langle x^3 \rangle$, $\langle x^4 \rangle$, $\langle x^6 \rangle$, and $\langle x^8 \rangle$ for the above wave functions. Work with nondimensionalized wave functions.

8. Consider the ground state of a two-dimensional linear quantum oscillator. Compute the energy of this state.

9. Compute the time period of a particle of mass m and energy E that executes a periodic motion in the following potentials:
    - (a) $U(x) = -U_0/\cosh^2 x$ with $-U_0 < E < 0$
    - (b) $U(x) = U_0 \tan^2 x$

11.3 Python's Quad & Multidimensional Integrals

In this section, we will describe how to compute multidimensional integrals using computers, and how to compute integrals using Python's *quad* functions. At the end, we illustrate how to deal with complex integrals.

Multidimensional Integrals

It is quite straightforward to generalise 1D quadrature schemes to higher dimensions. In the following discussion we illustrate how to compute the 2D integral $\int_a^b dx \int_0^{g(x)} dy f(x,y)$. We illustrate the computational domain (xy plane) in Figure 69. Here, the x coordinate varies from a to b, while, for a given x, the y coordinate varies from 0 to $g(x)$.

As shown in the figure, for the x integral, we choose abscissas at $\{x_0, x_1, \ldots, x_{n-1}\}$. After that, at each abscissa, we choose knots along the y direction. The coordinates of y-abscissas are $\{y_0, y_1, \ldots, y_{m-1}\}$. Now, the integral is performed as follows:

$$\int_a^b dx \int_0^{g(x)} dy f(x,y) = \sum_i w_i \int_0^{g(x)} dy f(x_i, y) = \sum_i w_i \sum_j w_{i,j} f(x_i, y_j).$$

Note that the weights along the y-direction will depend on the x coordinate. The above formula can be implemented using 1D integrals discussed earlier. Also, we can easily generalise the above formalism to three and higher dimensions.

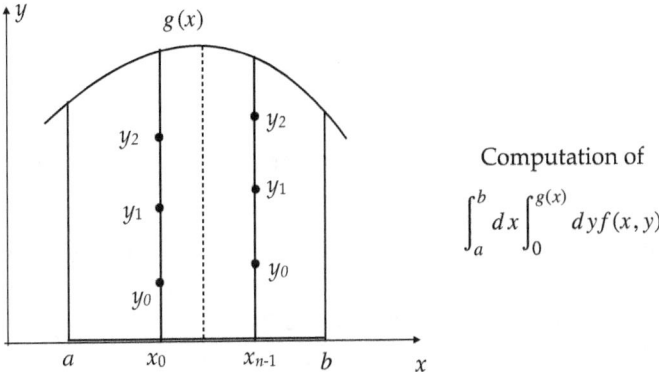

Figure 69: A diagram illustrating how to perform a 2D quadrature. We compute the function at the dotted points.

Python Functions for Integration

Fortunately, Python offers functions for numerical integration. Python's function *quad* (a part of *scipy.integrate* module) computes 1D integrals using Gaussian quadrature:

```
quad(function, lower_lim, upper_lim)
```

The usage of the function is as follow.

```
from scipy.integrate import quad
print (quad(lambda x: x², 0,1))   # 1D
```

The above code computes $\int_0^1 x^2 dx$ and yields ⅓ as an answer.

For 2D and 3D integrals, the corresponding functions are *dblquad* and *tplquad* respectively. In the following, *dblquad* and *tplquad* compute the following integrals:

$$\int_0^1 dx \int_0^x dy\, (xy); \qquad \int_0^1 dx \int_0^x dy \int_0^{x+y} dz\,(xyz).$$

```
from scipy.integrate import dblquad, tplquad

print (dblquad(lambda x,y: x*y, 0, 1, 0, lambda x: x))

print (tplquad(lambda x,y,z: x*y*z, 0, 1, 0, lambda x: x,
0, lambda x,y: x+y))
```

In the above examples, the lambda functions provide convenient means to pass the functions and integral limits as anonymous functions. The results from Python are 1/8 and 0.11805555555555555 (17/144), which are exact values of the integrals.

We also point out that *quad()* can handle improper integrals (whose one or both the limits are ∞ or −∞). For example,

```
In [121]: print(quad(lambda x: np.exp(-x**2), 0, inf))
(0.8862269254527579, 7.101318390472462e-09)
```

Here, the tuple contains the value of the integral and the associated error.

Python's functions *trapz* and *simps* integrate numerical data using trapezoid and Simpson's rules. For example,

```
In [92]: y = [1,2,3]
In [94]: from scipy.integrate import simps
In [95]: simps(y)
Out[95]: 4.0
```

Here, h is assumed to be unity. We could also give sampling points as arguments of *simps* and *trapz*. For example, for the abscissas at $x = $ [0.1, 0.2, 0.25], we employ the function *simps(y,x)* to compute the integral.

Important Tricks for Integral Computations

Even though *quad()* can handle improper and singular integrals, it is important to know how to handle such cases. In the following examples, we will illustrate some of the tricks for computing such integrals.

Example 1: For the integral $\int_0^\infty \exp(-x^2)dx$, one of the limits is at ∞. To avoid ∞, we make a change of variable $y = x/(1+x)$. In terms of y, the integral is

$$\int_0^1 \frac{\exp(-(y/(1-y))^2)}{(1-y)^2} dy, \quad \ldots(34)$$

which has finite limits. Incidentally, both the integrals, $\int_0^\infty \exp(-x^2)dx$ and Eq. (34), can be computed quite easily using Gauss quadrature.

Example 2: To evaluate $\int_1^\infty \frac{\exp(-x)}{(1+x)^2} dx$, we rewrite the integral as

$$\int_1^\infty \frac{\exp(-x)}{(1+x)^2} dx = \int_0^\infty \frac{\exp(-x)}{(1+x)^2} dx - \int_0^1 \frac{\exp(-x)}{(1+x)^2} dx$$

It is best to compute the first integral using Laguerre-Gauss quadrature and the second using Legendre-Gauss quadrature.

Example 3: The integral $\int_0^{\pi/2} \frac{\cos(x)}{x^{1/3}} dx$ is singular at $x = 0$. That is, the integrand $\to \infty$ as $x \to \infty$. We can avoid singularity by subtraction or by performing the integral by parts. The former trick is as follows:

$$\int_0^{\pi/2} \frac{\cos(x)}{x^{1/3}} dx = \int_0^{\pi/2} \frac{\cos(x) - 1}{x^{1/3}} dx + \int_0^{\pi/2} \frac{1}{x^{1/3}} dx$$

The first term is nonsingular. The second term, though singular, is easy to integrate.

Another way to solve the above integral is as follows. We employ integration by parts that yields

$$\int_0^{\pi/2} \frac{\cos(x)}{x^{1/3}} dx = \frac{3}{2} x^{2/3} \cos(x) \Big|_0^{\pi/2} + \frac{3}{2} \int_0^{\pi/2} x^{2/3} \sin(x) dx$$

In the above equation, the first term is zero, while the second term is nonsingular.

With this, we end our discussions on numerical integration.

****

Exercises

1. Compute the following integrals numerically:
   - $\int_0^1 \dfrac{x^4 \exp(x)}{(\exp(x) - 1)^2} dx$
   - $\int_0^\infty \dfrac{x^3}{\exp(x) - 1} dx$
   - $\int_0^\infty \exp(-x)(x^6 - 5x^5 + 3) dx$
   - $\int_0^1 dx \int_0^{x^2} dy \, \sin^2(xy)$
   - $\int_0^1 dx \int_0^x dy \int_0^{x+y} dz (x^2 y^3 z^4)$

2. Compute the integrals of Examples 1, 2, and 3 of this section.

3. Compute the following singular integral $\int_0^{\pi/2} \dfrac{\cos^2(x)}{x^{1/2}} dx.$

Chapter Twelve
NUMERICAL DIFFERENTIATION

Synopsis

"Nothing takes place in the world whose meaning is not that of some maximum or minimum."
— Leonhard Euler

This chapter describes numerical derivatives.

12.1 Computing Numerical Derivatives

Differentiation, which is inverse of integration, is an important operation in science and engineering. For example, the velocity of a particle is computed by taking derivative of its position. The population growth growth is computed by taking derivative of the population data. Also, physical systems are often described using differential equations where derivatives play an important role. In this chapter we will focus on numerical differentiation.

According to Newton and Leibniz, the derivative of a function $f(x)$ is

$$f'(x) = \lim_{h \to 0} \frac{f(x+h) - f(x)}{h}.$$

Mathematically, $h \to 0$, but h remains finite (but small) in numerical computations. Hence, numerical $f'(x)$ is an approximation of the actual derivative. To derive a simple formula for $f'(x)$, we start with the Lagrange polynomial with two points (x_i, x_{i+1}).

$$f(x) \approx P_2(x) = \frac{x - x_{i+1}}{x_i - x_{i+1}} f_i + \frac{x - x_i}{x_{i+1} - x_i} f_{i+1}.$$

The derivatives of the above function at both the points, x_i and x_{i+1}, are the same. Yet, by notation, we write them as

Forward difference: $f'(x_i) \approx P'_2(x_i) = D_+ f = \dfrac{f_{i+1} - f_i}{h_i}$,

Backward difference: $f'(x_{i+1}) \approx P'_2(x_{i+1}) = D_- f = \dfrac{f_{i+1} - f_i}{h_i}$,

where $h_i = x_{i+1} - x_i$. Here, the *forward difference* is the derivative computed at x_i looking toward the forward point x_{i+1}. The *backward difference* is the derivative computed at x_{i+1} looking backwards towards x_i. See Figure 70 for an illustration. The computed derivatives or slopes (the dashed lines of the figure) are approximations to the actual derivatives (solid lines).

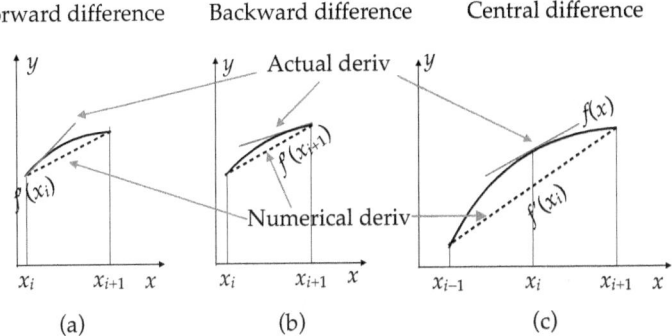

Figure 70: Schematic diagrams exhibiting (a) forward difference, (b) backward difference, and (c) central difference. The tangent lines are the actual derivatives, while the dashed lines represent the numerically-computed derivatives.

The accuracy of the derivatives improves with more number of points. We employ second-order Lagrange polynomial passing through three points (x_{i-1}, x_i, x_{i+1}):

$$f(x) \approx P_3(x) = \frac{(x - x_i)(x - x_{i+1})}{(h_{i-1} + h_i)(h_{i-1})} f_{i-1} + \frac{(x - x_{i-1})(x - x_{1+1})}{h_{i-1}(-h_i)} f_i$$

$$+ \frac{(x - x_{i-1})(x - x_i)}{(h_{i-1} + h_i)(h_i)} f_{i+1} \ldots (35)$$

The first and second derivatives of the above function at x_i are

$$f'(x_i) \approx P_2'(x_i) = -\frac{h_i}{(h_{i-1} + h_i)(h_{i-1})} f_{i-1} + \left(\frac{1}{h_{i-1}} - \frac{1}{h_i}\right) f_i + \frac{h_{i-1}}{(h_{i-1} + h_i)(h_i)} f_{i+1}$$

$$f''(x_i) \approx P_2'(x_i) = \frac{2}{(h_{i-1} + h_i)(h_{i-1})} f_{i-1} - \frac{2}{h_{i-1} h_i} f_i + \frac{2}{(h_{i-1} + h_i)(h_i)} f_{i+1}$$

The aforementioned complex expressions get simplified when the points are equidistant, that is, when $h_{i-1} = h_i = h$. Under this assumption, the first derivatives at the three points are

Forward difference: $f'(x_{i-1}) = D_+ f = \dfrac{-3f_{i-1} + 4f_i - f_{i+1}}{2h}$,

Backward difference: $f'(x_{i+1}) = D_- f = \dfrac{f_{i-1} - 4f_i + 3f_{i+1}}{2h}$,

Central difference: $f'(x_i) = \dfrac{1}{2}(D_+ + D_-)f = \dfrac{f_{i+1} - f_{i-1}}{2h}$.

The second derivatives at the three points are equal (see Eq. (35)):

$$f''(x_i) = \dfrac{f_{i+1} - 2f_i + f_{i-1}}{h^2}.$$

Note the usefulness of Lagrange interpolation formulas for the derivative computations.

We can generalise the above formulas to n points. The formulas for the qth derivatives ($q=1,2,3$) at $x = x_j$ are as follows:

Forward difference: $f^{(q)}(x_j) = \dfrac{1}{h^q} \sum\limits_{m=0}^{n-1} C_m f_{j+m}$

Backward difference: $f^{(q)}(x_j) = \dfrac{(-1)^q}{h^q} \sum\limits_{m=0}^{n-1} C_m f_{j-m}$

Central difference: $f^{(q)}(x_j) = \dfrac{1}{h^q} \sum\limits_{m=(1-n)/2}^{(n-1)/2} C_m f_{j-m}$

where the coefficients C_m are listed in Tables 24 and 25. As shown in the Table, C_m's follow the following properties.

1. The central difference scheme requires odd number of points.
2. The coefficients for the backward difference are related to those for the forward difference. For the first derivative using backward method, we read the coefficients of Table 24 from right to left but with sign reversed.
3. Note that $\sum C_m = 0$. It follows from the fact that the derivatives of a constant is zero.
4. The coefficients for the central difference are symmetric around the central point.

Table 24: Coefficients for the forward difference scheme.

C_0	C_1	C_2	C_3	C_4	C_5	C_6	C_7
$f'(x)$							
-1	1						
-3/2	2	-½					
-11/6	3	-3/2	⅓				
-25/12	4	-3	4/3	-1/4			
-137/60	5	-5	10/3	-5/4	1/5		
$f''(x)$							
1	-2	1					
2	-5	4	-1				
35/12	-26/3	19/2	-14/3	11/12			
15/4	-77/6	107/6	-13	61/12	-5/6		
203/45	-87/5	117/4	-254/9	33/2	-27/5	137/180	
$f'''(x)$							
-1	3	-3	1				
-5/2	9	-12	7	-3/2			
-17/4	71/4	-59/2	49/2	-41/4	7/4		
-49/8	29	-461/8	62	-307/8	13	-15/8	
-967/120	638/15	-3929/40	389/3	-2545/24	268/5	-1849/120	29/15

Table 25: Coefficients for the central difference scheme.

	C_{-4}	C_{-3}	C_{-2}	C_{-1}	C_0	C_1	C_2	C_3	C_4
$f'(x)$									
	-			-½	0	½			
			1/12	-2/3	0	2/3	-1/1		
		-1/6	3/20	-3/4	0	3/4	-3/2	1/60	
$f''(x)$									
				1	-2	1			
			-1/1	4/3	-5/2	4/3	-1/1		
		1/90	-3/2	3/2	-49/	3/2	-3/2	1/90	
$f'''(x)$									
			-½	1	0	-1	½		
		1/8	-1	13/8	0	-13/	1	-1/8	
	-7/240	3/10	-169/120	61/30	0	-61/30	169/120	-3/10	7/240

Errors in the Derivatives

We can estimate the errors in the numerical derivatives using the error formula for the Lagrange polynomials, which is Eq. (18) of Section 10.1. For n data points, the error is

$$E_n(x) = f(x) - P_n(x) = \frac{f^{(n)}(\zeta)}{n!} \prod_i (x - x_i)$$

Therefore, the error in the derivative computation is

$$f'(x_j) - P'_n(x_j) = \frac{d}{dx}E_n(x)|_{x=x_j} = \frac{f^{(n)}(\zeta)}{n!}\frac{d}{dx}\prod_i(x-x_i)$$

$$= \frac{f^{(n)}(\zeta)}{n!}\prod_{i,i\neq j}(x_j - x_i) \quad ...(36)$$

For equidistant points, the above error is $O(h^{n-1})$. We deduce this result using dimensional counting. The error formula also tells us that the first-derivative computed using n points is accurate for any polynomial of degree $(n-1)$. Also, by taking derivatives of Eq. (36), we derive that the errors in the computation of $f''(x)$ and $f'''(x)$ are $O(h^{n-2})$ and $O(h^{n-3})$ respectively.

Derivation Using Taylor Series

We can also derive the formulas for the derivatives using Taylor's series, which is

$$f(x \pm h) = f(x) \pm hf'(x) + \frac{h^2}{2}f''(x) \pm ....$$

Using the above formula we derive that

a $f(x-h)$ + b $f(x)$ + c $f(x+h)$ = $(a+b+c)f(x)$+ $(c-a)h\,f'(x)$
+ $(c+a)f'(x)\,h^2/2 + (c-a)f''(x)\,h^3/6 + ...$

For derivation of $f'(x)$ up to $O(h^2)$, we set

$a+b+c = 0$; $c-a = 1/h$; and $c+a = 0$.

whose solution is $b = 0$, $c = 1/(2h)$, and $a = -1/(2h)$. Hence,

$$f'(x_i) = \frac{f(x+h)-f(x-h)}{2h} = \frac{f_{i+1}-f_{i-1}}{2h}$$

with error as $(c-a)f'''(x)\,h^3/6 = f'''(x)\,h^2/6$. Using similar analysis, we can also calculate a formula for $f''(x)$.

It may be tempting to employ many points to compute the

derivatives. However, for large n with small h, the gains in accuracy is offset by the machine precision. For example, with 5 points and $h = 10^{-4}$, the error in derivatives is of the order of $h^4 \sim 10^{-16}$, which is close to machine precision. Hence, it is not advisable to use too many points for the derivative computations.

Using Python *Gradient* Function

Python's Numpy offers a function called *gradient* to compute numerical differences. For a given array, *gradient* computes second-order central differences in the interiors, and first- or second-order differences at the edges. The second argument of the gradient function is the spacing between the consecutive points.

```
In [207]: y
Out[207]: array([0.  , 0.25, 1.  ])

In [208]: gradient(y)   # first-derivative, same as
gradient(y,1)
Out[208]: array([0.25, 0.5 , 0.75])

In [210]: gradient(y,2) # gradient(y)/2
Out[210]: array([0.125, 0.25 , 0.375])
```

Example 1: We take $f(x) = x^2$ and compute the first and second derivatives using three points located at $x = 0$, ½, 1. The values of the function at these points are 0, 1/4, 1 respectively and h = ½. We employ the formulas of Tables 24 and 25 for derivative computations.

With two points, the forward first-order derivatives are

$f'(0) = (f(½) - f(0))/h = 0.5$ and
$f'(½) = (f(1) - f(½))/h = 1.5$,

while the backward first-order derivatives are

$f'(1) = (f(1) - f(1/2))/h = 1.5$ and
$f'(½) = (f(1/2) - f(0))/h = 0.5$.

All these derivatives differ from the exact values.
With three points, we obtain

forward difference $f'(0) = [-3 f(0) + 4f(½) - f(1)]/2h = 0$,

backward difference $f'(1) = [3 f(1) - 4f(½) + f(0)]/2h = 2$,

central difference $f'(1/2) = [f(1) - f(0)]/2h = 1$,

$f''(0) = f''(1/2) = f''(1) = [f(0) - 2f(½) + f(1)]/h^2 = 2$.

The derivatives with the three points are accurate. This is because the derivatives of a quadratic function can be computed exactly using three points.

Example 2: We compute the derivatives for $f(x) = \exp(x)$ using 3 points located at $x = 0, ½, 1$. The forward difference $f'(0)$, backward difference $f'(1)$, and central difference $f'(1/2)$ are 0.8766032543414677, 2.559960402576623, 1.718281828459045 respectively. They differ from the exact values. The second derivatives at these points are same (1.6833571482351548), and they too differ from the exact values.

We also remark that we can compute the accurate derivatives using Fourier transforms. We will discuss these computations in Chapter Fourteen. In addition, there are more complex and accurate methods, such as *compact schemes*. But, these topics are beyond the scope of this book.

In the next chapter, we will describe how to solve ordinary differential equations using computers.

****

Conceptual Questions

1. Why do the numerical derivatives have errors?
2. It is not recommended to use many points (say 8-10) for the derivative computations. Why?

3. Derive Eq. (36).
4. Derive a formula for the third derivative using four-point Lagrange interpolating polynomial.

Exercises

1. Discretize the function $f(x) = x^3$ using 2,3,4,5 points in $x = [0,1]$. Compute the first and second derivatives at each point using forward, backward, and central differences. Compute the errors in the computed derivatives, and compare them with the error laws discussed in this chapter. For what n do you expect accurate results?
2. Repeat Exercise 1 for $f(x) = 1/x$ in the interval $x = [1,2]$.
3. Repeat Exercise 1 for $f(x) = \sin x$ in the interval $x = [0, \pi/2]$.

CHAPTER THIRTEEN
ORDINARY DIFFERENTIAL EQUATION: INITIAL VALUE PROBLEMS

Synopsis

"An equation means nothing to me unless it expresses a thought of God." — Srinivas Ramanujan

In this chapter, we cover leading solvers of ordinary differential equations.

13.1 General Overview

Many natural laws are expressed using ordinary differential equations (ODE) and partial differential equations (PDE). For example, Newton's equation of motion is a second-order differential equation for the position of a particle. Schrödinger's equation, a PDE, describes the quantum world.The fluids flows in nature are described using Navier-Stokes equation. In this chapter we will describe how to solve ODEs using numerical algorithms. In Chapter Fifteen, Chapter Sixteen, and Chapter Nineteen, we will cover numerical solutions of PDEs.

Even though we come across differential equations of all orders in science and engineering, most of them are either first or second order equations. For example, Newton's equation of motion, $m\ddot{x} = F(x,\dot{x},t)$, is a second-order ODE in time; here, m and x are respectively the mass and position of the particle that is experiencing force $F(x,\dot{x},t)$. For numerical computations, it is convenient to work with first-order ODEs. Fortunately, a nth-order ODE can be reduced to n first-order ODEs. For example, $m\ddot{x} = F(x,t)$ is reduced to two first-order ODEs: $m\dot{x} = p$ and $\dot{p} = F(x,t)$.

A first-order ODE requires a single initial conditions, while n of them require n initial conditions. For example, Newton's equations, $m\dot{x} = p$ and $\dot{p} = F(x,t)$, require two initial conditions, $x(0)$ and $p(0)$. In this chapter, we solve ODEs for given initial conditions, hence such problems are referred to as *initial value problems*. In Chapter Eighteen, second order ODEs are solved using *boundary values*; such problems are referred to as *boundary value problems*.

In the following discussion, we will describe how to solve a first-order ODE numerically. Let us consider the following ODE with t as an independent variable and x as a dependent variable:

$$\frac{dx}{dt} = \dot{x} = f(x,t). \quad \ldots(37)$$

In this chapter, we solve the above equation given initial condition $x(t = 0)$.

For numerical computation of $x(t)$, we descretize the total time into $N-1$ steps with markers at $t_0, t_1, \ldots, t_n, t_{n+1}, \ldots, t_{N-1}$. We denote the variable x at these times as $x^{(0)}, x^{(1)}, \ldots, x^{(n)}, x^{(n+1)}, \ldots, x^{(N-1)}$. For simplicity, we assume the time markers to be equidistant with $t_{n+1} - t_n$

$= \Delta t$ for all n. See Figure 71 for an illustration. We contrast the dependent and independent variables using indices with superscripts and subscripts respectively.

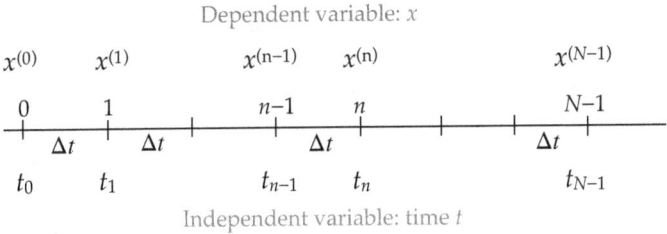

Figure 71: The total time is divided into $N-1$ steps. The time and x at the ith marker are t_i and $x^{(i)}$ respectively.

An integration of Eq. (37) from t_n to t_{n+1} yields

$$x^{(n+1)} - x^{(n)} = \int_{t_n}^{t_{n+1}} f(x,t) dt .$$

Now we employ some of the integration schemes studied in Section 11.1 to approximate the integral $\int_{t_n}^{t_{n+1}} f(x,t) dt$. The solution with different schemes are

Euler's forward method: $x^{(n+1)} = x^{(n)} + (\Delta t) f(x^{(n)}, t_n)$
Euler's backward method: $x^{(n+1)} = x^{(n)} + (\Delta t) f(x^{(n+1)}, t_{n+1})$
Midpoint method: $x^{(n+1)} = x^{(n)} + (\Delta t) f(x^{(n+\frac{1}{2})}, t_{n+\frac{1}{2}})$
Trapezoid method: $x^{(n+1)} = x^{(n)} + (\frac{1}{2})(\Delta t) [f(x^{(n)}, t_n) + f(x^{(n+1)}, t_{n+1})]$

These methods, called ODE solvers, prescribe how to advance from time t_n to t_{n+1}. We illustrate the *Euler forward*, *Euler backward*, and *midpoint methods* in Figure 72.

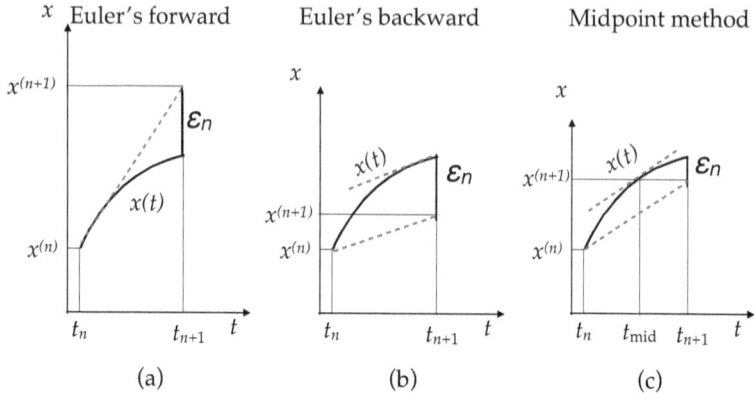

Figure 72: Schematic diagrams exhibiting (a) Euler's forward method, (b) Euler's backward method, and (c) midpoint method. The dashed lines are the actual slopes at the respective points. ε_n is the error between the actual value and the computed value at $t = t_{n+1}$.

In Euler's forward method, we compute $x^{(n+1)}$ using the slope at t_n. Since we go forward in time, the slope $f(x^{(n)}, t_n)$ can be easily computed. Such schemes are called *explicit schemes* because the unknown $x^{(n+1)}$ depends explicitly on the knowns: $x^{(n)}$, t_n, and t_{n+1}. The difference between the computed $x^{(n+1)}$ and the actual value, $f(x^{(n+1)}, t_{n+1})$ is the error ε_n.

In Euler's backward method, $x^{(n+1)}$ is computed using the slope $f(x^{(n+1)}, t_{n+1})$ at t_{n+1}. Since the slope depends on the unknown variable $f(x^{(n+1)}, t_{n+1})$ itself, this is an *implicit schemes*. In general, implicit schemes are more complex to implement.

In the *trapezoid method*, the slope is average of the slopes at $x^{(n)}$ and $x^{(n+1)}$. Therefore, this is called a *semi-implicit method*.

To advance from t_n to t_{n+1}, the *mid-point method* uses slope at $t_{n+\frac{1}{2}}$ and $x^{(n+\frac{1}{2})}$, which is an unknown; we need to come up with a way to estimate $x^{(n+\frac{1}{2})}$. However, an integration of Eq. (37) from t_{n-1} to t_{n+1} using midpoint method yields

$$x^{(n+1)} = x^{(n-1)} + (\Delta t) f(x^{(n)}, t_n).$$

This explicit scheme is called *Leapfrog method*. In a related method, a usage of Simpsons's ⅓ rule for the integration from t_{n-1} to t_{n+1} yields

$$x^{(n+1)} - x^{(n-1)} = \frac{1}{3}(\Delta t)\left[f(x^{(n-1)}, t_{n-1}) + 4f(x^{(n)}, t_n) + f(x^{(n+1)}, t_{n+1})\right].$$

In Leapfrog method, $x^{(n+1)}$ depends on $x^{(n)}$ and $x^{(n-1)}$, hence it is called multi-step method.

Later in this chapter, we will briefly describe all the above schemes. The next section covers Euler's forward method.

****

Conceptual Questions

1. Relate the ODE solvers to the numerical integration?
2. Why do the numerical solutions of ODEs have errors?
3. Derive an ODE solver that is based on Simpson's 3/8 rule.

13.2 Euler Forward Method, Accuracy & Stability

Euler's forward method is the simplest ODE solver. In this section we will solve the ODE $\dot{x} = f(x,t)$ using this method. The initial condition is $x(t = 0) = x^{(0)}$.

As described in the previous section, we descretize time into $N-1$ steps with markers at $t_0, t_1, \ldots, t_n, t_{n+1}, \ldots, t_{N-1}$. We time advance the ODE from t_0 to t_1 using

$$x^{(1)} = x^{(0)} + (\Delta t) f(x^{(0)}, t_0)$$

Similarly, we time advance the ODE from t_1 to t_2, ..., from t_n to t_{n+1}, ..., and finally, from t_{N-2} to t_{N-1}. The time stepping in the intermediate step is

$$x^{(n+1)} = x^{(n)} + (\Delta t) f(x^{(n)}, t_n)$$

The desired $x^{(N-1)}$ is the value of the dependent variable at $t = t_{N-1}$.

Example 1: We solve $\dot{x} = -x$ numerically using Euler's forward scheme described above. See the following Python code implementation of this scheme. The function, *Euler_explicit*, solves $\dot{x} = f(x,t)$ from $t = tinit$, to $t = tfinal$ with dt as the timestep. The numpy arrays t and x contain time and $x(t)$.

```
def f(x,t):
    return -100*x

def Euler_explicit(f, tinit, tfinal, dt, initcond):
    n = int((tfinal-tinit)/dt)+1    # n-1 divisions
    t = np.linspace(tinit,tfinal,n)
    x = np.zeros(n)
    x[0] = initcond

    for k in range(n-1):
        x[k+1] = x[k] + f(x[k],t[k])*dt
    return t,x
```

```
tinit = 0
tfinal = 1
dt = 0.01
initcond = 10
t,x = Euler_explicit(f, tinit, tfinal, dt, initcond)
```

We take $x(0) = 1$, final time = 10, and $(\Delta t) = 0.01$. The numerical result, shown in Figure 73(a) as a solid curve, matches quite well with the exact result $\exp(-t)$, which is shown as dashed curve.

Example 2: We solve $\dot{z} = -i\pi z$ numerically using $z(0) = 1$. The exact solution of this equation is $z(t) = \cos(\pi t) - i \sin(\pi t))$. We take the final time = 10, and $(\Delta t) = 0.01$. In Figure 73(b) we plot Im(z) vs. Re(z), where $z(t)$ is the numerical value of z at time t. The figure shows that $|z|$ increases with time. This is contrary to the exact solution for which $|z(t)| = 1$ (shown as dashed circle of radius 1). We will discuss the instability of the solution in later part of this section.

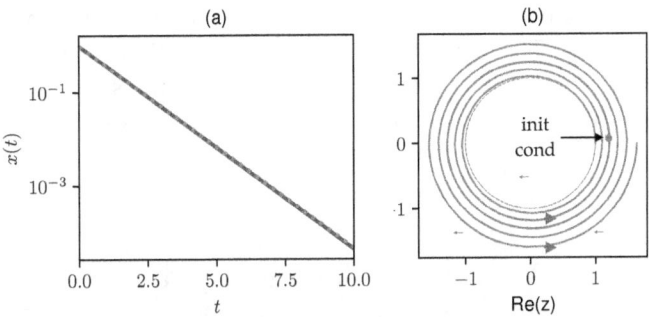

Figure 73: (a) Example 1: Plot of numerically-computed $x(t)$ vs. t (blue solid line). (b) Example 2: Plot of Im(z) vs. Re(z), shown using solid curve. In both the figures, the exact solutions are shown as dashed curves. In (a), the dashed curve is right on top of the solid curve.

Example 3: Let us take a nonlinear ODE, $\dot{x} = -t \exp(-x)$. We solve it numerically using Euler's forward scheme with $x(0) = 1$. We take final time = 2, and $(\Delta t) = 0.01$. The exact solution of the above equation is $x(t) = \log(e - t^2/2)$. In Figure 74(a) we plot the exact and numerical solutions, which are close to each other. We remark that the above solution is valid before the emergence of singularity at $t = \sqrt{2}e$.

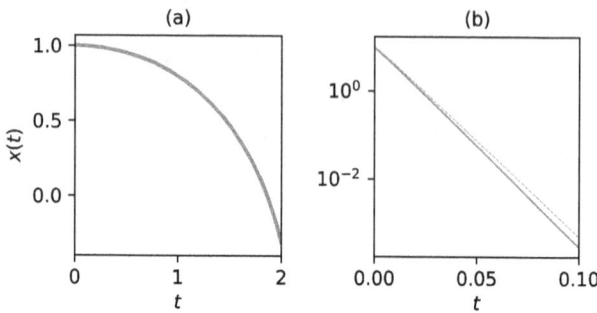

Figure 74: (a) Example 3 and (b) Example 4: Plots of numerically-computed $x(t)$ vs. t as solid curves and the exact solution as dashed curves.

Example 4: We solve another nonlinear ODE $\dot{x} = x^2 - 100x$ using $x(0)=10$ and $(\Delta t) = 0.001$. The exact solution is $x(t) = 100/(9 \exp(100\,t) - 1)$. In Figure 74(b) we exhibit the numerical and exact solutions. The numerical solution deviates slightly from the exact solution at late times.

Accuracy of Euler Method

Now we describe the errors in Euler's forward method. An application Taylor series yields,

$$x^{(n+1)} = x(t_n + \Delta t) = x(t_n) + (\Delta t)\dot{x}(t_n) + \frac{(\Delta t)^2}{2}\ddot{x}(t_n) + H.O.T.$$

$$= x^{(n)} + (\Delta t)f(x^{(n)}, t_n) + \frac{(\Delta t)^2}{2}\frac{df}{dt}\Big|_{t_n} + H.O.T. \quad ...(38)$$

where H.O.T. stands for higer order terms, and

$$df/dt = \partial_t f + \partial_x f \dot{x} = \partial_t f + f \partial_x f$$

Euler's forward method captures the first two terms of Eq. (38). Hence, for every time step, the error in this scheme is

$$\text{Error } \varepsilon_n = \text{Actual} - \text{Computed} = (½)(\Delta t)^2 \ddot{x}(x(n), t_n) \quad \ldots(39)$$

For Figure 72, $\ddot{x} < 0$ or $df/dt < 0$ due to negative curvature of $x(t)$. Hence, the above error is negative, or the actual value is lower than the numerical one. A question is whether the numerical errors would add up in every time step. Clearly, the error will accumulate if $x(t)$ is monotonic. This is an example of systematic error leading to the cumulative error in N steps (or in time T) as

$$\text{Net error} \approx (½)(\Delta t)(\Delta t) \ddot{x}(x(n), t_n) \approx (½) T (\Delta t) \ddot{x}(x(n), t_n).$$

However, if the curvature of $x(t)$ fluctuates significantly, then we expect the errors to be random, in which case

$$\text{Net error} \approx (½)N(\Delta t)(\Delta t) \ddot{x}(x(n), t_n) \sqrt{N} \approx (½)T (\Delta t) \ddot{x}(x(n), t_n)/\sqrt{N}$$

Example 5: Consider a DE $\dot{x} = \alpha x$ whose exact solution is $x(t) = x(0) \exp(\alpha t)$. In one step of this solution,

$$x^{(n+1)} = x^{(n)} \exp(\alpha(\Delta t)) = x^{(n)}(1 + \alpha(\Delta t) + (½)(\alpha(\Delta t))^2 + H.O.T.)$$

However, Euler's forward scheme yields $x^{(n+1)} = x^{(n)}(1+\alpha(\Delta t))$. Thus, to leading order, the error in this scheme is $(½)(\alpha(\Delta t))^2 x^{(n)}$, which is consistent with the formula of Eq. (39).

Stability of Euler Method

Stablity of an ODE is also an important issue. The notion of stability of an ODE differs from that of a dynamical system. We illustrate this concept for a simple ODE, $\dot{x} = \alpha x$. The stability of nonlinear DEs will be discussed after that.

The equation $\dot{x} = \alpha x$ has an exact solution, which is $x(t) = x(0) \exp(\alpha t)$. For $\alpha < 0$, the solution converges to zero as $t \to \infty$. We expect the numerical solution to converge in a similar manner. However, this is not guaranteed as we show below.

The solution of Euler's forward method, $x^{(n)} = x^{(0)} (1+\alpha(\Delta t))^n$, converges to zero asymptotically as long as $(\Delta t) < 2/|\alpha|$. However, for $|\alpha|(\Delta t) > 2$ or $(\Delta t) > 2/|\alpha|$ with $\alpha < 0$, $x^{(n)}$ oscillates around zero with its magnitude growing with time, which is contrary to the nature of the exact solution. Such a numerical scheme where numerical solution diverges contrary to the converging exact solution is called an *unstable scheme*. See Example 6 for an illustration. Note that for $\alpha > 0$, both exact and numerical solutions diverge. Clearly, the stability of ODEs are very different from that in mechanics, where a system is unstable if the fluctuations grow with time, and is stable otherwise.

Example 6: We analyse the stability of Euler's forward method for $\dot{x} = -100x$ ($\alpha = -100$). We solve the ODE using $\Delta t = 0.021$ and 0.001 and initial condition $x(0)=10$. For $\Delta t = 0.021$, $\alpha(\Delta t) = -2.1$. Hence, $x^{(n)} = x^{(0)} (1+\alpha(\Delta t))^n$ oscillates around 0, as shown in Figure 75. However, for $\Delta t = 0.001$, we find that $\alpha(\Delta t) = 0.1$, hence, the numerical solution (shown as the solid falling curve) is stable with the numerical result close to the exact result $10\exp(-100t)$.

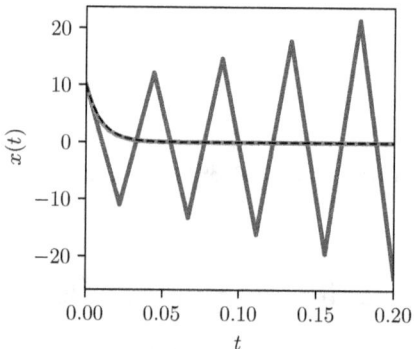

Figure 75: Solution of $\dot{x} = -100x$ using Euler's forward method using $(\Delta t) = 0.021$ (unstable, oscillatory curve) and 0.001 (stable, falling solid curve). The exact result (dashed curve) is close to the solution for $(\Delta t) = 0.001$.

Based on the stability issues, numerical schemes are classified into the following categories:

1. *Stable*: A Method is *stable* if it produces a bounded solution when the solution of the ODE is bounded.
2. *Unstable*: A method which is not stable is said to be *unstable*.

We have further classification of stable and unstable ODEs. They are

1. *Conditionally stable*: A method is conditionally stable if it is stable for a set of parameters, and unstable for another set of parameters.
2. *Unconditionally stable*: A method is unconditionally stable if it is stable for all parameter values.
3. *Unconditionally unstable*: A method is unconditionally unstable if it is unstable for all parameter values.

For complex α, exact solution is $x(t) = x(0)\exp(\alpha t)$. Here, the amplitude of $x(t)$ grows with time when $\text{Re}(\alpha) > 0$, and decreases when $\text{Re}(\alpha) < 0$. The numerical solution by Euler's forward scheme, $x^{(n)} = x^{(0)}(1+\alpha(\Delta t))^n$, behaves similar to the analytic solution, except when $|1+\alpha(\Delta t)| > 1$ with $\text{Re}(\alpha) < 0$. In this case, the exact solution converges to zero, but the numerical solution diverges. Hence, the system is unstable for $|1+\alpha(\Delta t)| > 1$ when $\text{Re}(\alpha) < 0$. As illustrated in Figure 76, the stable regime is inside the disk, while the unstable regime is the shaded region outside the disk (with $\text{Re}(\alpha) < 0$).

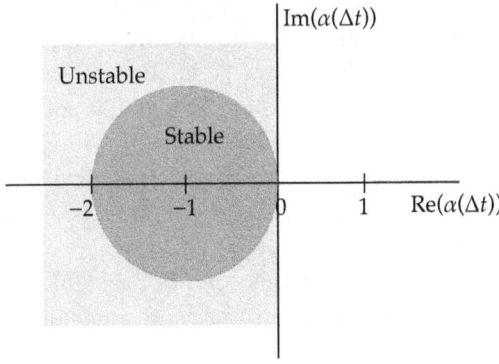

Figure 76: For $\dot{x} = \alpha x$, the stable region (disk) and unstable region (grey zone outside the disk) for Euler's forward method.

So far we dealt with stability of a linear equation $\dot{x} = \alpha x$. How is this result relevant to nonlinear equations, such as $\dot{x} = -t \exp(-x)$ of Example 3? For such equations, we linearize $f(x,t)$ around $(x^{(n)}, t_n)$ that yields

$$f(x,t) = f(x^{(n)}, t_n) + (x - x^{(n)})\frac{\partial f}{\partial x}\Big|_{(x^{(n)}, t_n)} + (t - t_n)\frac{\partial f}{\partial t}\Big|_{(x^{(n)}, t_n)}$$

Now we shift the origin to $(x^{(n)}, t_n)$ using a transformation: $x' = x - x^{(n)}$ and $t' = t - t_n$. In terms of these variables, the differential equation is

$$\dot{x}' = \beta + \alpha x' + \gamma t' \quad \ldots(40)$$

where $\beta = f(x^{(n)}, t_n)$, while $\alpha = \partial f/\partial x$ and $\gamma = \partial f/\partial t$ are the derivatives computed at $(x^{(n)}, t_n)$. Using the same arguments as for $\dot{x} = \alpha x$, we deduce that the equation $\dot{x}' = \alpha x' + \beta + \gamma t'$ would be locally unstable around $(x^{(n)}, t_n)$ when $\partial f/\partial x < 0$ and $|1 + (\Delta t)\partial f/\partial x| > 1$. As argued by Ferziger [1998], the homogeneous parts of Eq. (40), $\beta + \gamma t'$, in general, play insignificant role in the instability of the equation.

Thus, we can deduce the stability criteria for linear as well as nonlinear equations. Note that the above linearization process is similar to the computation of Lyapunov exponent in nonlinear dynamics.

Example 7: Let us explore the stability criteria for the Examples 1 to 4. In Table 26 we list the regions of stability and instability. In Example 4, $\partial f/\partial x = 2x - 100 \approx -100$ because x is small asymptotically. Therefore, Euler's forward method is stable for $\Delta t < 1/100$ and unstable for $\Delta t > 1/100$. We summarise these results in Table 26. In Example 3, $\partial f/\partial x = t \exp(-x) > 0$. Hence, we may expect $x(t)$ to grow. However, the other terms of the equation, in particular the homogeneous part of Eq. (40), make $x(t)$ to converge to 0.

Thus, Euler's forward method is conditional stable for rows 1, 3, and 5; unconditionally unstable for row 2; and unconditionally stable for row 4.

Table 26: Regions of stability and instability for Examples 1-4.

ODE	Stablity regime	Instablity regime
$\dot{x} = -x$	$\Delta t < 1$	$\Delta t > 1$
$\dot{z} = -i\pi z$	None	all Δt
$\dot{x} = \alpha x$	$\Delta t < 1/|\alpha|$ (for $\alpha < 0$)	$\Delta t > 1/|\alpha|$ (for $\alpha < 0$)
$\dot{x} = -t\exp(-x)$	all Δt	None
$\dot{x} = x^2 - 100x$	$\Delta t < 1/100$	$\Delta t > 1/100$

With this, we end our discussion on Euler's forward method.

****

Conceptual Questions

1. What is meant by instability of a differential equation solver? How is this notion of stability different from that in dynamics.
2. Argue that errors in Euler's forward method are of systematic type.

Exercises

1. Solve the following differential equations using Euler's forward method. Compare your results with analytical ones and estimate the errors. State the parameter regimes of stability for each of the ODEs.
    - $\dot{x} = 5x$ with $x(0) = 1$
    - $\dot{x} = -10x$ with $x(0) = 1$
    - $\dot{x} = -x^2$ with $x(0) = 1$
    - $\dot{x} = \sin(t)$ with $x(0) = -1$
    - $\dot{x} = \cos^2(t)$ with $x(0) = 0$
    - $\dot{x} = x^{-2}$ with $x(0) = 1$
    - $\dot{x} = x^3 - 50x$ with $x(0) = 10$

13.3 Implicit Schemes

In this section we describe Euler's backward method and Trapezoid method, both of which are implicit schemes.

Backward or Implicit Euler Method

Euler's backward method is similar to Euler forward method, except one critical difference: To time advance from t_n to t_{n+1}, we compute the slope at $t = t_{n+1}$. That is, for an ODE $\dot{x} = f(x,t)$,

$$x^{(n+1)} = x^{(n)} + (\Delta t) f(x^{(n+1)}, t_{n+1}) \quad \ldots(41)$$

The above equation is an implicit equation because the right-hand-side (RHS) contains the unknown $x^{(n+1)}$. Hence, Euler's backward method is called an *implicit scheme*.

Accuracy: In order to estimate the error for this scheme, we expand $f(x^{(n+1)}, t_{n+1})$ of Eq. (41) around $t = t_n$:

$$f(x^{(n+1)}, t_{n+1}) = \dot{x}|_{n+1} = \dot{x}|_n + (\Delta t)\ddot{x}|_n + \frac{1}{2}(\Delta t)^2 \dddot{x}|_n + \ldots + H.O.T.$$

where H.O.T. is the higher order terms. Therefore,

$$x^{(n+1)} = x^{(n)} + (\Delta t) f(x^{(n+1)}, t_{n+1})$$
$$= x^{(n)} + (\Delta t)\dot{x} + (\Delta t)^2 \ddot{x} + [(\Delta t)^3/2]\dddot{x} + H.O.T.$$

Comparison of the above with the solution of Eq. (38) yields the error in Euler's backward scheme as

$$\text{Error} = \text{Actual} - \text{Computed} = -(\tfrac{1}{2})(\Delta t)^2 \ddot{x}(x(n), t_n), \quad \ldots(42)$$

In comparison to the error for Euler's forward method (see Eq. (39)), the error for the implicit scheme has same magnitude, but of the opposite sign. The above observation is schematically shown in Figure

72 where $\ddot{x} < 0$.

Stability: After this, we explore the stability issues of Euler's backward method. We start with the analysis of $\dot{x} = \alpha x$ and test the stability for real and negative α. For this equation,

$$x^{(n+1)} = x^{(n)} + \alpha(\Delta t) x^{(n+1)}$$

Therefore,

$$x^{(n+1)} = x^{(n)} / (1 - \alpha(\Delta t)).$$

For negative α, $1/|(1-\alpha(\Delta t))| < 1$. Hence, the system is unconditionally stable. For complex α with Re(α) < 0, $1/|(1-\alpha(\Delta t))| = ((1-\alpha_{re}(\Delta t))^2 + (\alpha_{im}(\Delta t))^2)^{-½}$, which is also less than unity. Therefore, Euler's backward scheme is unconditionally stable for complex α as well. For nonlinear equations, an extension of the above analysis to that in Section 13.2 shows that Euler's backward method is also unconditionally stable for such equations.

We can rework all the examples of last section using Euler's backward method. The Examples 1 and 2 that are of the form $\dot{x} = \alpha x$ are straightforward to solve. For Examples 3 and 4, Euler's backward implementations are

$$x^{(n+1)} = x^{(n)} - \alpha(\Delta t)\, t_{n+1} \exp(-x^{(n+1)}) \quad ...(43)$$

$$x^{(n+1)} = x^{(n)} - \alpha(\Delta t)\, [(x^{(n+1)})^2 - 100\, x^{(n+1)}] \quad ...(44)$$

The former equation is solved using one of the methods to be discussed in Solving Nonlinear Algebraic Equation. The latter equation is quadratic that can be solved easily; however, we need to choose the root for which $x^{(n+1)} \approx x^{(n)}$. See Example 1 given below.

Example 1: We solve $\dot{x} = x^2 - 100x$ using Euler's backward method with $(\Delta t) = 0.02$. We take the initial condition as $x(0) = 10$. As shown in Figure 75, the numerical solution (solid line) is stable and is larger than the exact result (dashed line, $10\exp(-100t)$) for most part. Note that Euler's forward method is stable for $(\Delta t) < 0.01$. For time stepping, we solve Eq. (44) and take the root given below; the other root is unsuitable for time advancement.

$$x^{(n+1)} = \frac{1}{2(\Delta t)} \left[(100(\Delta t) + 1) - \sqrt{(100(\Delta t) + 1)^2 - 4(\Delta t)x^{(n)}} \right]$$

In the following code, the function Euler_implicit() produces t and x.

```
def Euler_implicit(tinit, tfinal, dt, initcond):
    n = int((tfinal-tinit)/dt)+1   # n-1 divisions
    t = np.linspace(tinit,tfinal,n)
    x = np.zeros(n,dtype=complex)
    x[0] = initcond

    for k in range(n-1):
        x[k+1] = ((100*dt+1)-np.sqrt((100*dt+1)**2
                 -4*dt*x[k]))/(2*dt)
    return t,x
```

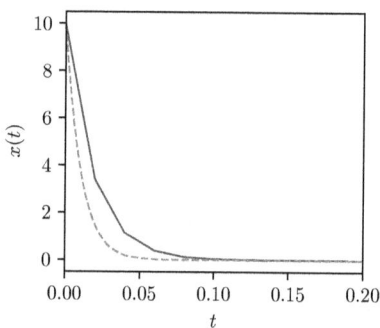

Figure 77: Solution of $\dot{x} = x^2 - 100x$ using Euler's backward method with $\Delta t = 0.02$ (solid curve). The exact result is shown as the dashed curve.

Trapezoid Method

Now we discuss the accuracy and stability issues of Trapezoid method where the time stepping is performed using the following formula:

$$x^{(n+1)} = x^{(n)} + (\tfrac{1}{2})(\Delta t) \, [f(x^{(n)}, t_n) + f(x^{(n+1)}, t_{n+1})] \, .$$

Since the above scheme is a combination of explicit and implicit schemes, hence it is called *semi-implicit method*.

In the above formula, an expansion of $f(x^{(n+1)}, t_{n+1})$ using Taylor series yields

$$x^{(n+1)} = x^{(n)} + (\Delta t)\, f(x^{(n)}, t_n) + \frac{(\Delta t)^2}{2} \frac{df}{dt} + \frac{(\Delta t)^3}{4} \frac{d^2 f}{dt^2} + H.O.T.$$

Thus, Trapezoid method is second order accurate, which is a significant improvement over Euler methods. The leading error for this method is

$$\text{Error} = \left(\frac{(\Delta t)^3}{3!} - \frac{(\Delta t)^3}{4} \right) \dddot{x}(t) = -\frac{(\Delta t)^3}{12} \dddot{x}(t) \ldots (45)$$

To analyse the stability of the above equation, we start with the equation $\dot{x} = \alpha x$. For this equation,

$$x^{(n+1)} = \left(\frac{1 + \alpha(\Delta t)/2}{1 - \alpha(\Delta t)/2} \right) x^{(n)}.$$

It is easy to show that

$$\left| \frac{1 + \alpha(\Delta t)/2}{1 - \alpha(\Delta t)/2} \right| < 1$$

for real but negative α, as well as for complex α with $\text{Re}(\alpha) < 0$. However, the above quantity is unity for purely imaginary α. We thus prove that the trapezoid method is unconditionally stable.

In summary, Euler's backward method is first oder accurate, while the trapezoid method is second order accurate. Both the methods are unconditionally stable, hence, we can choose any value of Δt for integration. However, an implementation of such schemes poses difficulties while solving the implicit nonlinear equations.

It is important to note that stability and accuracy are two different things. Stability is a must, that is, we need to choose either a unconditionally stable method, or an appropriate Δt for a conditionally stable method. Regarding accuracy, for a given accuracy, we can either choose appropriate Δt or higher order ODE solvers, which will be discussed in the next section.

****

Conceptual Questions

1. Show that the accuracies of forward and backward Euler methods are of the same order.
2. What are the advantages and disadvantages of backward or implicit ODE solvers?

Exercises

1. Solve the following differential equations using Euler's backward method. Compare your result with the analytical one.
   - $\dot{x} = 5x$ with $x(0) = 1$
   - $\dot{x} = -10x$ with $x(0) = 1$
   - $\dot{x} = x^{-2}$ with $x(0) = 1$
   - $\dot{x} = x^2 - 50x$ with $x(0) = 10$
2. Repeat Exercise 1 for trapezoid method.

13.4 Higher-order Methods

A major advantage of implicit schemes described in the previous section is that they are stable. However, solving implicit equations is a challenge. This difficulty is partially surmounted in predictor-corrector and Runge-Kutta methods where $x^{(n+1)}$ of the implicit term is estimated and plugged in. We describe these schemes below.

Predictor-Corrector (PC) Method

As described in the previous section, an implicit Scheme based on Trapezoid rule is

$$x^{(n+1)} = x^{(n)} + (\tfrac{1}{2})(\Delta t)[f(x^{(n)}, t_n) + f(x^{(n+1)}, t_{n+1})] \ldots (46)$$

In the RHS, $x^{(n+1)}$ of $f(x^{(n+1)}, t_{n+1})]$ is *predicted* as follows:

Predictor step: $x^{(n+1)*} = x^{(n)} + (\Delta t) f(x^{(n)}, t_n)$.

This value is now substituted for $x^{(n+1)}$ of the RHS of Eq. (46), that is,

Corrector step: $x^{(n+1)} = x^{(n)} + (\tfrac{1}{2})(\Delta t)[f(x^{(n)}, t_n) + f(x^{(n+1)*}, t_{n+1})]$.

The above scheme is accurate up to $O((\Delta t)^2)$. The proof is given in the previous section.

For the stability analysis, we solve the equation $\dot{x} = \alpha x$ using the above method that yields

$$x^{(n+1)} = (1 + \alpha(\Delta t) + (\alpha(\Delta t))^2/2)\, x^{(n)}.$$

Hence, the method is stable when $|1 + \alpha(\Delta t) + (\alpha(\Delta t))^2/2| < 1$, and it is unstable otherwise. Hence, the equation for the boundary between the stable and unstable regimes is $|1 + \alpha(\Delta t) + (\alpha(\Delta t))^2/2| = 1$. The following Python script draws the above boundary:

```
x = np.linspace(-3,3,100)
```

```
y = x.copy()
xv, yv = np.meshgrid(x,y)
zv = xv + 1j*yv
g = 1 + zv + zv**2/2
gmag = abs(g)

fig = plt.figure(figsize = (6,2.5))
ax1 = fig.add_subplot(1,2,1)
ax1.contour(xv, yv, gmag, 'k-',levels = [1])
# level = [1] generates contour for gmag=1.
```

In Figure 78(a) we plot the above boundary. In the figure, the inner region of the oval is stable, while the region outside the boundary is unstable.

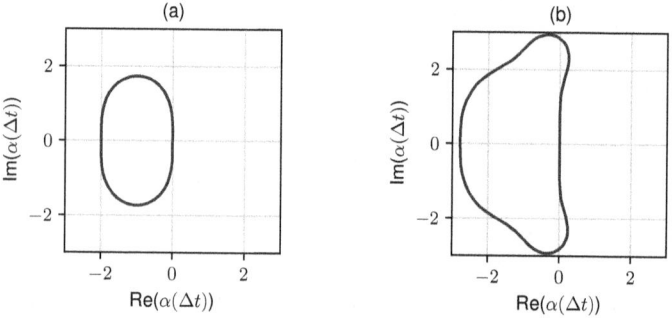

Figure 78: The boundary between the stable and unstable regions of (a) the predictor-corrector and RK2 methods; (b) RK4 method. The regions inside the curves are stable, while those outside with $Re(\alpha) < 0$ are unstable.

Runge-Kutta Methods

Runge-Kutta (RK) methods are similar to the predictor-corrector method. A major difference however is that RK methods make use of intermediate points between t_n to t_{n+1}. Here we describe the second-order, third-order, and fourth-order RK methods.

Second-order RK method (RK2): A ODE solver based on mid-point rule is

$x^{(n+1)} = x^{(n)} + (\Delta t) f(x^{(n+\frac{1}{2})}, t_{n+\frac{1}{2}})$ . ...(47)

In RK2 method, the intermediate point $x^{(n+\frac{1}{2})}$ is estimated using Euler's forward method, that is,

$k_1 = (\Delta t) f(x^{(n)}, t_n);\quad x^{(n+\frac{1}{2})*} = x^{(n)} + k_1/2$.

Now, we substitute the above in Eq. (47) that yields

$x^{(n+1)} = x^{(n)} + (\Delta t) f(x^{(n+\frac{1}{2})*}, t_{n+\frac{1}{2}})$ . ...(48)

A Python implementation of RK2 is as follows:

```
def RK2(f, tinit, tfinal, dt, initcond):
    n = int((tfinal-tinit)/dt)+1   # n-1 divisions
    t = np.linspace(tinit,tfinal,n)
    x = np.zeros(n)
    x[0] = initcond

    for k in range(n-1):
        xmid = x[k] + f(x[k],t[k])*dt/2
        x[k+1] = x[k] + f(xmid,t[k]+dt/2)*dt
    return t,x

initcond = 1.1
t_RK2,x_RK2 = RK2(f, tinit, tfinal, dt, initcond)
```

Thus, RK2 method involves two $f()$ computations per step. It is easy to show that this scheme has the accuracy of $(O((\Delta t)^2))$. Regarding stability, It is easy to show that the stability condition for the RK2 method is same as that for the predictor-corrector method. See Figure 78(a) for an illustration.

Third-order RK method (RK3): RK3 scheme involves more intermediate steps than RK2 method. The predictors for RK3 are

$k_1 = (\Delta t) f(x^{(n)}, t_n);\quad x^{(n+\frac{1}{2})*} = x^{(n)} + k_1/2$,
$k_2 = (\Delta t) f(x^{(n+\frac{1}{2})*}, t_{n+\frac{1}{2}});\quad x^{(n+1)**} = x^{(n)} - k_1 + 2k_2$,
$k_3 = (\Delta t) f(x^{(n+1)**}, t_{n+1})$.

Now, the corrector for RK3 is

$$x^{(n+1)} = x^{(n)} + (1/6)(k_1 + 2k_2 + 2k_3 + k_4).$$

Another version of RK3 is as follows:

$$k_1 = (\Delta t) f(x^{(n)}, t_n); \quad x^{(n+1/3)*} = x^{(n)} + k_1/3,$$
$$k_2 = (\Delta t) f(x^{(n+1/3)*}, t_{n+1/3}); \quad x^{(n+2/3)**} = x^{(n)} + (2/3) k_2,$$
$$k_3 = (\Delta t) f(x^{(n+2/3)**}, t_{n+2/3}),$$
$$x^{(n+1)} = x^{(n)} + (1/4)(k_1 + 3k_3).$$

RK3 method is third-order accurate, i.e., it has error of $O((\Delta t)^4)$. Note that RK3 involves three $f()$ computations per step.

Fourth-order RK method (RK4): The predictors for RK4 are

$$k_1 = (\Delta t) f(x^{(n)}, t_n); \quad x^{(n+1/2)*} = x^{(n)} + k_1/2,$$
$$k_2 = (\Delta t) f(x^{(n+1/2)*}, t_{n+1/2}); \quad x^{(n+1/2)**} = x^{(n)} + k_2/2,$$
$$k_3 = (\Delta t) f(x^{(n+1/2)**}, t_{n+1/2}); \quad x^{(n+1)***} = x^{(n)} + k_3,$$
$$k_4 = (\Delta t) f(x^{(n+1)***}, t_{n+1}).$$

Now, the corrector for RK4 is

$$x^{(n+1)} = x^{(n)} + (1/6)(k_1 + 2k_2 + 2k_3 + k_4).$$

A Python implementation of RK4 method is as follows:

```
def RK4(f, tinit, tfinal, dt, initcond):
    n = int((tfinal-tinit)/dt)+1    # n-1 divisions
    t = np.linspace(tinit,tfinal,n)
    x = np.zeros(n)
    x[0] = initcond

    for k in range(n-1):
        tmid = t[k]+dt/2
        k1 = dt*f(x[k],t[k])
        xmid_1 = x[k] + k1/2
        k2 = dt*f(xmid_1,tmid)
        xmid_2 = x[k] + k2/2
        k3 = dt*f(xmid_2,tmid)
        xend = x[k] + k3
```

```
k4 = dt*f(xend,t[k+1])

x[k+1] = x[k] + (k1+2*(k2+k3)+k4)*dt/6
return t,x

initcond = 1.1
t_RK4,x_RK4 = RK4(f, tinit, tfinal, dt, initcond)
```

For the equation, $\dot{x} = \alpha x$, RK4 method yields

$$x^{(n+1)} = \left(1 + \alpha(\Delta t) + \frac{1}{2}(\alpha(\Delta t))^2 + \frac{1}{6}(\alpha(\Delta t))^3 + \frac{1}{24}(\alpha(\Delta t))^4\right) x^{(n)}$$
$$+ H.O.T. \quad ...(49)$$

where H.O.T. stands for higher order terms. The above equation shows that RK4 method is fourth-order accurate, and it has error of $O((\Delta t)^5)$. RK4 method involves four $f()$ computations per step.

Using Eq. (49) we deduce that the boundary between the unstable and stable regions for RK4 method is

$$|1+\alpha(\Delta t)+(\alpha(\Delta t))^2/2+(\alpha(\Delta t))^3/6+(\alpha(\Delta t))^4/24| = 1.$$

We construct the boundary using a similar code as that used for predictor-corrector. We exhibit this boundary in Figure 78(b). The region inside (outside) the boundary is stable (unstable).

ODE Solver Based on Higher-order Derivative

For the equation, $\dot{x} = f(x,t)$, we can compute $x^{(n+1)}$ to higher orders using Taylor series. The series expansion yields

$$x^{(n+1)} = x^{(n)} + (\Delta t)\dot{x} + \frac{(\Delta t)^2}{2}\ddot{x} + H.O.T. \quad ... (50)$$

The second-order term is computed as

$$\ddot{x} = \frac{\partial f}{\partial t} + \dot{x}\frac{\partial f}{\partial x},$$

substitution of which in the series yields

$$x^{(n+1)} = x^{(n)} + \frac{(\Delta t)}{2}\left[2\dot{x} + (\Delta t)\frac{\partial f}{\partial t} + (\Delta t)f\frac{\partial f}{\partial x}\right].$$

which is accurate up to $O((\Delta t)^2)$. Higher order terms of Eq. (50) yield more accurate results.

Some of the multistep methods, e.g., Adam-Bashforth scheme, are derived using the above approach (see Chapra and Canale [2016]).

Using Python's *Odeint*

The function *odeint()* of Python's *scipy.integrate* module helps us solve ODEs. It's usage is shown below. It takes the function $f(x,t)$ of $\dot{x} = f(x,t)$, initial condition, and time array (t), and returns the values of the dependent variable $x(t)$ at each element of t.

```
from scipy.integrate import odeint

def f(x,t):
    return x**2-x

tinit = 0;  tfinal=2.0;   dt = 0.2
n = int((tfinal-tinit)/dt)+1
t = np.linspace(tinit,tfinal,n)

xinit = np.array(1.1)
x=odeint(f,xinit,t)
```

Example 1: We solve $\dot{x} = x^2 - x$ numerically in the interval [0,2] using $x(0) = 1.1$ and $\Delta t = 0.2$. The numerical results for Euler forward, RK2, RK4 methods, and ode_int() are shown in Figure 79(a). RK4 method and *ode_int()* yield results close to the exact result, but RK2 and Euler methods have significant errors.

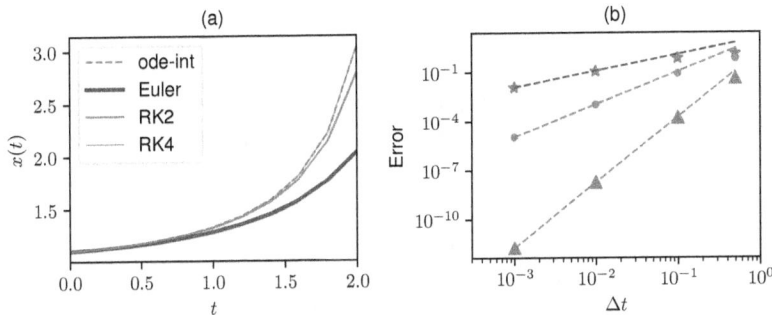

Figure 79: (a) Numerical solutions of $\dot{x} = x^2 - x$ using Euler forward, RK2, RK4 methods, and ode_int(). Here, $\Delta t = 0.2$ and $x(0) = 1$. (b) Plots of errors for Euler (stars), RK2 (dots), and RK4 (triangles) methods for various Δt. The errors for these schemes are proportional to Δt, $(\Delta t)^2$, and $(\Delta t)^4$ (dashed lines) respectively.

For the Euler-forward, RK2, RK4 methods, we compute the errors, which is the difference between the actual answer and the numerical results, at $t = 2$ with $\Delta t = 0.001, 0.01, 0.1$, and 0.5. These errors are plotted in Figure 79(b) using star, dots, and triangles. The figure shows that the respective errors are proportional to (Δt), $(\Delta t)^2$, and $(\Delta t)^4$ respectively, which are consistent with the theoretical formulas for small Δt. Naturally, we observe deviations from the theoretical estimates for $\Delta t = 0.5$. Note that the error in $x(t_{\text{final}})$ is an order lower than the error for individual steps.

With this, we end our discussion on higher-order methods.

****

Conceptual Questions

1. What are the advantages and disadvantages of RK2 and RK4 methods over implicit schemes?

Exercises

1. Solve the following differential equations using predictor-corrector, RK2, and RK4 methods. Compare your result with analytical one.
   - $\dot{x} = 5x$ with $x(0) = 1$
   - $\dot{x} = -10x$ with $x(0) = 1$
   - $\dot{x} = x^{-2}$ with $x(0) = 1$
   - $\dot{x} = x^2 - 50\,x$ with $x(0) = 10$
2. Solve the equations of Exercise 1 for $\Delta t = 0.0001, 0.001, 0.01,$ and 0.1, and study the errors. How do these errors vary with Δt?

13.5 Multistep Method

In this section, we briefly describe several *multistep methods*. In such methods, $x^{(n+1)}$ depends on $x^{(n)}$, as well as on x at earlier times, such as $x^{(n-1)}$, $x^{(n-2)}$, $x^{(n-3)}$. The name, multistep, comes due to this reason.

The simplest multistep method is leapfrog that will be described below.

Leapfrog Method

The time-stepping scheme for the *leapfrog method* is

$$x^{(n+1)} = x^{(n-1)} + 2(\Delta t) f(x^{(n)}, t_n) . \quad \ldots\ldots(51)$$

This method is very useful, specially for time-reversible systems because Eq. (51) is symmetric under time reversal ($t \to -t$). That is, if we go back in time from t_{n+1} to t_{n-1}, the prescription of leapfrog scheme,

$$x^{(n-1)} = x^{(n+1)} - 2(\Delta t) f(x^{(n)}, t_n)$$

is same as Eq. (51). It is easy to verify that Euler, RK2, and RK4 methods are not symmetric under time reversal.

Many physical systems are symmetric under time reversal operation. Some of the examples of such systems are a projectile motion in vacuum, planetary motion, motion of a charge particle in an electric field (Verma [2016]). Hamiltonian systems too are symmetric under time reversal (see Section 13.6). Leapfrog method is useful for solving these systems. Still, there are certain problems with this method, as we describe below.

For the equation $\dot{x} = \alpha x$, Eq. (51) becomes

$$x^{(n+1)} = x^{(n-1)} + 2\alpha(\Delta t) x^{(n)}, \ldots\ldots(52)$$

whose solution is of the form ρ^n with ρ determined from the quadratic equation $\rho^2 = 1 + 2\alpha(\Delta t)\rho$. The solutions of the quadratic equation are

$$\rho_{1,2} = \alpha(\Delta t) \pm \sqrt{(\alpha(\Delta t))^2 + 1}.$$

Therefore, a general solution of Eq. (52) after n steps is

$$x^{(n)} = c_1 \rho_1^n + c_2 \rho_2^n,$$

where c_1 and c_2 are constants that are determined using initial condition. Among the two solutions, ρ_1 is genuine, but ρ_2 is a spurious. This feature is evident from the Taylor expansion of $\rho_{1,2}$ (for small Δt):

$$\rho_1 \approx 1 + \alpha(\Delta t) + \frac{1}{2}(\alpha(\Delta t))^2 + H.O.T.$$

$$\rho_2 \approx -1 + \alpha(\Delta t) - \frac{1}{2}(\alpha(\Delta t))^2 + H.O.T.$$

where H.O.T. represents higher order terms. For small $\alpha(\Delta t)$, $\rho_2 \approx -1$, hence $(\rho_2)^n$ will induce oscillations in $x(t)$. This is a signature of the spurious solution. Thus, the leapfrog scheme is *unconditionally unstable* due to the presence of ρ_2. However, if the above instability arising due to ρ_2 could be suppressed (to be described below), then the solution would be second-order accurate.

We can suppress ρ_2 in a following manner. A first-order ODE requires only one initial condition. Hence, we can tweak $x^{(0)}$ and $x^{(1)}$ so as to make $c_2 = 0$. For example, our $x^{(0)}$ and $x^{(1)}$ satisfy the following relations:

$$x^{(0)} = c_1 + c_2,$$

$$x^{(1)} = c_1 \rho_1 + c_2 \rho_2.$$

If $x^{(1)} = \rho_1 x^{(0)}$, the constant $c_2 = 0$, and $c_1 = x^{(0)}$. This strategy can be used to turn off the spurious ρ_2 for the initial condition. Unfortunately, the spurious ρ_2 may reappear at a later stage due to the round-off errors. To overcome this difficulty, following measures are recommended:

1. Perform a step with another method often. It is better to use

second-order scheme such as RK2 method so as to match the accuracy of leapfrog method.
2. Once in a while, average the results of several successive steps to nullify the spurious oscillations.
3. Test whether $x^{(n+1)}/x^{(n)} = \rho_1$. A violation of this equality signals the presence of the spurious component ρ_2.

Once the spurious component of the solution has been suppressed, the leapfrog method works quite nicely. It is specially useful for solving time-reversible systems, such as Hamiltonian systems, Schrödinger's equation. We will address some of these systems later in this book.
In addition to the spurious component, the leapfrog method has several other disadvantages:

1. We need to store more variables (e.g., $x^{(n-1)}$ for the leapfrog method) in order to restart the system from the final value.
2. The leapfrog method requires two values, $x^{(0)}$ and $x^{(1)}$, for initialisation. For convenience, Euler's forward method is often used as a initial step. But, such a initialisation is prone to instability.

Adams-Bashforth Method

In this scheme,

$$x^{(n+1)} = x^{(n)} + (\Delta t) \sum_{m=0}^{k-1} \beta_{k,m} f(x^{(n-m)}, t_{n-m}),$$

with $\beta_{k,m}$ listed in Table 27 (Chapra and Canale [2016]).

Table 27: The coefficients $\beta_{k,m}$ for Adams-Bashforth method

β	$m=0$	$m=1$	$m=2$	$m=3$	$m=4$
$\beta_{1,m}$	1				
$2\beta_{2,m}$	3	−1			
$12\beta_{3,m}$	23	−16	5		
$24\beta_{4,m}$	55	−59	37	−9	
$720\beta_{5,m}$	1901	−2774	2616	−1274	251

As illustrations, we list the two lowest-order Adams-Bashforth schemes:

$$x^{(n+1)} = x^{(n)} + (\Delta t) f(x^{(n)}, t_n),$$

$$x^{(n+1)} = x^{(n)} + ((\Delta t)/2) [3 f(x^{(n)}, t_n) - f(x^{(n-1)}, t_{n-1})].$$

Note that the former is Euler's forward method.

Adams-Moulton Method

This scheme is very similar to Adams-Bashforth except that its RHS has a term dependent on $x^{(n+1)}$. In this scheme,

$$x^{(n+1)} = x^{(n)} + (\Delta t) \sum_{m=0}^{k-1} \beta_{k,m} f(x^{(n+1-m)}, t_{n+1-m}),$$

with $\beta_{k,m}$ listed in Table 28 (Chapra and Canale [2016]).

Table 28: The coefficients $\beta_{k,m}$ for Adams-Moulton method

β	$m = 0$	$m = 1$	$m = 2$	$m = 3$	$m = 4$
$\beta_{1,m}$	1				
$2\beta_{2,m}$	1	1			
$12\beta_{3,m}$	5	8	−1		
$24\beta_{4,m}$	9	19	−5	1	
$720\beta_{5,m}$	251	646	−264	106	−19

The three lowest-order Adams-Moulton schemes are listed below:

$$x^{(n+1)} = x^{(n)} + 2(\Delta t) f(x^{(n+1)}, t_{n+1}),$$

$$x^{(n+1)} = x^{(n)} + ((\Delta t)/2) [f(x^{(n+1)}, t_{n+1}) + f(x^{(n)}, t_n)],$$

$$x^{(n+1)} = x^{(n)} + ((\Delta t)/12) [5 f(x^{(n+1)}, t_{n+1}) + 8 f(x^{(n)}, t_n) - f(x^{(n-1)}, t_{n-1})].$$

With this, we end our discussion on multistep methods.

Conceptual Questions

1. Why is the leapfrog method unstable?
2. What are the benefits and disadvantages of multistep methods?

Exercises

1. Solve the following differential equations using leapfrog and second-order Adams-Bashforth methods. Compare your results with the analytical one.
   - $\dot{x} = 5x$ with $x(0) = 1$
   - $\dot{x} = -10x$ with $x(0) = 1$
   - $\dot{x} = x^{-2}$ with $x(0) = 1$
   - $\dot{x} = x^2 - 50\,x$ with $x(0) = 10$

13.6 Solving a System of Equations

So far we solved a single first-order ODE. However, in practice, we encounter a set of ODEs. For example, chemical reactions involving N species are described using N rate equations, which are first-order ODEs. In 3D, the dynamics of N particles is described using $3N$ second-order ODEs. In this chapter we discuss how to numerically solve such a set of ODEs.

Solving a Set of ODEs

We consider N first-order ODEs whose independent variable is t and dependent variables are $x_0, x_1, ..., x_{N-1}$. The ith equation of the set is written schematically as

$$\dot{x}_i = f_i(t, x_0, x_1, ..., x_{N-1}),$$

where the RHS function $f_i(x_j)$ could be linear or nonlinear functions of the variables: $x_0, x_1, ..., x_{N-1}$, and t.

To solve the above set of equations for a given initial condition $\{x_i(t=0)\}$, we discretize time into many intervals and evolve the equations from $t = 0$ to the final time. For example, if at time $t = t_n$, the dependent variables are $\{x_i^{(n)}\}$, then we time advance the variables using Euler's forward method as follows:

$$x_i^{(n+1)} = x_i^{(n)} + (\Delta t) f_i(t, x_0^{(n)}, x_1^{(n)}, ..., x_{N-1}^{(n)}),$$

where $(\Delta t) = t_{n+1} - t_n$. It is straightforward to compute the RHS and hence $\{x_i^{(n+1)}\}$. The other schemes such as RK2 can be implemented in a similar manner.

The time stepping equation in Euler's backward method, an implicit scheme, yields the following N coupled equations that may be either nonlinear or linear:

$$x_i^{(n+1)} = x_i^{(n)} + (\Delta t) f_i(t, x_0^{(n+1)}, x_1^{(n+1)}, ..., x_{N-1}^{(n+1)}).$$

Solving such a set of equations could be challenging. In Chapter Seventeen and Chapter Twenty, we will discuss how to solve such equations.

Now we will discuss how to solve coupled equations of mechanics.

Solving Equations of Motion in Mechanics

The equation of motion of a particle moving in 1D is $m\ddot{x} = f(x,\dot{x},t)$, where m is the mass of the particle; x, $\dot{x}$, $\ddot{x}$ are particle's position, velocity, and acceleration respectively; and $f(x,\dot{x},t)$ is the force on the particle. We can covert the above second-order ODE to the following two first-order ODEs:

$$m\dot{x} = p; \quad \dot{p} = f(x,p,t),$$

where p is the momentum of the particle. We can solve the above two equations using the methods described earlier. For a class of systems where the force $f(x) = -dV/dx$, the total energy, $p^2/2m + V(x)$, is constant in time; such systems are called *Hamiltonian* or *energy conserving systems*.

We take a concrete example. Consider a simple harmonic oscillator for which the force is $-x$ (ignoring the prefactor). For convenience, we set $m = 1$. Hence, the equations of motion for the oscillator are

$$\dot{x} = p; \quad \dot{p} = -x. \quad \ldots\ldots(53)$$

The above equations form a Hamiltonian system. We can solve these equations using Euler's forward scheme as follows:

$$x^{(n+1)} = x^{(n)} + (\Delta t)\, p^{(n)}; \quad p^{(n+1)} = p^{(n)} - (\Delta t)\, x^{(n)}. \quad \ldots(54)$$

Even though Euler's forward method yields a reasonably accurate solution to the oscillator for sufficiently small Δt, it has certain deficiencies. Equation (53) is symmetric under time reversal, but the Euler's time-stepping scheme is not (see Eq. (54)).

Fortunately, a modified version of leapfrog method discussed in Section 13.5 is suitable for solving Eq. (54). In *leapfrog method*, the position x and the momentum p are computed on a staggered time grid, as shown in Figure 80.

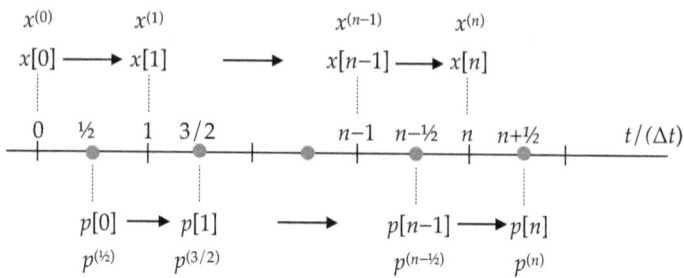

Figure 80: In the leapfrog method, $x(t)$ are computed at $t = (\Delta t), 2(\Delta t),$ ..., $n(\Delta t)$, .., while $p(t)$ are computed at $(\Delta t)/2, 3(\Delta t)/2, ..., (n+\frac{1}{2})(\Delta t)$. In a Python program, we store these variables in arrays $x[0:N-1]$ and $p[0:N-1]$.

In the first time step, we compute

$$p^{(\frac{1}{2})} = p^{(0)} - ((\Delta t)/2) \, x^{(0)}.$$

After this, we time advance both x and p using the following method:

$$x^{(n)} = x^{(n-1)} + (\Delta t) \, p^{(n-\frac{1}{2})} \, ; \, p^{(n+\frac{1}{2})} = p^{(n-\frac{1}{2})} - (\Delta t) \, x^{(n)} \, . \, \ldots \ldots (55)$$

The following Python code implements the above scheme. For the computation of energy, we interpolate the velocity field at the integer grid points of Figure 80.

```
def f(x,v):
    return -x     # force for the oscillator

def leap_frog(f, tinit, tfinal, dt, initcond):
    n = int((tfinal-tinit)/dt)+1    # n divisions
    t = np.linspace(tinit,tfinal,n)
    y = np.zeros((n,2))
    y[0][0] = initcond[0];  # position
    y[0][1] = initcond[1] +  f(y[0][0],y[0][1])*dt/2
    # init vel at t=1/2
```

```
for k in range(1,n):
    y[k][0] = y[k-1][0] + y[k-1][1]*dt
    y[k][1] = y[k-1][1] + f(y[k][0],y[k][1])*dt

return t, y
```

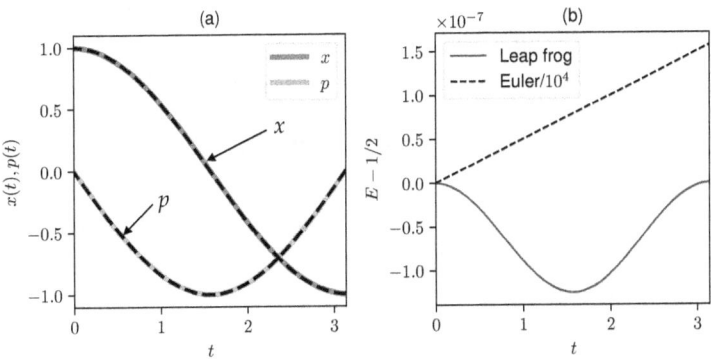

Figure 81: For a simple harmonic oscillator: (a) Plots of $x(t)$ and $p(t)$ computed using the leapfrog method (solid curves). The time-reversed $x(t)$ and $p(t)$ are shown as dashed black curves. (b) The error in energy, $E-1/2$, for the leapfrog and Euler methods.

In Figure 81(a), we exhibit the time series of $x(t)$ and $p(t)$ for initial condition $x(0) = 1$ and $p(0) = 0$, and $\Delta t = 0.001$. To check the correctness of our solution, we compute the total energy, $(x^2+p^2)/2$, whose exact value is ½ throughout the trajectory. As shown in Figure 81(b), the error in the energy of the order of 10^{-7}, which is due to the truncation error in the leapfrog method (see the Taylor series expansion in Section 13.5). In addition, the error is oscillatory, unlike the ever-increasing and large error of Euler's forward method (see Figure 81(b)). We also remark that more advanced schemes, e.g. Forest and Ruth [1990] and Position Extended Forest-Ruth Like (PFERL) methods (Omelyan et al. [2002]) provide more robust energy conservation.

According to the leapfrog method, we go from t_{n+1} to t_n using the following steps:

$$x^{(n)} = x^{(n+1)} - (\Delta t)\, p^{(n+\frac{1}{2})}\,;\; p^{(n-\frac{1}{2})} = p^{(n+\frac{1}{2})} + (\Delta t)\, x^{(n)}, \quad \ldots\ldots(56)$$

which are same as Eqs. (55). Thus, the time-advance equations for the leapfrog method are time-reversal symmetric. We demonstrate this feature in Figure 81(a) where the time-reversed $x(t)$ (from $t = \pi$ to $t = 0$), represented using dashed curves, overlaps with the forward time trajectories.

The above features are responsible for the approximate energy conservation observed for the leapfrog method. Another advantage of the leapfrog method is the it preserves the phase space volume during the evolution, a topic that is beyond the scope of this book.

A phase space plot, which is the plot of x vs. p, provides useful insights into the system dynamics. In Figure 82, we present the phase space plots of the simple harmonic oscillator, and that of Duffing oscillator, whose equation of motion is $\ddot{x} = x - x^3$. The three curves of Figure 82(b) are obtained by starting the ODEs with initial conditions $(x[0], p[0]) = (0.5, 0.5)$, $(0.4, 0)$, and $(-0.4, 0)$.

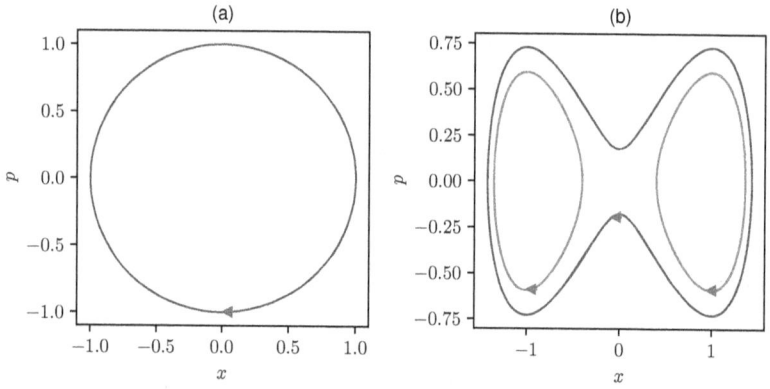

Figure 82: Phase space plots (a) of the simple harmonic oscillator ($\ddot{x} = -x$) and (b) of the Duffing oscillator ($\ddot{x} = x - x^3$).

It is important to note that in the phase space of a Hamiltonian system, a trajectory computed using Eq. (56) are same as the forward-time trajectory, except that it moves in anticlockwise direction. This time-reversed trajectory, however, is unphysical. But, an additional transformation $p \to -p$ (or flipping the trajectories around $p = 0$ axis) of the time-reversed trajectory yields a physically-realizable phase space trajectories. These observations are consistent with the fact that $t \to -t$ and $p \to -p$ together form the time-reversal operator for the Hamiltonian systems.

Many equations of physics violate time reversal symmetry. Some of the leading examples in this category are damped oscillator and forced oscillator. You can easily verify that these equations are not invariant under time reversal.

For solving mechanical systems, we could also use Python function *odeint()* to solve a system of equation. For example, a code segment for solving oscillator problem using *odeint()* is as follows:

```
def ydot_osc(y,t):
    return ([y[1], -y[0]])

yinit = np.array([1, 0])
y=odeint(ydot_osc,yinit,t)
```

With this, we end our discussion of this section.

****

Conceptual Questions

1. List examples of physical systems that are described by a set of ODEs.
2. Prove that the total energy is conserved for a simple harmonic oscillator. Show that its equation is time-reversal symmetric.
3. Read about three-body problem. Solve the equations for this system numerically.

Exercises

1. Using leapfrog method, solve the nondimensionalized forced oscillator $\frac{d^2 x'}{dt'^2} + x' = \cos\left(\frac{\omega_f}{\omega_0} t'\right)$, which is Eq. (17) of Section 9.2. What are the solutions for the oscillator whose parameters are $m = \frac{1}{2}$ kg, $\omega_0 = 10$ Hz, $\omega_f = 1$ Hz, and $F_0 = 0.1$ N. How does the result change when $\omega_0 = 0.1$ Hz or $\omega_0 = 1$ Hz?
2. Solve the equation for a damped oscillator without forcing. Choose appropriate parameters. Draw the phase space plots

for this system. It is better to use nondimensional equation of the system.

3. Repeat Exercise 2 for a forced damped oscillator.
4. Are the systems of Exercises 1, 2, and 3 time-reversible? Provide numerical justification for your answers.
5. Construct phase space plots for the Duffing oscillator whose equation of motion is $\ddot{x} = x - x^3$.
6. Solve $\ddot{x} = -x + x^3 + \sin(2t)$ using RK2 method for various initial conditions.
7. Solve Newton's equation of motion for a pendulum with a massless rod of length l and point bob of mass m. Plot the angle and angular velocity as a function of time. Also make the corresponding phase space plot. It is better to use non-dimensional equation and leapfrog method to solve this problem.
8. Lorenz equations play an important role in nonlinear dynamics. The Lorenz equations are $\dot{x} = P(y-x)$; $\dot{y} = x(r-z) - y$; $\dot{z} = xy - \beta z$. Make 3D plots of (x,y,z) for three sets of parameters: (1) $P = 10$, $r = 0.5$, $\beta = 1$; (2) $P = 10$, $r = 2$, $\beta = 1$; (3) $P = 10$, $r = 28$, $\beta = 1$. Choose various initial conditions.
9. Simulate a double pendulum with massless rods. Refer to Landau and Lifshitz [2013] for the equations. Numerically solve the equations of this system. Note that this system exhibits chaos.

13.7 Stiff Equations

Many natural and engineering systems involve several or many length and time scales. For example, a damped-forced oscillator has three time scales: the damping time scale, the time period of the oscillator, and the time period of the forcing. The length scales of Earth's atmosphere ranges from meters to thousands of kilometres.

Due to the underlying physics, the differential equations of multiscale systems have many length and time scales. An equation whose the lowest time scale and the largest time scale are far apart is called a *stiff equation*. Numerical computation of a such equation is quite challenging; this is the topic of the present section.

Solving $\dot{x} = x^2 - 10^6 x$

Let us consider an ODE: $\dot{x} = x^2 - 10^6 x$, which is a variant of Example 3 of Section 13.2. The timescales of this equation are $1/x$ and 10^{-6}. When x is $O(1)$, the two timescales are far apart, hence the system is *stiff*. Here, the linear term is *stiff* due to its very short time scale. The name "stiff" appears to originate from the fact that a stiff spring has very high frequency or very short time scale.

For the above equation, Euler's forward method is conditionally stable for $\Delta t < 10^{-6}$, which is too small for comfort. This difficulty is overcome using two methods.

Semi-implicit scheme: We employ a semi-implicit scheme for the stiff term that yields

$$x^{(n+1)} = x^{(n)} + (\Delta t)(x^{(n)})^2 - \frac{\Delta t}{2} 10^6 [x^{(n)} + x^{(n+1)}],$$

whose solution is

$$x^{(n+1)} = \left(\frac{1 - 10^6 (\Delta t)/2}{1 + 10^6 (\Delta t)/2} \right) x^{(n)} + (\Delta t)(x^{(n)})^2.$$

The above implementation is unconditionally stable, and we do not need a tiny Δt (10^{-6} or lower).

Exponential trick: We can combine the stiff term $-ax$ with $\dot{x}$ using a change of variable: $x' = x \exp(at)$. In terms of x',

$$\dot{x}' = x^2 \exp(at). \quad \ldots(57)$$

which is not stiff. Equation (57) can be easily solved as

$$x'^{(n+1)} = x'^{(n)} + (\Delta t)(x^{(n)})^2 \exp(at_n), \text{ or}$$
$$x^{(n+1)} = \left[x^{(n)} + (\Delta t)(x^{(n)})^2\right] \exp(-a(\Delta t)).$$

The above equation can have any Δt for time advancement, not a tiny Δt as in the original equation.

Solving a Set of Equation

Let us consider two linear equations:

$$\dot{x} + ax = y; \quad \dot{y} = -y,$$

or,
$$\begin{bmatrix} \dot{x} \\ \dot{y} \end{bmatrix} = \begin{bmatrix} -a & 1 \\ 0 & -1 \end{bmatrix} \begin{bmatrix} x \\ y \end{bmatrix}.$$

The eigenvalues of the matrix of the above equation are $-a$ and -1. Hence, the timescales of the above equations are $1/a$ and 1. When a is very large, the timescales $1/a$ and 1 are widely separated, thus making the above system stiff. For Euler forward method, the above equations are stable only for $\Delta t < 1/a$ that could be very demanding computationally.

For the above system of equations too, we can employ the strategies employed for $\dot{x} = x^2 - 10^6 x$. A semi-implicit implementation of the stiff term yields

$$x^{(n+1)} = x^{(n)} - a(\Delta t)\left(\frac{x^{(n)} + x^{(n+1)}}{2}\right) + (\Delta t)y^{(n)};$$

$$y^{(n+1)} = (1-\Delta t)y^{(n)}$$

or

$$x^{(n+1)} = \left(\frac{1-a(\Delta t)/2}{1+a(\Delta t)/2}\right)x^{(n)} + (\Delta t)y^{(n)};$$

$$y^{(n+1)} = (1-\Delta t)y^{(n)}$$

The first equation is stable for any Δt, but the second one is stable for $\Delta t < 2$. This is a major gain compared to original projection that $\Delta t < 1/a$.

We can also employ the exponential trick to the above equations. Using the change of variable, $x' = x\exp(at)$, the equation $\dot{x} + ax = y$ is transformed to

$$\dot{x}' = y\exp(at),$$

whose solution is

$$x^{(n+1)} = [x^{(n)} + (\Delta t)\, y^{(n)}]\exp(-a(\Delta t)).$$

The other equation, $\dot{y} = -y$, is easily time advanced using $y^{(n+1)} = (1-\Delta t)y^{(n)}$. Clearly, the new set of equations are unconditionally stable.

This is how we solve the stiff equations numerically. With this, we end this long chapter on ODE solvers.

****

Conceptual Questions

1. Why is solving an equation with two very different timescales a difficult problem?

Exercises

1. Solve the equation $\dot{x} = x^2 - 10^6 x$ using the methods described in this section.

2. Solve the equation $\dot{x} + ax = y;\ \dot{y} = -y$ for $a = 10^{10}$ using the methods described in this section.

3. Numerically solve the equation for a damped oscillator whose the viscous time scale is much larger than the time period of the oscillator.

4. Solve the equation $\dot{x} = \sin(t) - 10^5 x$ using the methods described in this section.

Chapter Fourteen
FOURIER TRANSFORM

Synopsis

"The scientists of today think deeply instead of clearly. One must be sane to think clearly, but one can think deeply and be quite insane." — Nikola Tesla

This chapter describes one-dimensional and multi-dimensional Fourier transforms.

14.1 Fourier Transform

Many natural phenomena have multiple scales. For example, Earth's atmosphere has structures whose sizes range from meter to thousands of kilometres. Stellar and galactic flows have even wider range of scales. Fourier transform is an important tool to analyse such multiscale systems.

In this chapter, we will first introduce Fourier transform. After this, we will describe how to compute Fourier transforms of 1D and multi-dimensional functions. In the next chapter, we will employ Fourier transform to solve partial differential equations; this technique is called *spectral method*.

One-dimensional Fourier Transform

We consider a periodic, piece-wise continuous and differentiable function $f(x)$ of period L. Hence, $f(x+L) = f(x)$. In 1807, Fourier showed that such a function can be expanded as the following infinite series:

$$f(x) = \sum_{n=-\infty}^{\infty} \hat{f}_n \exp(i k_n x), \ldots (58)$$

where $i = \sqrt{-1}$; $k_n = 2n\pi/L$ with n as an integer from $-\infty$ to $+\infty$; and $\hat{f}_n$ is the *Fourier coefficient* or *Fourier mode*. The constants k_n's are called *wavenumbers*. See Figure 83 for an illustration. In the following discussion, we assume that $f(x)$ could be real or complex. However, $\hat{f}_n$ is always complex.

The functions $\{\exp(ik_n x)\}$ form an *orthogonal basis* (just as orthogonal polynomials), that is,

$$\int_0^L \exp(i k_n x)\exp(-i k_m x) dx = L \delta_{m,n},$$

where *Kronecker delta function*, $\delta_{m,n} = 1$ if $n = m$, and 0 otherwise. Using the above orthogonality property, we can invert Eq. (58) as follows:

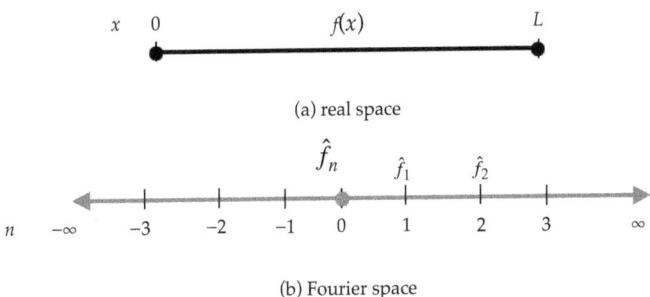

Figure 83: Fourier transform of $f(x)$ to $\hat{f}_n$. $f(x)$ is a periodic function with period of L. The index of $\hat{f}_n$ is an integer that takes values from $-\infty$ to ∞.

$$\hat{f}_n = \frac{1}{L}\int_0^L f(x)\exp(-ik_n x)dx. \quad\ldots(59)$$

In literature, Eqs. (59) and (58) are called *forward* Fourier *transform* (real to Fourier) and *inverse Fourier transforms* (Fourier to real) respectively. We use FT as a shorthand for Fourier transform. The space of wavenumbers is called *wavenumber space, Fourier space*, or *spectral space*. Note that the function f has two different representations: one in real space, and the other in spectral spaces.

The quantity $|f(x)|^2/2$ is the *energy density*, and its integral over the real space provides the *total energy* of the system. The quantity $|\hat{f}_n|^2/2$ is called the *modal energy*. Parseval's theorem relates the real space energy to the modal energy.

Parseval's theorem: The average energy in real space equals the sum of modal energies of all the Fourier modes. That is,

$$\frac{1}{L}\int_0^L dx \frac{1}{2}|f(x))^2| = \sum_{-\infty}^{\infty} \frac{1}{2}|\hat{f}_n|^2$$

.

Example 1: We compute the Fourier transform of $\cos(3x) + i\sin(3x)$,

$\sin(2x)$, $4\cos(4x)$, $8\cos^2(x)$ using Eq. (59). We assume that the box size is 2π. Note that the functions are periodic with a period of 2π. The results are

For $\cos(3x) + i\sin(3x)$: $\hat{f}_n = \delta_{3,n}$,
For $\sin(2x)$: $\hat{f}_n = \dfrac{1}{2i}(\delta_{2,n} - \delta_{-2,n})$,
For $4\cos(4x)$: $\hat{f}_n = 2(\delta_{4,n} + \delta_{-4,n})$,
For $8\cos^2(x)$: $\hat{f}_n = 4\delta_{(0)n} + 2(\delta_{2,n} + \delta_{-2,n})$.

We compute the total energy in Fourier space using the formula $\sum |\hat{f}_n|^2/2$ that yields ½, 1/4, 4, and 12 for the four cases. For example, for the last case,

$$E = \tfrac{1}{2}[4^2 + 2^2 + 2^2] = 12.$$

The above energy equals the average energy in real space. Verify the same!

Example 2: We compute the Fourier transform of $f(x) = \exp(-(x/a)^2/2)$, which is not a periodic function of x, using a trick. We consider $f(x)$ to be in a box of size L with $L \gg a$, and repeat this box on both sides (see Figure 84).

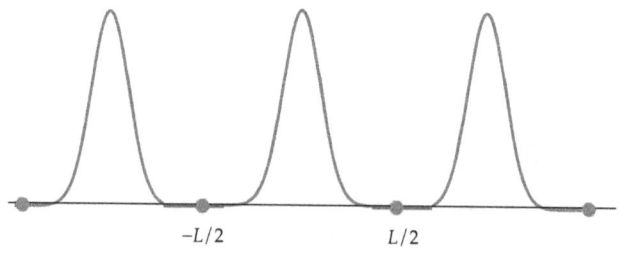

Figure 84: To compute the Fourier transform of $f(x) = \exp(-(x/a)^2/2)$, we keep $f(x)$ in a large box $[-L/2, L/2]$, and repeat it on both sides. We take Fourier transform of this periodic function.

Under these circumstances,

$$\hat{f}_n = \frac{1}{L} \int_{-L/2}^{L/2} \exp[-\frac{1}{2}(x/a)^2] \exp(-ik_n x) dx$$

$$= \frac{1}{L} \exp[-\frac{1}{2}(k_n a)^2] \int_{-L/2}^{L/2} \exp[-(x/a + ik_n a)^2/2] dx . \quad ...(60)$$

Numerical Fourier transform will yield the above result. Analytical form of the above integral, called error function, is quite complex to be discussed here.

For analytical calculations, we take $L \to \infty$, for which k_n becomes a continuum, while the sum of Eq. (58) becomes an integral. We perform the following transformation: $k_n \to k$; $\sum \to \int dn$; and $L\hat{f}_n = \hat{f}(k)\sqrt{2\pi}$ that leads to the following redefinitions of Fourier transforms:

$$f(x) = \frac{1}{\sqrt{2\pi}} \int_{-\infty}^{\infty} \hat{f}(k) \exp(ikx) dk, \quad .....(61)$$

$$\hat{f}(k) = \frac{1}{\sqrt{2\pi}} \int_{-\infty}^{\infty} f(x) \exp(-ikx) dx . \quad .....(62)$$

Under these definitions, the Fourier transform of $\exp(-(x/a)^2/2)$ is

$$\hat{f}(k) = a \exp[-\frac{1}{2}(ka)^2]. \quad .....(63)$$

In mathematics, Eqs. (61, 62) are called *Fourier transform*, while Eq. (58) is called *Fourier series*. However, in this book, following the convention of computational science, we will call Eqs. (58, 59) Fourier transforms.

We can compute $\{\hat{f}_n\}$ by performing integration of Eq. (59). We could employ one of the integration schemes of Chapter Eleven. However, optimised techniques, Discrete Fourier Transform (DFT) and Fast Fourier transform (FFT), are more common for the FT computations. These methods are topic of the next two sections.

****

Conceptual Questions

1. What benefits Fourier transform offer for analysing physical systems?

Exercises

1. Compute Fourier transforms of the following real functions that are periodic in domain $[0, 2\pi]$: $\cos(6x) + \sin(4x)$; $\cos^3(2x)$; $\sin^4(4x)$. Compute the total energy of these functions and verify Parseval's theorem.
2. Compute Fourier transforms of the following function in the domain $[-\infty, \infty]$.
    - $f(x) = \exp(-12.5\, x^2)$
    - $f(x) = \exp(-12.5\, |x|)$
    - $f(x) = \sin(20\, x)/x$

14.2 One-dimensional Discrete Fourier Transforms

In computers, forward Fourier transform and inverse Fourier transform are computed for discrete wavenumbers and discrete real space points. This method is called *Discrete Fourier Transform*, DFT in short.

For numerical computation, we discretize x and convert the integral of Eq. (59) to a sum. We divide the interval $[0, L]$ into N segments with the real space points at $x_j = jL/N$ with $j = 0{:}N{-}1$. Periodicity of the function implies that $f(x_N) = f(x_0)$, hence, $f(x_N)$ is not stored. See Figure 85.

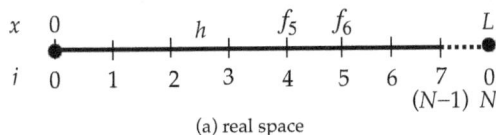

(a) real space

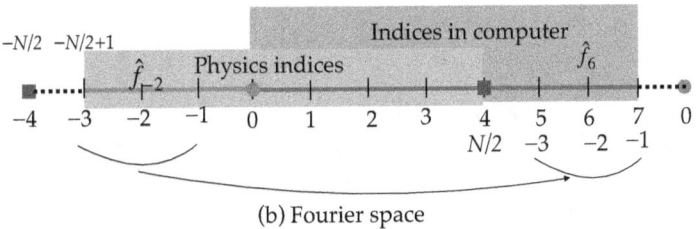

(b) Fourier space

Figure 85: For complex f: Storage of $\{f_j\}$ and $\{\hat{f}_n\}$ for $N = 8$, for which $f_0 = f_8$. Python stores $\hat{f}_n$ in an array with indices 0:7; the Fourier modes $\hat{f}_{-3}, \hat{f}_{-2}, \hat{f}_{-1}$ are transferred to $\hat{f}_5, \hat{f}_6, \hat{f}_7$ respectively.

The relationship between $\{f_j\}$ and $\{\hat{f}_n\}$ is linear, and there is a one-to-one transformation from one to other. It is customary to choose the wavenumber of the N Fourier coefficients from $-N/2+1$ to $N/2$. Under this arrangement, the formulas for the *Discrete Fourier Transform* (DFT) are

Inverse DFT: $$f_j = \sum_{n=-N/2+1}^{N/2} \hat{f}_n \exp\left[i\frac{2\pi j n}{N}\right], \quad \ldots..(64)$$

Forward DFT: $$\hat{f}_n = \frac{1}{N}\sum_{j=0}^{N-1} f_j \exp\left[i\frac{-2\pi j n}{N}\right]. \quad \ldots..(65)$$

It is easy to verify that the Fourier coefficients satisfy the property,

$$\hat{f}_n = \hat{f}_{n+N}.$$

Using this property, we shift the Fourier coefficients for $n = (-N/2+1)$: (-1) to $(N/2+1):(N-1)$. Under this arrangement, the Fourier coefficients are conveniently saved in an array with indices 0 to $N-1$. See Figure 85 for $N = 8$.

For DFT, Parseval's theorem translates to

$$\frac{1}{N}\sum_j \frac{1}{2}|f_j|^2 = \sum_n \frac{1}{2}|\hat{f}_n|^2.$$

DFT for Real $f(x)$

In a special case when $f(x)$ is real, $\{\hat{f}_n\}$ satisfy the *reality condition*, which is:

$$\hat{f}_{-n} = \hat{f}_n^*.$$

Consequently, we need to store only the Fourier coefficients for positive n's, i.e., for $0:N/2$. Also, note that among the Fourier modes, $\hat{f}_0$ and $\hat{f}_{N/2}$ are real; in fact, $\hat{f}_0$ is average of f_j's, while

$$\hat{f}_{N/2} = f_0 - f_1 + f_2 - f_3 + \ldots = \sum_{\text{even } j} f_j - \sum_{\text{odd } j} f_j$$

Hence, we have $(N-1)$ complex numbers for $\{\hat{f}_n\}$ with $n = 1$ to $(N/2-1)$, and 2 real numbers for $\hat{f}_0$ and $\hat{f}_{N/2}$. Thus, both $\{\hat{f}_n\}$ and $\{f_j\}$ consist of N

independent real numbers. See Figure 86 for an illustration.

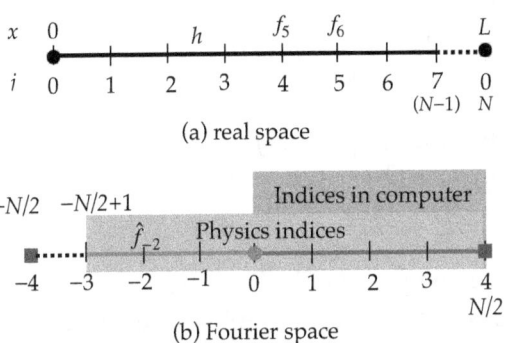

Figure 86: For real f: Storage of $\{f_j\}$ and $\{\hat{f}_n\}$ for $N = 8$. Python stores $\hat{f}_n$ in an array with indices $0:N/2$. Note that $\hat{f}_{-n} = \hat{f}_n^*$.

Forward and inverse DFTs prescribed above require N^2 addition and N^2 multiplications (N for each Fourier mode x N Fourier modes). In 1965, Cooley and Tukey devised an optimised algorithm, called *Fast Fourier Transform* (*FFT*), that can perform the above task using $O(N \log(N))$ floating-point operations. This is a big saving for large N. Python employs FFT for its Fourier transforms.

DFT using Python functions

Python's numpy module offers functions listed in Table 29. Note however that Python's *fft* and *ifft* have the following normalisation, which differs from our notation (Eqs. (64, 65)):

$$\text{ifft:} \quad f_j = \frac{1}{N} \sum_{-N/2+1}^{N/2} \hat{f}_n \exp\left[i\frac{2\pi j n}{N}\right]$$

$$\text{fft:} \quad \hat{f}_n = \sum_0^{N-1} f_j \exp\left[i\frac{-2\pi j n}{N}\right]$$

Hence, we need to be careful while matching the coefficients with our notation.

Table 29: Numpy's 1D FFT functions

Function	Operation
fft(f,N)	Forward FFT of complex f of size N
ifft(fk,N)	Inverse FFT of fk of size N
rfft(f,N)	Forward FFT of real f of size N
irfft(fk,N)	Inverse FFT of fk to real f; size = N

Example 1: We compute DFT of cos(3x)+i sin(3x), sin(2x), 4cos(4x), $8\cos^2(x)$ in a box of length 2π. We divide the box 2π into 15 segments and compute $\{f_j\}$ at the grid points (j = 0:15). We employ *fft* for the first function, and *rfft* for the rest of them. As expected, the results are same as that of Example 1 of the previous section. A code segment for fft computation is as follows:

```
L = 2*np.pi; N = 16;dx = L/N
j = np.arange(0,N)
x = j*dx
y = np.cos(3*x) + 1j*np.sin(3*x)
yk = np.fft.fft(y,N)/N
```

Computing Derivatives Using Fourier Transforms

We can compute accurate derivatives using Fourier transforms. Using Eq. (58) we deduce that

$$f'(x) = \frac{df(x)}{dx} = \sum_{-\infty}^{\infty} ik_n \hat{f}_n \exp(ik_n x) \quad .....(66)$$

Hence, the Fourier coefficients for $f'(x)$ are $\hat{f}'_n = ik_n\hat{f}$. Note that $f'(x)$ of Eq. (66) is exact as long as all the Fourier modes are included in the series. Since every signal has a wavenumber cutoff, denoted by k_{max}, the sum of Eq. (66) needs to be carried out from $-k_{max}$ to k_{max}, not $-\infty$ to ∞. Based on these input, we compute accurate $f'(x)$ using the following three steps:

1. Compute $\{\hat{f}_n\}$ for the given $f(x)$
2. Compute $\{ik_n\hat{f}_n\}$ using $\{\hat{f}_n\}$
3. Perform inverse transform of $\{ik_n\hat{f}_n\}$ that yields accurate $f'(x)$.

The aforementioned k_{max} is related to the minimum number of real-space points required for the FFT computation. We need two sampling points for the shortest wavelength λ_{min}. Hence, the minimum grid spacing (in real space) required is $h = \lambda_{min}/2$. Therefore, using $k_{max} = 2\pi/\lambda_{min}$, we deduce that

$$k_{max} h_{spectral} \approx \pi. \quad \ldots\ldots(67)$$

This condition is called *Nyquist criteria*. In addition, we require that $L \geq \lambda_{max}$.

Let us compare the spectral derivative with those computed using finite difference method. We consider $f(x) = \exp(ikx)$ and $\Delta x = h$. Based on the central-difference scheme,

$$f'(x_j) = [f(x_j+h) - f(x_j-h)]/(2h) = i\sin(kh) f(x_j)/h. \quad \ldots(68)$$

The exact derivative of $f(x)$ at $x = x_j$ is ikf_j. However, we approximate derivative using FD as $f'(x_j) = i\tilde{k}f_j$. Comparing this formula with Eq. (68), we deduce that

$\tilde{k}h = \sin(kh)$ for the central difference scheme.

Using similar calculation, for the fourth-order difference scheme, we can derive that

$$\tilde{k}h = (4/3)\sin(kh) - (1/6)\sin(2kh). \quad \ldots(69)$$

Note that $\tilde{k} = k$ for the spectral method due to its exact nature. To compare these results, we plot the three $\tilde{k}h$ in Figure 87. Note however that for all the method, $f'(x_j) \to ikf_j$ as $h \to 0$. As shown in Figure 87, $\tilde{k} \approx k$ up to $kh \approx \frac{1}{2}$.

We can also infer that for a given h, error in the FD derivatives decreases with the lowering of k. Hence, the error in FD derivative is maximum for $k = k_{max}$. Therefore, for an accurate computation, it is desirable that

$$k_{max} h_{FD} \leq \tfrac{1}{2} \quad \ldots\ldots(70)$$

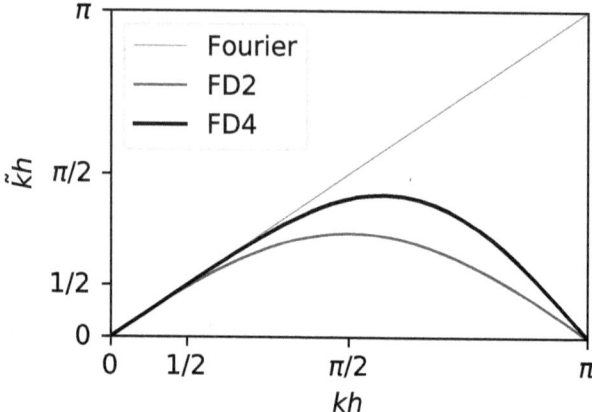

Figure 87: Plot of $\tilde{k}h$ vs. kh for Fourier transform, and second-order (FD2) and fourth-order (FD4) finite difference methods.

Note that Eq. (67) provides minimum h for the spectral calculation. Hence, a comparison of Eq. (70) with Eq. (67) shows that

$$h_{FD}/h_{spectral} \approx (\tfrac{1}{2})/\pi \approx 1/6.$$

Thus, for accurate derivative computations, the grid spacing for finite-difference should be approximately six times smaller than that for the Fourier method. Or, resolution of the shortest wave in the system requires 12 points in FD method compared to 2 in the spectral method. Note however that the requirement on h is less stringent for higher-oder finite-difference formulas.

Example 2: We compute the first derivative of $\cos(2x)$ using Fourier transform and finite difference method. The non-vanishing Fourier coefficients for $\cos(2x)$ are $\hat{f}_{-2} = \hat{f}_2 = 1/2$, multiplication of which with ik leads to $\hat{f}'_2 = i$ and $\hat{f}'_{-2} = -i$. The inverse Fourier transform of $\hat{f}'_n$

yields $f'(x) = -2\sin(2x)$, which is an exact answer. For the above computation, $N = 16$ is more than enough. A code segment for this computation is as follows:

```
kx = np.linspace(0, N//2, N//2+1)
fk_p = 1j*kx*fk    # fk is the Fourier transform of f(x)
fp = np.fft.irfft(fk_p,N)*N
```

We employ *np.gradient(f)/h* (central difference method) to compute the first derivative of $\cos(2x)$. As shown in Figure 88, the derivatives computed using Fourier transform (red dots) are accurate, while those using FD (blue stars) have significant errors. For the end points, the errors in FD derivatives are enhanced due to the limitations of the *gradient* function.

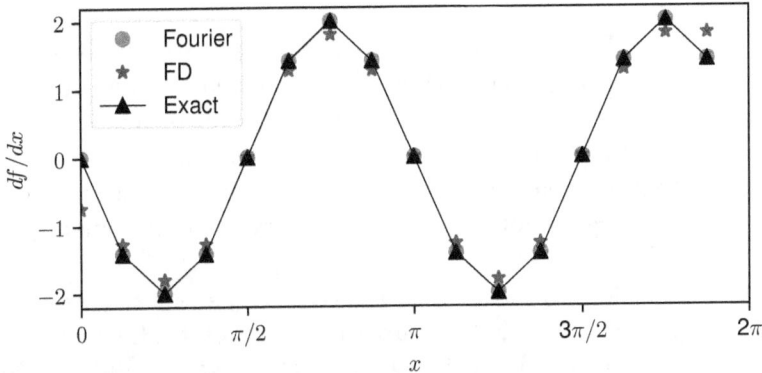

Figure 88: Example 2: Derivatives of $\cos(2x)$ computed using Fourier transform (dots) and Finite difference method (stars). The exact derivatives are shown using triangles. The spectral derivatives are exact, while FD derivatives have significant errors.

We can compute accurate higher-order derivatives using spectral method. For example, the Fourier coefficients of $f''(x)$ are $\hat{f}''_n = -k_n^2 \hat{f}_n$, whose inverse Fourier transform would yield exact $f''(x)$.

We end this section with a remark that *sine* and *cosine transforms* too are Fourier transforms. However, we do not discuss them here due to lack of space. Another important topic that is being skipped is *aliasing*.

In the next section, we will discuss multidimensional Fourier transforms.

****

Conceptual Questions

1. How does the derivatives computed using Fourier transform compare those computed using finite difference? Derive the formula of Eq. (69).

Exercises

1. Using Python's functions, compute the Fourier transforms of the following real functions that are periodic in domain $[0, 2\pi]$: $\cos(6x) + \sin(4x)$; $\cos^3(2x)$; $\sin^4(4x)$. Compute the total energy of these functions and verify Parseval's theorem.
2. Using Python's functions, compute Fourier transforms of the following complex function that is periodic in domain $[0, \pi]$: $\cos(2x) + i\sin(4x) + \cos(6x)$.
3. Consider $f(x) = \exp(-12.5\, x^2)$. What is the length scale of this system? Compute the Fourier transform of this function in the domain $[-5, 5]$. Is the numerical answer similar to the theoretical formula?
4. Verify Nyquist criteria using FFT functions of Python. For example, show that we need minimum four points to represent $\cos(2x)$.
5. Compute Fourier transforms of Bassel functions. Make appropriate assumptions on the limits.
6. Compute Fourier transforms of the following function in the domain $[-5, 5]$.
   - $f(x) = \exp(-12.5\, |x|)$
   - $f(x) = \sin(20\, x)/x$

14.3 Multidimensional Fourier Transform

It is straightforward to generalise the formalism of 1D Fourier transform to higher dimensions. We consider a periodic function $f(\mathbf{x})$ in a box $(L_1, L_2, .., L_d)$, where d is the space dimension. Note that the argument $\mathbf{x} = (x_1, x_2, .., x_d)$ is a vector.

The function $f(\mathbf{x})$ can be expanded in Fourier basis as follows:

Inverse transform: $f(\mathbf{x}) = \sum_{\mathbf{n}} \hat{f}_{\mathbf{n}} \exp(i\mathbf{k} \cdot \mathbf{x})$,

where the wavenumber component $k_l = 2\pi\, n_l/L_l$ with $l = 1{:}d$; and $\mathbf{n} = (n_1, n_2, ..., n_l, ..., n_d)$ is the lattice vector. Each n_l take values from $-\infty$ to $+\infty$. An inversion of the above equation yields

Forward transform: $\hat{f}_{\mathbf{n}} = \dfrac{1}{\prod_j L_j} \int d\mathbf{x} f(\mathbf{x}) \exp(-i\mathbf{k} \cdot \mathbf{x})$.

For the discrete Fourier transform, we discretize the real space into $\prod N_j$ small blocks, with N_1 sections along x_1, N_2 sections along x_2, ..., N_d sections along x_d. Hence, at the lattice point $(j_1, j_2, ..., j_d)$,

$$\mathbf{x} = \{(L_1/N_1)j_1, (L_2/N_2)j_2, ..., (L_d/N_d)j_d\}.$$

With this notation, multi-dimensional transform is

Inverse: $f_{\mathbf{j}} = \sum_{\mathbf{n}} \hat{f}_{\mathbf{n}} \exp\left(2\pi i \dfrac{j_l n_l}{L_l}\right)$,

Forward: $\hat{f}_{\mathbf{n}} = \dfrac{1}{\prod_j N_j} \sum_{\mathbf{j}} f_{\mathbf{j}} \exp\left(-2\pi i \dfrac{j_l n_l}{L_l}\right)$.

Note that for complex $f(\mathbf{x})$, the number of variables in real and Fourier spaces are the same. For example, in 2D, as shown in Figure 89, we have $N_x * N_y$ complex variables in both the spaces.

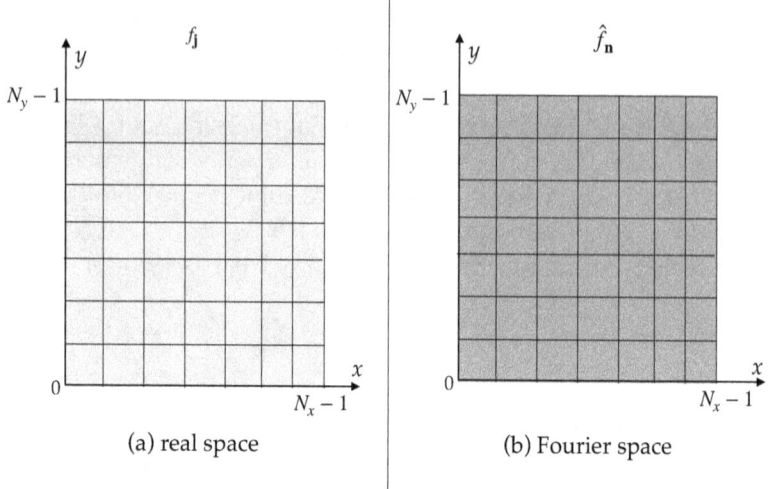

Figure 89: (a) A discretized 2D complex field $\{f_j\}$. (b) The Fourier coefficients $\{\hat{f}_n\}$ for the complex field. The number of complex variables in both real and Fourier spaces are $N_x * N_y$.

The Fourier coefficients $\{\hat{f}_n\}$ satisfy the following property:

$$\hat{f}_{(n_1+a_1N_1, n_2+a_2N_2, \ldots)} = \hat{f}_{(n_1, n_2, \ldots)},$$

where a_i are integers. The above properties hold for both real and complex fields. For real $f(x)$, the Fourier coefficients satisfy another important property, called *reality condition*:

$$\hat{f}_{(-n)} = \hat{f}^*_{(n)}.$$

Due to the reality condition, we save only half of the Fourier modes. We demonstrate this feature in Figure 90 for a 2D real $f(x)$. In Fourier space, only $\{\hat{f}_n\}$ with positive n_y (modes in the shaded region of Figure 90(b)) are stored inside the computer. As shown in the figure, $\hat{f}_{-2,-2} = \hat{f}^*_{2,2}$, hence $\hat{f}_{-2,-2}$ is not stored. However, all the Fourier coefficients are saved for $n_y = 0$. For this case, we need to manually set $\hat{f}_{-n_x, 0} = \hat{f}^*_{n_x, 0}$.

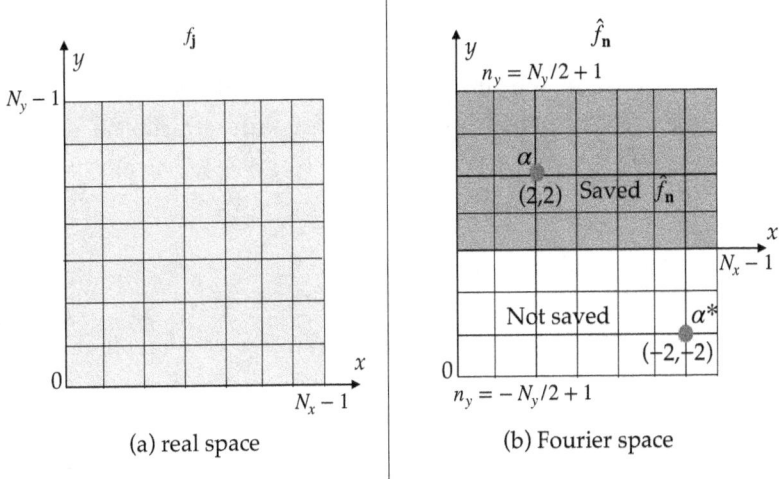

Figure 90: (a) 2D real field $\{f_j\}$. (b) The Fourier coefficients $\{\hat{f}_n\}$ of $\{f_j\}$. Only $\{\hat{f}_n\}$ in the shaded zone of (b) are stored in a computer due to the reality condition. Note that $\hat{f}_{-2,-2} = \hat{f}^*_{2,2}$.

Multidimensional DFT Using Python Functions

Python's numpy module offers functions for multidimensional FFT. These functions are listed in Table 30. The functions *fft2*, *ifft2*, *rfft2*, *irfft2* are for 2D fields, while, the functions *fftn*, *ifftn*, *rfftn*, *irfftn* are for *n*-dimensional fields. The forward transforms take the real-space field $\{f_j\}$ as input, while the inverse transforms take $\{\hat{f}_n\}$ as input.

Table 30: Numpy's multidimensional FFT functions.

Function	Operation
fft2(f)	Forward FFT for 2D complex *f*
ifft2(fk)	Inverse FFT for 2D complex *fk*
rfft2(f)	Forward FFT for 2D real *f*
irfft2(fk)	Inverse FFT for 2D *fk* (to real *f*)
fftn(f)	Forward FFT for n-dimensional complex *f*
ifftn(fk)	Inverse FFT for n-dimensional complex *fk*
rfftn(f)	Forward FFT for n-dimensional real *f*
irfftn(fk)	Inverse FFT for n-dimensional complex *fk* (to real *f*)

Example 1: Consider the functions, cos(x+y) and 8cos(x)sin(y), which are periodic in a $(2\pi)^2$ box. We compute the Fourier transforms of these functions as follows. Since cos(x+y) = (½) [exp(i(x+y)) + exp(−i(x+y))], we deduce that

$$\hat{f}_n = (½) [\delta_{nx,1} \delta_{ny,1} + \delta_{nx,-1} \delta_{ny,-1}]$$

That is, $\hat{f}_{1,1} = \hat{f}_{-1,-1} = ½$. Using similar arguments, we show that for 8 cos(x) sin(y),

$$\hat{f}_n = (-2i) [\delta_{nx,1} \delta_{ny,1} + \delta_{nx,-1} \delta_{ny,1} - \delta_{nx,1} \delta_{ny,-1} - \delta_{nx,-1} \delta_{ny,-1}]$$

The following Python code performs the above task.

```
L = 2*np.pi; Nx = 16; Ny = 16; dx = L/Nx; dy = L/Ny

f = np.zeros((Nx, Ny))
for jx in range(0,Nx):
    for jy in range(0,Ny):
        f[jx,jy] = 8*np.cos(jx*dx)*np.sin(jy*dy)

fk = np.fft.fftn(f)/(Nx*Ny)
```

Example 2: We compute the Fourier transform of 4 sin(2x +3y +4z) in a $(2\pi)^3$ periodic box using the similar procedure as Example 1. The result and the corresponding Python code given below.

$$\hat{f}_n = (-2i) [\delta_{nx,2} \delta_{ny,3} \delta_{nz,4} - \delta_{nx,-2} \delta_{ny,-3} \delta_{nz,-4}]$$

```
L = 2*np.pi; Nx = 16; Ny = 16; Nz = 16; dx = L/Nx; dy = L/Ny; dz = L/Nz

f = np.zeros((Nx, Ny, Nz))
for jx in range(0,Nx):
    for jy in range(0,Ny):
        for jz in range(0,Nz):
            f[jx,jy,jz] =
4*np.sin(2*jx*dx+3*jy*dy+4*jz*dz)
```

```
fk = np.fft.fftn(f)/(Nx*Ny*Nz)
```

Additional important properties of Fourier transforms are as follows. Here, for convenience, we index the Fourier mode with its wavenumber.

1. The Fourier transform of constant function, C, is $C \delta_{k,0}$.
2. For a n-dimensional field f, the derivative along x_j is $FT\left[\partial f/\partial x_j\right] = ik_j\hat{f}$.
3. The Fourier transform of a product of two real functions $f(x)$ and $g(x)$ is a convolution. That is, $(fg)_k = \sum_p f_{k-p} g_p$.
4. Parseval's theorem can also be written as follows: $\langle f(x)g(x)\rangle = \sum_p \Re[f_p^* g_p]$.
5. Fourier transform of the correlation function is the power spectrum. That is,

$$\frac{1}{L_x L_y L_z} \int d\mathbf{r} \langle f(\mathbf{r}) g(\mathbf{r}+\mathbf{l})\rangle \exp(-i(\mathbf{k}\cdot\mathbf{l})) = f(-\mathbf{k})g(\mathbf{k}).$$

With this, we end our discussion on Fourier transforms. In the next chapter, we will solve partial differential equations (PDEs) using Fourier transforms.

****

Exercises

1. Consider the velocity field $\mathbf{u}(x,y) = 4[\hat{x} \sin 2x \cos 2y - \hat{y} \cos 2x \sin 2y]$ that is periodic in a π^2 box. Using Python functions, compute the Fourier transforms of velocity field. Compute the average energy in real space and in Fourier space, and verify Parseval's theorem.

2. Consider a function $f(x,y,z) = 16(\sin 2x \cos 5y \sin 16z + \sin x + \cos y)$ that is periodic in a $(2\pi)^3$ box. Compute the Fourier transform and energy of $f(x,y,z)$.

3. Consider $f(x,y,z) = \exp[-12.5(x^2 + y^2 + z^2)]$. What is the length scale of this system? Compute the Fourier transform of this function in the domain $[-5:5, -5:5, -5:5]$.

4. Compute Fourier transform of $f(x,y) = \exp[-12.5((x-10)^2 + (y-5)^2)]$ defined in the domain $[0:20] \times [0:20]$.

Chapter Fifteen
SPECTRAL METHOD FOR PDES

Synopsis

"Science is a differential equation."
—Alan Turing

Using Fourier transforms, we can solve partial differential equations quite accurately. This is the topic of the present chapter.

15.1 General Procedure & Diffusion Equation

Partial differential equations (PDE) can be solved using Fourier transform. This procedure, called *spectral method*, is the topic of this chapter.

The basic steps of the spectral method are as follows. Consider the following PDE:

$$\frac{\partial \phi}{\partial t} = f(\phi, \frac{\partial \phi}{\partial x}, \frac{\partial^2 \phi}{\partial x^2}, t) \quad \ldots\ldots(71)$$

Here, the dependent variable $\phi(x,t)$ is a function of x and time t. The RHS of the equation contains a function dependent on ϕ and its spatial derivatives, as well on t. The domain of the space variable x is $[0:L]$.

In spectral method, we assume that the function ϕ is periodic with a period of L. We take Fourier transform of Eq. (71) that yields ODEs for each Fourier mode of the system:

$$\frac{d\hat{\phi}_k}{dt} = \hat{f}_k .$$

The conversion of a PDE to a set of ODEs is a major simplification. These ODEs can in turn be solved using the methods described in Chapter Thirteen. Note that every physical system has a finite number of Fourier modes.

In the next chapter, we will cover solution of PDEs using finite difference method. In this method, the spatial derivatives (e.g, $\partial_x \phi$) are computed using finite difference method, which was discussed in Chapter Twelve. Note that the spectral derivatives are much more accurate than the FD derivatives. Therefore, the solutions of PDEs computed using spectral method are more accurate than those using the FD method.

In this chapter, we solve the following equations using spectral method:

1. Diffusion equation
2. Wave equation

3. Burgers eqation
4. Navier-Stokes equation

Solving Diffusion Equation Using Spectral Method

The diffusion equation is

$$\partial_t \phi = \kappa \frac{\partial^2 \phi}{\partial x^2},$$

where $\partial_t \phi$ is a shorthand for $\partial \phi / \partial t$. The diffusion equation, which is one of the most important equations of physics, describes diffusion of temperature, pollution, etc. in a static medium. Note that the diffusion time L^2/κ, where L is the system size, is the time scale of the system. In a diffusion time, the field ϕ diffuses considerably, or ϕ_{max} goes down by a significant factor.

In 1807, Fourier devised Fourier series to solve the diffusion equation for a given initial condition $\phi(x, t=0)$. Fourier's procedure to solve the diffusion is as follows. The diffusion equation in Fourier space is

$$\frac{d}{dt}\hat{\phi}_k = -\kappa k^2 \hat{\phi}_k, \quad .....(72)$$

whose solution is

$$\hat{\phi}_k(t) = \hat{\phi}_k(t=0)\exp(-\kappa k^2 t). \quad .....(73)$$

For the initial condition, $\phi(x, t=0)$, we can compute

$$\hat{\phi}_k(t=0) = \frac{1}{L}\int_0^L \phi(x, t=0)\exp(-ikx)dx.$$

We arrive at the final $\hat{\phi}_k(t)$ by substituting $\hat{\phi}_k(t=0)$ in Eq. (73). An inverse Fourier transform of $\hat{\phi}_k(t)$ yields the final solution $\phi(x,t)$.

For a general initial condition, it is complex to derive an analytical solution for $\phi(x,t)$. However, it is quite easy to solve for $\phi(x,t)$ computationally. We illustrate this procedure using the following examples.

Example 1: We solve the diffusion equation in a 2π box with $\exp(-2(x-\pi)^2)$ as an initial condition. We choose $\kappa = 1$, $t_{\text{final}} = 1$ units. We take the box size to be 2π. The plots and a code segment for the above computation is given below:

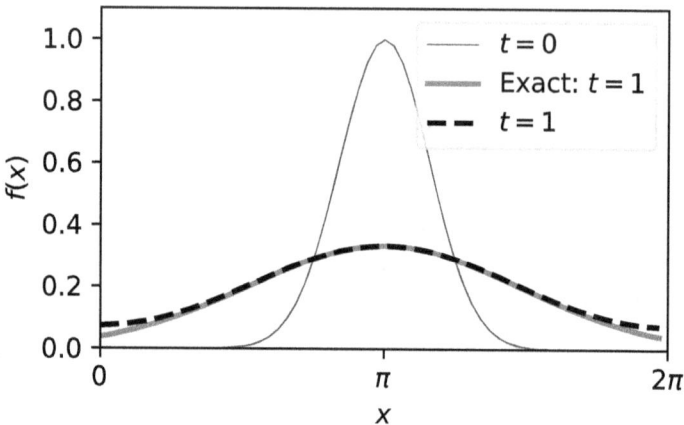

Figure 91: A figure depicting evolution of a initial function $\exp(-2(x - \pi)^2)$ (thin curve) under diffusion. The numerical solution (black dashed line) is close to the exact solution (for $L = \infty$), represented by thick solid curve (see Example 2 below).

```
kappa = 1; tf = 1
L = 2*np.pi; N = 64; h = L/N
j = np.arange(0,N); x = j*h

f = np.exp(-2*(x-pi)**2)   # init cond
fk = np.fft.rfft(f,N)/N
kx = np.linspace(0, N//2, N//2+1)

# Final states
fk_t = fk*np.exp(-kappa*kx**2*tf)
f_t = np.fft.irfft(fk_t,N)*N   # in Real space
```

In the above code, the array *f* contains the initial condition, while *fk* contains its Fourier coefficients. *fk_t* contains the Fourier coefficients at

$t = tf$. The inverse transform of fk_t yields f_t, which is the final result in real space. The initial and final real-space fields are shown in Figure 91. The field f spreads out as time progresses.

Example 2: We solve the diffusion in the infinite domain using Fourier transform following the formulas of Example 2 of Section 14.1. Here, the field variable is chosen as ϕ.

The Fourier transform of the initial condition $\phi(t=0) = \exp(-2(x-\pi)^2)$ is

$$\hat{\phi}(k, t = 0) = a \exp[-\frac{1}{2}(ka)^2]\exp(-ika),$$

where $a = \frac{1}{2}$. Hence,

$$\hat{\phi}(k, t) = a \exp[-\frac{1}{2}(ka)^2 - \kappa k^2 t]\exp(-ika),$$

whose inverse transform yields

$$\phi(x, t) = \frac{a}{a'} \exp\left[-\frac{1}{2a'^2}(x - \pi)^2\right],$$

where $a' = \sqrt{a^2 + \kappa t}$. With time, the above $\phi(x,t)$ spreads with decreasing amplitude. The exact solution $\phi(x,t=2)$ is shown in Figure 91, and it matches closely with the numerical solution (except at the ends).

CFL Condition

Even though Eq. (72) has an exact solution ($\hat{\phi}_k(t = 0)\exp(-\kappa k^2 t)$), it is important to understand the evolution of this equation with Euler's forward method (from t_n to t_{n+1}):

$$\hat{\phi}_k^{(n+1)} = \hat{\phi}_k^{(n)}[1 - \kappa k^2 (\Delta t)].$$

Note that $t_{n+1} - t_n = \Delta t$. Clearly, Euler's forward method is stable only if

$$|1 - \kappa k^2 (\Delta t)| < 1, \text{ or } \Delta t < \frac{2}{\kappa k^2}.$$

Note that the diffusion time scales for different modes are different. Hence we have a wide range of time scales making the diffusion equation stiff. However, for time integration, we need to choose a single Δt for all the modes, and it has to be the smallest Δt of the system. Therefore,

$$\Delta t < \frac{2}{\kappa k_{\max}^2}.$$

Note that $k_{\max} = 2\pi/\lambda_{\min} = 2\pi/(2h) = \pi N/L$, where h is the grid spacing, and N is the total number of discrete points. Hence,

$$\Delta t < \frac{2h^2}{\kappa \pi^2}.$$

Euler's forward method is unstable for Δt larger than $2h^2/(\kappa \pi^2)$. Other schemes, such as RK2 method, has a similar Δt requirement. The above constraint on Δt is called *Courant–Friedrichs–Lewy* (CFL) condition. Note that the wide range of Δt, from $2/(\kappa k_{\max}^2)$ to $2/(\kappa k_{\min}^2)$, makes the system stiff.

Example 3: For Example 1, we estimate Δt for Euler forward scheme based on CFL condition. Note that $\kappa = 1$, $L = 2\pi$, and $N = 64$. Therefore, $h = 2\pi/N = 2\pi/64$. Hence, according to the CFL criteria, minimum Δt is

$$(\Delta t)_{\min} = \frac{2h^2}{\kappa \pi^2} = \frac{2 \times 4\pi^2}{64^2 \pi^2} = \frac{1}{512} \approx 2 \times 10^{-3}.$$

Equation (72) can be solved exactly, hence the time marching procedures are not required for the diffusion equation. However, we need time marching schemes for nonlinear equations—Burgers and Navier-Stokes equations—that will be described later in this chapter.

The procedure to solve 2D and 3D diffusion equations is very similar. For them, we need to employ multidimensional FFTs. In later sections of this chapter we will solve more complex problems with spectral method.

****

Conceptual Questions

1. State applications of diffusion equations in physics, and in other areas of science and engineering.

Exercises

1. Solve the diffusion equation in a $[-\pi,\pi]$ box with $\exp(-8x^2)$ as an initial condition. Choose $\kappa = 1$ and $t_{final} = 5$ units. Make a movie of the profile. Compare the numerical result with analytical results for an infinite box.
2. Repeat Exercise 1 for a box $[-4\pi,4\pi]$. Also, study the variations of the solution with respect to κ.
3. Work out the asymptotic solution (large t) for Example 2.

15.2 Solving Wave, Burgers, and KdV Equations

In this section, we employ spectral method to solve several PDEs that exhibit wave motion. In particular, we will solve wave, Burgers, and KdV equations. The wave equation is linear, but Burgers and KdV equations are nonlinear.

Wave Equation

Many PDEs exhibit wave motion. Some of the leading examples are sound waves and electromagnetic waves. Here we solve the following PDE that exhibits wave motion:

$$\partial_t \phi + c \partial_x \phi = 0, \quad \text{.....(74)}$$

where c (a positive number) is the velocity of the wave.

We solve Eq. (74) for a given initial condition $\phi(x,t=0)$. Following the same procedure as that for the diffusion equation, we write Eq. (74) in Fourier space that yields the following set of ODEs:

$$\frac{d}{dt}\hat{\phi}_k = -ick\hat{\phi}_k. \quad (75)$$

The solution of the above equation is

$$\hat{\phi}_k(t) = \hat{\phi}_k(0)\exp(-ikct). \quad \text{.....(76)}$$

For the initial condition $\phi(x,t=0) = \zeta(x)$, $\hat{\phi}_k(0) = \hat{\zeta}_k$, which is substituted in Eq. (76). Hence, the solution for the wave equation is

$$\phi(x,t) = \sum_k \hat{\zeta}_k \exp[ik(x-ct)] = \sum_k \hat{\zeta}_k \exp[ikx'],$$

where $x' = x - ct$. From the above equation, we deduce that

$$\phi(x,t) = \zeta(x') = \zeta(x - ct).$$

Hence, $\phi(x,t)$ is $\zeta(x)$ travelling to the right with a velocity of c. The evolution of a wave packet is illustrated in Figure 92. Here, the wave packet moves to the right without any distortion (or dispersion). We remark that the wave equation $\partial_t \phi - c\partial_x \phi = 0$ yields a wave travelling to the left. Verify yourself!

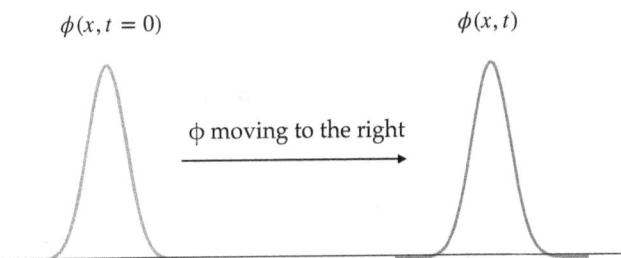

Figure 92: Under wave action, a wave packet moves to the right without distortion.

Equation (75) has a simple solution, hence, no computational method is required to solve this equation. However, it is important to see how ODE solvers could be used for solving the wave equation. The lessons learnt here will be useful for solving nonlinear wave equations.

Let us employ Euler's forward method to solve Eq. (75). Under this scheme,

$$\hat{\phi}_k^{(n+1)} = (1 - ick(\Delta t))\hat{\phi}_k^{(n)}$$

where $t_{n+1} - t_n = \Delta t$. The above equation is unconditionally unstable. Hence, we need to employ either an implicit scheme or the exponential trick to solve Eq. (75) computationally.

Next, we solve Burgers equation using numerical methods.

Burgers Equation

Burgers equation, given below, is a flow equation for a fully-compressible fluid:

$$\partial_t u + u\partial_x u = \nu\, \partial^2 u, \text{ or } \partial_t u + \partial_x(u^2/2) = \nu\, \partial_x^2 u,$$

where ν is the kinematic viscosity of the fluid. In comparison to the diffusion equation discussed in Section 15.1, Burgers equation has a nonlinear term, $u\partial_x u$.

In Fourier space, we obtain the following set of equations for the Fourier modes:

$$\frac{d}{dt}\hat{u}_k = -i\frac{k}{2}\widehat{u^2}_k - \nu k^2 \hat{u}_k = -\hat{N}_k - \nu k^2 \hat{u}_k, \quad \ldots(77)$$

where k is the wavenumber, and the nonlinear term involves a convolution: $\widehat{u^2}_k = \sum_p \hat{u}_p \hat{u}_{k-p}$. To solve Eq. (77), we can employ one of the methods discussed in Chapter Thirteen.

First, we employ Euler's forward method. Following the prescription of Section 13.2, we observe that $\partial f/\partial \hat{u}_k = -\nu k^2$, where f is the RHS of Eq. (77). Thus, the stability condition is unaffected by the nonlinear term, and it is dictated by the diffusive term. An application of Euler's forward scheme to Eq. (77) yields

$$\hat{u}_k^{(n+1)} = \hat{u}_k^{(n)}[1 - \nu k^2(\Delta t)] - (\Delta t)\hat{N}_k.$$

Following the result on the stability of diffusion equation, we deduce that the Euler's forward scheme is stable for Burgers equation when

$$|1 - \nu k^2 (\Delta t)| < 1, \text{ or } \Delta t < 2/(\nu k^2).$$

We need to choose the smallest Δt, which is $2/(\nu k_{max}^2) = 2h^2/(\nu \pi^2)$ with h as the grid spacing (see Section 15.1 for details). Note that Eq. (77) has a range of time scales: $2/(\nu k_{max}^2)$ to $2/(\nu k_{min}^2)$. In addition, the nonlinear term has its own time scale, which is of the order of h/u_{rms} (here, u_{rms} is root mean square velocity). The existence of so many time scales makes Eq. (77) stiff.

As discussed in Section 13.7, we can solve the stiffness problem by employing a semi-implicit scheme for the linear term or by using the exponential trick. Under one of the semi-implicit schemes, called Crank-Nicolson scheme,

$$\hat{u}_k^{(n+1)} = \hat{u}_k^{(n)} - \nu k^2 (\Delta t)\frac{1}{2}\left(\hat{u}_k^{(n)} + \hat{u}_k^{(n+1)}\right) - (\Delta t)\hat{N}_k,$$

or, $\hat{u}_k^{(n+1)} = \hat{u}_k^{(n)}\left[\dfrac{1-\nu k^2(\Delta t)/2}{1+\nu k^2(\Delta t)/2}\right] - (\Delta t)\hat{N}_k$

which is stable.

For the exponential trick, we make a change of variable, $\hat{u}'_k = \hat{u}_k \exp(\nu k^2 t)$, that transforms Eq. (77) to

$$\frac{d}{dt}\hat{u}'_k = -\hat{N}_k \exp(\nu k^2 t).$$

An application Euler's forward scheme to the above equation yields

$$\hat{u}_k^{(n+1)} = \left[\hat{u}_k^{(n)} - (\Delta t)\hat{N}_k^{(n)}\right]\exp(-\nu k^2(\Delta t)).$$

We could also employ more advanced time-stepping schemes, such as RK2 and RK4 methods, to integrate the Burgers equation.

A novice computation of the convolution, $\widehat{u^2}_k = \sum_p \hat{u}_p \hat{u}_{k-p}$ takes $O(N^2)$ floating-point operations, where N is the total number of Fourier modes. This computation is very expensive. Fortunately, FFT enables us to compute the convolution and nonlinear term using $O(N\log(N))$ operations, which is much faster than $O(N^2)$ for large N. As shown in Figure 93, we perform the following steps:

1. Transform $\hat{u}_k$ to $u(x)$ using IFFT
2. Compute $[u(x)]^2$
3. Perform forward FFT to compute FT of $[u(x)]^2$, which is $\widehat{u(x)^2}$
4. Multiply ik to $\widehat{u(x)^2}_k$ that yields the desired $\hat{N}_k = ik\widehat{u(x)^2}_k$.

In the above procedure, the array multiplication takes $O(N)$ operations, while FFT takes $O(N \log(N))$ operations. Hence, the overall time complexity of the computation for the nonlinear term is $O(N\log(N))$. Since $[u(x)]^2$ is computed in real space, the present method is also called a *pseudo-spectral method*.

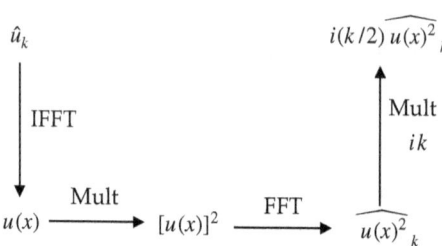

Figure 93: A schematic diagram illustrating computation of the nonlinear term $i k \widehat{u(x)^2}_k$.

Example 1: We simulate the Burgers equation in $x = [0, 2\pi]$ with $\nu = 0.1$ up to final time of 1 unit. We start with an initial state of $\sin(x)$, and choose $\Delta t = 0.001$ for time stepping. We employ the exponential trick, and time advance the nonlinear term using RK2 method. A code segment for the solution of Burgers equation is given below.

```
nu = 0.1; tf = 1; dt = 0.001; nsteps = int(tf/dt)
L = 2*np.pi; N = 64; h = L/N
j = np.arange(0,N); x = j*h

kx = np.linspace(0, N//2, N//2+1)
exp_factor_dtby2 = np.exp(-nu*kx**2*dt/2)
exp_factor = np.exp(-nu*kx**2*dt)

def comput_Nk(fk):
f = np.fft.irfft(fk,N)*N
    f = f*f
    fk_prod = np.fft.rfft(f,N)/N
    return (1j*kx*fk_prod)

f = np.sin(x) # initiation condition
```

```
fk = np.fft.rfft(f,N)/N    # FT(f)

for i in range(nsteps+2):
    Nk = comput_Nk(fk)
    fk_mid = (fk -(dt/2)*Nk)*exp_factor_dtby2
    Nk_mid = comput_Nk(fk_mid)
    fk = (fk -dt*Nk_mid)*exp_factor
```

The evolution of $u(x)$ at different times is shown in Figure 94. Clearly, $u(x)$ evolves from $\sin(x)$ to a well-formed shock by $t = 1$.

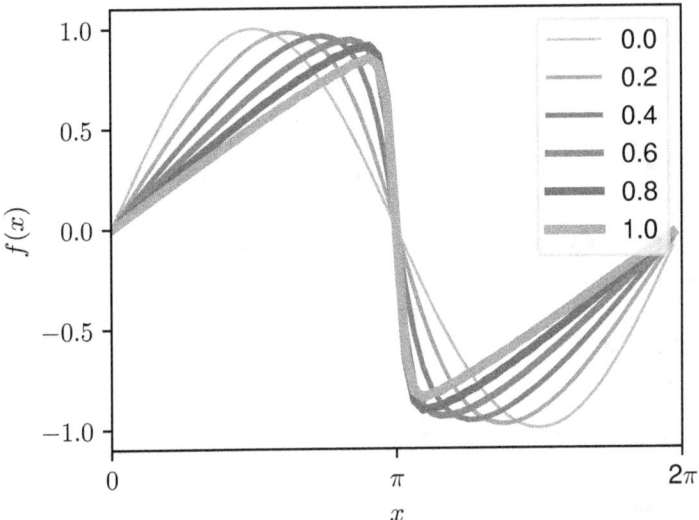

Figure 94: Example 1: Evolution of $u(x,t)$ for Burgers equation from $\sin(x)$ to a well-formed shock. The thickness of $u(x,t)$ increases with time.

In this example, according to the CFL condition,

$$(\Delta t)_{\min} = \frac{2h^2}{\nu \pi^2} = \frac{2 \times 4\pi^2}{0.1 \times 64^2 \pi^2} = \frac{10}{512} \approx 2 \times 10^{-2}.$$

On the other hand, based on the nonlinear term,

$\Delta t < h/U_{\text{rms}} \approx 1/64 \approx 0.015$.

For our computation, we choose $\Delta t = 0.001$, which is much smaller than both the limits.

KdV Equation

Korteweg–de Vries (KdV) equation describes solitons over shallow water. One version of the KdV equation is

$$\partial_t u + u \partial_x u = \kappa \, \partial_x^3 u \quad \ldots\ldots(78)$$

The nonlinearity of the KdV equation is same as that of Burgers equation. The only difference between the two equations is that the viscous term of the Burgers equation is replaced by a dispersive term ($\kappa \partial_x^3 u$) in the KdV equation. Consequently, $\int (u^2) \, dx$ is conserved for the KdV equation, but it decreases with time for the Burgers equation.

In Fourier space, the equation for the Fourier mode with wavenumber k is

$$\frac{d}{dt}\hat{u}_k = -\hat{N}_k - i\nu k^3 \hat{u}_k \quad \ldots\ldots(79)$$

where the nonlinear term $\hat{N}_k$ is same as that for the Burger equation. Therefore, KdV equation could be solved using FFT as in Burgers equation. An implementation of the diffusive term using Euler's forward method is unstable, hence either leapfrog method or the exponential trick is employed for the time integration.

Example 2: We simulate KdV equation for $\kappa = 0.1$ up to 2 time unit. We take $dt = 0.001$. The initial condition is chosen as $\sin(x)$. We employ exponential trick for absorbing the diffusion term, and time advance the nonlinear term using leapfrog method.

We exhibit the evolution of $u(x)$ in Figure 95. At $t = 2$, we observe several solitons, which are stable hump-like structures.

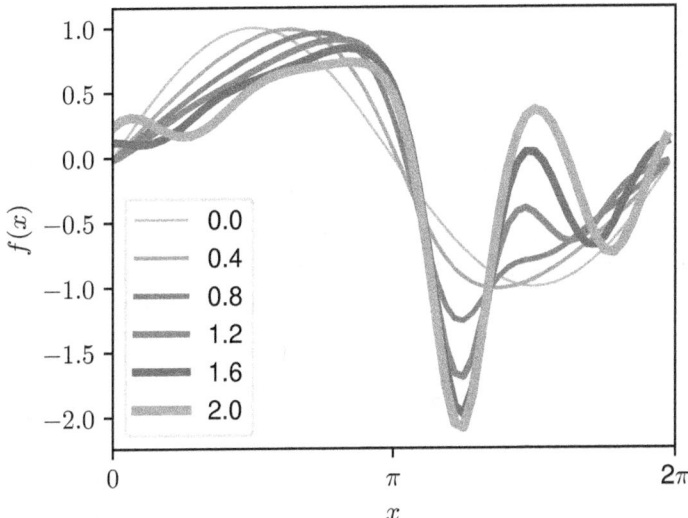

Figure 95: Example 2: Evolution of $u(x,t)$ for the KdV equation from $\sin(x)$ to structures called *solitons*. The thickness of $u(x,t)$ increases with time.

With this, we end our discussion on the spectral solutions of wave, Burgers, and KdV equations.

****

Conceptual Questions

1. The solution of Burgers equation shows sharp shocks for very small viscosity. What kind of numerical problems do you anticipate for such situations?
2. Study the analytical solution of dissipation-less Burgers equation (with $\nu = 0$). Try to simulate this equation using energy conserving time-stepping schemes.
3. Study the KdV equation and its soliton solutions. You may refer to Drazin [1989] on details.

Exercises

1. Solve the wave equation of Eq. (74) numerically in a periodic box of $[-4\pi, 4\pi]$. Take $c = 1$ and $\exp(-8x^2)$ as an initial profile.
2. For Exercise 1, make a movie of the wave motion.
3. Solve the Burgers equation of Example 1 using Euler's forward method and compare your results with that shown in Figure 94.
4. Solve Example 1 for $\nu = 10, 1, 0.01, 0.001$ with $\sin(x)$ as an initial condition. What are the grid requirements for these simulations?
5. Prove that the exact solution of Burgers equation with $\nu = 0$ is $u(x,t) = (x-a)/t$, with shocks in between the linear profiles. How does the solution with $\nu = 0.001$ compare with the exact solution?
6. Show that the KdV equation conserves the total energy $\int (1/2) u^2\, dx$. What is the value of the total energy for Example 2. Does RK2 method conserve the total energy? Do you get better handle on energy conservation with the leapfrog method?
7. Solve the KdV equation fo Example 2 with $\kappa = 0.02$. Compare your results with those of Example 2.
8. It has been shown that one of the exact solutions of the KdV equation is a travelling soliton, $(U/2)\,\mathrm{sech}^2[(\sqrt{U}/2)(x-Ut-x_0)]$. Here, U is the velocity of the soliton. Demonstrate it numerically.
9. Solve the KPZ equation, $\partial_t h = \dfrac{1}{2}(\partial_x h)^2 + \nu \partial_x^2 h$, numerically in a periodic box $[0, 2\pi]$. Take $\nu = 0.1$.

15.3 Spectral Solution of Naiver-Stokes Equation

In this section we will describe how to solve the Navier-Stokes equation using spectral method.

Solving the Navier-Stokes Equation

The Navier-Stokes equations describe fluid flows, which are seen everywhere—in kitchen sink, atmosphere, stars, etc. In general, flow properties depend on the box geometry, boundary condition, degree of compressibility of the fluid, initial condition, etc. However, we make a simplified picture in this section. We focus on an incompressible flow far away from the walls. To a good approximation, such a flow can be simulated in a periodic box using spectral method (Verma [2019]). This is what will be described in this section.

The Navier-Stokes equations under an incompressible limit are given below:

$$\partial_t \mathbf{u} + \mathbf{u} \cdot \nabla \mathbf{u} = -\nabla p + \nu \nabla^2 \mathbf{u}, \quad \ldots(80)$$

$$\nabla \cdot \mathbf{u} = 0, \quad \ldots(81)$$

where $\mathbf{u}, p$ are the velocity and pressure fields respectively, and ν is the kinematic viscosity. Equation (81) indicates that the fluid density is constant. Given initial condition, we solve the above equations in a periodic box of size $L_x \times L_y \times L_z$.

The numerical method for the above equations is very similar to that for Burgers equation, except two major differences:

1. Equation (80) has more terms than Burgers equation.
2. We need to take into account the pressure term that is solved using the constraint equation, Eq. (81).

We write down the following equation for the Fourier mode $\hat{u}_{\mathbf{k},i}$, where i takes values 1,2,3 for the three components of the velocity field:

$$\frac{d}{dt}\hat{u}_{\mathbf{k},i} = -ik_j\widehat{u_j(\mathbf{r})u_i(\mathbf{r})}_\mathbf{k} - ik_i\hat{p}_\mathbf{k} - \nu k^2\hat{u}_{\mathbf{k},i}$$
$$= -\hat{N}_{\mathbf{k},i} - ik_i\hat{p}_\mathbf{k} - \nu k^2\hat{u}_{\mathbf{k},i}, \quad .....(82)$$

$$k_i\hat{u}_{\mathbf{k},i} = 0.$$

Here, $\hat{p}_\mathbf{k}$ is the Fourier transform of the pressure field, and $\hat{N}_{\mathbf{k},i}$ is Fourier transform of the nonlinear term ($u_j\partial_j u_i$). Note that i in front of $\hat{N}_{\mathbf{k},i}$ is $\sqrt{-1}$. We divide the real space so that there are $M = N_1 \times N_2 \times N_3$ grid points. The wavenumber components of the modes are $(2\pi/L_i)n_i$, where n_i takes values from $[-N_1/2+1:N_1/2,-N_2/2+1:N_2/2, 0:N_3/2+1]$. The reality condition is $\hat{\mathbf{u}}_{-\mathbf{k}} = [\hat{\mathbf{u}}_\mathbf{k}]^*$.

The nonlinear term is computed using the following steps (see Figure 96):

1. Compute $\mathbf{u}(\mathbf{x})$ using IFFT($\hat{\mathbf{u}}(\mathbf{k})$).
2. Compute the products $u_i u_j$.
3. Compute the Fourier transform of $u_i u_j$ for all combinations.
4. Multiply FT($u_i u_j$) by ik_j that yields $ik_j\widehat{u_j(\mathbf{r})u_i(\mathbf{r})}_{\mathbf{k}'}$ which is the Fourier transform of the nonlinear term. This computation requires $O(M\log(M))$ operations.

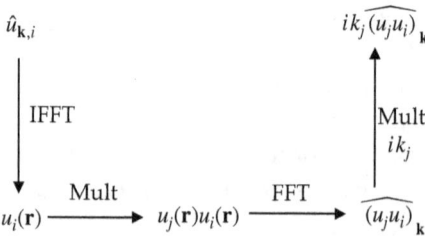

Figure 96: A schematic diagram illustrating computation of the nonlinear term $\hat{N}_{\mathbf{k},i} = ik_j\widehat{u_j(\mathbf{r})u_i(\mathbf{r})}_\mathbf{k}$.

Taking a divergence of Eq. (80) yields

$$-\nabla^2 p = \nabla \cdot [\mathbf{u} \cdot \nabla \mathbf{u}] = \nabla \cdot \mathbf{N},$$

whose Fourier transform provides the pressure as

$$\hat{p}_\mathbf{k} = i\frac{1}{k^2}\mathbf{k} \cdot \hat{\mathbf{N}}_\mathbf{k},$$

which is substituted in Eq. (82). We time advance $\hat{u}_{\mathbf{k},i}$ once all the terms of RHS have been computed. Application of Euler's forward method yields

$$\hat{\mathbf{u}}_\mathbf{k}^{(n+1)} = \hat{u}_\mathbf{k}^{(n)}[1 - \nu k^2(\Delta t)] + (\Delta t)[-\hat{N}_\mathbf{k} - i\mathbf{k}\hat{p}_\mathbf{k}^{(n)}]$$

As shown in Section 15.2, the method is stable only if

$$\Delta t < \tau_\nu = \frac{2h^2}{\nu \pi^2}.$$

The nonlinear term provides another timescale, $\tau_{NL} = h/u_{rms}$. The ratio of the two time scales is $\tau_\nu / \tau_{NL} \approx u_{rms}h/\nu \approx Re/N$, where Re is the Reynolds number. Note that $Re = u_{rms}L/\nu$, where L is the length scale of the system. Therefore, for viscous flows (Re ≤ 1), τ_ν is smaller of the two time scales, and hence Δt is choosen as τ_ν. However, for turbulent flows (Re ≫ 1),

$$\frac{\tau_\nu}{\tau_{NL}} \approx \frac{u_{rms}h}{\nu} \approx \frac{Re}{N} \approx \frac{Re}{Re^{3/4}} \approx Re^{1/4}.$$

Here, we use the fact that for turbulent flows, $N = Re^{3/4}$. The above relation shows that $\tau_{NL} < \tau_\nu$ for Re ≫ 1. Hence, for turbulent flows, Δt is determined by the nonlinear term, and CFL condition is not relevant in this case.

Example 1: Consider a spectral solver of the Navier-Stokes equation with $L = 1$, $\nu = 10^{-4}$, $N = 1000$, $u_{rms} = 1$. These parameters yield $h = L/N = 10^{-4}$. For this flow, $Re = u_{rms}L/\nu = 10^4$. Here, $\tau_\nu = Re/N = 10^{-2}$ and $\tau_{NL} = Re^{-1/4}\tau_\nu = 10^{-3}$. Hence, we choose Δt smaller than τ_{NL}.

We urge the students to write a Python code for solving the Navier-Stokes equations in 2D and 3D. In 1D, $\nabla \cdot \mathbf{u} = 0$ implies that $\mathbf{u}$ = constant, hence, 1D incompressible flows are uninteresting.

With this, we end our discussion on spectral solver of the Navier-Stokes equation.

****

Conceptual Questions

1. How does the time complexity of Navier-Stokes equation compare with that of Burgers equation? Why is it hard to perform large-resolution fluid simulations?

Exercises

1. Solve the incompressible Navier-Stokes equations in a 2D periodic box of dimension $(2\pi)^2$. Take Taylor Green vortex (u_x = sin(x) cos(y), u_y = −cos(x) sin(y)) as an initial condition, and ν = 0.1. Evolve the velocity field till 1 unit of time. You may use $(32)^2$ grid.
2. Repeat Exercise 1 in a 3D periodic box of dimension $(2\pi)^3$ with $(32)^3$ grid.
3. Solve Euler equation, which is Navier-Stokes equation without viscosity, in 2D and 3D. Employ random velocity field as an initial condition. Use leapfrog method for time stepping so as to conserve the total kinetic energy.

15.4 Spectral Solution of Schrödinger Equation

In this section, we will employ spectral method to solve the Schrödinger equation for several quantum systems. Needless to say that Schrödinger equation is one of the most important equations of physics.

In this section, we represent the wave function using symbol ψ. Note that the conservation of probability implies that $\int d\mathbf{r} |\psi(\mathbf{r})|^2 = 1$. To maintain this constraint, we employ energy-conserving schemes, such as leapfrog method. We also use exponential trick for time integration to overcome instability issues. A sketch of the spectral solver for the Schrödinger equation is as follows.

Time-dependent Schrödinger equation for a particle moving in a potential of $V(\mathbf{r})$ is

$$i\hbar \partial_t \psi = \left[-\frac{\hbar^2}{2m} \nabla^2 + V(\mathbf{r}) \right] \psi,$$

where $\hbar$ is the Planck constant, and m is the mass of the particle that is moving in a potential $V(\mathbf{r})$. We nondimensionalize the above equation using r_a as length scale and $\hbar/E_a$ as time scale, where E_a is the energy scale. We make a change of variable $t = t'(\hbar/E_a)$ and $\mathbf{r} = \mathbf{r}' r_a$, and derive the following nondimensional Schrödinger equation:

$$i \partial_{t'} \psi = \left[-\frac{\alpha}{2} \nabla^2 + V'(\mathbf{r}') \right] \psi,$$

where $\alpha = \hbar^2/(m r_a^2 E_a)$ and $V' = V/E_a$. We take Fourier transform of the above equation and obtain

$$\partial_{t'} \hat{\psi}_{\mathbf{k}'} = -i \frac{\alpha}{2} k'^2 \hat{\psi}_{\mathbf{k}'} - i \widehat{(V' \psi)}_{\mathbf{k}'}, \quad \ldots (83)$$

Time integration of the linear term using Euler's forward scheme is unstable, hence we employ the exponential trick and make a change of variable $\tilde{\psi}_{\mathbf{k}'} = \hat{\psi}_{\mathbf{k}'} \exp(i \frac{\alpha}{2} k'^2 t')$. As a result, Eq. (83) gets translated to

$$\partial_{t'}\tilde{\hat{\psi}}_{\mathbf{k'}} = -i\widehat{(V'\psi)}_{\mathbf{k'}} \exp(i\frac{\alpha}{2}k'^2 t').$$

whose integration using leapfrog method is

$$\hat{\psi}_{\mathbf{k'}}^{(n+1)} = \hat{\psi}_{\mathbf{k'}}^{(n-1)} \exp(-i\alpha k^2(\Delta t')) - i(2\Delta t')\widehat{(V'\psi)}_{\mathbf{k'}} \exp(-i\frac{\alpha}{2}k^2(\Delta t'))\ ..(84)$$

We could also employ more accurate time-marching schemes. In the following examples, we solve for the wave functions of a free particle and simple harmonic oscillator.

Example 1: We solve $\psi(x)$ for a free particle (mass m) whose initial wavefunction is $\exp(ik_0x)$. The energy of the particle is $(\hbar k_0)^2/2m$. We choose $1/k_0$ as the length scale. Therefore, $\alpha = 1$. Note that $V' = 0$. Therefore, Eq. (83) yields $\hat{\psi}_{k'}(t) = \hat{\psi}_{k'}(t=0)\exp(-ik^2t'/2)$. Since $\hat{\psi}_{k'}(t=0) = \delta_{k',1}$ we obtain $\hat{\psi}_{k'}(t) = \exp(-ik^2t'/2)\delta_{k',1} = \exp(-it'/2)$, whose inverse Fourier transform yields the following wavefunction at time t:

$$\psi(x,t) = \exp(ix' - it'/2) = \exp(ik_0x - i\hbar k_0^2 t/(2m)).$$

Since the above analytical solution is straightforward, we do not present a numerical solution for this problem.

Example 2: We solve $\psi(x)$ for a free particle with Gaussian packet as an initial condition. Here, $\psi(x, t=0) = (a\sqrt{\pi})^{-\frac{1}{2}} \exp(-(x/a)^2/2) \exp(ik_0x)$. We choose a as the length scale and $m/(\hbar a^2)$ as the time scale. Hence $\alpha = 1$. Nondimensional $\psi(x',t=0) = \pi^{-1/4} \exp(-x'^2/2) \exp(ik_0ax')$. Following the similar steps as those of Example 1, we obtain

$$\hat{\psi}_{k'}(t) = \hat{\psi}_{k'}(t=0)\exp(-ik^2t'/2). \quad .....(85)$$

The forward Fourier transform of $\psi(x,t=0)$ is

$$\hat{\psi}_{k'}(t=0) = \pi^{-1/4}\exp(-\frac{1}{2}(k'_0 - k')^2).$$

Substitution of the above in Eq. (85) and its subsequent inverse transform yields

$$\psi(x,t) = \left(\sqrt{\pi}(1+it')\right)^{-1/2}\exp(ik_0a(x'-it'/2))\exp\left(-\frac{(x'-k_0at')^2}{2(1+it')}\right).$$

The numerical solution of this problem is very similar to that of diffusion equation (see Example 1 of 15.1). Here, we consider $\psi(x)$ in a periodic box of length L, with $L \gg a$ and $L \gg 1/k_0$; in particular, we choose $a = 0.1$, $k_0 = 10$, and $x = [-5\pi, 5\pi]$. We employ forward and inverse Fourier transforms (complex to complex) to obtain the final result. A code segment for the above computation is given below:

```
tf = 2; L = 10*np.pi; N = 256; h = L/N
j = np.arange(0,N); x = j*h-L/2+h

# initcond
a = 0.1; k0 = 10; k0a = k0*a
f = 1/np.sqrt(np.sqrt(pi))*np.exp(-
x**2/2)*np.exp(1j*k0a*x)    # init cond
fk = np.fft.fft(f,N)/N
kx_pos = np.linspace(0, N//2, N//2+1)
kx_neg = np.linspace(-N/2+1,-1,N/2-1)
kx = np.concatenate((kx_pos, kx_neg))*(2*pi/L)

fk_t = fk*np.exp(-1j*kx**2*tf/2)
f_t = np.fft.ifft(fk_t,N)*N. # final solution in real
space
```

See Figure 97 for an illustration of the solution. The numerical result for the wavefunction at $t' = 2$ is very close to the analytical result.

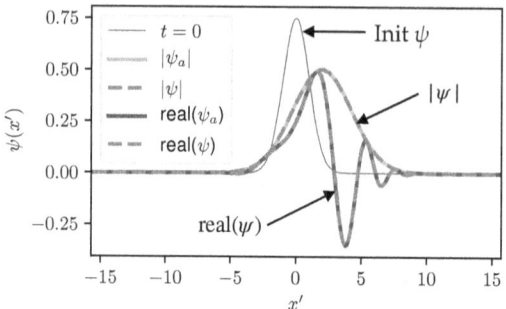

Figure 97: Example 2: Numerically computed wavefunction of a free particles with Gaussian initial condition (thin curve). The analytical solution (with subscript a) is close to the numerical solution.

Example 3: We numerically solve the wave function for a linear harmonic oscillator whose equation is

$$i\hbar \partial_t \psi = -\frac{\hbar^2}{2m}\frac{d^2\psi}{dx^2} + \frac{1}{2}m\omega^2 x^2 \psi,$$

where m, ω are respectively the mass and frequency of the oscillator. We choose $\hbar/E = 1/\omega$ as the time scale, and $\sqrt{\hbar/(m\omega)}$ as the length scale. Under this arrangement, the nondimensional equation for the oscillator is

$$i\partial_{t'}\psi = -\frac{1}{2}\frac{d^2\psi}{dx^2} + \frac{1}{2}x'^2\psi.$$

For the oscillator, in Eq. (84) we substitute $\alpha = 1$ and $V' = x'^2/2$ and solve for $\psi(x,t)$. For numerical computation, we take a finite box whose dimension is much larger than the length scale. In particular, we choose $L = 6\pi$ and $\psi(x',t=0) = (1/\sqrt{2})\,\pi^{-1/4}\exp(-x'^2/2)[1+\sqrt{2}x']$, which is a combination of the ground state and the first excited state.

We time advance the equation using leapfrog method (along with the exponential trick) up to 2 nondimensional time unit. In Figure 98 we present the numerically computed wavefunction at $t' = 0, 1, 2$. The final state matches with the exact wavefunction,

$(1/\sqrt{2})\,\pi^{-1/4}\exp(-x'^2/2)[\exp(-it'/2) +\sqrt{2}x'\exp(-3it'/2)]$, quite well.

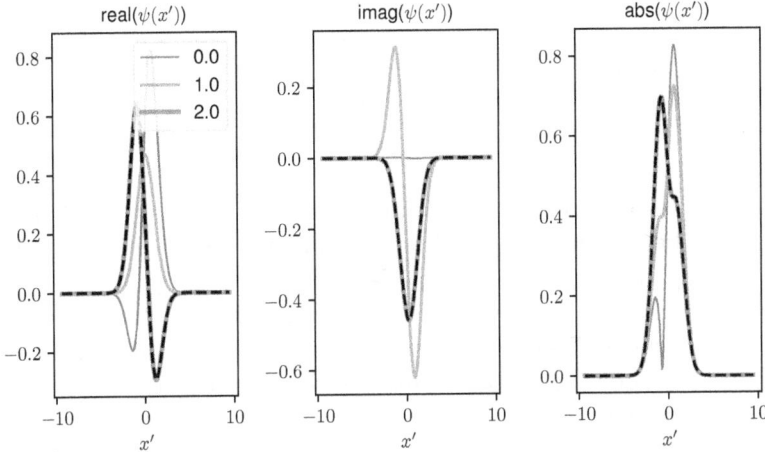

Figure 98: Numerically computed wavefunction of the simple oscillator of Example 3. The figure exhibits the real, imaginary, and absolute values of the wavefunction at $t' = 0, 1, 2$ using the curves with increasing thickness. The exact form of the final wave functions is represented using black-dashed curve.

Solving Gross–Pitaevskii Equation

Gross–Pitaevskii (GP) equation describes the behaviour of macroscopic wavefunction in quantum mechanics. The GP equation for the quantum wave function ψ is

$$i\hbar \partial_t \psi = \left[-\frac{\hbar^2}{2m} \nabla^2 + V(\mathbf{r}) + g|\psi|^2 \right] \psi, \quad \ldots(86)$$

where $\hbar$ is the Planck constant, g s a constant, and m is the mass of the quasi-particle that is moving in a potential $V(\mathbf{r})$. In spectral space, the equation for the Fourier mode $\hat{\psi}_\mathbf{k}$ is

$$i\hbar \partial_t \hat{\psi}_\mathbf{k} = \frac{\hbar^2 k^2}{2m} \hat{\psi}_\mathbf{k} + \widehat{(V\psi)}_\mathbf{k} + \widehat{(g|\psi|^2 \psi)}_\mathbf{k},$$

which can be solved following a similar procedure as employed for Navier-Stokes equation. We urge the students to solve the above equation for $V(\mathbf{r}) = 0$.

In summary, the solvers for Schrödinger and GP equations must ensure the following:

1. The conservation of quantum probability, i.e., $\int d\mathbf{r} \ |\Psi^2| = 1$.
2. The Schrödinger equation is symmetric under time-reversible operation ($t \to -t$ and $\Psi \to \Psi^*$)
3. Application of Euler's forward method of the linear term is unstable. Therefore, we need to employ an accurate and stable method. The simplest scheme is the leapfrog method with the exponential trick.

With this, we end our discussion on the Schrödinger and GP equations.

Assessment of Spectral Method

A major advantage of spectral method is its accuracy. As shown in this and previous chapter, the derivatives computed using Fourier transforms are accurate. This feature helps in accurate simulations of differential equations.

Spectral simulations have some limitations, which are listed below.

1. Fourier transform requires the functions to be periodic. This is a strong limitation considering that real applications involve more complex geometries and boundary conditions (e.g., flows in curved pipes, quantum devices with boundaries, etc.).
2. Using sine transforms, we could work with vanishing boundary conditions at the walls. More specialised functions, such as Bessel function and Legendre polynomials, enable us to employ spectral methods to cylindrical and spherical geometries.
3. Finite difference, finite volume, and finite elements methods are employed to solve complex applications with nonideal geometries. In the next chapter, we will discuss how finite

difference method is used for solving PDEs.

With this, we end our discussion on spectral methods.

****

Conceptual Questions

1. What are the complexities for the numerical simulation of Schrödinger equation?
2. Describe similarities and dissimilarities between the numerical methods for solving Navier-Stokes and Gross–Pitaevskii equations.

Exercises

1. Solve Schrödinger equation for a linear harmonic oscillator using RK2 method and compare the results with those of Example 3.
2. Solve Schrödinger equation for free particles in 2D and 3D. Use Gaussian packet as an initial condition.
3. Solve Schrödinger equation for a linear harmonic oscillator in 2D.
4. Solve Gross–Pitaevskii equation with $V = 0$ and $g = 1$. Nondimensionalize the equation before proceeding to solve the equation. Employ the leapfrog method along with the exponential trick. Compute the error in $\int d\mathbf{r}\ |\Psi^2|$.

Chapter Sixteen
SOLVING PDES USING FINITE DIFFERENCE METHOD

Synopsis

"Among all of the mathematical disciplines the theory of differential equations is the most important... It furnishes the explanation of all those elementary manifestations of nature which involve time."
— Sophus Lie

This chapter describes application of finite difference method for solving partial differential equations.

16.1 General Overview & Diffusion Equation Solver

In this chapter, we will discuss *finite difference* (*FD*) method for solving PDEs. FD method is less accurate than the spectral method, but they can be applied to complex geometries and boundary conditions. However, in this introductory book, we limit ourselves to simple geometries.

We will use this method to solve the following set of PDEs:

1. Diffusion equation
2. Wave equation
3. Burgers eqation
4. Navier-Stokes equation
5. Schrödinger equation

We consider the following 1D PDE for ϕ:

$$\frac{\partial \phi}{\partial t} = f(\phi, \frac{\partial \phi}{\partial x}, \frac{\partial^2 \phi}{\partial x^2}, t). \quad \ldots..(87)$$

The basic steps of the FD method for solving the above equation are as follows. We discretize the domain [0:L] at N equidistant points and label them as $x_0, x_1, \ldots, x_{N-1}$. The separation between two neighbouring points is h, and the function at x_i is denoted by ϕ_i. Note that the end points are located at x_0 and x_{N-1}. For vanishing boundary condition, $\phi_0 = \phi_{N-1} = 0$, but for periodic boundary condition, $\phi_0 = \phi_N$. See Figure 99 for an illustration.

At each x_i, we compute the RHS function of Eq. (87) and label it as f_i. It is best to use accurate and vectorized schemes (to be illustrated later) for the spatial derivative computation in f. The discretization process yields the following ODEs for ϕ_i's:

$$\frac{d}{dt}\phi_i(t) = f_i(t),$$

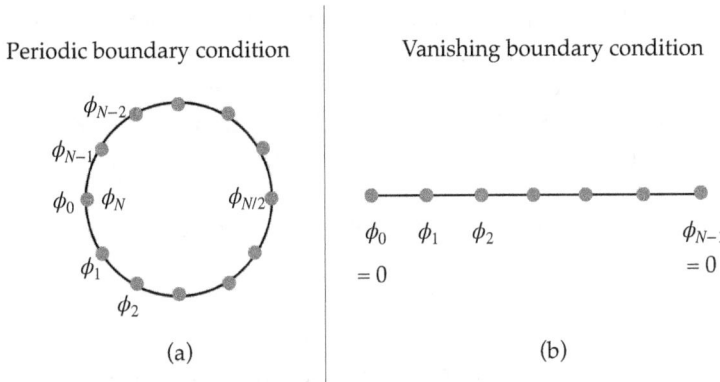

Figure 99: (a) Periodic boundary condition. Here, $\phi_0 = \phi_N$, but ϕ_N is not stored. (b) Vanishing boundary condition with $\phi_0 = \phi_{N-1} = 0$.

which can be solved using one of the time-stepping schemes. For example, with Euler's forward method, the time stepping from $t^{(n)}$ to $t^{(n+1)}$ is achieved using

$$\phi_i^{(n+1)} = \phi_i^{(n)} + (\Delta t) f_i .$$

As described earlier, we index space grid as x_i and time grid as $t^{(n)}$. Note that time varies from initial time $t^{(0)}$ to the final time t_{final}. See Figure 100 for an illustration.

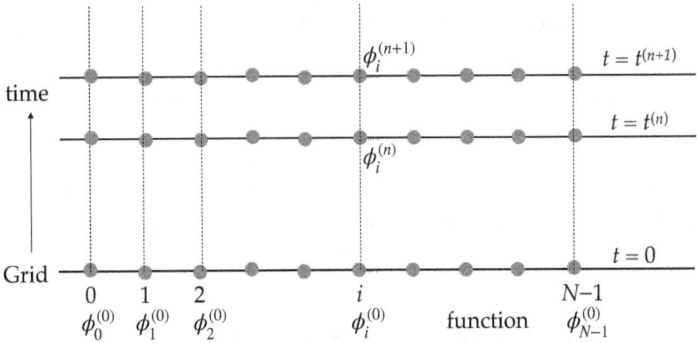

Figure 100: The domain x is discretized at N points. The functions at these points are $\{\phi_i\}$. The function evolves from $t = 0$ to the final time, t_{final}.

Thus, FD method helps in converting a PDE to a set of ODEs at discrete positions in real space. Solution of these ODEs yields the final solution. Note, however, that the solution has significant errors due to two-step discretization, first in space and then in time. In comparison, a spectral method has less error due to accurate spatial-derivative computation.

We start with solution of the diffusion equation using the FD method.

Solving Diffusion Equation Using FD Method

As discussed in Section 15.1, the diffusion equation is

$$\partial_t \phi = \kappa \frac{\partial^2 \phi}{\partial x^2},$$

with $\kappa > 0$ and real ϕ. We solve the above equation for a periodic boundary condition. For the same, we discretize the domain at N points. We compute $\partial^2 \phi / \partial x^2$ using the central difference. Consequently, the equation for ϕ_i is

$$\frac{d\phi_i(t)}{dt} = \frac{\alpha}{h^2}(\phi_{i+1} - 2\phi_i + \phi_{i-1}).$$

An application of Euler's forward scheme to the above equation yields

$$\phi_i^{(n+1)} = \phi_i^{(n)} + \frac{\kappa \Delta t}{h^2}(\phi_{i+1}^{(n)} - 2\phi_i^{(n)} + \phi_{i-1}^{(n)}). \quad \ldots\ldots(88)$$

The above equation is accurate up to $O(\Delta t)$. This equation is also unstable, as we demonstrate below.

CFL Condition for FD Method

The analytical solution of the diffusion equation shows that $\phi(x)$ vanishes asymptotically. We require similar convergence for the numerical solution. Note that $\phi(x)$ can be expanded as a Fourier series using exp(ikx), where k ranges from $2\pi/L$ to π/h. For stability, the coefficients for exp(ikx) must decrease with time. Therefore, to test the stability of Eq. (88), we substitute

$$\phi(x) = \exp(ikx)f(t) \quad \text{or} \quad \phi_i^{(n)} = \exp(ikx_i)f^{(n)}$$

in Eq. (88) and test if $f(t)$ grows or decays with time. The evolution equation for $f(t)$ is (show it!)

$$f^{(n+1)} = f^{(n)}\left[1 + \frac{2\kappa \Delta t}{h^2}(\cos(kh) - 1)\right]. \quad \ldots\ldots(89)$$

As shown in Figure 87, 0<kh<π or -1<cos(kh)<1. Clearly, $f^{(n)}$ decays with time when 0<cos(kh)<1. However, we may expect trouble when -1<cos(kh)<0. In particular, $f^{(n)}$ exhibits oscillatory growth if $(2\kappa(\Delta t)/h^2)(\cos(kh)-1) < -1$. The most unstable Fourier mode is one with the largest wavenumber ($kh = \pi$) for which cos(kh) = -1. Hence, a sufficient condition for stability is

$$\frac{4\kappa \Delta t}{h^2} < 1 \quad \text{or} \quad (\Delta t)_{\text{FD}} < \frac{h^2}{4\kappa}.$$

In Section 14.1 we showed that for the same accuracy, h for a FD method is 2π times smaller than that for a spectral method. Also, as shown in Section 15.1, for the stability of a spectral method,

$$(\Delta t)_{\text{SP}} < \frac{2h_{\text{SP}}^2}{\kappa \pi^2}.$$

Using these two limits and $h_{\text{FD}}/h_{\text{SP}} = 1/(2\pi)$, we obtain

$$\frac{(\Delta t)_{\text{FD}}}{(\Delta t)_{\text{SP}}} \approx \frac{h_{\text{SP}}^2/(4\kappa(2\pi)^2)}{2h_{\text{SP}}^2/(\kappa \pi^2)} \approx \frac{1}{32}.$$

That is, FD method requires approximately 1/32 smaller Δt compared to spectral method (for Euler forward scheme). Thus, for the same accuracy, both space and time requirements for the FD method are larger than the spectral method. We remark that the above calculations only provide estimates. The actual h and Δt may be even smaller than the prescription given by the CFL criteria.

The accuracy of Euler's forward method is $O(\Delta t)$. However, the accuracy of RK2 method is $O((\Delta t)^2)$. In RK2 scheme, the time advancement is given by the following:

$$\phi_i^{\text{mid}} = \phi_i^{(n)} + \frac{\kappa \Delta t}{2h^2}(\phi_{i+1}^{(n)} - 2\phi_i^{(n)} + \phi_{i-1}^{(n)}),$$

$$\phi_i^{(n+1)} = \phi_i^{(n)} + \frac{\kappa \Delta t}{h^2}(\phi_{i+1}^{\text{mid}} - 2\phi_i^{\text{mid}} + \phi_{i-1}^{\text{mid}}).$$

Note that CFL criteria for the RK2 method will yield a different prefactor for h^2/κ.

Example 1: We solve the diffusion equation in a 2π box with $\exp(-2(x-\pi)^2)$ as an initial condition. We take $\kappa = 1$, $N = 64$, $\Delta t = 0.001$, $t_{\text{final}} = 1$ units. Note $\Delta t < h^2/(4\kappa)$. hence, our method is stable.

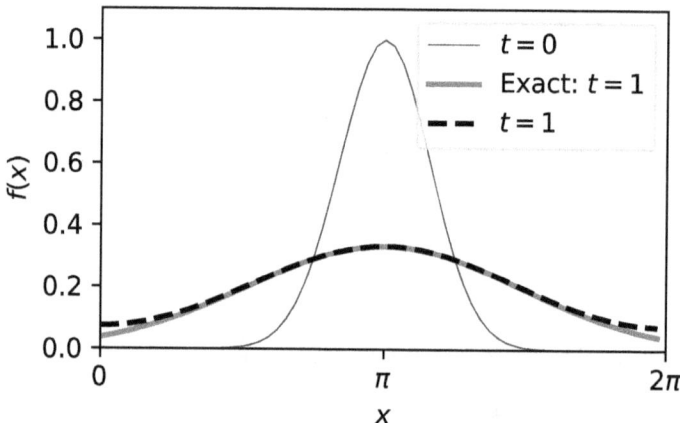

Figure 101: Evolution of a function $\exp(-2(x-\pi)^2)$ under diffusion. The numerical solution (black dashed line) is close to the exact solution (thick solid curve), except at the end points.

The initial and final fields are shown in Figure 101. The solution using FD method is quite close to the exact result (see Section 15.1), as well as to the spectral solution. At each x_i, the difference between the spectral and FD solutions is of the order of 10^{-4}. A code segment for the above computation is given below.

```
init_temp = np.exp(-2*(x-pi)**2)
f = np.zeros(N+2); f_mid = np.zeros(N+2);
f[1:N+1] = init_temp; f[0] = init_temp[-1];
f[N+1] = init_temp[0]

# Evolution wirh RK2 method.
for i in range(nsteps+2):
    f_mid[1:N+1] = f[1:N+1] +(prefactor/2)
              *(f[0:N]-2*f[1:N+1]+f[2:N+2])
    f_mid[0] = f_mid[N]; f_mid[-1] = f_mid[1]

    f[1:N+1] = f[1:N+1] + prefactor
              *(f_mid[0:N]-2*f_mid[1:N+1]+f_mid[2:N+2])
    f[0] = f[N]; f[-1] = f[1]
```

To speed up the code via vectorization, we save the field in array $f[1:N]$, and impose a condition that $f[0] = f[N]$ and $f[N+1] = f[1]$ due to periodic boundary condition (see Figure 102). With this arrangement, we can easily compute the second derivative, f'', using vectorized operations. See the code-segment above. We follow this convention for all our FD implementations.

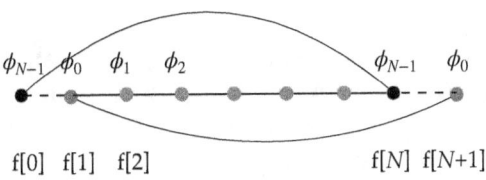

f[0] f[1] f[2]   f[N] f[N+1]

Figure 102: The field ϕ_i is saved in a numpy array $f[1:N]$. For vectorization, we impose a condition that $f[0] = f[N]$ and $f[N+1] = f[1]$.

Application of Implicit Scheme

The stability criteria for an explicit FD method yields very small Δt ($\sim h^2/(4\kappa)$) for small h (say 10^{-4}). Hence, it is better to employ a semi-implicit scheme that does not put such a strong constraint. One such scheme is Crank Nickelson method given below:

$$\phi_i^{(n+1)} = \phi_i^{(n)} + \frac{\kappa \Delta t}{2h^2}\left[(\phi_{i+1}^{(n)} - 2\phi_i^{(n)} + \phi_{i-1}^{(n)}) + (\phi_{i+1}^{(n+1)} - 2\phi_i^{(n+1)} + \phi_{i-1}^{(n+1)})\right], \text{ or}$$

$$-\frac{\kappa \Delta t}{2h^2}\phi_{i-1}^{(n+1)} + \left(1 + \frac{\kappa \Delta t}{h^2}\right)\phi_i^{(n+1)} - \frac{\kappa \Delta t}{2h^2}\phi_{i+1}^{(n+1)}$$
$$= \phi_i^{(n)} + \frac{\kappa \Delta t}{2h^2}\left[\phi_{i+1}^{(n)} - 2\phi_i^{(n)} + \phi_{i-1}^{(n)}\right]. \quad \ldots(90)$$

For periodic boundary condition, we have N equations for $\phi_0, \phi_1, \ldots \phi_{N-1}$ of the form of Eq. (90) (see Figure 99). The equations for ϕ_i's can be written in the following matrix form:

$$\begin{pmatrix} X & Y & & & Y \\ Y & X & Y & & \\ & Y & X & Y & \\ & & \ddots & \ddots & \ddots \\ Y & & & Y & X \end{pmatrix} \begin{pmatrix} \phi_0 \\ \phi_1 \\ \phi_2 \\ \ldots \\ \phi_{N-1} \end{pmatrix} = \begin{pmatrix} r_0 \\ r_1 \\ r_2 \\ \ldots \\ r_{N-1} \end{pmatrix}, \quad \ldots(91)$$

where $X = (1+\kappa(\Delta t)/h^2)$, $Y = -\kappa(\Delta t)/(2h^2)$, and r_i's are the RHS of Eq. (90). The matrix in the above equation is a variant of a tridiagonal matrix, which will be solved in Section 20.1.

For the vanishing boundary condition, $\phi_0 = \phi_{N-1} = 0$, the corresponding matrix equation is (leaving out ϕ_0 and ϕ_{N-1}, which are zeros)

$$\begin{pmatrix} X & Y & & & \\ Y & X & Y & & \\ & Y & X & Y & \\ & & \ddots & \ddots & \ddots \\ & & & Y & X \end{pmatrix} \begin{pmatrix} \phi_1 \\ \phi_2 \\ \phi_3 \\ \ldots \\ \phi_{N-2} \end{pmatrix} = \begin{pmatrix} r_1 \\ r_2 \\ r_3 \\ \ldots \\ r_{N-2} \end{pmatrix}. \quad \ldots(92)$$

This equation too is solved using a variant of tridiagonal matrix solver.

With this, we end our discussion on the FD implementation of the diffusion equation.

****

Conceptual Questions

1. State the advantages and disadvantages of spectral and FD methods for solving the diffusive equation.

Exercises

1. Solve Example 1 for different gird sizes and Δt, and identify the optimum Δt and grid size.
2. Solve 1D diffusion equation for κ = 10, 1, 0.1, 0.01 for vanishing boundary condition. Choose appropriate Δt.
3. Solve the diffusion equation in a 2D box with κ = 0.1. Take $\exp(-50r^2)$ as an initial condition. Make sure to employ vectorization for the 2D solution.
4. Solve the diffusion equation in a 3D box with κ = 0.1. Take $\exp(-50r^2)$ as an initial condition.
5. Consider $\partial_t \phi = -\partial^4_x \phi$, which is a variant of the diffusion equation. Solve this equation using FD method. Compare the errors for this equation with that for the original diffusion equation.

16.2 Solving Wave Equation

In this section we will solve the following wave equation using the FD method:

$$\partial_t \phi + c \partial_x \phi = 0, \quad \ldots\ldots(93)$$

where c, a positive number, is the speed of the wave. The above equation represents a wave travelling rightwards with speed c. Note that the above equation is also called *advection equation* since the field ϕ is advected by the wave motion.

We employ central-difference scheme for the space-derivative computation and Euler's forward method for time stepping that yields

$$\phi_i^{(n+1)} = \phi_i^{(n)} - \frac{c\Delta t}{2h}(\phi_{i+1}^{(n)} - \phi_{i-1}^{(n)}).$$

The above equation is unstable. To prove this statement, we substitute $\phi_i^{(n)} = \exp(ik\,x_i)f^{(n)}$ in the above equation that yields

$$f^{(n+1)} = f^{(n)}[1 - ic\Delta t \frac{\sin kh}{h}].$$

Since $|1 - ic(\Delta t)\sin(kh)/h| > 1$, the above integration scheme is unstable for all Δt.

However, *upwind scheme* given below is stable:

$$\phi_i^{(n+1)} = \phi_i^{(n)} - \frac{c\Delta t}{h}(\phi_i^{(n)} - \phi_{i-1}^{(n)}). \quad \ldots..(94)$$

Here, the spatial derivative is computed using Euler's backward scheme. Substitution of $\phi_i^{(n)} = \exp(ik\,x_i)f^{(n)}$ in Eq. (94) yields

$$f^{(n+1)} = f^{(n)}\left[1 - \frac{c\Delta t}{h}\{1 - \exp(-ikh)\}\right] = f^{(n)}[1 - \alpha + \alpha \exp(-ikh)],$$

where $\alpha = c(\Delta t)/h$. For stability,

$$|1 - \alpha + \alpha \exp(-ikh)| < 1, \text{ or } (1-\alpha)(1-\cos(kh)) > 0.$$

Since $\cos(kh) < 1$ or $(1 - \cos(kh)) > 0$, the stability condition leads to

$$\alpha = c(\Delta t)/h < 1. \quad \ldots(95)$$

Physical interpretation of the above result is as follows. A disturbance takes h/c unit of time to cover the grid distance of h. Hence, Δt should be less than h/c for a proper temporal resolution of the disturbance evolution.

Let us examine the nature of solution with central difference and upwind schemes. The error in central difference scheme is $h\partial^3\phi/\partial x^3$, a dispersive term (see KdV equation) because of which this scheme is unstable. On the other hand, upwind scheme has error of the form $h\partial^2\phi/\partial x^2$, which is dissipative, as in Burgers equation.

What about the wave travelling to the left? The equation for such waves is $\partial_t\phi - c\partial_x\phi = 0$. It is straightforward to show that Eq. (94) is unstable for time-stepping $\partial_t\phi - c\partial_x\phi = 0$. An appropriate time-marching scheme for a left-moving wave is

$$\phi_i^{(n+1)} = \phi_i^{(n)} + \frac{c\Delta t}{h}(\phi_{i+1}^{(n)} - \phi_i^{(n)}). \quad \ldots(96)$$

Substitution of $\phi_i^{(n)} = \exp(ik\, x_i) f^{(n)}$ in the above equation yields

$$f^{(n+1)} = f^{(n)}\left[1 + \frac{c\Delta t}{h}\{\exp(ikh) - 1\}\right] = f^{(n)}[1 - \alpha + \alpha \exp(ikh)].$$

Following the same procedure as that for the right-moving wave, we deduce the same stability condition of the wave equation with Eq. (95).

A careful inspection of Eqs. (94, 96) reveal that the information propagates from site $i-1$ to i for the right-moving wave, and from site $i+1$ to i for the left-moving wave. The upwind scheme gets its name due to the above reason. This observation is consistent with *causality*.

Example 1: We solve the wave equation for $c = 10$. We use $L = 10\pi$, $h = L/128$, and $\Delta t = 0.001$. Note $\Delta t < h/c$. We run the program till $t = 1$ with RK2 scheme. We take a Gaussian waveform, shown as black dashed curve in Figure 103, as an initial condition. Figure 103 illustrates that the solution is unstable and diffusive for the central difference scheme, but it is stable but dissipative for the upwind scheme. A code segment for upwind scheme is given below:

```
c = 10; tf = 1; dt = 0.001; nsteps = int(tf/dt)

for i in range(nsteps+2):
    f[1:N+1] = f[1:N+1] - prefactor*(f[1:N+1]-f[0:N])
    f[0] = f[N]; f[-1] = f[1]
    if (i%500 == 0):
        ax2.plot(x, f[1:N+1], lw = i/500*1)
```

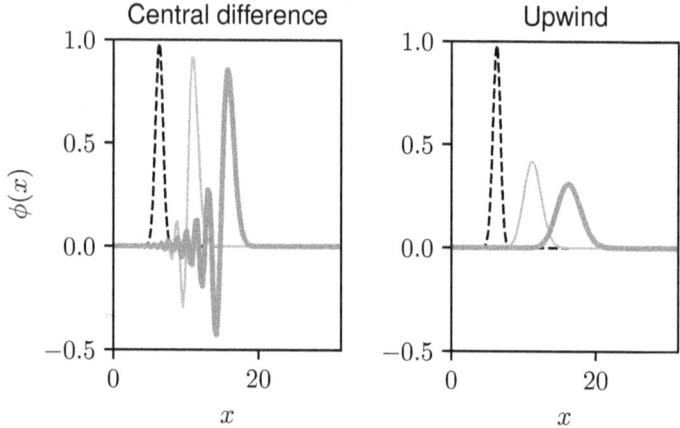

Figure 103: Numerical solution of the wave equation using FD method: (a) Central difference scheme, which is unstable. (b) Upwind scheme, which is stable but dissipative. The dashed, thin, and thick curves represent the waves at $t = 0, 0.5, 1$ respectively.

Note that spectral solution discussed in Section 15.2 has an exact solution. But, the solution using FD method is approximate. The implementation of spectral method with Euler method is unconditionally unstable. For the FD implementation, Euler forward time-advancement with central-difference spatial derivative is unstable. However, upwind implementation of FD method is conditionally stable.

With this, we end our discussion on the wave equation.

****

Conceptual Questions

1. Compare the complexities of spectral and FD solutions of a wave equation.

Exercises

1. Solve the wave equation $\partial_t \phi = \partial_x \phi$ numerically using the central difference and upwind schemes. Compare the results with that for $\partial_t \phi = -\partial_x \phi$.
2. For Exercise 1, study how the accuracy of the solution depends on parameters h and c?

16.3 Burgers and Navier-Stokes Equations

In this section we will employ FD method to solve Burgers and Navier-Stokes equations that contains advection and diffusion terms. See Ferziger [2019] for more details.

The Burgers equation is

$$\partial_t u + u \partial_x u = \nu \partial_x^2 u,$$

where u is the velocity field, and ν is the kinematic viscosity of the fluid. Note, however, that the advection velocity u is not constant.

This system has two time scales for stability analysis: $\tau_\nu = h^2/\nu$ from the diffusion term, and $\tau_{NL} = h/u_{rms}$ from the advection term, where h is the grid size. The ratio $\tau_\nu/\tau_{NL} = u_{rms} h/\nu = \text{Re}/N$, where N is number of grid points. We choose smaller of the two timescales as Δt.

We employ upwind scheme for the nonlinear term, and central difference scheme for the diffusion term. Euler's forward scheme is employed for time-stepping. Consequently,

$$u_i^{(n+1)} = u_i^{(n)} - \frac{\Delta t}{h} u_i^{(n)}(u_i^{(n)} - u_{i-1}^{(n)}) + \frac{\nu \Delta t}{h^2}(u_{i+1}^{(n)} - 2u_i^{(n)} + u_{i-1}^{(n)}) \text{ (for } u_i^{(n)} > 0)$$

$$u_i^{(n+1)} = u_i^{(n)} - \frac{\Delta t}{h} u_i^{(n)}(u_{i+1}^{(n)} - u_i^{(n)}) + \frac{\nu \Delta t}{h^2}(u_{i+1}^{(n)} - 2u_i^{(n)} + u_{i-1}^{(n)}) \text{ (for } u_i^{(n)} < 0)$$

Alternatively, we could also apply RK2 for the nonlinear term and central difference for the diffusion term. These schemes provide convergent solutions for a reasonable length of time.

Example 1: We solve the Burgers equation for $\nu = 0.1$, $N = 128$, and $\Delta t = 0.001$. We take $\sin(x)$ as the initial condition and carry out our simulation till $t_{final} = 1$ unit using RK2 method. We exhibit the evolution of $u(x)$ in Figure 104 with the final profile (purple-thick curve) exhibiting a clear shock front.

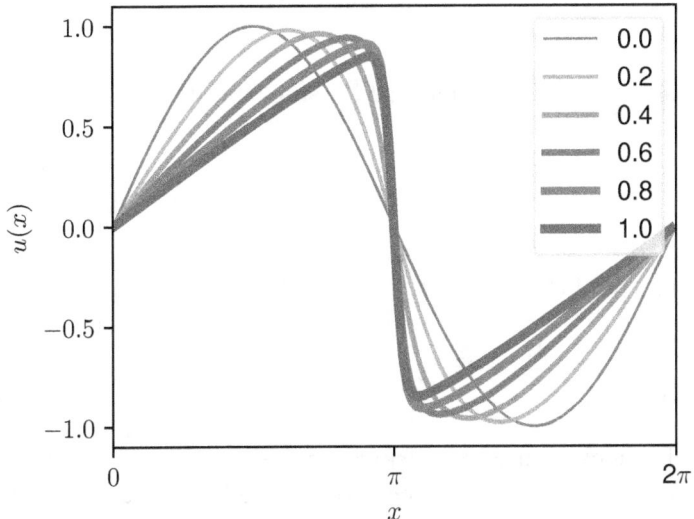

Figure 104: Numerical solution of Burgers equation with $\nu = 0.1$, $N = 128$. The solution $u(x,t)$ at $t = 0, 0.2, 0.4, 0.6, 0.8$, and 1 are exhibited in the plot.

Incompressible Hydrodynamic Equations

Now, we provide a brief discussion on how to solve *incompressible Navier-Stokes equations* using FD method. The governing equations are

$$\partial_t \mathbf{u} + \mathbf{u} \cdot \nabla \mathbf{u} = -\frac{1}{\rho} \nabla p + \nu \nabla^2 \mathbf{u} ; \quad \nabla \cdot \mathbf{u} = 0,$$

$$\nabla^2 p = -\rho \nabla \cdot [\mathbf{u} \cdot \nabla \mathbf{u}].$$

Further, we assume that the density is constant. The last equation is *pressure Poisson equation*. Here we present a simple method, called *pressure correction* (*Chorin's projection*), to solve these equations.

The numerical scheme involves the following steps. First, given $\mathbf{u}^{(n)}$, we compute the intermediate velocity field $\mathbf{u}^*$ using the following equation:

$$\frac{u^* - u^{(n)}}{\Delta t} = -u^{(n)} \cdot \nabla u^{(n)} + \nu \nabla^2 u^{(n)}.$$

The pressure, $p^{(n+1)}$ is determined using the following Poisson equation:

$$\nabla^2 p^{(n+1)} = \frac{\rho}{\Delta t} \nabla \cdot u^* . \quad \ldots(97)$$

Now, using u^* and the pressure, $p^{(n+1)}$, we advance to $u^{(n+1)}$:

$$u^{(n+1)} - u^* = -\frac{\Delta t}{\rho}(\nabla p^{(n+1)}).$$

Note that the above procedure ensures that $\nabla \cdot u^{(n+1)} = 0$.

A Python implementation of the above procedure is quite complex, and hence it is not presented here. In the next section, we will present FD implementation of Schrödinger equation.

****

Conceptual Questions

1. Compare the accuracies of spectral and FD solutions of the Burgers equation.

Exercises

1. Solve Burgers equation for $\nu = 10, 1, 0.01, 0.001$ with $\sin(x)$ as an initial condition. What are the grid requirements for these simulations?
2. Compare the errors in the solution of Example 1 with the corresponding spectral solution.
3. Solve KdV equation $\partial_t u + u \partial_x u = \kappa \, \partial^3 u$ with $\kappa = 0.1$ using FD method. Compare your FD solution with the spectral one.
4. Write a Python program for solving 2D incompressible Navier-Stokes equation.

16.4 Schrodinger Equation

In this section we will solve time-dependent Schrödinger equation using FD method. Since $\int |\psi|^2 \, dx$ is conserved, we employ leapfrog method that conserves this quantity.

For simplicity, we solve 1D nondimensional Schrödinger equation for Hamiltonian $H = -(½)\partial_{xx} + V(x)$. The Schrödinger equation is

$$i \partial_t \psi = H\psi.$$

We decompose ψ into its real and imaginary parts: $\psi = R + iI$. The equations for R and I are as follows:

$$\partial_t R = [-(½)\partial_{xx} + V(x)] I$$

$$\partial_t I = -[-(½)\partial_{xx} + V(x)] R$$

Note that the above equations have a similar form as those for the position and momentum of an oscillator ($\dot{x} = p; \dot{p} = -x$). Hence, following the method adopted for a linear oscillator (see Section 13.6), we time advance R and I as follows:

$$R^{(n)} = R^{(n-1)} + (\Delta t)[-(½)\partial_{xx} + V(x)] I^{(n-½)}$$

$$I^{(n+½)} = I^{(n-½)} - (\Delta t)[-(½)\partial_{xx} + V(x)] R^{(n)}$$

See Figure 105 for an illustration. Note, however, that as a first step, we time advances $I_i^{(0)}$ to $I_i^{(½)}$, after which we employ the above procedure. We remark that the numerically-computed wavefunction is approximate.

Following the convention of FD methods, we discretize the space domain at N points. At the ith site, the evolution equations (with central difference scheme) are

$$R_i^{(n)} = R_i^{(n-1)} + (\Delta t) [-(I_{i+1}^{(n-½)} - 2I_i^{(n-½)} + I_{i-1}^{(n-½)})/(2h^2) + V_i I_i^{(n-½)}],$$

$$I_i^{(n+½)} = I_i^{(n-½)} + (\Delta t)[(R_{i+1}^{(n)} - 2R_i^{(n)} + R_{i-1}^{(n)})/(2h^2) - V_i R_i^{(n)}].$$

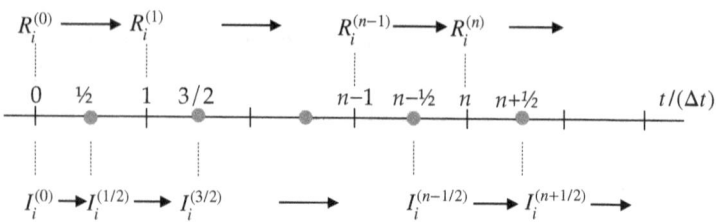

Figure 105: In the Schrödinger-equation solver using leapfrog method, R_i are computed at $t = (\Delta t), 2(\Delta t), \ldots, n(\Delta t), \ldots$, while I_i's are computed at $(\Delta t)/2, 3(\Delta t)/2, \ldots (n+½)(\Delta t), \ldots$.

Example 1: We solve $\psi(x)$ for a free particle ($H = -(½)\partial_{xx}$) with nondimensional Gaussian wave packet $\psi(x, t=0) = \pi^{-1/4} \exp(-x^2/2) \exp(ix)$ as an initial condition. We employ the leapfrog method described above. A Python implementation of the above is as follows:

```
# initcond
a = 0.1; k0 = 10; k0a = k0*a
init_f = 1/np.sqrt(np.sqrt(pi))*np.exp(-x**2/2)
         *np.exp(1j*k0a*x)

R = np.zeros(N+2);
R[1:N+1] = np.real(init_f); R[0] = np.real(init_f[-1]);
R[N+1] = np.real(init_f[0])
I = np.zeros(N+2);
I[1:N+1] = np.imag(init_f); I[0] = np.imag(init_f[-1]);
I[N+1] = np.imag(init_f[0])

# Goto t=dt/2 using Euler method
I[1:N+1] = I[1:N+1] + (dt/
(4*h**2))*(R[2:N+2]-2*R[1:N+1]+R[0:N])
I[0] = I[N]; I[-1] = I[1]

for time_ind in range(nsteps+2):
    R[1:N+1] = R[1:N+1]- (dt/(2*h**2))*(I[2:N+2]
                    -2*I[1:N+1]+I[0:N])
    R[0] = R[N]; R[-1] = R[1]
```

```
I[1:N+1] = I[1:N+1]+ (dt/(2*h**2))*(R[2:N+2]
                    -2*R[1:N+1]+R[0:N])
I[0] = I[N]; I[-1] = I[1]

# Goto t=dt/2 using Euler method
R[1:N+1] = R[1:N+1] - (dt/(4*h**2))
                    *(I[2:N+2]-2*I[1:N+1]+I[0:N])
R[0] = R[N]; R[-1] = R[1]
```

In Figure 106, we plot the $|\psi|$, real(ψ), and imag(ψ) at $t' = 2$. The initial wave packet is shown as black dashed curve. In the figure, we also plot the exact values, which are $|\psi_a|$ and real(ψ_a). The numerical result for the FD code is very close to the analytical result.

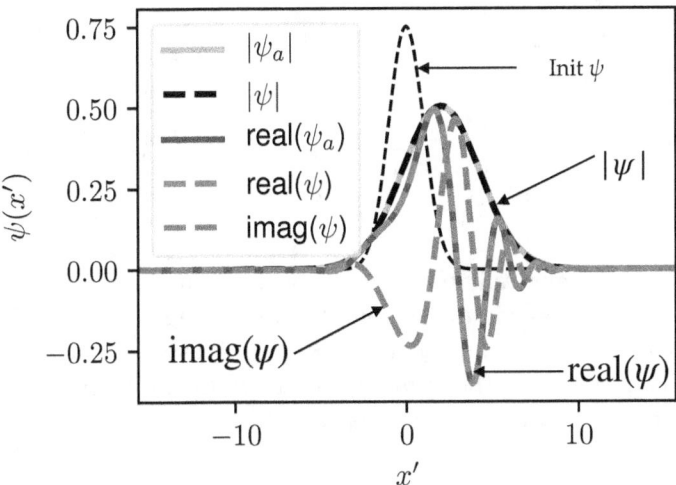

Figure 106: Example 1: Numerically computed wavefunction of a free particles at $t' = 2$. The Gaussian wave packet (black-dashed curve) is the initial condition. The subscript a represents the analytical solution of the wavefunction. The FD solution is close to the exact results.

Example 2: We solve for the wavefunction of a linear harmonic oscillator whose Hamiltonian is $H = -(½)\partial_{xx} + (½) x^2$. We employ same initial condition and parameters as those used for the spectral method, that is, $L = 6\pi$, $\Delta t = 0.001$, $t_f = 2$, and $\psi(x', t=0) = (1/\sqrt{2})\, \pi^{-1/4} \exp(-$

$(x')^2/2)[1 +\sqrt{2}x']$. The numerical results for $t' = 0, 1, 2$ are shown in Figure 107. The final state is close to the exact wavefunction, $(1/\sqrt{2})$ $\pi^{-1/4}$ $\exp(-(x')^2/2)[\exp(-it'/2)+\sqrt{2}x'\exp(-3it'/2)]$ (shown as black dashed curve). The plots are very similar to that for spectral solution of the same problem (see Figure 98).

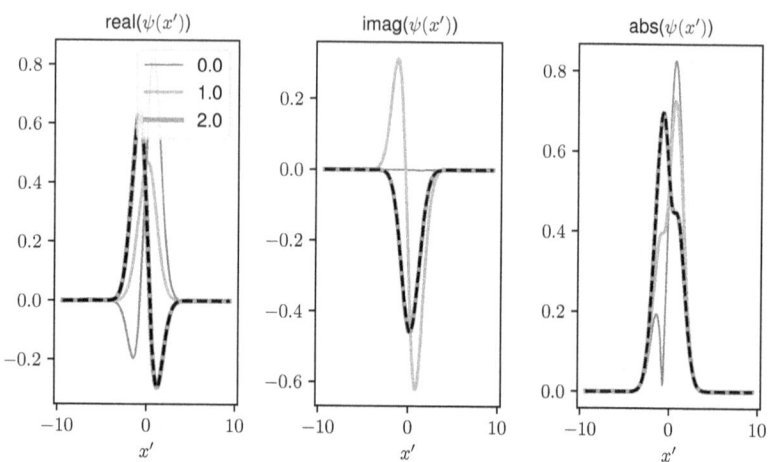

Figure 107: Numerically computed wavefunction of a simple oscillator of Example 2. The figure exhibits the real, imaginary, and absolute values of the wavefunction at $t' = 0, 1, 2$ using the curves with increasing thickness. The numerical solution is close to the exact wave function, represented using the black-dashed curves.

Solving Schrödinger Equation Using split-operator Method

We present an alternative time-stepping scheme called *split-operator method* for the Schrödinger equation. In this method, we start with

$$|\psi(t + \Delta t)> = \exp(-i\hat{H}\Delta t/2)\exp(-i\hat{H}\Delta t/2)|\psi(t)>,$$

or, $\exp(i\hat{H}\Delta t/2)|\psi(t + \Delta t)> = \exp(-i\hat{H}\Delta t/2)|\psi(t)>.$

Now we expand the exponential operator to the first-order in Taylor series that yields

$$[1 + i\hat{H}\Delta t/2]|\psi(t+\Delta t)> = [1 - i\hat{H}\Delta t/2]|\psi(t)> . \quad \ldots(98)$$

Scalar product of Eq. (98) with $<x|$ yields the following equation

$$[1 + i(\Delta t/2)(-\partial_{xx}^2 + V)]\psi(x, t+\Delta t) =$$
$$[1 - i(\Delta t/2)(-\partial_{xx}^2 + V)]\psi(x, t) . \quad \ldots(99)$$

Following the standard procedure, we discretize ψ in real space. We denote the wavefunction at position x_i at time t and at time $t+\Delta t$ using $\psi_i^{(n)}$ and $\psi_i^{(n+1)}$ respectively. By employing central difference scheme for ∂^2_{xx}, the discretized version of Eq. (99) is

$$-i\frac{\Delta t}{2h^2}\psi_{i-1}^{(n+1)} + \left[1 + i\frac{\Delta t}{2}V(x_i) + i\frac{\Delta t}{h^2}\right]\psi_i^{(n+1)} - i\frac{\Delta t}{2h^2}\psi_{i+1}^{(n+1)}$$
$$= +i\frac{\Delta t}{2h^2}\psi_{i-1}^{(n)} + \left[1 - i\frac{\Delta t}{2}V(x_i) - i\frac{\Delta t}{h^2}\right]\psi_i^{(n)} + i\frac{\Delta t}{2h^2}\psi_{i+1}^{(n)}.$$

This is a tridiagonal matrix, which can be solved using a matrix solver (see Section 20.1). By time stepping the above equation for sufficiently large number of steps, we obtain the final $\psi(x,t)$.

With this, we stop our discussion on FD implementation of solvers for the Schrodinger equation.

Assessment of FD Method

In this chapter we introduced FD method for simple problems. FD method is very powerful, and it is heavily used for simulating systems with complex geometries and complex boundary conditions. Some of the leading applications are flows in pipes and Earth's atmosphere, electromagnetic waves for radar applications, stresses in structures, etc. The grids for such problems are typically nonuniform and complex. These topics are covered in specialised books on FD methods, e.g., Ferziger et al. [2019].

Note that the PDEs with complex geometries and complex boundary conditions are difficult (often impossible) to simulate using spectral method. This is a major drawback of spectral method compared to FD method. However, for the same grid resolution, the errors in a FD method is larger than that in a spectral method. Or, for a similar accuracy, we need higher grid resolution for a FD method compared to a spectral method. Thus, FD and spectral methods have their advantages and disadvantages.

****

Conceptual Questions

1. State the merits and demerits of spectral and FD implementations of Schrödinger-equation solver.

Exercises

1. Solve Schrödinger equation for a linear harmonic oscillator using RK2 method in time. Take the parameters of Example 2. Compare your results with those of Example 2.
2. Solve the Schrödinger equation for a free particle in 2D and in 3D. Use Gaussian packet as an initial condition.
3. Solve the Schrödinger equation for a linear harmonic oscillator in 2D.
4. Solve Gross–Pitaevskii equation with $V = 0$ and $g = 1$ using FD method. Compute the error in $\int d\mathbf{r} \ |\Psi^2|$ in this method.

Chapter Seventeen
SOLVING NONLINEAR ALGEBRAIC EQUATIONS

Synopsis

"A view of nature as dense and nonlinear is at the core of our contemporary science. Process and order emerge subtly." — Gregory Benford

In this chapter, we describe leading methods for solving algebraic nonlinear equations.

17.1   Root Finders

Root finding of a nonlinear equation is an important exercise in science and engineering. Some applications requiring roots are as follows: computation of roots of polynomials for Gauss quadrature; finding fixed points of nonlinear equations and nonlinear maps; finding minima or maxima during optimisation.

In this chapter, we will discuss how to find roots for a single nonlinear equation. The methods discussed here can be generalised to multiple nonlinear equations. In Section 20.1, we will discuss methods for solving a set of linear equations.

In this chapter, we will describe the following root-finding algorithms: *Bisection method, Newton-Raphson's method, Secant method,* and *Relaxation method*. Our objective is to solve equations of the form $f(x) = 0$. We start with the bisection method.

Bisection Method

Consider one of the roots of equation $f(x) = 0$. In bisection method, we adopt the following strategy:

1. We plot $f(x)$ vs. x and identify two points x_l and x_r that are on the left and right sides of the root x^*. Thus, we bracket the root between x_l and x_r. See Figure 108 for an illustration.
2. We compute the mid point $x = (x_l+x_r)/2$.
3. If $|f(x)| \le \varepsilon$, where ε is the tolerance level, then we have found the root. We stop here.
4. Otherwise, $|f(x)| > \varepsilon$. Now, if $x < x^*$, x replaces x_l, otherwise x replaces x_r.
5. We repeat the above process till $|f(x)| \le \varepsilon$.

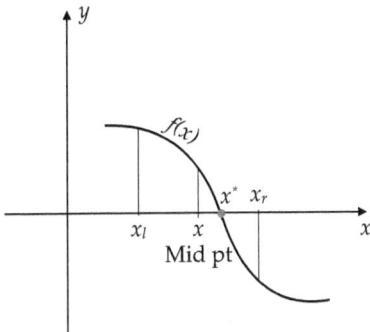

Figure 108: Root finder using bisection method. We start with x_l and x_r, and approach the root iteratively.

Now we estimate the error in the bisection method. Let us denote the two starting points as x_0 and x_1, and later x's as $x_2, x_3, \ldots x_n$, etc. Note that

$$x_{n+1} = (½)(x_n + x_{n-1}). \quad \ldots..(100)$$

Hence, the error, $\varepsilon_n = x^* - x_n$, evolves as

$$\varepsilon_{n+1} = (½)(\varepsilon_n + \varepsilon_{n-1}).$$

Hence, the error, which is average of the two previous steps, converges slowly.

Example 1: Using the bisection method, we find root of the equation $f(x) = \exp(x) - 6$. The correct answer is $\log(6) \approx 1.791759469228055$. First, we plot the function $f(x)$ in Figure 109(a), and choose $x_0 = 3$ and $x_1 = 1$, which are on the opposite sides of the root. After this, we compute x_n's iteratively using Eq. (100). We plot x_n vs. n in Figure 109(b), according to which, for a tolerance level of $\varepsilon = 0.001$, the iteration converges to 1.7890625 in 9 steps. A code segment is given below:

```
def f(x):
    return np.exp(x)-6

eps = 0.001; N = 10
```

```
x = np.zeros(N); x[0] = 3; x[1] = 1

for i in range(2,N):
    mid = (x[i-2] + x[i-1])/2
    if (abs(mid-x[i-1]) < eps):
        x[i] = mid
        break
    if f(x[i-2])*f(mid) > 0:
        x[i] = mid
    else:
        x[i-1] = x[i-2]; x[i] = mid
    print("i, mid = ", i, mid)

print ("estimated root ", mid)
```

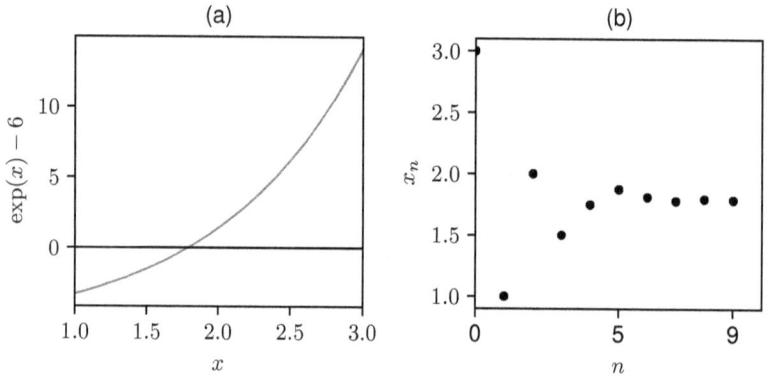

Figure 109: Example 1: Finding the root of $f(x) = \exp(x)-6$ using the bisection method. (a) plot of $f(x)$ vs. x. (b) Plot of x_n vs. n.

Example 2: We employ bisection method to compute the root of $f(x) = x^{1/3}$. We choose $x_0 = 1.7$ and $x_1 = -0.4$ and iterate Eq. (100). For a precision of 10^{-5}, the solution converges to $x^* \approx 0$ in 18 iterations.

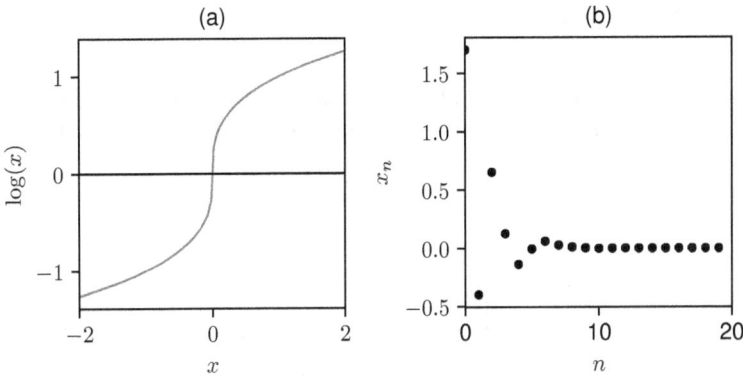

Figure 110: Example 2: Finding the root of $f(x) = x^{1/3}$ using bisection method. (a) plot of $f(x)$ vs. x. (b) Plot of x_n vs. n.

Newton-Raphson Method

The Newton-Raphson method provides a faster convergence to the root than the bisection method. In this method, we start with x_0 and compute x_1 using the slope at x_0. As shown in Figure 111,

$$f'(x_0) = \frac{f(x_0)}{x_0 - x_1}, \text{ hence, } x_1 = x_0 - \frac{f(x_0)}{f'(x_0)}.$$

For the $(n+1)$th step,

$$x_{n+1} = x_n - \frac{f(x_n)}{f'(x_n)}. \quad \ldots(101)$$

The process is continued until $|x_{n+1} - x_n| < \varepsilon$, or till the tolerance level is met.

Now let us analyse the error for this method. At the root x^*, $f(x^*) = 0$. Rewriting of Eq. (101) and its Taylor expansion around x^* yields

$$x^* - x_{n+1} = x^* - x_n + \frac{f(x^*) - \epsilon_n f'(x^*) + (1/2)\epsilon_n^2 f''(x^*) + H.O.T.}{f'(x^*) - \epsilon_n f''(x^*) + H.O.T.},$$

or, $\epsilon_{n+1} \approx -\dfrac{1}{2}\epsilon_n^2 \dfrac{f''(x*)}{f'(x*)}$, ...(102)

where H.O.T. stands for higher order terms. In the above analysis, the denominator too is expanded using Taylor series. Thus, the error converges as ϵ_n^2 as long as $f''(x^*)/f'(x^*)$ is finite.

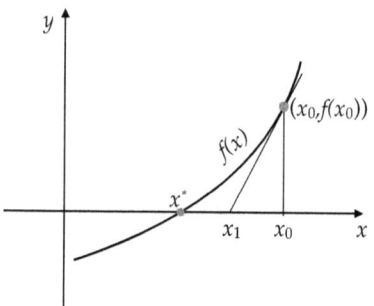

Figure 111: Root finder using Newton-Raphson method.

The quadratic convergence of Newton-Raphson method is a faster than the linear convergence of bisection method. However, Newton-Raphson method fails to converge if $|f''(x^*)/f'(x^*)|$ is large. For this case, the iteration diverges, that is, $\epsilon_{n+1} > \epsilon_n$. See Figure 112 for an illustration.

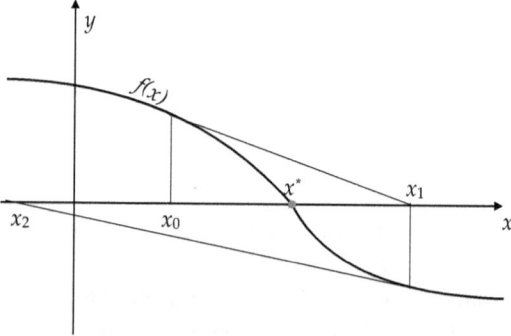

Figure 112: Newton-Raphson method fails to converge when $|f''(x^*)/f'(x^*)|$ is large. In this case, we go further away from the root, or $\epsilon_{n+1} > \epsilon_n$.

Example 3: We solve for the root of $f(x) = \exp(x) - 6$ using Newton-Raphson method. We start with $x_0 = 3$ and iterate using Eq. (101). For the tolerance level of $\varepsilon = 0.001$, the iteration converges to 1.7917594693651107 in 5 iteration. See Figure 113(a) for an illustration. A code segment for the computation is given below:

```
for i in range(1,N):
    x[I] = x[i-1] - f(x[i-1])/np.exp(x[i-1])
    if (abs(x[i]-x[i-1]) < eps):
        break

print ("estimated root ", x[i])
```

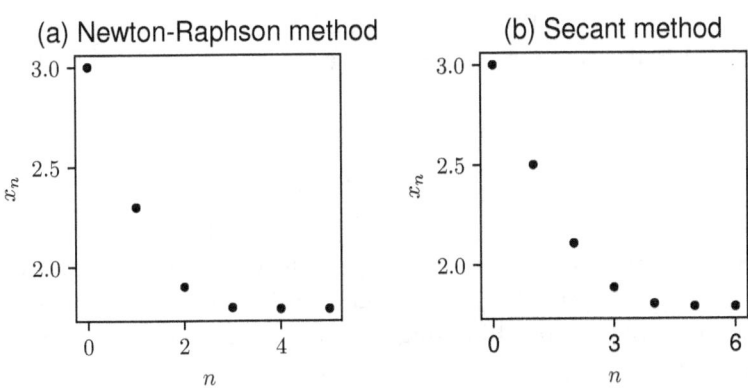

Figure 113: Finding the root of $f(x) = \exp(x) - 6$. Plots of x_n vs. n for (a) Newton-Raphson method (Example 3); (b) secant method (Example 5).

Example 4: Newton-Raphson method fails to compute the root of $f(x) = x^{1/3}$. We start with $x_0 = 1$ and iterate Eq. (101). As shown in Figure 114(a), the solution x_n diverges from the root $x^* \approx 0$. This is because of the divergence of $|f''(x^*)/f'(x^*)|$ near the origin.

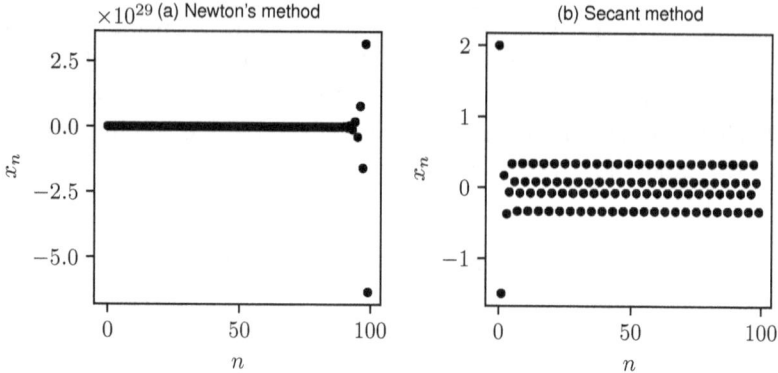

Figure 114: For $f(x) = x^{1/3}$. Plots of x_n vs. n for (a) Newton-Raphson method (Example 4); (b) secant method (Example 6). Both these methods fail to find the roots of the equation.

Secant Method

Often, it may be impractical to compute the derivative of a function. It is specially so when $f(x)$ is provided as a time series. In that case, we estimate $f'(x_n)$ of Eq. (101) using two neighbours $(x_{n-1}, f(x_{n-1}))$ and $(x_n, f(x_n))$ (see Figure 115):

$$f'(x_n) \approx \frac{f(x_n) - f(x_{n-1})}{x_n - x_{n-1}}.$$

Substitution of the above $f'(x_n)$ in Eq. (101) yields

$$x_{n+1} = x_n - f(x_n) \frac{x_n - x_{n-1}}{f(x_n) - f(x_{n-1})}. \quad \ldots..(103)$$

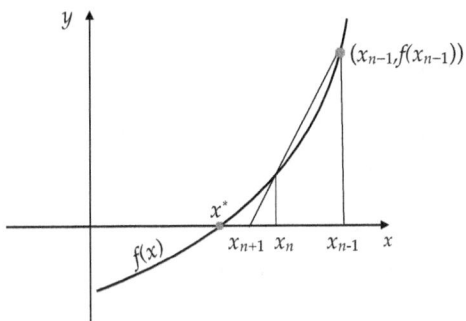

Figure 115: Root finder using Secant method.

This method is called secant method due to the secant passing through the points $(x_n, f(x_n))$ and $(x_{n-1}, f(x_{n-1}))$. Also, the convergence of the secant method is similar to that of Newton-Raphson method, that is, errors converge as in Eq. (102).

Example 5: We solve for the root of $f(x) = \exp(x) - 6$ using the secant method. We start with $x_0 = 3$ and $x_1 = 2.5$, and take tolerance level of $\varepsilon = 0.001$. The iteration of Eq. (103) converges to 1.791764077555014 in 6 steps. See Figure 113(b) for an illustration.

Example 6: The secant method fails to compute the root of $f(x) = x^{1/3}$ because $|f''(x^*)/f'(x^*)|$ diverges near the origin. However, unlike Newton-Raphson method, x_n's oscillate around 4 values near the origin. See Figure 114(b) for an illustration.

Relaxation Method

Often, we need to solve equations of the form $f(x) = x$, which is equivalent to finding the roots of $F(x) = f(x) - x$. Let us denote the solution of $f(x) = x$ by x^*, that is, $f(x^*) = x^*$. Following the notation of dynamical systems, we refer to x^* as a *fixed point* (FP).

To find x^*, we start with $x = x_0$ and compute $x_1 = f(x_0)$. After this we compute $x_2 = f(x_1)$, and continue further. The $(n+1)^{th}$ step is

$$x_{n+1} = f(x_n) . \quad \ldots\ldots(104)$$

For some fixed points, called *stable fixed points*, the iteration converges, that is, $|x_{n+1} - x_n| < \varepsilon$. The fixed points for which the iteration does not converge are called *unstable fixed points*. Figure 115 illustrates these points. The left FP is stable, while the one in the middle is unstable. The diagram of Figure 115 is also called a *web diagram* because the arrows form a web.

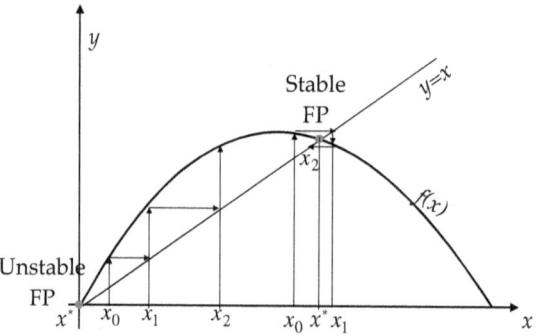

Figure 116: The web diagram for finding the fixed points of $f(x) = x$ using the relaxation method.

The relaxation method has a simple criteria for convergence. We show below that the iterations converge to the *stable fixed point* x^* when $|f'(x^*)| < 1$. On the other hand, the iterations diverge when $|f'(x^*)| > 1$. We prove the above statement using the following arguments.

We subtract x^* from Eq. (104) that yields

$$x_{n+1} - x^* = f(x_n) - x^* = f(x_n) - f(x^*) .$$

Using Taylor expansion of $f(x_n)$ around x^* and ignoring the higher order terms, we obtain

$$x_{n+1} - x^* = (x_n - x^*)f'(x^*),$$

or, $\varepsilon_{n+1} = \varepsilon_n f'(x^*)$.

Clearly, $|\varepsilon_{n+1}| < |\varepsilon_n|$ when $|f'(x^*)| < 1$. Hence, $|f'(x^*)| < 1$ is the necessary condition for the convergence of the relaxation method. The iteration process diverges when $|f'(x^*)| > 1$.

How do we compute the unstable FP considering that the iterations diverge for this case? Figure 116 provides us a hint. The reversed arrows converge to the unstable fixed point. Hence, the iteration

$$x_n = f^{-1}(x_{n+1})$$

will lead us to the unstable FP. Note that reversal of the arrows is equivalent to going back in time.

Example 7: We find the solutions of $f(x) = 2.5\,x(1-x) = x$ (see Figure 117(a)) using the relaxation method. This equation has two solutions: $x^* = 0$ and $x^* = 1 - 1/2.5 = 0.6$. Note that $f'(0) = 2.5$ and $f'(0.6) = -0.5$. Hence, $x^* = 0$ is an unstable FP, while $x^* = 0.6$ is a stable FP. To reach to the stable FP, we start with $x_0 = 0.1$ and iterate that takes us to $x^* = 0.6$. The small black dots of Figure 117(b) represent x_n's during the iteration.

To obtain the unstable FP using relaxation method, we start with $x_{n+1} = 0.2$ and iterate backwards, that is, $x_n = f^{-1}(x_{n+1})$. We finally reach near the FP, $x^* = 0$. The large red circles of Figure 117(b) represent x_n for this iteration. Note that $f^{-1}(y)$ has two solutions. However, we employ

$$x = f^{-1}(y) = \frac{a - \sqrt{a^2 - 4ay}}{2a}$$

with $a = 2.5$; this solution takes us to $x^* = 0$.

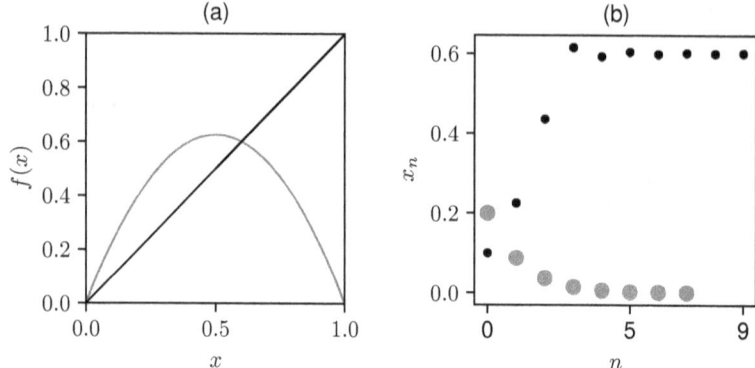

Figure 117: Example 7: Finding the roots of $f(x) = 2.5\ x(1-x)$. (a) Plot of $f(x)$ vs. x. (b) Plot of x_n vs. n; small black dots converge to the root $x^* = 0.6$, while the large red circles converge to $x^* = 0$.

Python's root finder

Python's scypy module has several functions for finding the roots of equations. These functions are *brentq, brenth, ridder,* and *bisect,* whose arguments are the function and the bracketing interval. Here we discuss how to use the function *brentq*. The following code segment finds the roots of $g(x) = x^2 - 1$ and $f(x) = \sin(\pi x) - x$.

```
In [15]: from scipy import optimize

In [308]: g = lambda x: x**2 - 1

In [309]: optimize.brentq(g, 0.5, 1.5)       # finds the
root in the interval [0.5, 1.5]
Out[309]: 0.9999999999999993

In [310]: optimize.brentq(g, -1.5, -0.5)
Out[310]: -0.9999999999999993

In [312]: f =lambda x: np.sin(np.pi*x) - x

In [313]: optimize.brentq(f,-0.1, 0.1)
Out[313]: 0.0
```

```
In [314]: optimize.brentq(f,0.5, 1)
Out[314]: 0.7364844482410411
```

Assessment of Root Finders

Let us review the root finders discussed in this chapter. The bisection method is quite robust and simple, and it is guaranteed to converge. The convergence however is slow. On the other hand, Newton-Raphson and secant methods converge quickly. These two methods however fail if $|f''(x^*)/f'(x^*)|$ diverges. We illustrate this issue using $f(x) = x^{1/3}$ as an example. The bisection method can find the root of $f(x) = x^{1/3}$, but Newton-Raphson and secant methods fail to do so.

The relaxation method is an efficient and direct method to find the solution of $f(x) = x$. This method is very useful in dynamical systems.

In the next chapter, we will employ root finders to solve boundary value problems.

****

Conceptual Questions

1. Provide examples in physics where we need to find roots of nonlinear equations.
2. What are the merits and demerits of the bisection, Newton-Raphson, and secant methods for finding roots of nonlinear equations.

Exercises

1. Find root of $f(x) = \log(x)$ using the bisection, Newton-Raphson, and secant methods. Compare their convergence rates.
2. Find all the roots of $f(x) = 65 x^5 - 70 x^3 + 15x$ numerically.
3. Give an example of a function for which Newton-Raphson

method fails to find roots.
4. Find the solutions of $\sin(\pi x) = x$ using relaxation method.
5. Find the root of $f(x) = \tan(2x) - x$ in the interval $[-1/2, 1]$ using relaxation and Newton-Raphson methods.

Chapter Eighteen
BOUNDARY VALUE PROBLEMS

Synopsis

"There is geometry in the humming of the strings, there is music in the spacing of the spheres."
—Pythagorus

This chapter describes methods for solving boundary value problems.

18.1 Shooting Method

In Chapter Thirteen, we solved ordinary differential equations (ODE) given initial conditions. In this chapter, we will solve the differential equations given *boundary conditions*. Such problems are called *boundary value (BV) problems*.

The solution of a nth-order ODE requires n boundary values. For example, Newton's equation, $m\ddot{x} = F(x,\dot{x},t)$, requires two boundary conditions, say $x(t{=}0)$ and $x(t{=}1)$. The equations for eigenvalue problems such as $d^2y/dx^2 = -a^2 y$, as well as time-independent Schrödinger equation, require two boundary conditions. The solution of the equation of a beam, which is a fourth-order ODE, requires four boundary conditions.

In this section, we will solve second-order ODEs using shooting method.

Shooting Method

We consider a second-order ODE, $y'' = f(x,y)$, in the domain $[x_0, x_1]$. The boundary conditions to be used are the function values y_0 and y_1 at the ends, x_0 and x_1. Note that x is the independent variable, while $y(x)$ is the unknown function. See Figure 118 for an illustration.

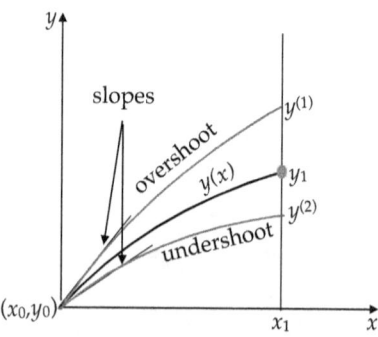

Figure 118: An illustration of the shooting method.

To solve the ODE using initial values at $x = x_0$, we require $y(x_0)$ and $y'(x_0)$. Unfortunately, we do not have $y'(x_0)$. In the shooting method, we determine $y'(x_0)$ using trial and error. The basic idea is the following. With the correct slope $y'(x_0)$, the trajectory will hit $y = y_1$ at $x = x_1$. To obtain the correct slope, we start with two guess values: a slope larger than $y'(x_0)$ leads to an overshoot to $y^{(1)}$, and a slope lower than $y'(x_0)$ leads to an undershoot to $y^{(2)}$ (see Figure 118). We start with these guesses and slowly converge to $y'(x_0)$ using the method described in Chapter Seventeen. This is akin to a shooting exercise, which is the reason for the name *shooting method*.

In this excercise, we have to solve for the required *slope* using the following equation:

$y(\text{slope}, x=1) = y_1$.

Since we do not know the form of the equation, we cannot employ Newton-Raphson method. However, we can employ bisection method.and keep adjusting the slope until the error ε falls within a given tolerance limit. We illustrate the shooting method using the following examples.

Example 1: We solve the following equation

$$d^2y/dx^2 = -a^2 y. \quad \ldots(105)$$

In the domain [0,1]. We consider two cases: $a = 1$ with $y(0) = 0$ and $y(1) = 0.5$; and $a = 5$ with $y(0) = 0$ and $y(1) = 0.1$.

In Figure 119 we illustrate the evolution of $y(x)$ towards the final solution for $a = 1$ and 5. For the former, we take first two slopes, $y'(0)$, as 0.1 and 2, but for the latter, the first two slopes are 0.1 and -1. The latter choice of -1 is somewhat counterintuitive. We solve for $y(x)$ given the initial conditions $(y(0), y'(0))$. In the figure, the initial curves are shown using dashed curves.

We employ bisection method to obtain the desired $y'(0)$. For the tolerance limit $\varepsilon = 0.01$, we converge to the final answer in 6 iterations. The numerical solutions are close to the respective exact solutions.

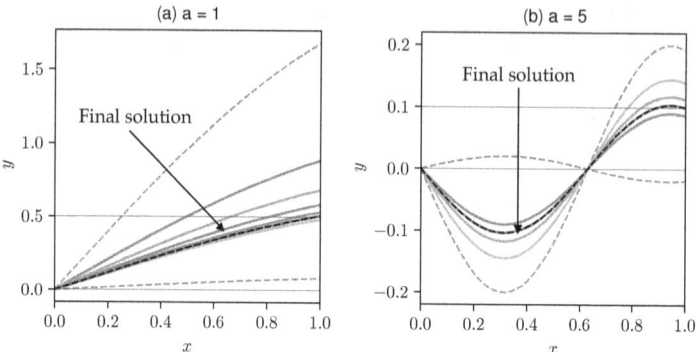

Figure 119: The solutions of $y'' = -a^2 y$ using the shooting method for (a) $a = 1$; $y(0) = 0$; $y(1) = 0.5$; (b) $a = 5$; $y(0) = 0$; $y(1) = 0.1$. The first two trial solutions are shown as the dashed curves below and above the real solution (black dashed curve). The final solutions are close to the respective exact results.

For boundary condition $y(0) = 0$ and $y(1) = A$, the equation $y'' = -a^2 y$ has an exact solution, $y(x) = A\sin(ax)/\sin(a)$. The slope at $x = 0$ is $Aa/\sin(a)$; the shooting method endeavours to reach this slope. Note that the slope is negative for $a = 5$, consistent with the numerical solution.

A code segment for the above problem is given below:

```
def ydot(y,x):
    return ([y[1], -a**2*y[0]])

end_val = 0.1; a = 5; tollerance = 0.01;
x = np.linspace(0,1,100)
slope_t = -1
yinit = np.array([0, slope_t])
y = odeint(ydot, yinit, x)
ax2.plot(x,y[:,0],'r--', lw=1)

slope_b = 0.1
yinit = np.array([0, slope_b])
y = odeint(ydot, yinit, x)
ax2.plot(x,y[:,0],'g--', lw=1)

iter = 0
while ((abs(y[-1,0]-end_val) > tollerance) and (iter < 20) ):
    slope_mid = (slope_t+slope_b)/2
    yinit = np.array([0, slope_mid])
```

```
y = odeint(ydot, yinit, x)
ax2.plot(x,y[:,0])

if (y[-1,0]>end_val):
    slope_t = slope_mid
else:
    slope_b = slope_mid
iter = iter +1
```

Example 2: Let us explore if we can apply shooting method to find solution of the equation $d^2y/dx^2 = -a^2y$ with $y(0) = y(1) = 0$. For the given the boundary conditions, the equation has solution $y = A \sin(ax)$ only for $a = n\pi$, where n as a positive integer. When $a = n\pi$, the numerical solution reaches $y(1) = 0$ for any slope; hence we can not adjust the slope using the shooting method.

This problem can not be solved using the shooting method; it belongs to the category of eigenvalue finder, which will be discussed in the next section.

Example 3: Let us solve $\ddot{x} = -a^2 x$ for boundary condition $x(t = 0) = 0$ and $x(t = 1) = A$. Physically, we start the mass of the oscillator from the origin in such a way that it reaches $x = A$ at $t = 1$. Clearly, this problem is same as Example 1 with a change of variable $x \to t$ and $y \to x$.

Example 4: We solve the equation of a pendulum $ld^2\phi/dt^2 = -g \sin\phi$ given boundary condition $\phi(0) = 0$ and $\phi(1) = \pi/4$. That is, we require the pendulum to start from $\phi(0) = 0$ and reach $\phi = \pi/4$ at $t = 1$ sec. We take $l = 1$ m and $g = 9.8$ m/sec^2. We solve the above problem using shooting method. We start with the first two slopes of 0.1 and 5 (shown as dashed curve). For the tolerance level of 0.01, we reach the final solution in 8 iteration. We employ the bisection method for iterations. See Figure 120 for an illustration.

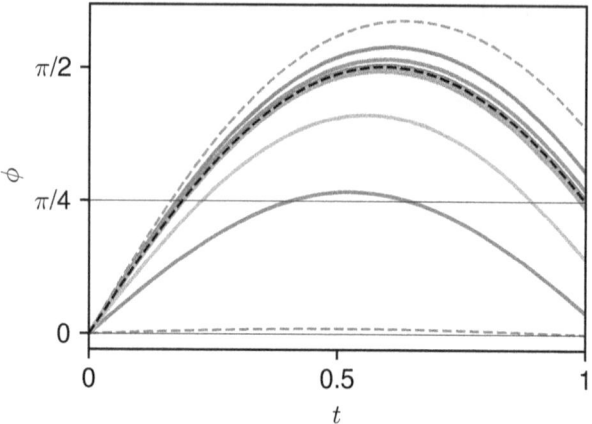

Figure 120: Solution of $d^2\phi/dt^2 = -g\sin\phi$ using the shooting method. The first two trial solutions are the dashed curves. The final curve is the black dashed curve.

With this, we end our discussion on shooting method.

****

Conceptual Questions

1. Provide examples of boundary value problems in science and engineering.
2. What are the key differences between ODE solvers with boundary values and initial values?

Exercises

1. The shells from the Bofors gun leave the muzzle with an speed of 1 km/sec. The shell is required to hit a target 10 km away. Use shooting method to compute the angle of launch of the shell. Assume the surface to be flat. Ignore air friction.

2. Redo Exercise 1 in the presence of air drag. Assume kinematic viscosity of air to be 0.1 cm²/sec, and cannon balls to have a diameter of 20 cms.
3. Solve the equation $\ddot{x} = -x - \gamma \dot{x}$ with $\gamma = 0.1$ for the boundary conditions $x(0) = 0$ and $x(1) = 1$.
4. Numerically solve the equation $\varepsilon y'' + y' = 0$ for $\varepsilon = 0.001$ and the boundary conditions $y(0) = 0$ and $y(1) = 1$. This is a stiff equation.

18.2 Eigenvalue Calculation

Computing eigenvalues of ODEs is important exercise in science and engineering. For example, in quantum mechanics, we compute the energy eigenvalues of time-independent Schrödinger equation; we determine the eigenvalues of vibrating strings and drums; etc. In this section, we briefly describe how to compute eigenvalues of ODEs for given boundary conditions.

Solving $y'' = \lambda y$

Here, we solve for the eigenvalue λ of the equation

$$y'' = \lambda y \quad \ldots(106)$$

for the boundary condition $y(0) = 0$, $y(2) = 0$. Recall Example 2 of Section 18.1 where we showed that the equation $y'' = \lambda y$ with vanishing boundary condition has a solution only for specific values of λ.

The exact solution of the above equation is

$$y(x) = A \sin(\sqrt{-\lambda} x) \ldots(107)$$

with negative λ and arbitrary A. Since $y(2) = 0$, we obtain $2\sqrt{-\lambda} = n\pi$, where n is an integer. This relation yields the *eigenvalues* as $\lambda_n = -(n\pi/2)^2$; the first two eigenvalues are $-\pi^2/4$ and $-\pi^2$.

For the vanishing boundary condition, the solution $y(x)$ of Eq. (106) can be multiplied by any factor, which is related to the arbitrariness of A of Eq. (107). Thus, the slope of $y(x)$ is not unique, and we can choose any value for $y'(0)$.

We choose $y'(0) = B$. Under these condition, the end point depends on λ. We need to solve the following nonlinear equation of λ:

$$y(\lambda, x=2) = 0.$$

We employ one of the solvers discussed in Chapter Seventeen and compute λ for which y(2) = 0. The function $y(x)$ that satisfies Eq. (106) is called *eigenfunction* corresponding to the eigenvalue λ. In the following discussion we employ secant method to compute λ. A code segment for computing the first eigenvalue is given below. Here, we fix the slope to 0.1.

```
def ydot(y,x):
    return ([y[1], a*y[0]]).   # a = λ

yinit = np.array([0, 0.1]) #slope = 0.1
a = -2
y = odeint(ydot, yinit, x)
yend = y[-1,0]
ax1.plot(x,y[:,0],'r--', lw=1)

a_prev = a;   a = -1

iter = 0
while ((abs(a-a_prev) > tollerance) and (iter < 10)):
    y = odeint(ydot, yinit, x)
    ax1.plot(x,y[:,0])

    yend_prev, yend = yend, y[-1,0]
    a_prev, a = a, a - yend*(a-a_prev)/(yend-yend_prev)
    iter = iter + 1
```

For the first eigenvalue, we start the iteration process $\lambda = -2$ and -1 and employ the secant method to reach the desired λ within precision of 0.01. In 4 iterations we converge to −2.47, which is quite close to the exact value $-\pi^2/4$. In Figure 121(a), we exhibit $y(x)$ computed at each iteration. The initial $y(x)$ is shown as a red dashed curve. The final curve (after 4 iteration) is quite close to the exact solution, which is exhibited as black dashed curve.

Equation (106) has infinite many eigenvalues (see Eq. (107)). We can obtain these eigenvalues by starting the iteration with guessed value of λ. The second eigenvalue (-9.869606001069714 ≈ π^2) can be reached by starting the iterations with $\lambda = -11$ and -8. We illustrate the second eigenfunction in Figure 121(b).

Next, we compute the eigenvalues and eigenfunctions for a quantum particle moving in a potential.

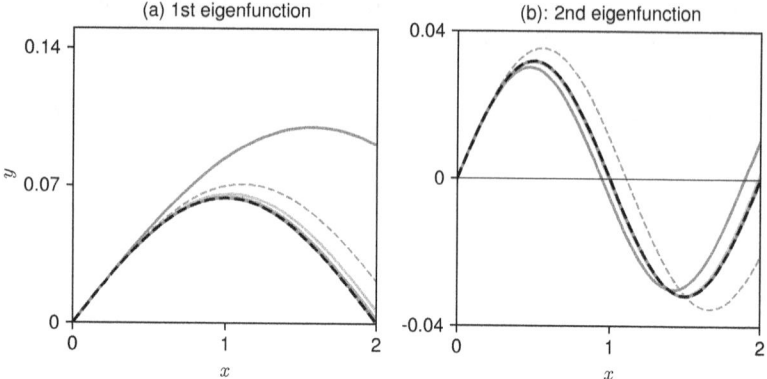

Figure 121: First two eigenfunctions of equations $y'' = \lambda y$ with the condition that $y(1) = 0$. For the two cases, the final solutions is close to the exact solutions, which are shown as the thick dashed curves. The initial $y(x)$ is shown as the thin dashed curve.

Solving Eigenvalues with Potentials

Now we make Eq. (106) a bit more complex by introducing a potential $V(x)$:

$$-(\tfrac{1}{2})y'' + V(x)y = Ey. \quad \ldots(108)$$

The time-independent nondimensionalized Schrödinger equation has the above form with $y(x)$ as the wavefunction of a particle moving under a potential $V(x)$. In addition to Schrödinger equation, Eq. (108) describes many other physical systems, for example, a wave moving in a medium whose refractive index varies in space.

We can solve Eq. (108) following the procedure described earlier in this section. Let us solve Schrödinger equation in the domain [−1, 1] with the following potential:

$$V(x) = \frac{1}{1.1 - x^2}. \quad \ldots(109)$$

Note that $V(x)$ takes a large value near the wall, hence it is similar to a square-well potential. In Figure 122(a,b) we plot the eigenfunctions of the ground state and the first excited state respectively. The final curves are exhibited by black dashed curves. The corresponding energies (eigenvalues E) are 2.30 and 6.24 respectively (within precision of 0.01). Figure 122(a) also illustrates the potential $V(x)$ as a chained curve.

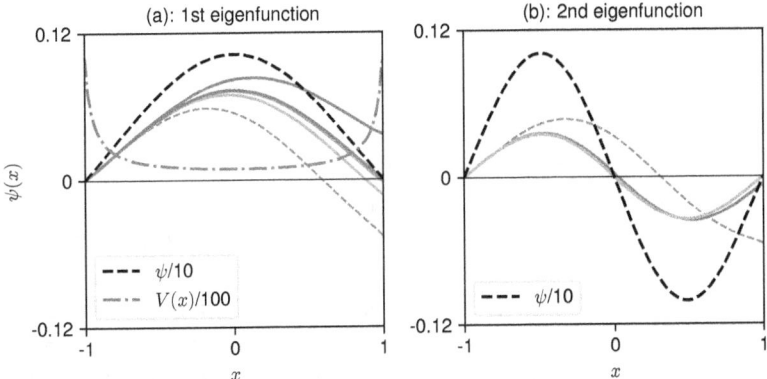

Figure 122: The eigenfunctions of equations $-(\frac{1}{2})y'' + V(x)y = Ey$: (a) Ground state, (b) the first excited state. The normalized potential $V(x)/100$ is exhibited using the chained curve in (a), and the initial $y(x)$ using the thin dashed curves in both the plots. The final $y(x)$ are shown using the thick dashed curves.

Typically, the iterative solution of Eq. (108) is not normalized, that is $\int_{-1}^{1} |y(x)|^2 dx \neq 1$. However, we can easily construct the normalised wave function as follows:

$$y_{\text{norm}}(x) = \frac{1}{\sqrt{\int_{-1}^{1} |y(x)|^2 dx}} y(x).$$

The potential $V(x) = 0$ for a particle in a box. Therefore, the governing equation is $y'' = -2Ey$. For vanishing boundary condition at -1 and 1, the two lowest eigenvalues E for the particle in a box are $\pi^2/8$ (~1.23) and $\pi^2/2$ (~4.93). These values are lower than those with the potential $V(x)$ of Eq. (109), which is expected because positive $V(x)$ increases the energy eigenvalue.

With this, we end our discussion on eigenvalue computation of ODEs.

****

Exercises

1. Compute the third and fourth eigenvalues of ODE $y'' = \lambda y$ for the boundary condition $y(0) = y(2) = 0$.
2. Compute the third and fourth eigenvalues for the quantum problem discussed in this section (with potential $V(x)$ of Eq. (109).
3. Solve for the eigenvalues and eigenfunctions of a quantum oscillator. Employ the boundary condition that the eigenfunctions vanish at $x = \pm\infty$. For numerical simulation, solve the nondimensional Schrödinger equation in a large box.
4. Compute the eigenvalues and eigenfunctions of the equation $x^2 y'' + xy' + (x^2 - a^2)y = 0$ for the boundary conditions $y(0) = y(1) = 0$.
5. Compute the eigenvalues and eigenfunctions of the equation $x^2 y'' + xy' + (x^2 - a^2)y = 0$ for the boundary conditions $y(0) = 1$ and $y(1) = 0$.

Chapter Nineteen
SOLVERS FOR LAPLACE AND POISSON EQUATIONS

Synopsis

"Today's scientists have substituted mathematics for experiments, and they wander off through equation after equation, and eventually build a structure which has no relation to reality." — Nikola Tesla

Solution of Laplace and Poisson equations are covered in this chapter.

19.1 Solving Laplace Equation

Laplace equation plays an important role in science and engineering. Some applications of Laplace equation are as follows:

1. In electrostatics, the electric potential (ϕ) in the absence of any source is described by $\nabla^2 \phi = 0$.
2. In magnetostatics, the equation for the vector potential (**A**) in a current-free region is $\nabla^2 \mathbf{A} = 0$.
3. The equation for the gravitational potential in the absence of any source: $\nabla^2 \phi = 0$.
4. The equation of the stream function in irrotational hydrodynamics: $\nabla^2 \phi = 0$.
5. The equation of a membrane under static condition: $\nabla^2 \phi = 0$.

In Cartesian geometry, the Laplace equation in 2D and 3D are as follows:

$$\frac{\partial^2 \phi}{\partial x^2} + \frac{\partial^2 \phi}{\partial y^2} = 0 \text{ in 2D}$$

$$\text{and } \frac{\partial^2 \phi}{\partial x^2} + \frac{\partial^2 \phi}{\partial y^2} + \frac{\partial^2 \phi}{\partial z^2} = 0 \text{ in 3D}$$

in a domain Ω. Three kinds of boundary conditions (BC) are employed for the Laplace equation:

1. *Dirichlet boundary condition*: Specify ϕ at the boundary of the domain Ω.
2. *Neumann boundary condition*: The normal derivative of ϕ is specified at the boundary.
3. Mixed boundary condition: Some regions of the boundary have Dirichlet BC, while the other regions have Neumann BC.

Before we start to solve the above equation numerically, it is best to state some of the important properties of Laplace equation. They are

1. *Uniqueness theorem*: The solution of the Laplace equation is uniquely determined given the boundary condition.

2. In 3D, the average value of ϕ over a sphere is equal to its value at the center of the sphere.
3. In 2D, the average value of ϕ over a disk is equal to its value at the center of the disk.

It is important to note that the solution of 1D Laplace equation, $d^2\phi/dx^2 = 0$, is trivial. It is $\phi(x) = ax+b$; the constants a and b are determined using the boundary condition.

Direct Method for Laplace Equation

In the following discussion, we solve Laplace equation in 2D. For simplicity, we discretize the domain uniformly along x and y directions, and denote the grid spacing by h. See Figure 123(a) for an illustration. Using

$$\frac{\partial^2 \phi}{\partial x^2} = \frac{\phi_{i+1,j} - 2\phi_{i,j} + \phi_{i-1,j}}{h^2},$$

$$\frac{\partial^2 \phi}{\partial y^2} = \frac{\phi_{i,j+1} - 2\phi_{i,j} + \phi_{i,j-1}}{h^2},$$

we derive the following discrete equation for the Laplace equation:

$$\frac{\phi_{i-1,j} - 2\phi_{i,j} + \phi_{i+1,j}}{h^2} + \frac{\phi_{i,j-1} - 2\phi_{i,j} + \phi_{i,j+1}}{h^2} = 0$$

or, $\phi_{i,j} = \frac{1}{4}(\phi_{i-1,j} + \phi_{i+1,j} + \phi_{i,j-1} + \phi_{i,j+1})$, ...(110)

which is the third property of the Laplace equation that the average value of ϕ in a small neighbourhood is equal to its value at the center. Here, we replace "a circle" with "a square", and the averaging is performed over the four nearest neighbours.

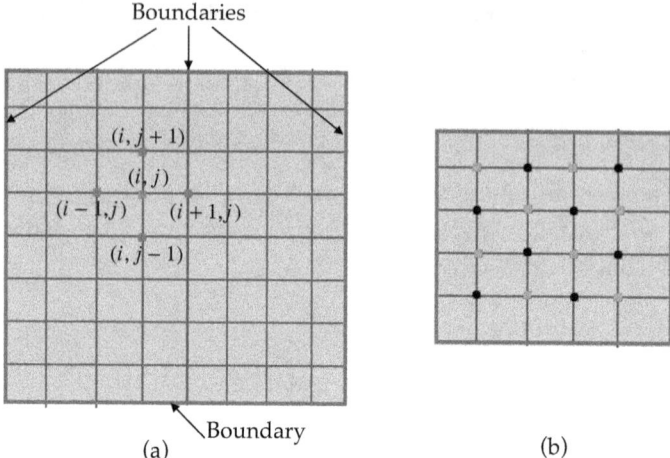

Figure 123: (a) The grid for Laplace equation. $\phi_{i,j}$ is average of ϕ's of the nearest neighbours. (b) The red and black grid points for the Red-Black method, here presented using light and dark colours.

For Dirichlet boundary condition, we specify ϕ at the boundary. Hence, we have Eq. (110) for every point of the grid except those at the boundary. We can write these equations in a matrix form as follows:

$$A \begin{bmatrix} \phi_{0,1} \\ \dots \\ \phi_{0,m} \\ \phi_{1,0} \\ \phi_{1,1} \\ \dots \end{bmatrix} = 0,$$

where A is a banded matrix with nonzero entries as 1, −4, 1. Note that the column vector excludes the points at the boundaries (e.g., $\phi_{0,0}$). We can solve for ϕ using matrix methods, which will be described in Section 20.1.

The iterative methods for solving Laplace equation are simpler than the direct method. In the following discussion, we will describe several such methods. We start with the Jacobi method.

Iterative Procedure: Jacobi Method

In Jacobi method for Dirichlet boundary condition, we set up the given boundary condition at the edges. The initial ϕ inside the domain could be set to zero (or any other value). However, it is better to start with an approximate solution if it is known. After this initial setup, we recompute ϕ inside the domain using the following formula:

$$\bar{\phi}_{i,j} = \frac{1}{4}(\phi_{i-1,j} + \phi_{i+1,j} + \phi_{i,j-1} + \phi_{i,j+1}). \quad \dots(111)$$

We test if

$$\max(|\bar{\phi} - \phi|) < \varepsilon,$$

where ε is the tolerance limit. If the error is larger than ε, we continue the iteration. Otherwise, we stop the iteration and report $\bar{\phi}$ as the desired solution.

Example 1: We compute the potential ϕ in a charge-free square. The left wall is kept at a potential of 1 unit, while the other walls have zero potential. For the computation, we employ a 66x66 grid, with the edges taking the boundary values.

We start with $\phi = 1$ at the left wall, and zero elsewhere. Boundary conditions on ϕ are maintained throughout the computation. We solve for ϕ at the 64x64 (inner) grid points by iterating Eq. (111) till $\max(|\bar{\phi} - \phi|) < \varepsilon = 10^{-6}$. The final potential is shown in Figure 124. A Python implementation of Jacobi method is given below. Note that the code is vectorized.

```
y   = np.zeros([N+2,M+2])
y[0,:]=V

while (error > eps):
    yp[1:N+1,1:M+1] = y[0:N,1:M+1] +y[2:N+2,1:M+1] \
                    + y[1:N+1,0:M] +y[1:N+1,2:M+2]
    yp[1:N+1,1:M+1] /= 4

    error = np.max(np.absolute(yp[1:N+1,1:M+1]-
y[1:N+1,1:M+1]))
```

```
y = yp.copy()
```

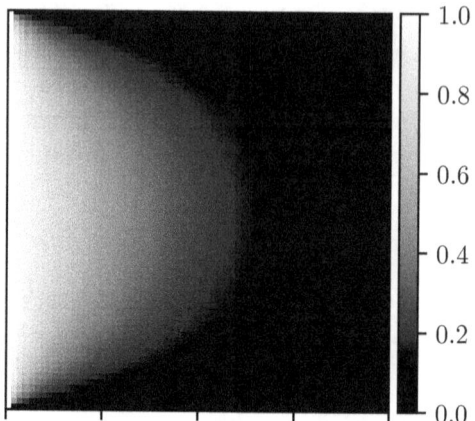

Figure 124: Example 1: The final potential ϕ computed using Jacobi method.

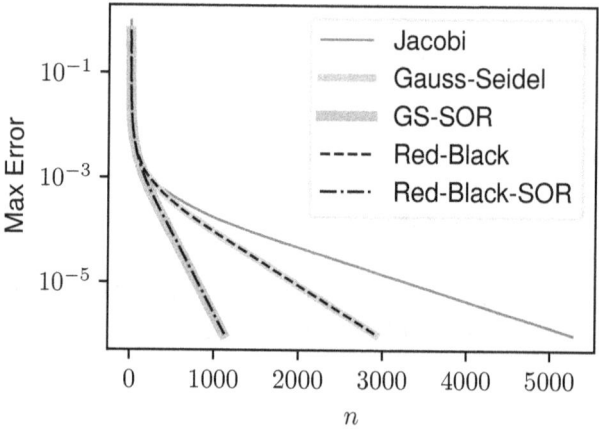

Figure 125: Plot of maximum error vs. Iteration (n) shows the convergence of various solvers of Laplace equation. The Jacobi method has the slowest convergence, while the Gauss-Seidal and Red-Black methods have next best results. SOR improves the convergence considerably.

The final solution was obtained using 5273 iterations, and it took approximately 0.25 second on my MacBook Pro (16 inch, 2019 model). Figure 125 exhibits the convergence of the error. The error falls sharply in the beginning, after which the convergence is exponential.

Next, we present several methods that converge faster than the Jacobi scheme.

Gauss-Seidel Method

Jacobi method employs ϕ of the previous step to update $\phi_{i,j}$ (see Eq. (111)). Note however that when we reach $\phi_{i,j}$ in the loop, we have already updated all the points up to (i,j). In Gauss-Seidel scheme, we use these already updated values for computing new $\phi_{i,j}$, that is,

$$\bar{\phi}_{i,j} = \frac{1}{4}(\bar{\phi}_{i-1,j} + \phi_{i+1,j} + \bar{\phi}_{i,j-1} + \phi_{i,j+1}), \quad \dots(112)$$

where $\bar{\phi}$ represents the updated variables.

A simple way to implement Gauss-Seidel scheme is to employ a single array for ϕ, and update the same using Eq. (112). Customarily, this kind of update is written as

$$\bar{\phi}_{i,j} \leftarrow \frac{1}{4}(\phi_{i-1,j} + \phi_{i+1,j} + \phi_{i,j-1} + \phi_{i,j+1}).$$

A python implementation of the above loop is as follows:

```
while (error > eps):
    yp = y.copy()    # prev step
    for i in range(1,N+1):
        for j in range(1,M+1):
            y[i,j] = (y[i-1,j] +y[i+1,j] + y[i,j-1] \
                     +y[i,j+1])/4

    error = np.max(np.absolute(yp[1:N+1,1:M+1] \
                   - y[1:N+1,1:M+1]))
```

For the system of Example 1, the Gauss-Seidel method takes 2918 iterations (less than Jacobi method) to converge to the desired accuracy, but the time taken is approximately 15 seconds, which is much larger than that for the Jacobi method. This is because the

Gauss-Seidel loop cannot be vectorized. Note however that the convergence of Gauss-Seidel method is faster than that for the Jacobi scheme (see Figure 125).

Next, we present Red-Black method, which is a vectorized implementation of Gauss-Seidel scheme.

Red-Black Method

In this scheme, we classify the grid points as red and black, as shown in Figure 123(b). The red grid-points are updated first, and then the black grid-points are updated. Fortunately, this process can be vectorized, as shown in the following code segment.

```
while (error > eps):
    tmp  = y.copy()   # copy of y
    y[1:N:2,1:M:2] = (y[0:N-1:2,1:M:2]
                      +y[2:N+1:2,1:M:2] \
                      + y[1:N:2,0:M-1:2] \
                      +y[1:N:2,2:M+1:2])/4

    y[2:N+1:2,2:M+1:2] = (y[1:N:2,2:M+1:2]
                      +y[3:N+2:2,2:M+1:2] \
                      + y[2:N+1:2,1:M:2] \
                      +y[2:N+1:2,3:M+2:2])/4

    y[1:N:2,2:M+1:2] = (y[0:N-1:2,2:M+1:2]
                      + y[2:N+1:2,2:M+1:2] \
                      + y[1:N:2,1:M:2] \
                      + y[1:N:2,3:M+2:2])/4

    y[2:N+1:2,1:M:2] = (y[1:N:2,1:M:2]
                      + y[3:N+2:2,1:M:2] \
                      + y[2:N+1:2,0:M-1:2] \
                      + y[2:N+1:2,2:M+1:2])/4

    error = np.max(np.absolute(tmp[1:N+1,1:M+1] \
                      -y[1:N+1,1:M+1]))
```

For Example 1, the Red-Black method converges to the desired accuracy in 2934 iterations (approximately same as Gauss-Seidel method), and it takes 0.20 second, which is much smaller than that for Gauss-Seidel method. The speedup is due to the vectorisation of the loop. Also, note that the convergence of Red-black algorithm is same as that for Gauss-Seidel method (see Figure 125).

Successive Over-relaxation (SOR)

The basic idea of over-relaxation method is that we overshoot the updated $\phi_{i,j}$ with ω, along with a compensation of $(1-\omega)\phi_{i,j}$. That is,

$$\bar{\phi}_{i,j} \leftarrow \frac{\omega}{4}(\phi_{i-1,j} + \phi_{i+1,j} + \phi_{i,j-1} + \phi_{i,j+1}) + (1-\omega)\phi_{i,j}. \quad (113)$$

We recover Gauss-Seidel method for $\omega = 1$. The convergence is faster for ω between 1 and 2. Unfortunately, SOR method works only for the Gauss-Seidel scheme, not for the Jacobi method. The following code segment illustrates the SOR scheme:

```
sor = 1.5
for i in range(1,N+1):
    for j in range(1,M+1):
        y[i,j] = sor*(y[i-1,j] +y[i+1,j] \
            + y[i,j-1] +y[i,j+1])/4 + (1-sor)*y[i, j]
```

For Example 1, SOR implementation of Gauss-Seidel scheme with ω = 1.5 convergence to the desired accuracy in 1116 iterations, and it takes 7.6 seconds. This convergence is faster than that for Gauss-Seidel. See Figure 125 for an illustration.

An implementation of SOR scheme in the Red-Black method yields additional speedup. For Example 1, this method converge to the final solution in 1131 iterations in 0.10 seconds. This is the fastest convergence for Example 1. See Figure 125 for an illustration. We summarise the convergence results in Table 31.

Table 31: Number of iterations and time taken for different solvers of Laplace equation.

Scheme	Iterations	Time
Jacobi	5273	2.5
Gauss-Seidel	2918	15
Red-Black	2934	0.20
Gauss-Seidel-SOR	1116	7.6
Red-Black-SOR	1131	0.10

For Neumann condition, the procedure a bit more complex, and it is not covered here. I recommend the following video for this problem: https://www.youtube.com/watch?v=yWU9x8F3zHU. Another topic that is skipped in this chapter is *multigrid method*.

With this, we end our discussion on Laplace equation.

****

Conceptual Questions

1. Compare the time complexities of various methods for solving Laplace equation.

Exercises

1. Solve Example 1 for various grids, e.g., 130x130, and examine the dependence of the convergence on the grid size.
2. Example 1 employs second order scheme for the computation of $\nabla^2 \phi$. Redo the exercise using fourth order scheme for the derivative computation. Compare the convergence.
3. Consider a box of unit dimension. Given that the left, right, bottom, and top walls are kept at a electric potential of 1, 2, 3, 4 Volts respectively, compute the potential inside the box using Jacobi, Gauss-Seidel, Red-Black, and SOR methods. Compare the time taken by these methods.
4. Solve for the electric potential inside a box of dimension 2x1x1. The left wall of the box is at kept at a potential of 1 Volt, while the other walls are at zero potential.

19.2 Solving Poisson Equation

Poisson equation is used to describes many physical phenomena. For example, for a given charge density ρ, the electric potential ϕ is described by $\nabla^2\phi = -4\pi\rho$ (in CGS units). The equation for the gravitation potential for a given mass density is similar. In addition, the pressure field of incompressible flows is described by the Poisson equation (see Eq. (97)). In this section, we will describe how to solve the Poisson equation numerically.

The Poisson equation is

$$\nabla^2\phi = f.$$

The above equation is solved for given f and boundary condition. The computation methods for Poisson equation are very similar to those for Laplace equation.

The discretized version of the Poisson equation at the grid point (i,j) is

$$\frac{1}{h^2}(-4\phi_{i,j} + \phi_{i-1,j} + \phi_{i+1,j} + \phi_{i,j-1} + \phi_{i,j+1}) = f_{i,j},$$

where h is the grid spacing. We can write the equations as the following matrix equation:

$$A \begin{bmatrix} \phi_{0,1} \\ \cdots \\ \phi_{0,m} \\ \phi_{1,0} \\ \phi_{1,1} \\ \cdots \end{bmatrix} = \begin{bmatrix} f_{0,1} \\ \cdots \\ f_{0,m} \\ f_{1,0} \\ f_{1,1} \\ \cdots \end{bmatrix},$$

where A is a banded matrix. This equation is solved using matrix methods, which will be described in Section 20.1.

However, the iterative methods are simpler to implement. In Jacobi method, ϕ is updated using the following equation:

$$\bar{\phi}_{i,j} = \frac{1}{4}(\phi_{i-1,j} + \phi_{i+1,j} + \phi_{i,j-1} + \phi_{i,j+1}) - \frac{h^2}{4}f_{i,j}.$$

The implementation of Jacobi method for Poisson equation is same is that for Laplace equation.

Example 1: We solve the equation $\nabla^2 \phi = \exp(-20\ r^2)$ in a 2D box $[-1:1,-1:1]$ with The potentials ϕ at all the side walls are kept at zero. We employ a grid of 64x64 inside the box, hence, $h = 2/64$. We use the Jacobi scheme for iteration, and obtain the final solution for tolerance of 10^{-6}. Figure 126(a) illustrates the source term $\exp(-20\ r^2)$, while Figure 126(b) shows the final solution. The following Python code implements the above procedure.

```
N = 64; M = 64; h = 2/64

y = np.zeros([N+2,M+2])
# set BC
y[0,:]= 0; y[N+1,:]=0
y[:,0]=0; y[:,M+1]=0
yp = y.copy()

# setup the source term
f = np.zeros([N+2,M+2])
xc = np.linspace(-1,1,N+2)
yc = np.linspace(-1,1,M+2)
xv, yv = np.meshgrid(xc,yc)
f = np.exp(-20*(xv**2 + yv**2))

eps = 1e-6;  error = 1

# Jacobi method
while (error > eps):
    yp[1:N+1,1:M+1] = (y[0:N,1:M+1] +y[2:N+2,1:M+1]
                + y[1:N+1,0:M] +y[1:N+1,2:M+2])/4
    yp[1:N+1,1:M+1] = yp[1:N+1,1:M+1]
                + h**2*f[1:N+1,1:M+1]

    error = np.max(np.absolute(yp[1:N+1,1:M+1]
                -y[1:N+1,1:M+1]))
    y = yp.copy()
```

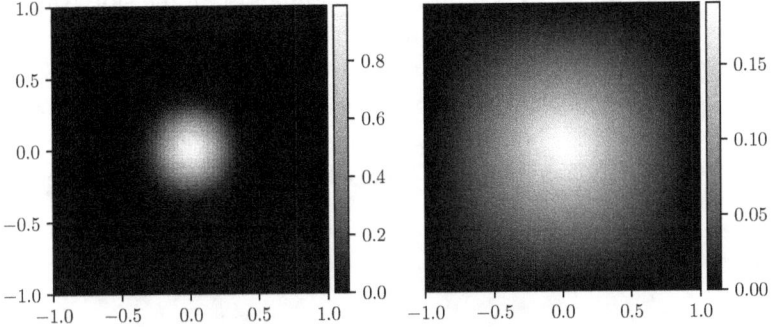

Figure 126: Example 1: (a) The source term $\exp(-20r^2)$. (b) The potential ϕ generated by the source term.

We can solve Poisson equation using Gauss-Seidel, Red-Black, and SOR methods. The codes are very similar to those for Laplace equation, hence they are not discussed here.

With this, we end our discussion on Poisson Equation.

****

Conceptual Questions

1. State scientific and engineering applications of Poisson equation.
2. What are the differences between the numerical methods for solving Laplace and Poisson equations?

Exercises

1. For Example 1, plot the potential $\phi(r)$ as a function of r.
2. Solve Example 1 when the source is replaced by a disk of radius 1 with unit charge density. That is, $f = 1$ inside the disk.
3. Solve for the electric potential inside a 2D box of dimension 2x2 that contains a charge source density of $\exp(-20\, r^2)/4\pi$ at

the centre of the box (r is the distance from the centre of the source). Use CGS units. The potentials at all the side walls are kept at zero. Compute the potential inside the box.

4. Solve for the electric potential inside a box of dimension 2x1x1. A charged ball of charge density of $\exp(-20\ r^2)/4\pi$ is at the centre of the box. Use CGS units. The left wall of the cube is at kept at a potential of 1 Volt, while the other walls are at zero potential.

CHAPTER TWENTY
LINEAR ALGEBRA SOLVERS

Synopsis

"Learning by doing, peer-to-peer teaching, and computer simulation are all part of the same equation." — Nicholas Negroponte

This chapter describes briefly several numerical methods of linear algebra.

20.1 Solution of Algebraic Equations

Linear algebra finds applications in all branches of science and engineering. In this book, we came across a set of linear algebraic equations in the following applications:

1. Splines
2. Solving equations for the implicit ODE solvers
3. Solution of Laplace and Poisson's equation.

Some other physics applications of linear algebra are

1. The dynamics of a linear dynamical systems is described by $\dot{x} = A\,x$, where x is a vector, and A is a matrix.
2. Quantum mechanics
3. Linear circuits are expressed using a set of linear equations.

There are numerous numerical solvers in linear algebra. In this chapter, we will discuss only two solvers: Solvers for linear algebraic equations and eigenvalues. For detailed discussions of computational algorithms of linear algebra, a reader is referred to Chapra and Canale [2016].

Solution of a Set of Linear Equations

A system of linear equations is described as

$$Ax = b,$$

where x is an unknown vector, A is a matrix, and b is a known vector. For example, the equations $x_0 + x_1 = 1$ and $x_0 - x_1 = 2$ are written concisely as

$$\begin{bmatrix} 1 & 1 \\ 1 & -1 \end{bmatrix} \begin{bmatrix} x_0 \\ x_1 \end{bmatrix} = \begin{bmatrix} 1 \\ 2 \end{bmatrix},$$

where A = $\begin{bmatrix} 1 & 1 \\ 1 & -1 \end{bmatrix}$, x = $[x_0, x_1]$ is the unknown vector, and b = [1,2] is the known vector. The solution of the above equation is x = A^{-1}b, where A^{-1} is the inverse of A:

$$A^{-1} = \frac{1}{\det(A)} \text{adj}(A). \quad \ldots\ldots(114)$$

Here, adj(A) is the adjoint of A, and det(A) is the determinant of the matrix, which is defined as the following for a $n \times n$ matrix:

$$\det(A) = \sum \text{sign} \times a_{0,j_0} a_{1,j_1} \ldots a_{n-1,j_{n-1}},$$

where sign = +1 for even permutations of j_i's, and sign = −1 for odd permutations. Note that det(A) has $n!$ terms, hence the number of computations required to compute the determinant is $O(n^n)$, which is enormous for large n. Therefore, the inverse of a matrix and the solution of Ax = b are not computed using Eq. (114). Gauss elimination, to be discussed below, is one of the popular methods for solving linear equations.

Gauss Elimination Method

We write equation Ax = b as

$$\begin{bmatrix} a_{00} & a_{01} & a_{02} & \cdots \\ a_{10} & a_{11} & a_{12} & \cdots \\ a_{20} & a_{21} & a_{22} & \cdots \\ \cdots \\ a_{n-1,0} & a_{n-1,1} & a_{n-1,n-1} \end{bmatrix} \begin{bmatrix} x_0 \\ x_1 \\ x_2 \\ \cdot \\ x_{n-1} \end{bmatrix} = \begin{bmatrix} b_0 \\ b_1 \\ b_2 \\ \cdot \\ b_{n-1} \end{bmatrix}$$

and solve for x in three steps:

a. Reduce the matrix A to an upper triangular matrix in the following manner.
b. Solve for x_{n-1} from the equation of the last row.
c. Solve for other x_i's using back substitution.

The above steps are described below in more detail.

(a) *Gauss elimination*: First we eliminate a_{i0} from rows $i = 1:(n-1)$ by subtraction of (row 0)×(a_{i0}/a_{00}). This operation yields

$$\begin{bmatrix} a_{00} & a_{01} & a_{02} & \cdots \\ 0 & a_{11}^{(1)} & a_{12}^{(1)} & \cdots \\ 0 & a_{21}^{(1)} & a_{22}^{(1)} & \cdots \\ \cdots \\ 0 & a_{n-1,1}^{(1)} & a_{n-1,n-1}^{(1)} \end{bmatrix} \begin{bmatrix} x_0 \\ x_1 \\ x_2 \\ \vdots \\ x_{n-1} \end{bmatrix} = \begin{bmatrix} b_0 \\ b_1^{(1)} \\ b_2^{(1)} \\ \vdots \\ b_{n-1}^{(1)} \end{bmatrix}$$

with the coefficients revised as $a_{ij}^{(1)} = a_{ij} - a_{i0}\dfrac{a_{0j}}{a_{00}}$. The element a_{00}, which is called pivot, plays a critical role here. After this step, we eliminate a_{i1} from rows $i = 2:(n-1)$, and so on. This process finally leads to

$$\begin{bmatrix} a_{00} & a_{01} & a_{02} & \cdots \\ 0 & a_{11}^{(1)} & a_{12}^{(1)} & \cdots \\ 0 & 0 & a_{22}^{(2)} & \cdots \\ \cdots \\ 0 & 0 & 0 & a_{n-1,n-1}^{(n-1)} \end{bmatrix} \begin{bmatrix} x_0 \\ x_1 \\ x_2 \\ \vdots \\ x_{n-1} \end{bmatrix} = \begin{bmatrix} b_0 \\ b_1^{(1)} \\ b_2^{(2)} \\ \vdots \\ b_{n-1}^{(n-1)} \end{bmatrix} \quad \ldots\ldots(115)$$

Here, $a_{ij}^{(m)}$ represents the the matrix element after m^{th} level of elimination.

(b): Solution of the last equation yields $x_{n-1} = \dfrac{1}{a_{n-1,n-1}^{(n-1)}} b_{n-1}^{(n-1)}$.

(c) *Back substitution*: We solve for x_{n-2} using the second last equation, which is

$$a_{n-2,n-2}^{(n-2)} x_{n-2} + a_{n-2,n-1}^{(n-2)} x_{n-1} = b_{n-2}^{(n-2)}.$$

We continue this process till all x_n's have been computed.

Let us analyse the time complexity of this algorithm. The number of multiplications during the elimination process is

$$(n-1)*n + (n-2)*(n-1) + \ldots = O(n^3).$$

The number of multiplication during the back substitution process is

$$1+2+\ldots+(n-1) = O(n^2).$$

Hence, the total number of multiplication required for this algorithm is $O(n^3)$, which is much smaller than $O(n^n)$ multiplications required for the computation of A^{-1} using Eq. (114). This is the reason why we choose Gauss elimination for solving a set of linear equations.

Example 1: Let us solve the following equation using Gauss elimination method.

$$\begin{bmatrix} 1 & 1 & 0 \\ 3 & 2 & 1 \\ 0 & 1 & 3 \end{bmatrix} \begin{bmatrix} x_0 \\ x_1 \\ x_2 \end{bmatrix} = \begin{bmatrix} 3 \\ 10 \\ 11 \end{bmatrix}.$$

Step 1: row 2 − (row 1)x3

$$\begin{bmatrix} 1 & 1 & 0 \\ 0 & -1 & 1 \\ 0 & 1 & 3 \end{bmatrix} \begin{bmatrix} x_0 \\ x_1 \\ x_2 \end{bmatrix} = \begin{bmatrix} 3 \\ 1 \\ 11 \end{bmatrix}.$$

Step 2: row 3 + row 2

$$\begin{bmatrix} 1 & 1 & 0 \\ 0 & -1 & 1 \\ 0 & 0 & 4 \end{bmatrix} \begin{bmatrix} x_0 \\ x_1 \\ x_2 \end{bmatrix} = \begin{bmatrix} 3 \\ 1 \\ 12 \end{bmatrix}.$$

The final matrix is of the upper triangular form. We solve for x_2 using the equation of the third row, $4 x_2 = 12$, which yields $x_2 = 3$. After this, we compute x_0 and x_1 using back substitution. The equation of the second row is $-x_1 + x_2 = 1$ that yields $x_1 = 2$. Substitution of x_1 in the equation of the first row, $x_0 + x_1 = 3$, yields $x_0 = 1$. Thus, the solution of the three linear equations is $\mathbf{x} = [1,2,3]$.

Gauss elimination method has several problematic issues:

1. Consider a new equation, $A\mathbf{x} = \mathbf{b}'$. To solve for this system of equations, we will need to redo the whole elimination operation. Instead, it is preferable to compute the inverse of A, using which we compute $\mathbf{x}$ for any $\mathbf{b}$ ($\mathbf{x} = A^{-1}\mathbf{b}$). The following discussion contains the procedure for computing A^{-1} in $O(n^3)$ steps.
2. The aforementioned method breaks down if the pivots (a_{ii}) at any stage is zero. This issue however can be salvaged by interchanging rows so that the pivot is nonzero.

After this, we discuss another important topic called *LU decomposition*.

LU Decomposition

Any matrix A can be decomposed into a product of a lower diagonal matrix (L) and an upper diagonal matrix (U), along with a permutation matrix P for pivoting. That is,

$$A = PLU.$$

The above decomposition of A is called *LU decomposition*. The U matrix has the same form as that of Eq. (115). However, in L, the lower part of the matrix are nonzero, and the diagonals are all 1:

$$L = \begin{bmatrix} 1 & 0 & 0 & \cdots \\ l_{10} & 1 & 0 & \cdots \\ l_{20} & l_{21} & 1 & \cdots \\ \cdots & & & \\ l_{n-1,0} & l_{n-1,1} & l_{n-1,2} & 1 \end{bmatrix}.$$

In this short chapter, we do not detail the process of LU decomposition that takes $O(n^3)$ operations. Refer to Chapra and Canale [2016] for more details.

After the *LU* decomposition, we can compute $\mathbf{x}$ for the equation $A\mathbf{x} = \mathbf{b}$ as follows. First,

$LU \mathbf{x} = P^{-1} \mathbf{b} = \mathbf{b}'$.

Then, we solve for $\mathbf{y}$ from the equation $L\mathbf{y} = \mathbf{b}'$, after which solve for $\mathbf{x}$ using the equation $U\mathbf{x} = \mathbf{y}$.

We can compute the inverse of a matrix using LU decomposition. We compute $\mathbf{x}_i$ satisfying the following equation:

$$A \mathbf{x}_i = \begin{bmatrix} 0 \\ 0 \\ \vdots \\ 1 \\ \vdots \\ 0 \end{bmatrix}.$$

The vector in the RHS has 1 in the ith row and zeros everywhere else. This process is carried out to compute $\mathbf{x}_i$'s for $i = (0:n-1)$. It is easy to show that

$$A^{-1} = [\mathbf{x}_0, \mathbf{x}_1, \ldots, \mathbf{x}_i, \ldots, \mathbf{x}_{n-1}].$$

Python's *scipy.linalg* module has functions to solve linear equations, as well as for *LU* decomposition. We illustrate these functions using the following code segment:

```
In [176]: from scipy import linalg

In [177]: A = np.array([[1,1,0], [3,2,1], [0,1,3]])
     ...:
     ...: b = np.array([3,10,11])

In [178]: x = linalg.solve(A,b)   # solves Ax = b

In [179]: x
Out[179]: array([1., 2., 3.])
```

The statement $P, L, U = linalg.lu(A)$ yields

$$L = \begin{bmatrix} 1 & 0 & 0 \\ 0 & 1 & 0 \\ 1/3 & 1/3 & 1 \end{bmatrix}; \quad U = \begin{bmatrix} 3 & 2 & 1 \\ 0 & 1 & 3 \\ 0 & 0 & -1/3 \end{bmatrix}; P = \begin{bmatrix} 0 & 0 & 1 \\ 1 & 0 & 0 \\ 0 & 1 & 0 \end{bmatrix}$$

You can easily verify that $PLU = A$. Note that we use *numpy.dot(A,B)* for the matrix multiplication of two matrices A and B. We can compute x using the following statements:

```
In [184]: y = linalg.solve(L, np.dot(linalg.inv(P),b))
   ...:
   ...: x = linalg.solve(U, y)
```

The other useful linear algebra functions are

1. *np.det(A)* to compute the determinant of matrix A
2. *np.trace(A)* to compute the trace of matrix A
3. *np.inv(A)* to compute the inverse of a matrix A
4. *np.norm(a)* to compute the norm of a vector or a matrix.
5. *np.inner(a,b)* and *np.outer(a,b)* for computation of inner and outer products of two vectors a and b
6. *np.linalg.matrix_power(A, n)* to compute A^n
7. *np.linalg.expm(A)* to compute exp(A)
8. *np.eye(n,n)* to create an $n \times n$ identity matrix

You can easily verify these functions.

Solving Equations with Tridiagonal Matrix

Tridiagonal matrices have nonzero entries on the main diagonal, as well as on one diagonal above and one diagonal below the main diagonal. Solution of the equation $Ax = b$, where A is a tridiagonal matrix, is easier compared to the full Gauss-elimination described above. This is because we need to eliminate the lower diagonal only. The back-substitution too is less demanding compared to the solution for full upper triangular matrix.

It is easy to verify that the Gauss elimination and backward substitution for a tridiagonal matrix have computational complexities of $O(n)$. You can easily write a program for the same.

Here, we will use Python's *scipy.linalg.solve_banded(l_and_u, ab, b)* function to perform the above task. The arguments of *solve_banded* are

1. *l_and_u*: A tuple containing the number of non-zero lower and upper diagonals in a banded matrix. Note that a *banded matrix* may have more than one nonzero diagonals above and below the main diagonal.
2. *b*: The vector **b**
3. *ab*: Banded matrix containing upper, middle, and lower diagonals. For example, for the matrix,

$$A = \begin{bmatrix} 1 & 1 & 0 \\ 3 & 2 & 1 \\ 0 & 1 & 3 \end{bmatrix}, \text{the matrix ab} = \begin{bmatrix} - & 1 & 1 \\ 1 & 2 & 3 \\ 3 & 1 & - \end{bmatrix}.$$

In the matrix *ab*, the top row is the upper diagonal, the middle row is the main diagonal, and the bottom row is the lower diagonal. We can put any number for – in the matrix *ab*. However, it cannot be left blank.

We illustrate the above functions as follows:

```
In [192]: ab = np.array([[0,1,1],[1,2,3],[3,1,0]])

In [193]: b = np.array([3,10,11])

In [195]: linalg.solve_banded((1,1), ab, b)
Out[195]: array([1., 2., 3.])
```

I make a passing remark that $Ax = b$ can also be solved iteratively. These topics are however beyond the scope of this book. Refer to Ferziger [1998].

****

Conceptual Questions

1. State specific examples in science and engineering where linear algebra is used.
2. What is the time complexity of Gauss elimination method?
3. How many multiplication are required for solving $Ax = b$, where A is a upper triangular matrix?

Exercises

1. Solve the following equations using Python functions: $x + y = 2$; $x - y = 3$.
2. Solve the following equations using Python functions: $2y + z = -6$; $x-2y-3z = 0$; $-x+y+2z = 3$.
3. Perform LU decomposition of the matrix $numpy.array([[1,4,7], [2,5,8], [3,6,9]])$. Does it have an inverse?
4. Consider a matrix $A = np.array([[1,2,3],[2,1,4],[3,4,2]])$. Compute the determinant, trace, norm, and inverse of A. In addition, compute $\exp(A)$ and A^3.
5. Consider five points $\{(2,1/2), (3,1/3), (4,1/4), (5,1/5), (6,1/6)\}$. Construct a spline that goes through these points. Use free-end boundary conditions.
6. Consider matrix equations for the implicit scheme discussed in Section 16.1. Solve Eqs. (91) and (92) for $N = 8$.

20.2 Eigenvalues and Eigenvectors

Eigenvalues and eigenvectors play an important role in science and engineering applications, especially in the field of dynamical systems and quantum mechanics. In this section, we provide a brief description on how to compute eigenvalues and eigenvectors of a matrix.

Typically, for a matrix A and vector x, the vector Ax is not in the same direction as x. However, for some special vectors, the vector Ax is in the same direction as the original vector x. Such special vectors are called *eigenvectors*. In Figure 127(a), Ax and x are not in the same direction. However, in Figure 127(b), Ax_0 and x_0 are in the same direction, so are Ax_1 and x_1; hence, x_1 and x_2 are the eigenvectors.

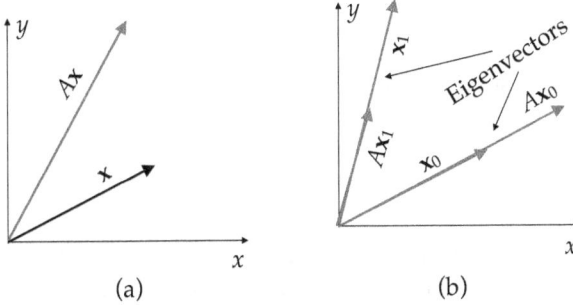

(a)　　　　　　　　　(b)

Figure 127: (a) For a typical vector x, Ax is not in the same direction of x. (b) The eigenvector x_0 and Ax_0 are in the same direction, so are the second eigenvector x_1 and Ax_1.

Eigenvector x_i satisfies the following equation:

$$A x_i = \lambda_i x_i,$$

where λ_i is the *eigenvalue* corresponding to x_i. Note that λ_i could be real or complex. For a $n \times n$ matrix, there are n eigenvalues, but the number of eigenvectors are n or less. Note that the eigenvalues need not be distinct (Mathews and Walker [1970]).

The eigenvalues and eigenvectors have many interesting properties, but we will not discuss them here. In addition, we will not discuss the *QR algorithm* which is often used for the computation of eigenvalues and eigenvectors.

Numpy.linalg has several functions for computing eigenvalues and eigenvectors of a matrix. They are

1. *numpy.linalg.eigen(A)*: It provides the eigenvalues and eigenvectors of any matrix A.
2. *numpy.linalg.eigh(A)*: It provides the eigenvalues and eigenvectors of Hermitian or real-symmetric matrix A.
3. *numpy.linalg.eigvals(A)*: It returns only the eigenvalues (sans eigenvectors) of any matrix A.
4. *numpy.linalg.eigvalsh(A)*: It returns only the eigenvalues (sans eigenvectors) of a Hermitian matrix A.

We illustrate the usage of the above functions using the following examples.

Example 1: Consider the following matrix:

$$A = \begin{bmatrix} 2 & 1 \\ 1 & 2 \end{bmatrix}.$$

Using the function *eigh(A)*, we find the eigenvalues to be 1 and 3, and the corresponding eigenvectors to be $x_0 = [-1/\sqrt{2}, 1/\sqrt{2}]$ and $x_1 = [1/\sqrt{2}, 1/\sqrt{2}]$ respectively. The eigenvectors, illustrated in Figure 128, are perpendicular to each other. See below for the Python code:

```
In [83]: eigh(A)
Out[83]:
(array([1., 3.]), array([[-0.70710678,  0.70710678],
       [ 0.70710678,  0.70710678]]))
```

Example 2: Find the eigenvalues of the matrix np.array([[1,1,0], [3,2,1], [0,1,3]]) using Python functions.

```
In [212]: A = np.array([[1,1,0], [3,2,1], [0,1,3]])

In [213]: vals, vecs = np.linalg.eig(A)

In [214]: vals
```

Out[214]: array([-0.41421356, 2.41421356, 4.   ])

In [215]: vecs
Out[215]:
array([[0.56151667, 0.33655677, 0.22941573],
       [-0.79410449, 0.47596315, 0.6882472],
       [0.23258782, -0.81251992, 0.6882472]])

In *vecs*, the eigenvectors are arranged as columns. These vector are orthogonal.

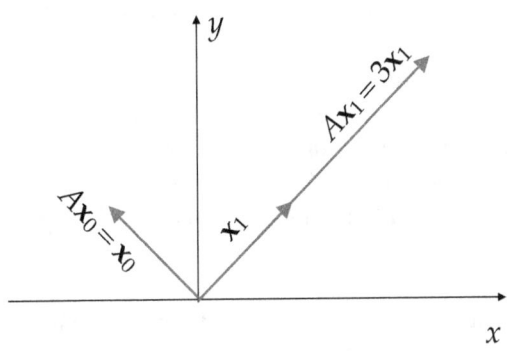

Figure 128: Example 1: Illustrations of eigenvectors x_0 and x_1 of the matrix [[2,1], [1,2]], Note that $Ax_0 = x_0$ and $Ax_1 = 3x_1$.

Example 3: Find the eigenvalues of the matrix array([[1,1,1], [1,1,1], [1,1,1]]).

In [216]: A = np.array([[1, 1,1], [1, 1,1],[1,1,1]])

In [217]: vals, vecs = linalg.eigh(A)

In [218]: vals
Out[218]: array([-2.37213427e-17, 8.88178420e-16,
3.00000000e+00])

In [219]: vecs

```
Out[219]:
array([[ 0.       ,  0.81649658, -0.57735027],
       [-0.70710678, -0.40824829, -0.57735027],
       [ 0.70710678, -0.40824829, -0.57735027]])
```

Here, the two eigenvalues are zeros.

Example 4: We can solve $\dot{x} = Ax$ using the properties of eigenvalues. When A has n distinct eigenvectors with x_i's as the corresponding eigenvectors, it is easy to show that the general solution of $\dot{x} = Ax$ is

$$x(t) = \sum c_i\, x_i \exp(\lambda_i t).$$

The coefficients c_i's are computed using the initial condition.

Example 5: Let us compute the largest eigenvalue of a matrix A iteratively. Here, we use a property that a vector along the largest eigenvalue gets stretched maximally. We start with a vector x_0 and compute $Ax_0 = x_1$, and then $Ax_1 = x_2$, and so on. After many iterations, the resulting vector is along the eigenvector corresponding to the largest eigenvalue. We compute the largest eigenvalue using $norm(dot(A,x))/norm(x)$.

The following iterative procedure yields the largest eigenvalue and the corresponding eigenvector in 20 iterations. These results match with those of Exercise 2.

```
In [25]: A = np.array([[1,1,0], [3,2,1], [0,1,3]])

In [26]: x =np.array([1, 1, 1])

In [27]: x = x/norm(x)
In [31]: for i in range(20):
   ...:      x = dot(A,x)
   ...:      x = x/norm(x)
   ...:
In [32]: x    # (vector S)
Out[32]: array([0.22941573, 0.6882472 , 0.6882472 ])

In [34]: norm(dot(A,x))/norm(x)
Out[34]: 4.0000000001217835
```

With this, we end our discussion on eigenvalues and eigenvectors of a matrix. We have not covered many important topics, e.g., singular value decomposition (SVD), due to lack of space and time.

****

Conceptual Questions

1. State the importance of eigenvectors and eigenvalues in science and engineering.
2. Consider Example 4. Show that $x(t) = \sum c_i x_i \exp(\lambda_i t)$ is a general solution of $\dot{x} = Ax$.

Exercises

1. Compute eigenvalues and eigenvectors of the following matrices:
   - numpy.array([[1,4,7], [2,5,8], [3,6,9]])
   - numpy.array([[1,1], [1,−1]])
   - numpy.ones([5,5])
   - np.array([[0,1], [−1,0]])
2. Compute largest eigenvalue of the array([[1,4,7], [2,5,8], [3,6,9]]) using the iterative procedure discussed in this section. Also, compute the smallest eigenvalue iteratively. Find the corresponding eigenvectors.
3. Solve the equation $\ddot{x} = -x - \gamma \dot{x}$ with $\gamma = 0.1$ using matrix method. Take initial conditions as $x(0) = 1$ and $\dot{x}(0) = 0$.
4. Consider a matrix $A = \begin{bmatrix} \cos\theta & \sin\theta \\ -\sin\theta & \cos\theta \end{bmatrix}$. Compute the eigenvalues and eigenvectors of this matrix for a given θ. What does this matrix do to a vector? Illustrate it using an example.

Chapter Twenty-One
MONTE CARLO METHODS AND DATA SCIENCE

Synopsis

"Creativity is the ability to introduce order into the randomness of nature." — Eric Hoffer

"AI is one of the most important things humanity is working on. It is more profound than, I dunno, electricity or fire." — Sundar Pichai

In this chapter, we show how random numbers help us solve important problems encountered in statistical physics and daily lives.

21.1 Random numbers

Many natural processes are random or *stochastic*. Here we list some examples:

1. The velocity of the particles in a thermodynamic system is random.
2. The velocity field in a turbulent signal is random.
3. The height of human beings is random.
4. The stock market indices are random.
5. The income distribution of people follows a random distribution. The distribution however is nontrivial.
6. Quantum measurements on all occasions yield random values. For example, the decay time of elementary particles are random around a mean.

The above systems generate a large amount of data. We need tools to understand the patterns in such data. In addition to plots (see Chapter Seven), we require more sophisticated tools, e.g., regression and machine learning. In this chapter, we will briefly discuss regression analysis, and make an introductory remarks on machine learning.

The stochastic processes are modelled using random numbers. For example, simple diffusion of a gas molecule is modelled as a random walk; earth-quakes and phase transitions using random processes; etc. Such methods are called *Monte Carlo methods*.

Random Numbers

Considering the importance of random variables, all programming languages generate random numbers. Note, however, that the random numbers generated by computers are *pseudo random numbers*. These numbers are generated by deterministic algorithms, yet, they appear random due to the usage of large prime numbers.

In the following, we describe several popular random distributions:

Uniform distribution: The random variables are distributed evenly in a domain $[a,b]$. The probability distribution function, PDF in short, $P(x)$

is given by

$$P(x) = 1/(b-a).$$

See Figure 129(a) for an illustration. Note that $\int_a^b dx\, P(x) = 1$.

Gaussian or Normal distribution: Here, the random variables are distributed as follows:

$$P(x) = \frac{1}{\sigma\sqrt{2\pi}} \exp\left[-\frac{1}{2}\left(\frac{x-\mu}{\sigma}\right)^2\right],$$

where μ is the *mean* of the variables, and σ is the *standard deviation* (*std* in short). Note that at $x = \mu \pm \sigma$, $P(x)$ falls by a factor of $1/\sqrt{e}$. See Figure 129(b) for an illustration; here $\mu = 5$ and $\sigma = 5$.

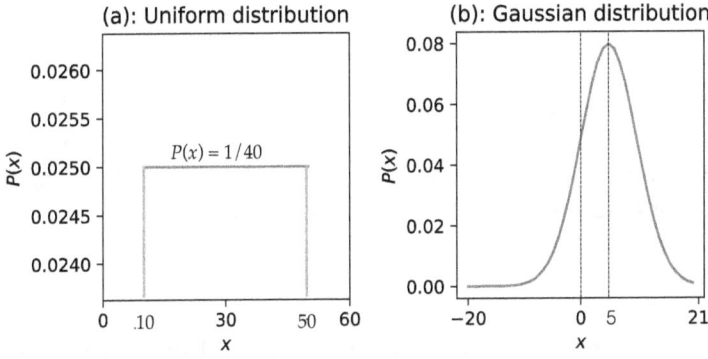

Figure 129: (a) Uniform probability distribution $P(x) = 1/40$ in the interval [10,50]. (b) Normal probability distribution with mean = 5 and std = 5.

Python offers several functions to generate random numbers. They are given below (reproduced from 3.3):

random.rand(shape): Returns a float array of given *shape* with random numbers sampled from a uniform distribution in [0,1].

random.randn(shape): Returns a float array of given *shape* with random numbers sampled from a Gaussian (normal) distribution.

random.randint(low, high=None, size=None, dtype=int): Returns an integer array of given size with random numbers sampled from a uniform distribution in [*low, high*]. If high is None, the random numbers are sampled from [0, *low*).

We illustrate the usage of the above functions using several examples.

Example 1: We employ the following Python statement to generate an array x containing 500 random numbers with uniform distribution in the interval [0,1]:

```
In [35]: x = np.random.rand(500)
```

We can change the range of the random numbers to [a,b] using the following trick. We multiply x with ($b-a$) and then add a to the same:

```
In [36]: a=10; b=50
In [37]: y = np.random.rand(500)*(b-a)+a
```

You can verify the minimum and maximum elements of y. The probability distribution $P(y) = 1/(b-a)$ in the band [a,b]. See Figure 129(a) for an illustration.

Example 2: We generate a random array x of 500 elements with normal distribution (mean $\mu = 0$, standard deviation $\sigma = 1$) using the following Python statement.

```
In [40]: x = np.random.randn(500)
```

For a different choice of μ and σ, we employ the following statement.

```
In [41]: mu = 5; sig = 5
In [42]: x = mu + sig*np.random.randn(500)
```

Example 3: We generate random integers using the function

np.random.randint(). The following statement generates 1000 numbers between 0 and 10.

```
In [56]: x = np.random.randint(0,11,1000)
```

Example 4: The heights of human males and females follow a Gaussian distribution. To verify the same, we download the relevant data from the website https://www.kaggle.com/mustafaali96/weight-height as a *csv* file. To read the data from this file, we employ *Pandas' read_csv()* function. The file contains the data of 5000 men and 5000 women. Note that the heights are in inches. A Python script for the analysis of the histogram and PDF for human males is given below:

```
import pandas as pd
dat = pd.read_csv("weight-height.csv")

h_male = np.array(dat['Height'][0:5000])
h_female = np.array(dat['Height'][5000:10000])
w_male = np.array(dat['Weight'][0:5000])
w_female = np.array(dat['Weight'][5000:10000])

fig = plt.figure(figsize = (6, 3))
ax1 = fig.add_subplot(1,2,1)

num_bins = 50
n, bins, patches = ax1.hist(h_male, num_bins)

ax2 = fig.add_subplot(1,2,2)
mu = np.mean(h_male)
st = np.std(h_male)
my_bins = (bins[1:num_bins+1] + bins[0:num_bins])/2
h = bins[1]-bins[0]
P2 = h*np.exp(-0.5*((my_bins-mu)/st)**2)
       /(st*np.sqrt(2*np.pi))

ax2.plot(my_bins, n/5000, 'b-', label='n/5000')
    ax2.plot(my_bins, P2, 'r--', label='Gaussian-fit')
```

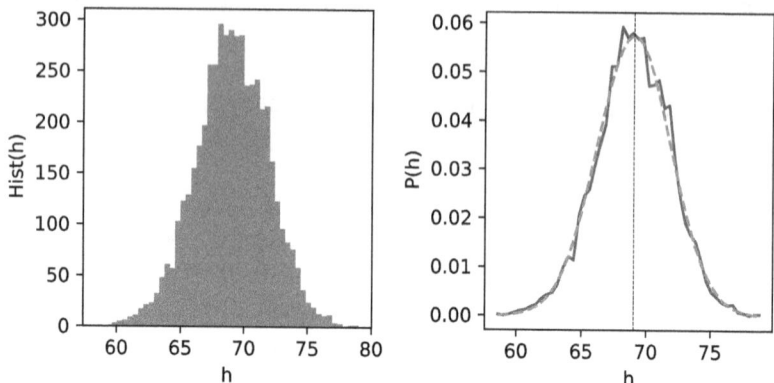

Figure 130: (a) Histogram of heights of males (height in inches). (b) PDF of height. In (b), the solid curve represents the PDF of the data, while the dashed curve is the associated Gaussian PDF.

We exhibit the histogram and associated PDF in Figure 130. The average and std of male height are 69 inches and 2.86 inches respectively. We compute a Gaussian PDF using the mean and std, and exhibit it as the dashed curve in Figure 130(b); this PDF matches well with the PDF of the data. Thus, we provide a numerical demonstration that the heights of human males follow a Gaussian distribution.

With this, we end our discussion on random numbers.

****

Conceptual questions

1. State natural processes that are random in nature.
2. Are the computer generated random numbers really random?

Exercises

1. Generate 500 random integers between 1 and 5.
2. Generate 500 random numbers with uniform distribution in

the interval [0,10].

3. Generate 500 Gaussian random numbers whose mean is 5 and std is 1. Plot the PDF of the generated numbers.
4. Download the data on female heights from the website https://www.kaggle.com/mustafaali96/weight-height. Plot the PDF of height and show this to be a Gaussian.
5. Repeat Exercise 1 for weights of males and females.
6. Download the daily rainfall data of your city for many years. Plot the histogram and PDF of the data.

21.2 Integration Using Random Numbers

In Chapter Eleven, we performed numerical integration of smooth functions. However, the methods described in this chapter are not suitable for functions that fluctuate strongly. One such function is $f(x) = \cos^2(1/(x(1-x))$, which is exhibited in Figure 131(b). Monte Carlo method provides a convenient way to compute integrals for such rapidly varying functions. We will illustrate this method using several examples.

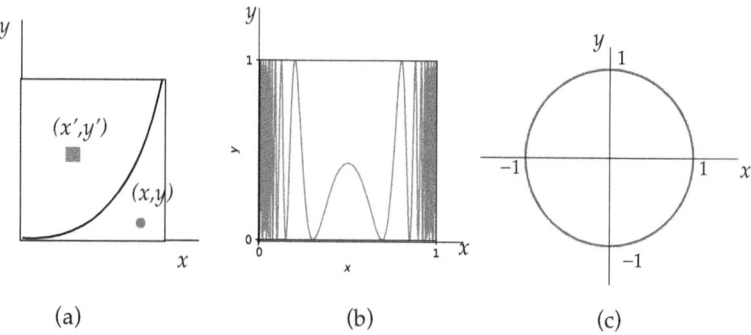

Figure 131: (a) Plot of $y = x^2$. (b) Plot of $f(x) = \cos^2(1/(x(1-x)))$. (c) Plot of a circle whose equation is $x^2 + y^2 = 1$

Example 1: We integrate $y = x^2$ in domain [0,1]. Note that y lies in the band [0,1]. To integrate the above function, we generate N pairs of random numbers with uniform distribution in the interval [0,1], and assign them to (x,y). We count all the points below the $y = f(x)$ curve, and ignore the ones above the curve. The integral is approximated using the ratio of the number of points below the curve and the total number of points.

In Figure 131(a), the red dot are below the curve, while the blue squares are above the curve. A Python code segment for the quadrature computation is given below:

```
def f(x):
    return x**2
```

```
N = 1000000
count = 0
for i in range(N):
    x = np.random.rand()
    y = np.random.rand()
    if y<f(x):
        count += 1

print("Integral = ", count/N)
```

We observe that the the integral fluctuates around a mean. For $N = 10^6$, one of the outcomes is 0.333967, which is close to the actual answer of 1/3. The error for the integral is approximately 0.00063367, which is $O(\sqrt{N})$ or 10^{-3}.

Example 2: Following the same approach Example 1, we compute the integral of $f(x) = \cos^2(1/(x(1-x)))$, which is plotted in Figure 131(b). For 10^6 random number pairs with uniform distribution, the answer fluctuates wildly ranging from 0.614 to 0.616. Clearly, the error is of the order of 10^{-3}, which is $O(\sqrt{N})$. The Monte Carlo method is very useful for this example because Newton-Cotes and Gauss quadratures are not suitable here.

Example 3: We compute the volume of a d-dimensional sphere of radius unity using Monte Carlo method. We generate many sets of d random numbers in the interval $[-1,1]$ with uniform distribution and assign them to x_i (see Figure 131(c)). The point $(x_0, x_1, ..., x_{d-1})$ is inside the sphere if $\sum x_i^2 < 1$. The integral is proportional to the number of points inside the sphere. The following Python code segment implements the above algorithm.

```
d=2
N = 10000
count = 0
for i in range(N):
    x = 2*np.random.rand(d)-1
    if sum(x**2) < 1:
        count += 1
```

```
print("Integral = ", 2**d*count/N)
```

The integrals fluctuate significantly. One instance of the integral for $d = 2$ is 3.1532, rather than π. For $d = 3$ and 10, the code yields 4.2288 and 2.8672 respectively. The numbers are close to the exact results, with error of the order of 10^{-2}.

The above examples illustrate that Monte Carlo method is a handy tool for integration, but the results have significant errors, which are of the order of $O(\sqrt{N})$, where N is the number of points used.

****

Conceptual Questions

1. For quadrature, what are the advantages and disadvantages of Monte Carlo method over Newton-Cotes method.
2. Why is the error in Monte Carlo quadrature $O(\sqrt{N})$, where N is the number of points used for the integration.

Exercises

1. Compute the integral $\int_0^1 \tanh^2(x^2) dx$ using Monte Carlo method.
2. Compute the integral $\int_0^1 x^{-1/2}/(\exp(x)+1)\, dx$ using Monte Carlo method.
3. Compute the volume of a d-dimensional sphere for $d = 4$ to 20, and compare your results with the exact formula.

21.3 Regression Analysis

In Chapter Ten, we discussed how to interpolate a function through a given n data points. The interpolation algorithms, however, work well for small n, and they are impractical for large data sets (e.g., for $n > 10$). Note that large data sets exhibit significant spread due to random errors, hence *regression analysis* is better suited for such data. This is the topic of this section.

For regression analysis, it is best to plot the data and then attempt various best-fit curves to the data. We pick the curve with minimum error as the best-fit curve. Python's *polyfit()* is a useful function for regression analysis. In the following discussion, we will consider linear and nonlinear regression.

Linear Regression

Many systems exhibit linear behaviour. For example, the voltage across a resistor is proportional to the current passing through it. The force on a spring is proportional to the displacement of the spring. In the following discussion, we will take a demographic example.

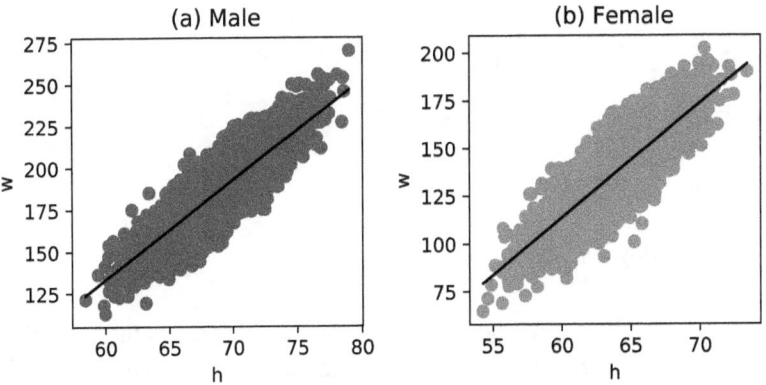

Figure 132: Plots of *height* (h) vs. *weight* (w) for 5000 men (a) and 5000 women (b). The dots represent the sample data, and the straight line in the middle is the best-fit curve obtained using linear regression. Data taken from https://www.kaggle.com/mustafaali96/weight-height.

It has been observed that the weight of a healthy individual is proportional to his/her height. We download the height and weight data of 5000 men and women from the website https://www.kaggle.com/mustafaali96/weight-height. Here, the height is in inches, and weight is in pounds. First we plot the height vs. weight data for men and women separately. The data plotted in Figure 132 exhibits linear relations between the weights and heights, both for men and women. In the following, we perform linear regression on this data set.

The process of linear regression is as follows. We postulate a linear relation between the height h and weight w of a population:

$$w = a h + b,$$

with a and b as unknown constants. Most data points do not lie on the linear curve, hence the function $w = a h + b$ is an approximate or guessed relationship, not an exact one.

We derive the constants a and b by minimising the squared error E:

$$E = \sum_i (w_i - a h_i - b)^2, \quad \ldots(116)$$

where w_i and h_i are the weight and height of ith individual. The minimization criteria,

$$\partial_a E = 0 \text{ and } \partial_b E = 0,$$

yield the following conditions:

$$\langle wh \rangle - a \langle wh \rangle - b \langle h \rangle = 0,$$

$$\langle w \rangle - a \langle h \rangle - b = 0,$$

where $\langle f \rangle$ stands for the average of variable f. Using the above equations, we derive the following expressions for a and b:

$$a = \frac{\langle wh \rangle - \langle w \rangle \langle h \rangle}{\langle h^2 \rangle - \langle h \rangle^2}, \quad \ldots(117)$$

$$b = \langle w \rangle - a \langle h \rangle . \quad \ldots(118)$$

Thus, we determine the approximate relationship $w = ah + b$, which is a straight line. This curve is called *best-fit curve*, and the procedure is called *linear regression*. Note that we could use measures other than Eq. (116) for computing error. For example, we could minimise the absolute error, which is $E = \sum_i |w_i - a h_i - b|$.

We also state the formulas for the standard deviations in a and b, which are σ_a and σ_b respectively:

$$\hat{w}_i = a h_i + b,$$

$$S_{w/h} = \left(\frac{(w_i - \hat{w}_i)^2}{n - 2} \right)^{1/2},$$

$$\sigma_b = \frac{S_{w/h}}{\sqrt{\sum (h_i - \langle h \rangle)^2}},$$

$$\sigma_a = S_{w/h} \left(\frac{\sum h_i^2}{n \sum (h_i - \langle h \rangle)^2} \right)^{1/2}.$$

Python's *polyfit()* provides us a and b. The usage of the function is as follows:

```
p1, res1, _, _, _ = np.polyfit(h_male,w_male,1, full=True)
```

where p1[0] = a, p1[1] = b, and res1 = $\sum (w_i - \hat{w}_i)^2$.

Example 1: For the data of Figure 132, we compute a and b using the formulas of Eqs. (117) and (118). The statistics for both men and women are listed in Table 32. We verify that the output of polyfit provides the same a and b as Eqs. (117) and (118).

Note that Python lists the above numbers with 16 significant digits. However, they are not as accurate, as is evident from the standard deviations listed in the table. For example, σ_h = 2.9 inches for the males, hence, it is not prudent to report $\langle h \rangle$ with more than 1 significant digit after the decimal point.

Table 32: Example 1: Statistics of the weights (in pounds) and heights (in inches) of males and females.

Statistics	Male	Female
$\langle h \rangle$	69.0	63.7
$\langle w \rangle$	187.0	135.9
σ_h	2.9	2.7
σ_w	19.8	19.0
a	5.96	5.99
b	−224.5	−246.0
σ_a	0.049	0.053
σ_b	3.4	3.4

Nonlinear Regression

Many physical phenomena or statistical data exhibit nonlinear behaviour. For example, turbulent drag is approximated as (a Re + b Re^2), where Re is the Reynolds number. Python's *polyfit()* provides a way to fit a polynomial of any degree for a dataset. The following Python code helps us fit a second order polynomial to a function

$$y = 0.2\,x + 0.3\,x^2 - 1 + \eta,$$

where where η is random number with uniform distribution in [0,1].

```
n = 21
x = np.arange(n)
y = 0.2*x + 0.3*x**2 -1 + np.random.rand(n)

p, res, _, _, _ = np.polyfit(x, y,3, full=True)

fig = plt.figure(figsize = (5, 2.5))
ax = fig.add_subplot(1,1,1)
ax.plot(x, y, 'ro')
ax.plot(x, np.polyval(p, x), 'k-')
```

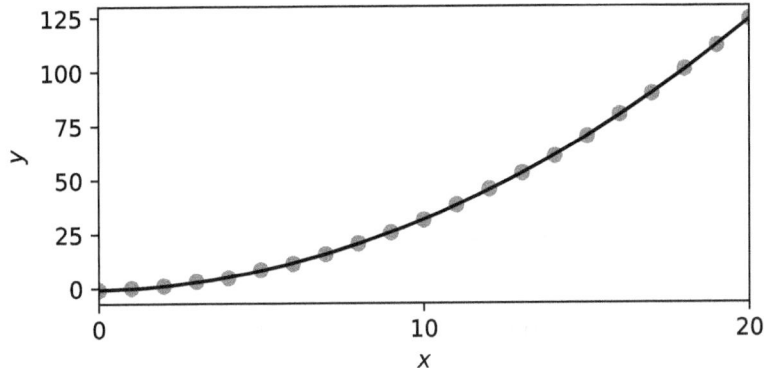

Figure 133: Plot of $y = 0.2\,x + 0.3\,x^2 - 1 + \eta$ (dots) along with best fit curve (solid curve)

The function np.polyfit(x, y,3, full=True) produces the following

```
p = array([-8.18369917e-05,  3.02199806e-01,
1.95317325e-01, -6.49026781e-01])
res = 1.75563867
```

The best-fit curve is

$$y = p[0]\,x^3 + p[1]\,x^2 + p[2]\,x + p[3],$$

which is close to the original function. For example, $p[1] \approx 0.302$ and $p[2] \approx 0.195$. We depict the data, as well as the best-fit curve in Figure 133.

Often, the functional form is a power law, and not a polynomial. For such a scenario, it is best to take a logarithmic of both sides and then employ linear regression.

Example 2: The time period of a pendulum is $T = 2\pi\sqrt{l/g}$, where l is the length of the pendulum, and g is the acceleration due to gravity. We take logarithm of the equation that yields

$\log(T) = (½) \log(l) + b$.

To verify the above law, we measure different sets of (l, T), and apply linear regression analysis to $(\log(l), \log(T))$. We expect the slope of the best-fit curve to be close to ½.

With this, we end our discussion on regression analysis.

****

Conceptual Questions

1. How are interpolation and regression analysis different?

Exercises

1. For x = 0:100:1, generate $y = 0.2x + 0.3x^2 - 1 + 5\eta$, where η is random number with uniform distribution in [0,1]. Use *polyfit*() to construct the best-fit curve to the data. Comment on the quality of the best-fit curve. What happens to the regression parameters when the noise is 10 η.
2. Download the population data for India from *https:// www.worldometers.info/world-population/india-population*. Plot the yearly data and derive the best-fit curve for the data. Do the same analysis for the world data.
3. Download the Covid data for the most-affected countries and study the growth rates of the pandemic during the initial phases.

21.4 Applications in Statmech

In statistical mechanics and thermodynamics, we deal with a large number of particles. Hence, there is significant randomness in such systems. For example, the average energy of the particles in a closed thermodynamic system fluctuates around a mean. Monte Carlo methods are often employed to simulate thermodynamic and stat-mech systems. In this section, we will discuss two important examples of statistical physics.

Simulating Ising Phase Transition

Ising model is often used to study phase transition. In this model, the spins that take values +1 or −1 are placed on a d-dimensional grid. The energy of the Ising system is

$$E = -J \sum S_i S_j ,$$

where J is the coupling constant, and the sum is performed over nearest neighbours. In Figure 134(a), we illustrate the nearest neighbours of Ising spin X.

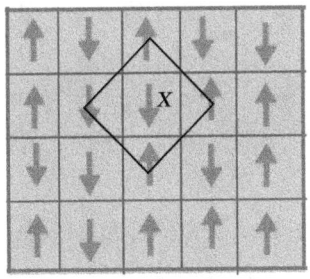
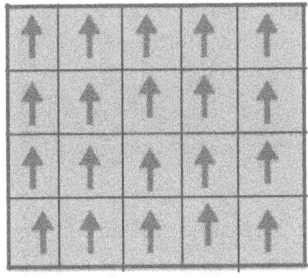

(a) Disordered phase (b) Ordered phase

Figure 134: Illustrations of the Ising spins: (a) a disordered phase; (b) an ordered phase. In (a), the corners of the square represent the nearest neighbours of the spin X.

In dimensions 2 and higher, the Ising system exhibits *phase transition* at some critical temperature T_c. The Ising system remains in a disordered phase (with random spins) for $T > T_c$, but it becomes ordered for $T < T_c$ (see Figure 134 for an illustration). The mean magnetization $\langle M \rangle$ is defined as

$$\langle M \rangle = (M_\uparrow - M_\downarrow) / (M_\uparrow + M_\downarrow),$$

where $M_\uparrow$ and $M_\downarrow$ represent the number of up and down spins respectively. Clearly, $\langle M \rangle \approx 0$ for $T > T_c$, and $\langle M \rangle \approx 1$ or -1 for $T < T_c$.

For a large number of spins, the available states is enormous. This feature makes the simulation of phase transition very difficult. However, there are interesting and practical algorithms that are quite successful in simulating phase transition. One such algorithm is *Metropolis algorithm*, which is described below for $d = 2$ (Newman [2013]).

Metropolis algorithm employs *Boltzmann distribution*, according to which the probability of a spin configuration α is

$$P(E_\alpha) = \frac{\exp\left(-\frac{E_\alpha}{k_B T}\right)}{\sum_\alpha \exp\left(-\frac{E_\alpha}{k_B T}\right)},$$

where E_α is the energy of the configuration α, k_B is the Boltzmann constant, and $Z = \sum_\alpha \exp(-E_\alpha/k_B T)$ is the partition function. Based on the above, we deduce that

$$\frac{P(E_\alpha)}{P(E_\beta)} = \exp\left(-\frac{E_\alpha - E_\beta}{k_B T}\right).$$

For numerical simulations, the probability employed for the transition from state α to state β is as follows:

$$P_{\alpha \to \beta} = 1 \text{ if } E_\beta < E_\alpha,$$

$$P_{\alpha \to \beta} = \exp\left(-\frac{E_\beta - E_\alpha}{k_B T}\right) \text{ if } E_\beta > E_\alpha. \quad \ldots(119)$$

Details of Metropolis algorithm is as follows. After initialisation, we loop with the following steps:

1. The energy of the current configuration = E_α.
2. Randomly pick a site (i,j) and flip its spin.
3. Compute the energy of the new configuration (E_β).
4. If the new energy $E_\beta < E_\alpha$, accept the configuration as the next configuration.
5. If $E_\beta > E_\alpha$, accept the new configuration with a probability of $\exp(-(E_\beta - E_\alpha)/k_B T)$ (see Eq. (119)).
6. Repeat the process from 1 until average magnetisation saturates to a constant value.

A Python implementation of the above algorithm for a 2D Ising model is given below:

```
N = 100; M = 100
max_steps = 100000
E = np.zeros(max_steps+1)
m = np.zeros(max_steps+1)
T = 10
eps = 0.01

# create random array A(1 to N,1 to M)
# The boundary values are zeros
A = np.random.randint(0,2,(N+2,M+2))
A[0,:]=0; A[N+1,:]=0
A[:,0]=0; A[:,M+1]=0
for i in range(1,N+1):
    for j in range(1,M+1):
        random_no = np.random.rand()
        if (A[i,j] == 0):
            if (random_no > 0.7):   # bias toward -1
                A[i,j] = -1
            else:
                A[i,j] = 1

def energy(A):
    return (-np.sum(A[1:N+1,1:M+1]*A[0:N,1:M+1]   \
        +  A[1:N+1,1:M+1]*A[2:N+2,1:M+1]  \
        +  A[1:N+1,1:M+1]*A[1:N+1,0:M]    \
        +  A[1:N+1,1:M+1]*A[0:N,2:M+2]))


Enow = energy(A)
```

```
E[0] = Enow
m[0] = np.sum(A)/(N*M) # magnetization

#for step in range(1,nsteps):
step = 0
while ((abs(m[step])< eps) or ((1-abs(m[step]))< eps))
            or (step < max_steps):
    step += 1
    i = np.random.randint(1,N+1)
    j = np.random.randint(1,M+1)
    A[i,j] = -1*A[i,j]
    Enext = energy(A)
    dE = Enext-Enow
    if np.random.rand() < np.exp(-dE/T):
        Enow = Enext  # accept change
    else:
        A[i,j] = -1*A[i,j]
        # back to old config; reject change
    E[step] = Enow
    m[step] = np.sum(A)/(N*M)

print("Avg mag = ", np.sum(A)/(N*M))
```

We simulate the 2D Ising spins on a 100x100 grid. We vary the nondimensionalized constant $\bar{T}$, which is $k_B T/J$, as a parameter. Since $\bar{T}_c = 2/\log(1+\sqrt{2}) = 2.26918$ for the 2D Ising Model, we simulate the model for $\bar{T} = 1, 2,$ and 10. We set the spins at the boundary to 0, and start with a random initial configuration whose $\langle M \rangle \approx 0.7$. Also, the energy computation, which is the most expensive operation of the simulation, has been vectorized. We run our simulation for 10^5 time steps.

In Figure 135 we exhibit the evolution of $\langle M \rangle$ as a function of time (here, iteration of the simulation). We observe that $\langle M \rangle \to 0$ for $\bar{T} = 10$, while $\langle M \rangle \to 1$ for $\bar{T} = 1$ and 2. Thus, $\bar{T}_c$ lies between 2 and 10. Note that the number of iterations required for saturation increases as we go closer to the critical temperature. This phenomena is called *critical slowing down*.

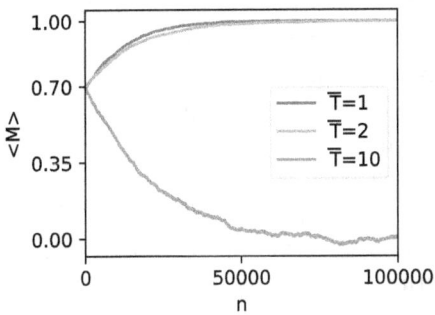

Figure 135: A plot exhibiting the evolution of ⟨M⟩ as a function of time (n). ⟨M⟩ → 0 for $\bar{T}$ = 10, but ⟨M⟩ → 1 for $\bar{T}$ = 1 and 2.

Simulating Self-organized Criticality

It has been observed that the correlation function of spins exhibits a power law near the phase transition. This is termed as *critical behaviour*. Note, however, that phase transition in Ising system is achieved by tuning the temperature. Interestingly, there are systems that approach criticality without external tuning. This phenomena, called *self-organised criticality* (Bak et al. [1988]), is a topic of the present discussion.

In 1988, Bak et al. considered a 2D grid with open boundaries. Each grid point contains sands ranging from 0 to 3, hence it is called a *sandpile*. In Figure 136, we illustrate different snapshots of a sandpile on a 4x4 grid.

We initialise the sandpile with random numbers in the range 0 to 3. After initialization, we update the sandpile as follows:

1. A sand is dropped at a random location, say (i,j), of the sandpile.
2. If the number of sands at the site (i,j) is less than 3, the new sand is added at that site.
3. If the number of sands at (i,j) is 3, then the new sand makes the total count = 4. At this point, the current site becomes critical. The following operations are performed consequently.

- The four sands at the site are distributed uniformly (one each) among the four nearest neighbours. The current site becomes empty.
- As a result of the redistribution of the sand, some neighbour(s) of (i,j) may become critical. The sands at the new critical sites are distributed to the neighbours.
- If the sites at a boundary become critical, then the sands crossing the boundary are lost.
- The above process is continued until none of the site is critical.

4. After the sandpile has stabilised, we repeat the process starting from (1).

(a)	(b)	(c)	(d)
2 0 2 1	2 0 2 1	2 0 2 1	2 0 2 1
1 0 1 2	1 *1* 1 2	1 1 1 2	1 1 2 *3*
1 **3** 2 2	*2 0 3* 2	2 0 **3** *3*	2 *1 1 0*
1 2 0 3	1 *3* 0 **3**	1 3 *1 0*	1 3 2 *1*
	Avalanche = 1	Avalanche = 1	Avalanche = 2
		Sand lost = 2	Sand lost = 1

Figure 136: Four snapshots of a sandpile. A new sand falls at site whose occupation number is in bold. This event affects sites are those with italicized occupation numbers. In frame (a), a sand is dropped at (2,1) making the count of sands at that site to go to 4. The 4 sands at (2,1) are distributed to the neighbours. In frame (b), a new sand arrives at (3,3). The critical site (3,3) distributes its sands to two of its neighbours, while the other two sands are lost at the boundary. In frame (c), a new sand arrives at (2,2). The critical site (2,2) distributes its sands to its neighbours. However, the distribution makes the site (2,3) critical. The sands from this site are sent to its neighbours, but one sand is lost at the boundary. The frame (d) is the final state.

We illustrate the above processes in Figure 136. The new sand arrives at a site whose occupation number is in bold, while the affected sites are those with italicized occupation numbers. The figure contains four consecutive snapshots, while the figure caption explains the transitions.

A Python implementation of the above algorithm is given below. Note that the function *update()* is recursive.

```
N = 4; M = 4
nsteps = 40
cnt = np.zeros(nsteps, dtype = int)

A = np.random.randint(0,4,(N,M))

def update(A, i, j, step):
    if (A[i,j] == 4):
        A[i,j] = 0
        cnt[step] += 1
        if (i+1)<N:
            A[i+1,j] += 1;
            update(A, i+1, j, step)
        if (i-1)>=0:
            A[i-1,j] += 1
            update(A, i-1, j, step)
        if (j+1)<M:
            A[i,j+1] += 1;
            update(A, i, j+1, step)
        if (j-1)>=0:
            A[i,j-1] += 1
            update(A, i, j-1, step)
        return
    else:
        return

for step in range(nsteps):
    i = np.random.randint(N)
    j = np.random.randint(M)
    A[i,j] += 1
    update(A, i, j, step)
    print(step, i, j, cnt[step],'\n', A, '\n')
```

We perform numerical simulation of sandpile model on a 32x32 grid. We carry out our simulation for 10000 iterations, and compute the size of the avalanches. The maximum size of the avalanches is 2206. We make histogram of occurrences of avalanches of size s, and plot it in Figure 137. Using the best-fit curve we deduce that $N(s) \sim s^{-2.25}$, which is a power law. We remark however that the our exponent (-2.25) differs from that of Bak et al. [1988]; the difference may be due to smaller size of the domain.

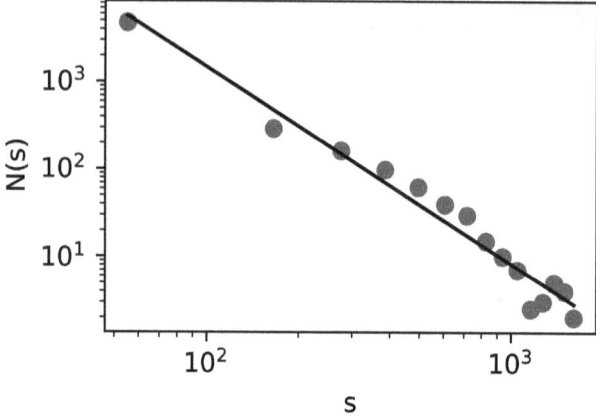

Figure 137: For the SOC simulation, the avalanche size distribution, $N(s)$ vs. s. The best-fit curve to the data is $N(s) \sim s^{-2.25}$, which is shown in the figure as a straight line.

With this we end our discussion on applications of Monte Carlo methods to statistical physics.

****

Conceptual Questions

1. Explain why Metropolis algorithm works while simulating equilibrium statistical systems.

Exercises

1. Simulate 2D Ising model for $\bar{T}$ = 2, 2.5, 3, 4. Compute the decay/growth rate of $\langle M \rangle$ for these runs.
2. Solve Exercise 1 with completely random initial condition, i.e., with $\langle M \rangle = 0$. It would take much longer time to reach a steady state.
3. Solve 1D and 3D Ising models numerically using appropriate

initial condition.
4. For the Ising system, compute the time scales for the decay and growth of $\langle M \rangle$ during the phase transition.
5. For the sandpile model, study the properties of interval distribution between large events, say avalanches greater than 100.
6. Simulate a 3D sandpile model. Make appropriate rules yourself.

21.5 Machine Learning

Artificial intelligence (*AI*) and *machine learning* (*ML*) are buzz words today. ML is being widely used in all fields of science and engineering, as well as in daily lives, such as self-driving cars, e-marketing, finance, etc. In the following discussion, we illustrate applications of AI using several examples.

AI tools help computers recognise characters. Such applications are used in postal department for reading hand-written addresses, and in income tax department for reading the income-tax return forms.

A character-recognition program works as follows. We collect samples of hand-written characters along with their identification. This sample data, called *training set*, is supplied to a AI software who employs ML algorithms to learn the characters. A computer learns better using large (in thousands) and varied training sets. After the training, the program is ready for testing. Test cases are provided to the program. If the software recognises the characters accurately, the program is ready for deployment.

Figure 138 illustrates a sample of numeral characters that could be used for training and testing a program for character recognition. The present table contains only 160 characters, but more are needed for training.

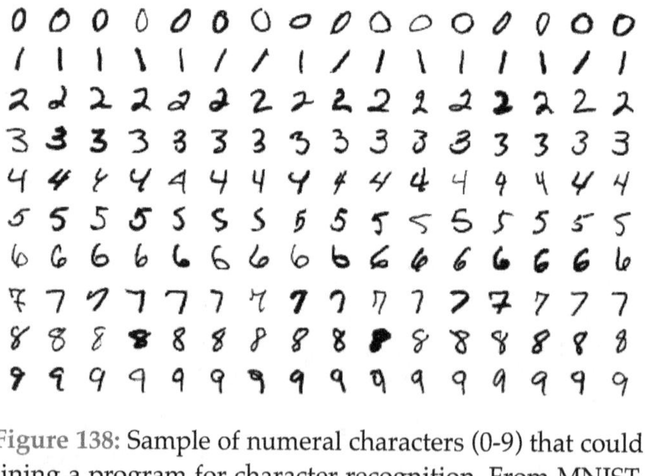

0 0 0 0 0 0 0 0 0 0 0 0 0 0 0 0
1 1 1 1 1 1 1 1 1 1 1 1 1 1 1 1
2 2 2 2 2 2 2 2 2 2 2 2 2 2 2 2
3 3 3 3 3 3 3 3 3 3 3 3 3 3 3 3
4 4 4 4 4 4 4 4 4 4 4 4 4 4 4 4
5 5 5 5 5 5 5 5 5 5 5 5 5 5 5 5
6 6 6 6 6 6 6 6 6 6 6 6 6 6 6 6
7 7 7 7 7 7 7 7 7 7 7 7 7 7 7 7
8 8 8 8 8 8 8 8 8 8 8 8 8 8 8 8
9 9 9 9 9 9 9 9 9 9 9 9 9 9 9 9

Figure 138: Sample of numeral characters (0-9) that could be used for training a program for character recognition. From MNIST database of wikipedia. Source wikipedia.org.

Another popular example of AI is how to contrast images of apple and oranges using a software. We train the software using a large number of images of apple and oranges. Modern tools easily identify the correct fruit.

There are many more AI applications. Some of them are

1. Speech to text conversion. *Youtube* often generates subtitles in movies using such applications.
2. Language translations, e.g., English ⟷ French
3. Self-driving cars
4. In piloting of aeroplanes
5. E-marketing, as in amazon
6. Weather forecasting

With these introductory remarks we close our discussion on machine learning and artificial intelligence.

Epilogue

"Bramhan cannot be expressed or described, because it transcends names, classifications, or characterizations. It cannot be known by reasoning, but its existence may be apprehended intuitively."
— Shankarcharya

Now, we are at the end of our journey. In this book, I covered basics of Python programming and important numerical methods. Once you master these techniques, you can solve moderately difficult problems of scientific computing. I recommend that you use the ideas learnt here in your other courses, such as quantum mechanics, statistical physics, mathematical physics, classical mechanics. This exercise will help you understand the theoretical concepts better. And, do not simply trust what is written in books, but verify them by writing your own codes.

I summarised good programming practices in Chapter Six. I reiterate them here; I strongly recommend that you follow these rules seriously:

1. Think of algorithm first, then write pseudocode, and then write your program. Write your algorithm in a piece of paper. Do not start typing your code right away.
2. Think of extreme cases! Most codes break for these cases.
3. Code slowly!
4. Code in parts, and test each part. Python gives you this flexibility.
5. Code with confidence!
6. First write a code that works, and then make it efficient.
7. Comment your code!

What Next?

The tools discussed in this book will enable you to solve moderate-size problems, but not large ones, e.g., weather prediction codes and Monte Carlo simulations of billion particles. We need the following advanced tools for solving large-scale problems:

1. *Structured Programming:* Computer programs for large-scale

problems may have millions of lines of codes. Also, such programs are written by a large team of coders. So far, large codes are written in compiler languages, e.g., C, C++, Fortran, Java. Hence, you will have to learn one or several of these languages. Note, however, that in recent times, large codes are being written in Python as well.

2. *Object-oriented programming:* It is easier to organise large codes in the framework of Object-oriented programming. Here, you can solve a large problem using Top-down approach, i.e., by breaking the problem into smaller pieces. Each piece could then be programmed independently. This feature is useful for a collaborative development of codes. Modern languages such as C++, Java, and Fortan 90 offer such features.

3. *Parallel programming:* Complex problems, such as weather forecasting, require enormous computing time (see Section 1.3). For such applications, you need to write *parallel programs* that could run on many computers. For writing parallel programs, you will need to learn many tools and paradigms. Also, you need sufficient knowledge of the computer hardware for writing such efficient programs.

4. Using libraries and tools: A large number of software and computing tools have been developed so far. For example, FFTW (*Fastest Fourier transform in the West*) is a very useful library. Scipy is a large collection of scientific programs. In addition, there are efficient tools for handling large data, visualisation, code development, etc. These libraries greatly help in solving large-scale problems efficiently.

Hence, advanced scientific computing requires the above skills, which are part of a field called *High Performance Computing* (HPC). Those interested should learn these techniques.

Computing in Modern Science and Engineering

Computing has opened a major window of opportunity in all areas of science and engineering. As we discussed in Section 1.7, attempts are being made to solve grand-challenge problems using computers. Some of the leading problems are as follows:

1. Turbulence
2. Human brain
3. Universe, stars, and planets
4. Oceans and Atmospheres
5. Human body
6. Complex materials and Drugs
7. Human behaviour and Artificial Intelligence (AI)

Future hardware and computing tools will be even more powerful, and they will accelerate the pace of research in complex systems. I encourage young students to learn advanced computing so that they can venture into these challenging areas of science and engineering.

Limits of Numerical Computation

The present success of computing has led to interesting conjectures. For example, Sundar Pichai, Google's CEO, argues that "AI is one of the most important things humanity is working on. It is more profound than, I dunno, electricity or fire." No one can doubt the power of computers. However, not all problems can be solved using computers. In the following discussion, we state some of the unsolvable problems.

It has been theoretically proven that "halting problem" is unsolvable by computers. The solution of "halting problem" would be a computer program that can detect infinite loops in any arbitrary code. Turing showed that no one can write this general and useful computer program.

Another way to see the limitation of computers is as follows. The number of computer programs is countably infinite (same as integers). However, the number of real functions, e.g., $f(x)$, is uncountably infinite. Hence, there are many $f(x)$ that can not be generated by computer programs. It is normally assumed that we can find approximate solutions to all functions. But, that is an assumption.

It is fascinating that every object of nature follows laws of nature accurately. For example, an electron in a Hydrogen atom follows the Schrödinger equation accurately; and a projectile follows the trajectory precisely. As discussed in this book, most numerical methods have significant errors, even with enormous memory and computing power. Some researchers argue that nature is a large computer. If so, how does a natural system know/compute its future trajectory (or wave function) precisely? Many natural systems appear to follow nonclassical computing. This is a difficult question that needs more thought.

At present, many researchers believe that human intelligence can be simulated in a computer. Recent developments in AI has been remarkable. Self-driving cars are a major achievement of AI. The present chess champion is a computer. Yet, some people debate that these activities are just fast and efficient computations, and they cannot match human intelligence. I personally believe that human emotions and intuition are too complex to be programmable. This issue is being debated vigorously at present.

Irrespective, the present computers are very powerful, and they can help us solve challenging scientific problems.

With this, I conclude this book and wish you happy computing!

Appendix A: Errors in Lagrange Interopolation

As stated in Section 10.1, the error for Lagrange interpolation is

$$E_n(x) = f(x) - P_n(x) = \frac{f^{(n)}(\zeta)}{n!} \prod (x - x_i). \quad \ldots(120)$$

The derivation of the above formula is somewhat complex and it involves Rolle's and Taylor's theorems. We state them first.

Preliminaries

Rolle's theorem: Consider a function $f(x)$ that takes values $f(a)$ and $f(b)$ at $x = a, b$ respectively. Then, according to the mean value theorem, $\exists c \in (a,b)$ such that

$$f'(c) = \frac{f(b) - f(a)}{b - a}.$$

Taylor's Theorem: If $f(x)$ is differentiable $(n+1)$ times in $[a,b]$ and $x_0 \in [a,b]$, then for every $x \in [a,b]$, $\exists \zeta(x)$ such that

$$f(x) = P_n(x) + R_n(x),$$

$$P_n(x, x_0) = f(x_0) + f'(x_0)(x - x_0) + \frac{f''(x_0)}{2!}(x - x_0)^2 + \ldots$$
$$+ \frac{f^{n-1}(x_0)}{(n-1)!}(x - x_0)^{n-1}, \quad \ldots (121)$$

$$R_n(x) = \frac{1}{n!} f^n(\zeta(x))(x - x_0)^n$$

Proof: Consider a function

$$g(t) = [f(x) - P_n(x,t)] - \left(\frac{x-t}{x-x_0}\right)^n [f(x) - P_n(x,x_0)],$$

where $P_n(x,t)$ is the expansion given by Eq. (121), but around t (not x_0). Note that $P_n(x,x) = f(x)$. Therefore, $g(x) = g(x_0) = 0$. We consider t in the domain $[x,x_0]$.

Applying Rolle's theorem, we deduce that $\exists \zeta$ in the domain $[x, x_0]$ such that $g'(\zeta) = (g(x)-g(x_0))/(x-x_0) = 0$. Therefore,

$$0 = -[\frac{d}{dt}P_n(x,t)]_{t=\zeta} + n\frac{(x-\zeta)^{n-1}}{(x-x_0)^n}[f(x) - P_n(x,x_0)].$$

Using Eq. (121) we deduce that

$$[\frac{d}{dt}P_n(x,t)]_{t=\zeta} = \frac{f^n(\zeta)}{(n-1)!}(x-\zeta)^{n-1}.$$

Therefore, using the above two equations, we deduce that

$$R_n(x) = f(x) - P_n(x,x_0) = \frac{1}{n!}f^n(\zeta(x))(x-x_0)^n.$$

Q.E.D.

Example 1: We estimate e using Taylor series. We expand the series around $x = 0$ that yields

$$P_3(1) = e^x|_{x=1} = 1 + x + \frac{x^2}{2!} = 1 + 1 + \frac{1}{2} = 2.5.$$

We estimate the error as follows. Since

$R_3(x) = \exp(\zeta) \, x^3/3!$,

and x and $\zeta \in [0,1]$, $1/6 < R_3 < e/6$, or $0.166667 < R_3 < 0.453047$. Therefore $2.666667 < e < 2.953047$ (adding R_3 the estimate of to 2.5). Note that the actual value of $e = 2.7182818...$ lies within the aforementioned error band.

For $x = -1$, the actual value is $1/e = 0.3678794412...$, and the estimate $P_3(x) = 1/2$. The error bound is $(-1/(6e), -1/6) = (-0.061313, -0.166667)$. Therefore, we deduce that $1/e$ lies in the bound $(0.333333, 0.438687)$.

Errors in Lagrange Interpolation

The proof of Eq. (120) is in the similar lines as that for Taylor's theorem. First we define

$$g(t) = f(t) - P(t) - [f(x) - P(x)] \prod_i \frac{(t - x_i)}{(x - x_i)},$$

where x_i are the given data points, and $P(t)$ is the extrapolating n-th order polynomial. It is easy to see that $g(t=x_i) = 0$ and $g(t=x) = 0$. Hence $g(t) = 0$ at $n+1$ points. Therefore, according to Rolle's theorem, $g'(t) = 0$ at n points. Continuing this argument, we conclude that the second derivative of g, $g^{(2)}(t) = 0$ at $n-1$ points, ..., and $g^{(n)}(t) = 0$ at one point. We denote this point of vanishing $g^{(n)}(t)$ by ζ. By setting $g^{(n)}(\zeta) = 0$ we obtain

$$f^{(n)}(\zeta) - P^{(n)}(\zeta) - [f(x) - P(x)] \frac{n!}{\prod(x - x_i)} = 0.$$

Since $P_n(x)$ is a $(n-1)$th order polynomial, $P^{(n)}(\zeta) = 0$. Hence the error

$$E = f(x) - P(x) = \frac{f^{(n)}(\zeta)}{n!} \prod(x - x_i).$$

Q.E.D.

Appendix B: Improving Accuracy Using Richardson Method

Richardson proposed a clever scheme to increase the accuracy of a computation using iterations. The idea is as follows.

Imagine that we compute a quantity $I(h)$ using h as a small parameter. For example, $I(h)$ could be the value of an integral with h as the grid spacing. We expand $I(h)$ as a series expansion:

$$I(h) = I + c_1 h + c_2 h^2 + H.O.T. \quad \dots(122)$$

where H.O.T. stands for the higher order terms. The exact result is I, but numerical value differs from it due to the errors arising because of finite h. With $h/2$, the numerical value is improved, but the accuracy is still $O(h)$:

$$I(h/2) = I + \frac{1}{2} c_1 h + \frac{1}{4} c_2 h^2 + H.O.T. \dots(123)$$

Interestingly, using the above two equations, we can improve the accuracy of the numerical value to $O(h^2)$ using the following trick:

$$I_1(h) = 2I(h/2) - I(h) = I + c_2' h^2 + c_3' h^3 + H.O.T.$$

This was the scheme proposed by Richardson. The accuracy is improved even further by computing the following:

$$I_2(h) = \frac{1}{3}(4I_1(h/2) - I_1(h)) = I + \frac{1}{4} c_3'' h^3 + H.O.T.$$

We can carry out this process iteratively. At the nth step, the accuracy of numerical value is $O(h^{n+1})$:

$$I_n(h) = \frac{2^n I_{n-1}(h/2) - I_{n-1}(h)}{2^n - 1} = I + O(h^{n+1}).$$

Note that the above scheme is quite general, and it can be applied to all kinds of numerical methods—quadrature, derivatives, ODE solvers, etc.

References

Books

1. S. C. Chapra and R. P. Canale, *Numerical Methods for Engineers*, 7th Edition, McGraw Hill (2016).
2. P. G. Drazin and R. S. Johnson, *Solitons: An Introduction*, Cambridge University Press (1989).
3. J. H. Ferziger, *Numerical Methods for Engineering Application*, John Wiley & Sons (1998).
4. J. H. Ferziger, M. Perić, and R. L. Street, *Computational Methods for Fluid Dynamics*, Springer (2019).
5. A. Gezerlis, *Numerical Methods in Physics with Python*, Cambridge University Press (2020).
6. A. K. Gupta, *Scientific Computing in Python*, 2nd edition, Techno World (2020),
7. C. Hill, *Learning Scientific Programming with Python*, 2nd edition, Cambridge University Press (2020).
8. A. Kiusalaas, *Numerical Methods in Engineering with Python 3*, 3rd edition, Cambridge University Press (2013).
9. L. D. Landau and E. M. Lifshitz. *Mechanics, Course of theoretical physics*, Elsevier (2013).
10. M. Lutz, *Learning Python*, 2nd edition, O'Reilly Media (2013).
11. J. Mathews and R. L. Walker, *Mathematical methods of physics*, WA Benjamin (1970).
12. M. Newman, *Computational Physics*, Amazon Digital Service (2013).
13. J. M. Stewart, *Python for Scientists*, Cambridge University Press (2014).
14. M. K. Verma, *Introduction to Mechanics*, 2nd edition, Universities Press (2016).
15. M. K. Verma, *Energy Transfers in Fluid Flows*, Cambridge University Press (2019).

I am particularly fond of Ferziger's book on Numerical Methods because it connects various numerical algorithms in a coherent manner.

Journal Papers

1. P. Bak, C. Tang, and K. Wiesenfeld, Self-organized criticality, Phys. Rev. A, **38**, 364 (1988).
2. E. Forest and R. D. Ruth, Physica D: Nonlinear Phenomena 43, 105 (1990).
3. P. Omelyan, I. M. Mryglod, and R. Folk, Computer Physics Communications 146, 188 (2002).

Subject Index

1's complement, 47
2's complement, 47
32-bit processor, 62
64-bit processor, 62

&, !, ^, <<, >>, 71
\n, \u, \x, \a, \b, 76-77

Accuracy, 222
add_subplot(), 189
Anaconda Python, 31
and operator, 69
Animation using Python, 205
Applications of computers, 35
Application software, 21
arange(), 93
Argument passing in Python, 145
axes object, 188
Artificial intelligence, 502
ASCII, 75, 215-216

Binary format, 213, 215
Binary point, 51
Binary search, 175
Binary system, 42, 51
Bisection method, 422
Bitwise operators, 71
Boundary value problems
    Shooting method, 435
    Eigenvalue solver, 442
Break statement, 129
Built-in namespace, 143
Burgers equation, 380, 412
Byte, 11

Central Processing Unit, 9
CPU, 9
Characters, 74
chr(), 74
complex(), 78
Complex float, 62
Comparative operators, 68
Computational scientist, 6
Compute Server, 12
Concatenation, 76
Conditional statements, 121

Control flow diagram, 119
Contour plot, 192
Conversion between number systems, 44, 52
CSV format, 215, 481
Cubic splines, 260-264

Decimal system, 42, 50
Decoding, 75
Density plot, 193
Derivatives, 300
    Backward, 300
    Central, 301
    Error, 304
    Forward, 300
    gradient(), 306
Dictionary, 106
Diffusion equation, 373, 402
dtype(), 91

Eigenvalues & eigenvectors (ODEs), 442
Eigenvalue (matrix) solver, 471
Enclosing namespace, 142
Encoding, 75
Error, 218
    Absolute error, 224
    In Arithmetic, 227
    In subtraction, 227
    Logical error, 227
    Numerical error, 227
    Propagation, 234
    Random error, 235
    Relative error, 230
    Round-off error, 60, 230
    Series expansion, 231
    Syntax error, 226
    Systematic error, 225, 235
Escape sequences, 77
Euler method (ODE), 314-322

Fast Fourier Transform (FFT), 359-369
figure object, 188
Files in Python, 210
float(), 78

Subject Index

Finite-difference method for PDEs
  Boundary condition, 400
  Burgers equation, 412
  Central difference, 402
  CFL condition, 402
  Diffusion equation, 402
  Formalism, 400
  Implicit scheme, 406
  Navier-Stokes equation, 412
  Schrödinger equation, 415
  Split-operator method, 418
  Upwind scheme, 408
  Wave equation, 408
Floating point numbers, 50, 54
for loop, 125
for-else, 130
Formatting of strings, 79
Fourier transform, 351
  Derivative computation, 360-363
  Multidimensional, 365
  Reality condition, 358, 366, 388
Fraction, 50
Function as Python object, 138
Functions in Python, 133
Function parameter, 135

Gauss elimination, 463
Gauss-Seidel method, 453
Gaussian quadrature, 279
  Error, 283
  Hermite-Gauss, 290
  Legendre-Gauss, 283
  Leguerre-Gauss, 286
getsizeof(), 66
Global namespace, 143
Global variables 148
Good programming practices, 166
Google Colab, 33
GPU, 12, 15
Gross-Pitaevskii eqn, 395

Hardware, 12
Hard disk, 11

Hexadecimal system, 43, 54
HDF5 format, 215, 217-218
High performance computing, 15
Histogram, 201

id(), 66
if statement, 121
if-else statement, 122
if-elif-else statement, 123
Immutable objects, 110
Infinite loop, 129
Integers, 42
Integers in computers, 45
Interconnect, 16
interp1d(), 256
index(x), 83
Input units, 12
int(), 78
Integration, 267
  dblquad(), 294
  Gaussian quadrature, 279
  Multidimensional, 294
  Newton-Cotes, 268
  quad(), 294
  tplquad(), 295
Ipython, 25, 31

Jacobi method, 451
Jupyter Notebook, 33

KdV equation, 384
Key:value, 106
Keywords, 67

Lagrange interpolation, 250
  Error, 252, 509
lagrange_interpolate(), 253
Lambda function, 139
Laplace equation, 448
  Direct method, 449
  Gauss-Seidel method, 453
  Iterative methods, 451
  Jacobi method, 451
  Red-black method, 454
  Successive over-relaxation (SOR), 455

Subject Index

len(), 84
Limits of computation, 507
Linear algebra solvers, 462
  Gauss elimination, 463
  LU decomposition, 466
  Tridiagonal matrix, 468
  Eigenvalues (matrix), 471
  Eigenvectors (matrix), 471
Linear search, 173
linspace(), 93
List, 82
Local namespace, 142
Logical operators, 69
Logical variables, 67
LU decomposition, 466

Machine learning, 502
Mantissa, 55
Matplotlib, 25, 184
Memory, 10
Memory complexity, 17
meshgrid(), 102
Metropolis algorithm, 485
Module, 141
Monte Carlo method, 468
  Metropolis algorithm, 494
  Phase transition, 493
  Quadrature, 484
  Random numbers, 478
  Regression analysis, 487
  Sandpile model, 497
  Self-organized criticality, 497
Multidimensional arrays, 95
Mutable objects, 114

Namespace, 142
Navier-Stokes equation, 387, 412
Newton-Cotes formulas, 268
  Error, 272
  Multi-interval, 276
  Simpson's rule, 270-271, 296
  Trapezoid rule, 270, 296
Newton-Raphson method, 425
Nondimensionalization, 237
  of classical oscillator, 240
  of equations, 238

of Hydrogen atom, 242
of quantum oscillator, 241
of projectile with drag, 238
Nonlinear algebraic equation solvers, 421
  Bisection method, 422
  Newton-Raphson, 425
  Python's functions, 432
  Relaxation method, 429
  Secant method, 428
Numerical methods, 245
Numpy, 25, 91
Numpy arrays, 91
Negative integers, 46
not operator, 70

Object code, 22
Octal system, 43
ODE solver, 309
  Adam-Bashforth, 337
  Euler backward, 322
    Stability, 323
  Euler forward, 310, 314
    Accuracy, 316
    Stability, 317
  Implicit, 312, 322
  Leapfrog, 335
  Mechanics, 341
  Multistep method, 335
  odeint(), 332
  Predictor-corrector, 327
  Runge-Kutta, 328
  Semi-implicit, 312
  Stiff equations, 347
  System of ODEs, 340
  Trapezoid method, 320
Operating System (OS), 20
or operator, 69
ord(), 74
Output units, 12
Ordinary differential equation solvers, See ODE solver

Partial differential equation solvers
  Finite difference, 399
  Laplace equation, 448-456

Subject Index

Poisson equations, 457-460
Spectral method, 371-397
Pie diagram, 202
Pingla-Virahanka-Fibonacci numbers, 161
Plotting using Python, 183
Poisson equation, 457-460
polyfit(), 490
pop(), 82
Precedence of operators, 46, 59, 69
Precision, 60, 222
Primality test, 164
Prime factors, 168
Prime numbers, 168
Processor, 9
Prutor, 33
Pyplot, 184
Python, 24
Python files, 27
Python modules, 25, 144
Python Notebooks, 33
Python objects, 109
Python variables, 65, 67
Python vs. C, 28

Radial-polar plot, 200
range(), 87
rand(), *randn*(), *randint*(), 98, 479-480
Reading in Python, 212, 216, 217, 218
Reading an image, 219
Real numbers, 50
Real numbers in computers, 56
Recursive functions, 155
Regression analysis, 487
Relaxation method, 429
Repeat until, 130
Richardson method, 512
Round-off error, 60, 224
Runge-Kutta method, 328

Sandpile model, 497
Schrödinger equation, 391, 407
Scipy, 26

Scopes of Python variables, 144
Search, linear, 173
Search, binary, 175
Secant method, 428
Self-organized criticality, 497
shape(), 99
Shooting method, 436
Sierpinski triangle, 158
Significant digits, 223
Simple statements, 120
Simpson's integration rule, 270-271, 296
size(), 84, 97
Slicing, 85
Software, 20
Sorting an array, 178
Spectral method for PDEs, 371
    Burgers equation, 380
    CFL condition, 375
    Diffusion equation, 373
    Formalism, 372
    Gross-Pitaevskii eqn, 395
    KdV equation, 384
    Navier-Stokes equation, 387
    Schrödinger equation, 391
    Wave equation, 378
Splines, 260
    Cubic, 270, 264
    B-splines, 266
Spyder, 32
SSD, 11
Sublime editor, 26
Supercomputer, 15
Surface plot, 195
Strings, 76
System software, 20
Systematic error, 225, 235

Time complexity, 17
Tower of Hanoi, 156
Trapezoid integration method, 270, 296
Truncation errors, 60
Truth table, 69
Tuple, 89
Turtle, 159

Subject Index

Vector plot, 196
Vectorization, 103
Von Neumann Architecture, 8

Wave equation, 378, 408
while loop, 128
Writing in Python, 211, 216-218

www.ingramcontent.com/pod-product-compliance
Lightning Source LLC
Chambersburg PA
CBHW051539240526
45465CB00028B/884